AlgebraicThinking • Foundations

*a*ᵗ
AlgebraicThinking

FOUNDATIONS
THIRD EDITION

Authors

Dr. Brian E. Enright

and

Linda L. Mannhardt

Leslie G. Baker

Copyright © 2004 by National Training Network

All rights reserved. No part of the material protected by this copyright notice, except the Reproduction Pages contained within, may be reproduced or utilized in any form by any means, electronic or mechanical, including photocopying, recording, or by any information storage and retrieval system, without written permission from National Training Network, Inc.

ISBN 978-1-57290-033-2

Table Of Contents

Lesson		Page
1	Gathering Data – Bar Graphs	1
2	Bar Graphs and Line Graphs	4
3	Collect...Organize...Display	9
4	Mean, Median, and Mode	14
5	SOLVE – Study the Problem	18
6	SOLVE – Organize the Facts	22
7	SOLVE – Line Up a Plan (1 Step)	27
8	SOLVE – Verify the Plan with Action (1 Step)	33
9	SOLVE – Line Up a Plan (2 Steps)	36
10	SOLVE – Verify the Plan with Action (2 Steps)	41
11	SOLVE – Examine the Results	45
12	Review of SOLVE	50
13	Evaluation of SOLVE	52
14	Fact Masters	53
15	Commutative Property	59
16	Associative Property	63
17	Distributive Property	67
18	Property Review – Sign Language	72
19	Let's Bring Some Order to This!	74
20	Order of Operations	81
21	Review – Scavenger Hunt	88

Lesson		Page
22	Evaluation of Properties and Order of Operations	91
23	Points, Lines, and Planes (Oh My!)	92
24	Angles	98
25	Concept of Fractions	106
26	Equivalent Fractions	110
27	Ratios	124
28	Compare and Order Fractions	132
29	Decimal Fractions	138
30	Converting Fractions and Decimals	145
31	Percent Fractions	150
32	Review	156
33	Evaluation of Fractions, Decimals, and Percents	158
34	Adding Fractions	159
35	Adding Fractions	164
36	Adding Fractions	171
37	Adding Fractions	176
38	Adding Fractions	180
39	Adding Fractions	186
40	Subtracting Fractions	190
41	Subtracting Fractions	195
42	Review of Adding and Subtracting Fractions	199
43	Mixed Numbers and Improper Fractions	202

Lesson		Page
44	Adding Mixed Numbers	211
45	Subtracting Fractions and Mixed Numbers	218
46	Review and Quiz	226
47	Multiplying Fractions and Whole Numbers	227
48	Dividing Fractions	238
49	Dividing Fractions – Reciprocals	251
50	Multiplying and Dividing Mixed Numbers	256
51	Review and Quiz on Multiplying and Dividing Fractions and Mixed Numbers	265
52	Review of Fractions/Mixed Number Operations	266
53	Scavenger Hunt	268
54	Evaluation of Fractions/Mixed Numbers	271
55	Simple Probability	272
56	How to Count – Sample Space	278
57	Compound Probability	283
58	Combinations and Permutations	290
59	Geometry – Polygons	298
60	Geometry – Triangles	303
61	Geometry – Quadrilaterals	308
62	Area and Perimeter	315
63	Area of Triangles and Parallelograms	322
64	Area of Trapezoids	327

Lesson		Page
65	Addition and Subtraction of Decimals	332
66	Multiplying Decimals with Models	338
67	Multiplying Decimals without Models	343
68	Dividing Decimals with Models	349
69	Dividing Decimals by Whole Numbers	357
70	Dividing Decimals by Decimals	363
71	Decimal Review	369
72	Evaluation of Decimals	373
73	Circles – Area and Circumference	374
74	Exponential and Scientific Notation	379
75	Exponential and Scientific Notation	386
76	Writing and Evaluating Variable Expressions	390
77	Variable Expressions	395
78	Expressions Review	398
79	Evaluation of Expressions	401
80	Comparing and Ordering Integers	402
81	Adding Integers	407
82	Adding Integers – Think Maximum	416
83	Subtracting Integers – Same Signs	419
84	Subtracting Integers – Different Signs	425
85	Review of Addition and Subtraction of Integers	432
86	Evaluation of Addition and Subtraction of Integers	434

Lesson		Page
87	Multiplying Integers	435
88	Dividing Integers	442
89	Review of Integers – Integer Card Game	447
90	Evaluation of Integers	452
91	Functions	453
92	Coordinate Plane – Abandon Ship	457
93	Translations	461
94	Reflections	466
95	Spreadsheets	471
96	Keep It Balanced	477
97	Revenge of the Word Problems	485
98	Solving Multiplication and Division Equations	491
99	Return of the Word Problems	498
100	Review of One-Step Equations	505
101	Evaluation of One-Step Equations	507
102	Solving Proportions	508
103	The Word Problems Returned	516
104	Finding a Percent of a Number	524
105	Using Proportions to Find the Percent of a Number	532
106	Finding Percents Using Equations	539
107	Evaluation of Proportions	544
108	Congruent and Similar Figures	545

Lesson		Page
109	Metric Units of Length	554
110	Metric Units of Capacity and Weight	561
111	Customary Units of Length	566
112	Customary Units of Capacity and Weight	571
113	Geometric Solids	574
114	Volume of Prisms	580
115	Evaluation of Measurement and Geometry	585
116	Two-Step Equations	586
117	Two-Step Equations	591
118	Review of Two-Step Equations	595
119	Evaluation of Two-Step Equations	598
120	Inequalities on the Number line	599
121	Solving Inequalities	604
122	Negatives in Multiplication and Division Inequalities	609
123	More One-Step Inequalities	613
Appendix A	Prime and Composite Numbers	618
Appendix B	Finding the Greatest Common Factor and the Least Common Multiple	623

Appendix 1: Stem and Leaf Plots 626

Appendix 2: Divisibility 631

Appendix 3: Sample Space 636

Appendix 4: Probability - Results as Decimals, Percents, and Ratios 641

Lesson	Page

Appendix 5: More Probability 645

Appendix 6: Identify and Compare the Relationship Between Parts of a Circle. . . 650

Appendix 7: Determine the Area and Perimeter of Composite Figures 653

Appendix 8: Comparing and Ordering Rational Numbers on a Number Line 658

Appendix 9: Functions Without Integers. 663

Appendix 10: Plotting Points in the Coordinate Plane 670

Appendix 11: Polygons in the Coordinate Plane. 677

Appendix 12: Rotations. 685

Appendix 13: One-Step Equations – No Integers. 690

Appendix 14: One-Step Equations – Revenge of the

               Word Problems – No Integers. 698

Appendix 15: Solving Multiplication and Division Equations – No Integers 704

Appendix 16: One-Step Equations - Return of the Word Problems 711

Appendix 17: Review of One-Step Equations. 718

Appendix 18: Interpreting Circle Graphs. 722

Appendix 19: Percent of Discount, Sales Tax. 727

Appendix 20: Distance Between Two Points Using a Drawing and a Scale 732

Appendix 21: Finding the surface area of cubes and rectangular prisms 738

Appendix 22: Histograms 744

AlgebraicThinking • Foundations   Warm Up 1

Warm Up 1: Uniquely You

Answer each of these questions to show your uniqueness!

1. What is your favorite food?

2. What is your favorite color?

3. What month were you born in?

4. What type of movie would you choose to go see – drama, comedy, science fiction, horror, or romance?

5. List five things you did over the summer.

Lesson 1

AlgebraicThinking • Foundations

Use Question 2 from your Warm Up. Make a table of the favorite colors in your class and the number of students who chose each color.

Favorite Color	Number of Students

Use the table above to create a bar graph.

AlgebraicThinking • Foundations

Lesson 1

Use Question 4 from your Warm Up. Gather data from your classmates. Then use the data to make a bar graph.

Type of Movie	Number of Students

Use the table above to create a bar graph.

Warm Up 2: Division Tower

Follow the division problems from top to bottom. Use the answer for each problem as the dividend in the next problem.

3,888 ÷ 6 = _____

÷ 6 = _____

÷ 2 = _____

÷ 9 = _____

÷ 3 = _____

÷ 2 = _____

Algebraic Thinking • Foundations Lesson 2

Bar Graphs and Line Graphs

There are many different kinds of graphs. The kind of graph you choose to display your data depends on the type of data you have. If you want to compare quantities, you would use a **bar graph.** If you want to show how an amount changes over time, you would use a **line graph.**

The graph below is a bar graph. **Bar graphs** compare quantities.

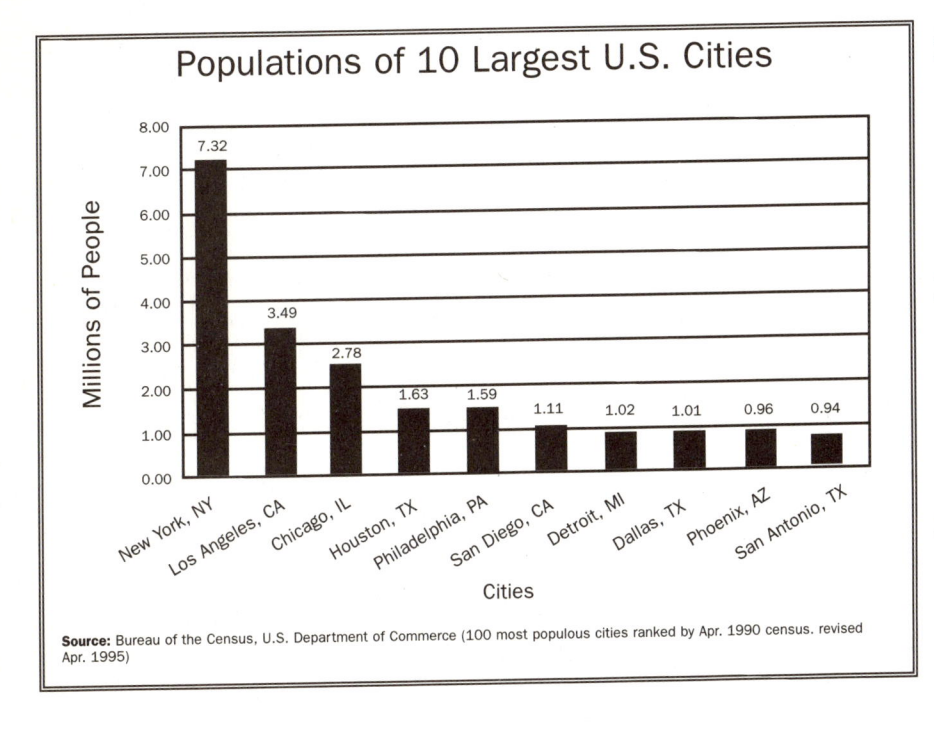

Populations of 10 Largest U.S. Cities

(Bar graph showing Millions of People vs Cities)
- New York, NY: 7.32
- Los Angeles, CA: 3.49
- Chicago, IL: 2.78
- Houston, TX: 1.63
- Philadelphia, PA: 1.59
- San Diego, CA: 1.11
- Detroit, MI: 1.02
- Dallas, TX: 1.01
- Phoenix, AZ: 0.96
- San Antonio, TX: 0.94

Source: Bureau of the Census, U.S. Department of Commerce (100 most populous cities ranked by Apr. 1990 census. revised Apr. 1995)

1. What quantities are compared in this bar graph?

2. What was the population of Houston?

3. Which city had a population of 3.49 million?

4. What is the label for the vertical axis?

5. What is the label for the horizontal axis?

6. The scale for this graph goes from _____ to _____ in units of 1.

7. Each bar in a bar graph should have the same _____ .
   (height or width)

8. List the things to remember about bar graphs.

5

Lesson 2   **Algebraic Thinking • Foundations**

The graph below is a line graph. A **line graph** shows how a quantity changes over time.

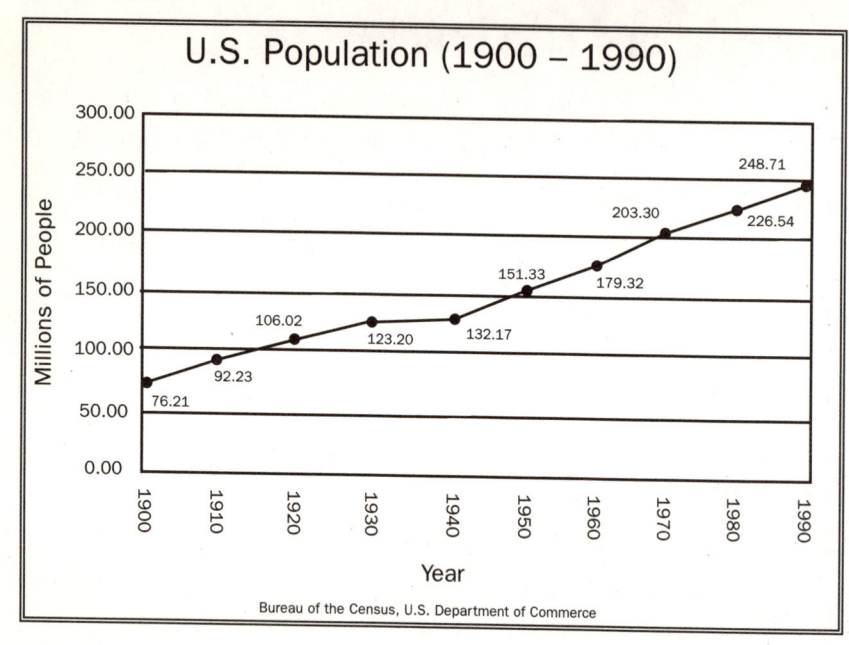

U.S. Population (1900 – 1990)

Millions of People: 0.00, 50.00, 100.00, 150.00, 200.00, 250.00, 300.00
Year: 1900, 1910, 1920, 1930, 1940, 1950, 1960, 1970, 1980, 1990
Data points: 76.21, 92.23, 106.02, 123.20, 132.17, 151.33, 179.32, 203.30, 226.54, 248.71

Bureau of the Census, U.S. Department of Commerce

9. What was the population of the United States in 1950?

10. About when did the population of the United States go over 200 million?

11. What is the label for the vertical axis?

12. What is the label for the horizontal axis?

13. The scale for this graph goes from _____ to _____ in units of 50.

14. Would units of 5 be a good choice for the scale on this graph? Why or why not?

15. List the things to remember about line graphs.

Algebraic Thinking • Foundations

Lesson 2

16. Three students created the graphs below. Indicate what is wrong with each graph.

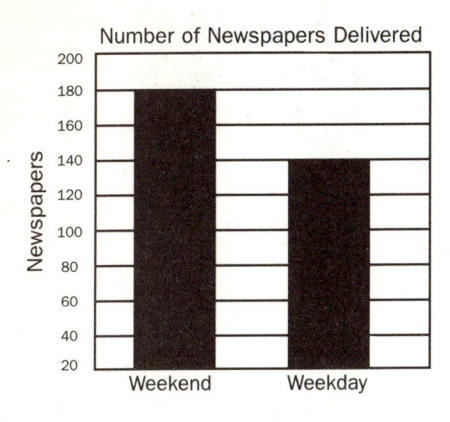

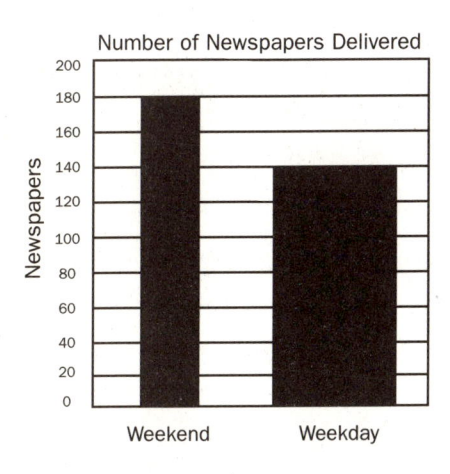

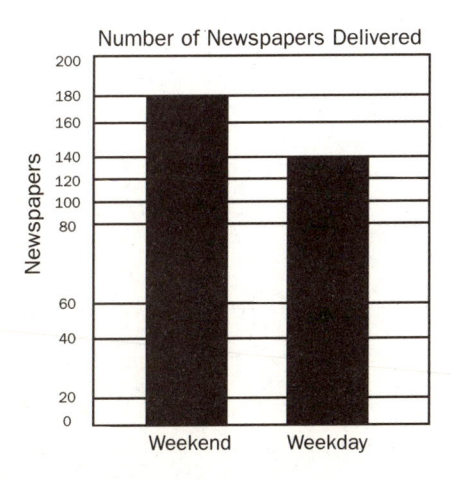

Lesson 2

Algebraic Thinking • Foundations

Practice it!

Directions: In problems 1 – 4, decide what scale you would use to graph the data. Choose 1, 5, 10, 50, 100, 1,000, or 5,000 as units to count by.

1. 2 lb, 3 lb, 5 lb, 1 lb, 4 lb, 3 lb

2. $100, $300, $250, $200, $150

3. 2,500, 10,000, 25,000, 5,200, 30,500, 37,500, 25,100

4. 25 ft, 20 ft, 30 ft, 20 ft, 30 ft, 55 ft, 80 ft, 10 ft

5. Correctly graph the data from Problem 16 on page 7.

6. Would you graph the data in the table below using a line graph or a bar graph? Graph the data.

Year	Population of U.S.
1790	3,929,000
1800	5,308,000
1810	7,240,000
1820	9,638,453
1830	12,860,702
1840	17,063,353
1850	23,191,876
1860	31,443,321
1870	38,558,371
1880	50,189,209
1890	62,979,766

Warm Up 3: Fast Track

Follow the track from top to bottom. Use the answer as the first number in the next problem.

178 + 22 = _____

_____ ÷ 10 = _____

_____ • 5 = _____

_____ − 52 = _____

_____ ÷ 8 = _____

_____ + 6 = _____

_____ ÷ 2 = _____

_____ + 17 = _____

_____ + 9 = _____

_____ ÷ 4 = _____

_____ + 18 = _____

_____ • 10 = _____

Lesson 3

AlgebraicThinking • Foundations

Collect ... Organize ... Display

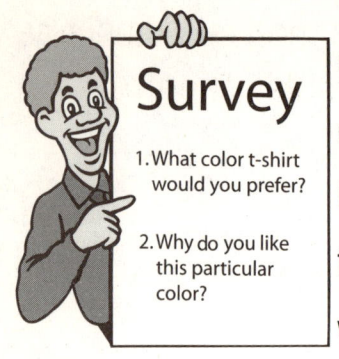

Survey
1. What color t-shirt would you prefer?
2. Why do you like this particular color?

Companies use surveys to find out the preference of consumers before they make a product. The band is going to sell t-shirts as a fundraiser. They asked the students at their middle school what color they would like the t-shirt to be. One student wrote her results in a list. Help her organize it into a **frequency table** and then a **line plot**.

white, white, red, white, gray, blue, green, green, green, white, blue, yellow, yellow, white, gray, red, gray, white, green, blue, red, black, red, black, blue, white, white, gray, white, yellow, red, blue, white, white, red, white, white

Color	Tally	Frequency

10

AlgebraicThinking • Foundations

Lesson 3

Use the number cube provided by your teacher. Roll the number cube 30 times and record your results in the frequency table. Then make a line plot of your results.

Number	Tally	Frequency
1		
2		
3		
4		
5		
6		

A number cube is said to be fair. That is, each number has an equally likely chance of coming up as the other numbers. In **theoretical probability,** each outcome is equally likely to occur. Since the number cube is fair, each number on the cube is equally likely to occur.

When you rolled the number cube 30 times, you completed a simple **experimental probability** situation. Experimental probability involves a simulation. How close did each number get to coming up 1 time in every 6 rolls? We will learn more about probability in a later lesson.

Try This! Sixth and seventh graders were asked, "How many video game cartridges/discs do you have at home?" The results are in the list below. Make a frequency table to show the data.

7, 14, 5, 16, 15, 14, 8, 8, 7, 9, 11, 12, 14, 12, 15, 8, 9, 10, 18, 5, 8, 18, 8, 9, 10, 8, 10, 7, 11, 11, 14, 14, 14, 7, 8, 15, 14, 7, 8, 10, 7, 8, 15, 14, 15, 14, 8, 8, 7, 9, 11, 10, 7, 11, 12, 15, 8, 9, 10, 18, 5, 8, 10, 8, 10, 7, 10, 8, 14, 14, 7

Lesson 3   **Algebraic**Thinking • **Foundations**

When preparing to make your frequency table, it is a good idea to consider the **range** of the data. You can find the range of numerical data by finding the difference between the greatest value and the least value.

1. What is the range of the data given on the previous page?

2. How does the range help you in making a frequency table?

3. Make a frequency table to show the data. (Use notebook paper.)

4. Make a line plot to show the data. (Use notebook paper. Put only one "X" between the blue lines on your paper. That will help you keep things straight.)

Practice it!

Directions: *Create a frequency table and a line plot for the data in each set. Use notebook paper or graph paper.*

1. Grades on a math test: 95, 90, 85, 95, 90, 100, 90, 85, 80, 75, 90, 100, 90, 95, 90, 85, 80, 90, 95, 90, 85, 95, 90, 85, 80, 95

2. Number of TVs per household: 2, 3, 5, 4, 6, 6, 4, 1, 1, 2, 2, 3, 2, 4, 2, 5, 2, 5, 2, 5, 4, 4, 2, 2, 5, 4, 2, 2, 3, 5, 4, 3, 3, 2, 2, 3, 5, 4

3. Color of eyes: blue, green, blue, brown, brown, hazel, brown, brown, green, brown, brown, blue, hazel, green, brown, green, brown, blue, green, hazel, hazel, brown, brown, blue, green, blue, brown, brown, hazel

4. Favorite fruit: apples, oranges, apples, bananas, grapes, bananas, apples, pears, oranges, apples, oranges, oranges, bananas, lemons, apples, oranges, grapes, oranges, apples, oranges, apples, oranges, apples, bananas

Algebraic Thinking • Foundations

Lesson 3

Directions: Use the frequency table and the pictograph to answer the questions.

Time Spent Working on Homework Each Day

Time	Tally	Frequency
30 min	|||||	5
1 h	||||| ||||| ||||| ||||| ||||| ||||| |||||	35
1 h 30 min	||||| ||||| ||||| ||||| |||||	25
2 h	||||| ||||| |||||	15
2 h 30 min	||||| |||||	10
3 h or more	|||||	5

Time Spent Working on Homework Each Day

Time	Students
30 min	🧍
1 h	🧍 🧍 🧍 🧍
1 h 30 min	🧍 🧍 🧍
2 h	🧍 🧍
2 h 30 min	🧍
3 h or more	🧍

🧍 = 10 students

5. How many students were surveyed in all?

6. What amount of time did the most students say they worked on homework?

7. What is the difference between the number of students who spent 1 hour compared to 2 hours on homework each day?

8. How would the pictograph show 90 students?

9. How would the pictograph change if 30 students said that they worked on homework for $1\frac{1}{2}$ hours?

10. In order to represent the number 2 in the pictograph, the value of the picture might have to be changed. Why might it need to be changed?

13

Warm Up 4: Pattern Patrol

Find the pattern in each list of numbers. Then give the next three numbers in the pattern.

1. 12, 18, 24, 30, ___, ___, ___, . . .

   What's the pattern? _____

2. 1, 2, 3, 5, 8, 13, ___, ___, ___, . . .

   What's the pattern? _____

3. 75, 60, 45, ___, ___, ___, . . .

   What's the pattern? _____

4. 2, 4, 8, 16, ___, ___, ___, . . .

   What's the pattern? _____

Algebraic Thinking • Foundations　　　　　　　　Lesson 4

Mean, Median, and Mode

A set of data is often described by measures of central tendency. There are three of them. List them here.

_____

_____

_____

Directions: *Complete this activity to learn about the mean (average). You will need some beans or counters.*

1. Find the mean of 7 and 3. _____
    a. Count out two groups – a group of 7, and a group of 3.
    b. Combine the groups. Then separate the items **evenly** into two groups.
    c. The mean is the number of items in each group.

2. Find the mean of 11, 6, and 7. _____
    a. Count out three groups – a group of 11, a group of 6, and a group of 7.
    b. Combine the groups. Then separate the items **evenly** into three groups.
    c. The mean is the number of items in each group.

3. Find the mean of 4, 7, 5, and 8. _____
    a. Count out four groups – a group of 4, a group of 7, a group of 5, and a group of 8.
    b. Combine the groups. Then separate the items **evenly** into four groups.
    c. The mean is the number of items in each group.

4. Use the above method to find the mean of 9 and 7.

5. Find the mean of 2, 5, 3, 7, 8, and 5. _____

6. When you combine the groups, you are finding the total number of items. What math operation are you modeling?

7. When you separate the items into equal groups, what math operation are you modeling?

8. Write the two steps for finding the mean, or average.

Lesson 4 **AlgebraicThinking • Foundations**

Outliers are data items that are very high or very low. When there are outliers, the **median** is a better measure of central tendency. The median is the middle number when the data are put in order from least to greatest or greatest to least.

9. Find the median of the data in each set.

About how many times do you go to a park during a week?				
0	2	3	1	4
3	5	3	2	2
5	1	0	1	8
3	2	1	4	

How many videos did you rent last week?				
2	4	7	4	3
6	7	3	5	4
2	1	3	8	7
2	3	2	6	5

The **mode** is the item that occurs the most often in the data. There can be more than one mode for a set of data.

10. Find the mode of the data below.

11. What is the mode of the data about "going to the park"?

12. What is the mode of the data about "renting videos"?

What is your favorite color for a new car?		
Silver	Silver	Black
Green	Red	Blue
Blue	Silver	Silver
Green	Yellow	White

AlgebraicThinking • Foundations

Lesson 4

Practice it!

Directions: *Order the data. Then find the mean, median, and mode for each set of data.*

1. Hours spent outside after school
   2, 3, 1, 1, 3, 2, 2, 1, 2, 1, 2, 2, 4

2. Runs scored in a baseball game
   1, 3, 7, 6, 7, 6, 5, 5, 4, 3, 4, 8, 12, 8, 11

3. Fee charged to baby-sit (per hour)
   $3, $4, $2, $3, $2, $3, $3, $3, $3, $4

4. Hours students spent on homework last night
   3, 3, 5, 2, 1, 3, 2, 3, 2, 3, 4, 1, 2, 3, 4, 3, 7, 3

5. Theatres at 15 movie cinemas
   12, 6, 14, 24, 10, 12, 6, 2, 4, 8, 12, 15, 16, 20, 19

6. Lockers at 10 schools
   750; 600; 1,200; 1,100; 750; 850; 900; 1,050; 1,155; 625

17

Warm Up 5   Algebraic Thinking • Foundations

Warm Up 5: Tic-Tac-Toe

Julie and Sam played a game of tic-tac-toe. Find out who won by matching each answer on the board to the correct problem. Put the appropriate letter over that space on the board.

Julie played the X

29 + 72 =
47 + 32 =
25 + 50 =
49 + 34 =

Sam played the O

36 + 58 =
63 + 29 =
91 + 76 =
82 + 20 =

167	82	79
94	75	92
83	102	101

Who won the game?_____

Algebraic Thinking • Foundations Lesson 5

Solve

1. Kevin wants to do 500 sit-ups every week. On Sunday and Monday he started off slow, doing only 50 sit-ups each day. However, he picked up the pace on Tuesday and Wednesday. He did 100 sit-ups each of those days. He only did 75 on Thursday and 50 on Friday. On Friday, he also did 20 pull-ups. How many sit-ups must he do on Saturday to reach his goal?

    • Highlight the question.

    • What is the problem asking me to find? _____
    _____

2. Angela needs $65 to buy a pair of jeans she has been wanting. She gets paid $4 per hour to baby-sit. Her parents gave her $20 for a good report card, and she baby-sat for 6 hours. How much more money will she need to buy the jeans?

    • Highlight the question.

    • What is the problem asking me to find? _____
    _____

Lesson 5   **AlgebraicThinking** • Foundations

3. When Edwin Moses won a gold medal in the 400-meter hurdles, it was his 90th win in a row. His time was 47.75 seconds. How many more wins did he need to have one hundred wins in a row?

    •   Highlight the question.

    •   What is the problem asking me to find? _____
        _____

4. Lindsay walked her horse around a track 7 times. Each lap took 30 minutes. How many hours did Lindsay walk her horse?

    •   Highlight the question.

    •   What is the problem asking me to find? _____
        _____

5. At a restaurant, 2 pounds of shrimp will feed 3 people. How many pounds of shrimp are needed for 18 people?

    •   Highlight the question.

    •   What is the problem asking me to find? _____
        _____

AlgebraicThinking • Foundations   Homework 5

Name _____

Directions: *Review your addition skills. Find each sum. (No calculators!)*

1. 8 + 3 =

2. 18 + 3 =

3. 28 + 3 =

4. 38 + 3 =

5. 7 + 5 =

6. 7 + 15 =

7. 7 + 25 =

8. 7 + 35 =

9. 6 + 5 =

10. 5 + 6 =

11. 4 + 7 =

Directions: *Answer each question.*

12. Write three addition sentences with a sum of 15.

13. Write three addition sentences with a sum of 5.

14. Write three addition sentences with a sum of 10.

15. Write three addition sentences with a sum of 4.

Warm Up 6: Money Sense

In how many different ways can you make 50 cents using quarters, dimes, and nickels?

Algebraic Thinking • Foundations Lesson 6

s**O**lve

> Yesterday's lesson showed you how to **S**tudy the problem so that you can understand the problem. Today's lesson will help you learn how to **O**rganize the facts. Facts are listed in many ways, and you must learn how to find them. Some of the facts you will find in a problem will not help you solve the problem. You must learn how to ignore those facts.

Definition of a Fact

A fact is any piece of information contained in a problem. There are many different kinds of facts, but <u>most facts deal with numbers</u>. For example, a fact could be the number of points a team scored in a game. Another fact might be the temperature of something hot or cold. A fact might also explain how much something costs.

Directions: *These are the steps we will perform when we complete step O.*

O. _____

_____

_____

Directions: *Perform steps S and O with your teacher.*

1. The running back for the Southern High School wears his lucky number 48 on his jersey. During his last three games, he carried the ball 58 yards, 49 yards, and 53 yards. What was the total yardage for those last three games?

S. What is the problem asking me to find? _____

_____

O. _____

_____

23

Lesson 6   **AlgebraicThinking** • Foundations

Directions: *Perform steps S and O on each problem. Don't forget to highlight the question and answer the question "What is the problem asking me to find?" Then identify the facts. Eliminate the unnecessary facts and make a list of the necessary facts.*

2. Shelly and Mario went shopping. Mario had $19. Shelly had $35, and she bought a knit vest for $13. How much money does Shelly have now?

   S. What is the problem asking me to find? _____

   _____

   O. _____

   _____

3. Joanna has grown 3 inches since last year. She has 16 tops, but 7 do not fit her anymore. How many tops still fit her?

   S. What is the problem asking me to find? _____

   _____

   O. _____

   _____

AlgebraicThinking • Foundations   Lesson 6

4. Toshi went to a store 20 minutes from his home. He bought 2 shirts for $24. If he gave the clerk a $50 – bill, how much change should he receive?

S. What is the problem asking me to find? _____

_____

O. _____

_____

5. The Shoe Shop was planning a 5-day sale. They had 165 pairs of shoes in the store before the sale started. They sold 46 on the first day of the sale. How many pairs of shoes were left for the last 4 days of the sale?

S. What is the problem asking me to find? _____

_____

O. _____

_____

Homework 6   **AlgebraicThinking** • Foundations

Name _____

Directions: *Review your subtraction skills. Find each difference. (No calculators!)*

1. 12 – 9 =

2. 22 – 9 =

3. 32 – 9 =

4. 42 – 9 =

5. 22 – 19 =

6. 32 – 19 =

7. 42 – 19 =

8. 52 – 19 =

9. Write three subtraction problems that have a difference of 10.

10. Write three subtraction problems that have a difference of 100.

Algebraic Thinking • Foundations

Warm Up 7: Operation Word Wall

Make a list of words that have to do with each operation.

Addition	Multiplication
Subtraction	**Division**

Lesson 7   **AlgebraicThinking** • Foundations

In the last lessons you learned how to Study the Problem and how to Organize the Facts. Today you will learn how to make plans to solve problems. This step is called "Line up a Plan." Your plans will include one of the four operations (+, − , • , ÷).

Directions: *Perform steps S, O, and L on each problem with your teacher.*

1. Melissa bought 2 CDs for a total of $28. She said it was a gift for her 4-year-old niece, but everyone knew it was for her! One of the CDs cost $13. How much did the second CD cost?

   S. What is the problem asking me to find? _____

   _____

   O. _____

   _____

   L. _____

   _____

   _____

   _____

28

AlgebraicThinking • Foundations

Lesson 7

2. In order to run for president of his school, Philip needed to have some students sign a petition. On the first day, 25 students signed. Fifty students signed on the second day. Seventy-five signed on the third day, and 100 signed on the fourth day. How many students signed Philip's petition?

S. What is the problem asking me to find? _____

_____

O. _____

_____

L. _____

_____

_____

29

Lesson 7

AlgebraicThinking • Foundations

3. When Roberto started lifting weights, he could only bench-press 10 pounds. After 4 weeks, he could bench-press 20 pounds. At the end of five months, Roberto was able to bench-press 80 pounds. How many more pounds could Roberto bench-press after five months than when he started?

S. What is the problem asking me to find? _____

O. _____

L. _____

AlgebraicThinking • Foundations

Lesson 7

Directions: *Work this problem with your partner.*

4. Kathy planted a garden. She planted 6 rows with 12 bean plants each. How many bean plants did she plant in her garden?

   S. What is the problem asking me to find? _____
   _____

   O. _____
   _____

   L. _____
   _____
   _____
   _____

31

Homework 7 — **AlgebraicThinking** • Foundations

Name _____

Directions: *Read each problem carefully. Highlight the question. Then circle the question to the right that best tells what is being asked in the problem. List the steps you would go through to recreate the scene with objects.*

1. The aerobics instructor at a local health club likes for her students to exercise in rows. Yesterday, she put them in rows of 8. There were 3 rows. How many people were exercising in all?

   a. How many rows are there?

   b. How many people are there?

_____
_____
_____
_____

2. Kristin and Lindsay jog every day. Kristin jogs 3 miles, and Lindsay jogs 10 miles. How many more miles does Lindsay jog than Kristin does in one week?

   a. How many miles does Lindsay jog?

   b. How many *more* miles does Lindsay jog?

_____
_____
_____
_____

AlgebraicThinking • Foundations

Warm Up 8: Uniquely You

Directions: *Answer each one of the questions to show your uniqueness.*

1. What are your three favorite foods?

2. What is the best gift you ever received? Why?

3. What is the best gift you ever gave? Why?

4. What are the three best things about school?

Lesson 8   **AlgebraicThinking • Foundations**

Directions: *Complete steps S, O, L, and V with your partner.*

1. Kristin and Lindsay jog every day. Kristin jogs 15 miles in a week. Lindsay jogs 32 miles in a week. How many more miles does Lindsay jog in a week?

    S. What is the problem asking me to find? _____
    _____

    O. _____
    _____

    L. _____
    _____

    V. _____
    _____

2. Simon and his friends enjoy building airplane models. Simon spent 4 hours on his 747 model. Michael spent 3 times that amount of time on his DC-10 jet. Thomas worked on his model for 7 hours. How many hours did Michael spend on his model?

    S. What is the problem asking me to find? _____
    _____

    O. _____
    _____

    L. _____
    _____

    V. _____
    _____

AlgebraicThinking • Foundations					Homework 8

Name _____

Directions: *It's time to be creative. You will practice writing word problems today.*

Tonight when you go home, find an article in the newspaper, cut it out, and attach it to this paper. Underline a few of the facts in the article. Use those facts to write a mathematical word problem.

_____
_____
_____
_____
_____
_____
_____
_____
_____
_____
_____
_____
_____
_____
_____
_____

Warm Up 9: Add Another

Directions: *Add one number to each box so that the sum will equal 100.*

25
48

31
54

12
70

43
18

AlgebraicThinking • Foundations   Lesson 9

Today will we continue to practice step L, Line up a Plan. Some plans will require you to choose more than one operation or steps to solve the problem. Work with your teacher on the following problems.

1. In order to improve its image, the Clown Brothers Carnival Co. agreed to give all the parking fees to the local schools to buy computer equipment. Parking cost $3 per car. On the night of the carnival, 400 parking spaces were empty in the lot. The lot could park 6,000 cars. How much money was raised parking cars?

    S. What is the problem asking me to find? _____

    O. _____

    L. _____

2. This summer, the principal of a school bought 12 computers. In November, he bought 10 more computers. The computers cost $1,300 each. How much money did the principal spend on computers?

    S. What is the problem asking me to find? _____

    O. _____

    L. _____

Lesson 9   **AlgebraicThinking** • Foundations

3. Frank worked for a lawn service during the summer. He earned $10 for each yard he mowed and $6 for each set of hedges he trimmed. He mowed 3 hours each day. How much did he make last week if he mowed 4 yards and trimmed 3 sets of hedges?

   S. What is the problem asking me to find?_____
   _____

   O. _____
   _____

   L. _____
   _____

AlgebraicThinking • Foundations Lesson 9

Directions: *Complete the following problems with your partner.*

4. Bob worked at a grocery store for $5 per hour. He worked 19 hours last week. He owes a friend $25 for a concert ticket. How much money will he have after he pays his friend back?

   S. What is the problem asking me to find?_____

   _____

   O. _____

   _____

   L. _____

   _____

5. The band needs to purchase 60 new uniforms for the upcoming school year. The jacket and pants for each uniform will cost $240. The hats will cost $36 each, and the special mascot overlay will cost $28 each. How much money will the band need to pay for the uniforms?

   S. What is the problem asking me to find?_____

   _____

   O. _____

   _____

   L. _____

   _____

Homework 9   **AlgebraicThinking** • Foundations

Name _____

Directions: *Write a word problem using the following facts. Then solve the problem. (You don't have to use all the facts.)*

Facts:

- The largest stadium in the world was the Strahov Stadium in Prague, Czech Republic. It was completed in 1934 and could accommodate 240,000 spectators. (It is no longer in use.)

- The largest stadium in the United States is Michigan Football Stadium in Ann Harbor, MI. It has a seating capacity of 102,501. However, on September 11, 1993, the stadium was overcrowded when 106,851 people saw Ohio State beat Michigan 27-23.

AlgebraicThinking • Foundations

Warm Up 10: Pattern Patrol

Directions: *Write the next three terms of each pattern.*

1. 2, 4, 6, 8, ... ___ ___ ___

2. 1, 2, 4, 8, ... ___ ___ ___

3. 1, 2, 3, 1, 2, 3, ... ___ ___ ___

4. 3, 6, 9, 12, ... ___ ___ ___

5. 1, 1, 2, 3, 5, 8, 13, ... ___ ___ ___

6. J, F, M, A, M, J, ... ___ ___ ___

7. 1, 10, 100, 1,000, ... ___ ___ ___

8. 1, 2, 3, 1, 2, 3, 4, 1, 2, 3, 4, 5, 1, 2, 3, ... ___ ___ ___

Lesson 10   **Algebraic Thinking • Foundations**

Directions: *Work through the following problems with your partner. Show each part of the steps S, O, L, and V from the SOLVE method.*

1. Anjulie had $35. She bought two classic movies that were on sale for $7 each and one new release for $15. How much change should Anjulie receive from the cashier?

   S. What is the problem asking me to find? _____
   _____

   O. _____
   _____

   L. _____
   _____

   V. _____
   _____

2. Janet bought 6 single stamps and 2 books of stamps. Each book had 20 stamps. How many stamps did she buy?

   S. What is the problem asking me to find? _____
   _____

   O. _____
   _____

   L. _____
   _____

   V. _____
   _____

Algebraic Thinking • Foundations   Lesson 10

3. Sandra needed to earn $35 to buy a new pair of jeans to wear to a party next week. She had a baby-sitting job on Thursday that paid $5 per hour. She baby-sat for 4 hours. How much more money will she need to buy the jeans?

S. What is the problem asking me to find? _____
_____

O. _____
_____

L. _____
_____

V. _____
_____

Homework 10 — **AlgebraicThinking • Foundations**

Name _____

Add or subtract.

1. 743
     37
  + 122

2. 846
  − 271

3.   47
     68
  + 92

4. 586
  + 902

5. 708
  − 536

6.   79
  − 18

7. 926
  + 39

8. 256
  − 78

AlgebraicThinking • Foundations

Warm Up 11: Pattern Patrol

Find the next three terms in each pattern.

1. A, C, B, D, C, E, D, F, E, G, F, ... ___ ___ ___

2. 1, 4, 9, 16, 25, ... ___ ___ ___

3. 100, 11000, 1110000, ... ___ ___ ___

4. M, T, W, T, ... ___ ___ ___

5. 10, 5, 20, 10, 30, 15, 40, 20, 50, 25, ... ___ ___ ___

Lesson 11   **AlgebraicThinking • Foundations**

Congratulations on your hard work with SOLVE. Today you will learn the final step, "E", which stands for Examine the Results. In this step you will check your work. If it is correct, write your answer in a complete sentence. Remember what you wrote in "S" to help with writing your sentence. If your answer is not correct, now is the time to revise your work.

Directions: *Complete the following problems with your teacher.*

1. The organizers of a large outdoor concert decided to have 28 different groups perform. After the first month of planning, 16 groups were signed up. How many more groups are needed to sign up?

   S. What is the problem asking me to find? _____

   O. _____

   L. _____

   V. _____

   E. _____

AlgebraicThinking • Foundations

Lesson 11

2. Jackie and Traci sold raffle tickets for the French Club fundraiser. Each ticket sold for $2. Traci sold 43 tickets. The two girls sold 97 tickets between them. How much money did Jackie collect for the fundraiser?

S. What is the problem asking me to find? _____

O. _____

L. _____

V. _____

E. _____

Directions: *Complete the following problems with your partner. Show all 5 steps of SOLVE.*

3. A dolphin jumped 11 feet to catch a fish from the aquarium keeper. Then the dolphin jumped twice as high to catch the next fish. How high did the dolphin jump the second time?

S. What is the problem asking me to find? _____

O. _____

L. _____

V. _____

E. _____

Lesson 11   Algebraic Thinking • Foundations

4. Justin has been collecting baseball cards for years. He bought 137 cards the first year and 143 cards the second year. He plans on putting them in a binder that will hold seven cards per page. How many pages must the binder have to hold Justin's collection?

   S. What is the problem asking me to find? _____

   O. _____

   L. _____

   V. _____

   E. _____

5. Jessica decided to join a CD club. She gets the first 10 CDs for one dollar. Part of the agreement is that she will buy 6 CDs within 2 years at a cost of $17 each. When she has completed her agreement, how much will she have spent on CDs?

   S. What is the problem asking me to find? _____

   O. _____

   L. _____

   V. _____

   E. _____

AlgebraicThinking • Foundations Homework 11

Name _____

Directions: *The answers to the questions have been given! But what are the questions? Write questions for the answers.*

The Maracaña Municipal Stadium in Rio de Janeiro is the largest stadium in the world still in use. It has a normal capacity of 205,000. Only 155,000 of those can be seated. A World Cup soccer final between Brazil and Uruguay attracted 199,854 people on July 16, 1950.

Answers:
1. 50,000

2. 44,854

3. 5,146

Warm Up 12: Ducks and Cows

Farmer Ben only has ducks and cows. He can't remember how many of each he has, but he really doesn't need to remember. He does know that he has 22 animals, which is his age. He also remembers that those animals have a total of 56 legs, which is his father's age. How many of each animal does Farmer Ben have?

AlgebraicThinking • Foundations   Lesson 12

SOLVE Problems for Review

1. There are 16 cheerleaders on the Mustang Varsity cheerleading squad. At the last home basketball game, the cheerleaders led a cheer every four minutes. The game lasted 96 minutes. How many times did the cheerleaders cheer for the Mustangs that night?

2. Jessica received $25 for her birthday from her grandparents. She went to the mall to buy 2 CDs that cost $11 and $13. How much change should she receive back?

3. Sara makes a call to a teen talk line. The cost of the call is $3 for the first two minutes plus $1 for each additional minute. If she talks for 10 minutes, how much will the call cost?

4. John set a goal of swimming 20 laps in the pool every week during the summer. On Monday and Wednesday, he swam 5 laps each day. On Tuesday and Thursday, he swam 2 laps each day. How many laps does he need to swim on Friday to complete his laps for the week?

5. James' father wants to lose 25 pounds. He lost 3 pounds each week for each of the last 5 weeks. How much weight has he lost?

6. Jerry spent three dollars on each of five magazines at the supermarket, while waiting on his mom to do the shopping. He was thirsty, so he went outside to the soft drink machine and bought a drink for a dollar. Someone outside was working to raise money for a local charity, so he donated two dollars. How much did his trip to the supermarket cost him?

Warm Up 13

Warm Up 13: Taxi Ride

Directions: *Use SOLVE to answer the problem below.*

Chris wanted to ride a taxi from the library to the mall. The cab driver said there was a $2 fee plus $1 per mile. Chris knew the library was 11 miles from the mall. How much would his ride cost?

S. What is the problem asking me to find? _____

O. _____

L. _____

V. _____

E. _____

AlgebraicThinking • Foundations   Warm Up 14

Warm Up 14: You're the Teacher

Brent has finished the problems below. It is your job to find his mistakes, explain what he did wrong, and show the correct answer for each problem.

Brent's Work	What are his mistakes?	Correct Answers

1.   375
     + 167
     ―――
       532

* *

2.   265
     + 375
     ―――
     6,710

* *

3.   137
     + 128
     ―――
       265

* *

4.   843
     + 736
     ―――
       579

Lesson 14 **AlgebraicThinking • Foundations**

Use the following number tiles for your cups. Place one set of the numbers 1 – 9 in the group cup and place one set of the numbers 1 – 9 in the items cup.

1	2	3	4	5	6	7	8	9
1	2	3	4	5	6	7	8	9

Choose facts with your groups and items cups and model them with squares and beans below.

_____ groups with _____ items per group = _____

_____ groups with _____ items per group = _____

_____ groups with _____ items per group = _____

_____ groups with _____ items per group = _____

AlgebraicThinking • Foundations Lesson 14

Use the centimeter grid paper to make pictures of multiplication facts. Make sure you use at least two colors.

Lesson 14 **Algebraic**Thinking • Foundations

Use the centimeter grid paper to make pictures of multiplication facts. Make sure you use at least two colors.

AlgebraicThinking • Foundations Lesson 14

Grid for Basic Multiplication Facts

X	0	1	2	3	4	5	6	7	8	9
0	0	0	0	0	0	0	0	0	0	0
1	0	1	2	3	4	5	6	7	8	9
2	0	2	4	6	8	10	12	14	16	18
3	0	3	6	9	12	15	18	21	24	27
4	0	4	8	12	16	20	24	28	32	36
5	0	5	10	15	20	25	30	35	40	45
6	0	6	12	18	24	30	36	42	48	54
7	0	7	14	21	28	35	42	49	56	63
8	0	8	16	24	32	40	48	56	64	72
9	0	9	18	27	36	45	54	63	72	81

Homework 14 **AlgebraicThinking** • Foundations

Name _____

Directions: *Find the median and mode for each set of data.*

1. 7, 8, 4, 3, 6, 9, 12, 9, 5, 11, 9

median _____ mode _____

2. 98, 82, 47, 56, 82, 65, 47, 73

median _____ mode _____

3. 16, 21, 35, 18, 25, 21, 21, 16, 37, 39

median _____ mode _____

Algebraic Thinking • Foundations

Warm Up 15: Tic-Tac-Toe

Ryan and Shelly played a game of tic-tac-toe. Find out who won the game by matching each answer on the board to the correct problem. Put the appropriate letter on the board.

Ryan played the X
A. 251 • 32 =
B. 480 ÷ 20 =
C. 145 − 78 =
D. 253 • 12 =

Shelly played the O
E. 385 • 12 =
F. 1,386 ÷ 9 =
G. 658 − 267 =
H. 25 • 24 =

391	5,428	154
600	8,032	4,620
24	3,036	67

Who won the game? _____

Lesson 15

AlgebraicThinking • Foundations

Directions: *Record what you are directed to on the cards in each envelope that you are given.*

Envelope #1:

Envelope #2:

* * * * * * * * * * * * * * * * * *

The Commutative Property says: _____

_____

* * * * * * * * * * * * * * * * * *

Envelope #3:

Envelope #4:

Algebraic Thinking • Foundations   Lesson 15

Directions: *Answer each of the questions below with your partner. Use what you have just discovered to correctly answer the questions.*

True or false:

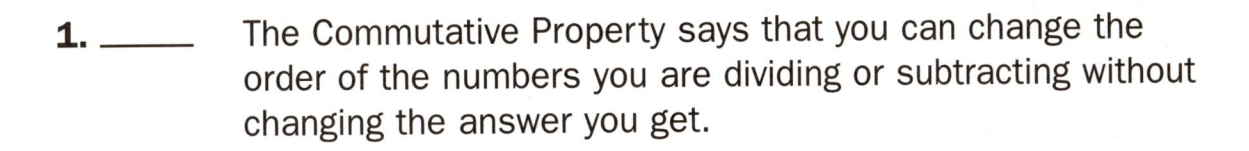

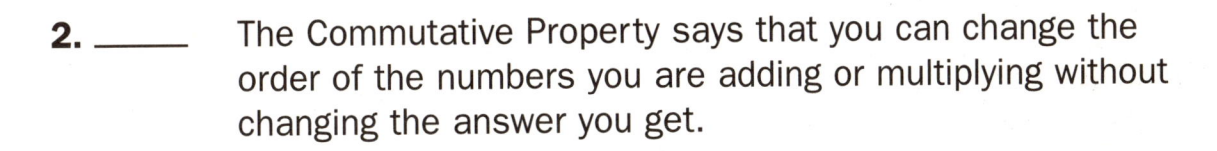

1. _____   The Commutative Property says that you can change the order of the numbers you are dividing or subtracting without changing the answer you get.

2. _____   The Commutative Property says that you can change the order of the numbers you are adding or multiplying without changing the answer you get.

3. _____   The Commutative Property says that 4 + 5 = 5 + 4.

4. _____   The Commutative Property says that 6 ÷ 3 = 3 ÷ 6.

5. _____   The Commutative Property says that 6 − 8 = 8 − 6.

6. _____   The Commutative Property says that 5 • 7 = 7 • 5.

Write an example of why the Commutative Property does or does not work for each of the four basic operations (addition, subtraction, multiplication, or division).

Addition   Subtraction

Multiplication   Division

Homework 15 **Algebraic Thinking** • Foundations

Name _____

Divide.

1. 4)32   2. 6)24

3. 7)49   4. 5)35

5. 9)54   6. 2)16

7. 10)30   8. 8)72

9. 6)12   10. 7)56

AlgebraicThinking • Foundations Warm Up 16

Warm Up 16: Division Tower

Follow the division problems from top to bottom. Use the answer for each problem as the dividend in the next problem.

4,320 ÷ 9 = _____

                 ____ ÷ 2 = ____

                               ____ ÷ 6 = ____

                                           ____ ÷ 5 = ____

                                                     ____ ÷ 4 = ____

Lesson 16

AlgebraicThinking • Foundations

Directions: *Record what you are directed to on the cards in each envelope that you are given.*

Envelope #1:

Envelope #2:

* * * * * * * * * * * * * * * *

The Associative Property says: _____

_____

64

Algebraic Thinking • Foundations

Lesson 16

1. The Associative Property says: _____
   _____

2. Finish the examples below.
   a) 8 − (4 − 1) =   b) (8 − 4) − 1 =

3. From the examples in #2, do you think the Associative Property holds true for subtraction? _____

4. Write another example (of your own) and explain why you feel that the Associative Property does or does not hold true for subtraction.

5. Finish the examples below.
   a) (16 ÷ 4) ÷ 2 =   b) 16 ÷ (4 ÷ 2) =

6. From the example in #5, do you think the Associative Property holds true for division? _____

7. Write another example (of your own) and explain why you feel that the Associative Property does or does not hold true for division.

65

Homework 16 — **AlgebraicThinking • Foundations**

Name _____

Directions: *It's time to practice your multiplication skills. Draw a picture to model each problem and then give the product. (No calculators!)*

EXAMPLE 2 • 4 = 8 (The first number (2) is the number of groups. The second number (4) is the number of objects in each group.)

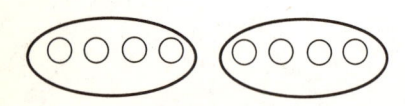

1. 3 • 4 =

2. 5 • 4 =

3. 2 • 6 =

4. 10 • 2 =

5. 1 • 3 =

6. 3 • 1 =

7. 6 • 4 =

8. 4 • 5 =

9. Write three problems that have a product of 12.

10. Write four problems that have a product of 36.

AlgebraicThinking • Foundations

Warm Up 17

Warm Up 17: SOLVE the Problem

Use the SOLVE method to answer the word problem.

The fans for both teams wanted to cheer their football teams on to a championship victory. Tickets to a regular season game were only $4, but tickets to the championship game were $7 each. At the gate, programs sold for $3 each. If 4,000 fans turned out to support the teams, how much money did the stadium make from selling tickets?

S

O

L

V

E

Lesson 17   **AlgebraicThinking • Foundations**

Directions: *Work through the SOLVE method for each word problem with your teacher.*

Problem #1:

The manager at Pizza Plaza gives two employees an overtime bonus. They each worked a different amount of overtime, so one received $40 and the other received only $25. Later, he decided to triple the bonus for each of the two people. How much did he end up giving the two employees for their overtime hours?

S

O

L

V

E

Problem #2:

A tutor was helping three students one evening. She gave one student 6 problems to work on, the second got 4 problems, and the third was given 10 problems. She decided that since they were doing so well, she would only give each student half the amount of problems for homework that they had done earlier. How many total problems did she assign the three students for homework?

S

O

L

V

E

AlgebraicThinking • Foundations   Lesson 17

Use this page to record any notes on Commutative or Associative properties!

Lesson 17　　　　　　　　　　　　　　　　**AlgebraicThinking • Foundations**

Directions: *For #1 – 8, tell whether the Distributive Property states that the number sentence is True or False. Be careful, especially on #6 – 8. THINK, THINK, THINK!*

1. 3(7 – 4) = 3 • 7 – 3 • 4 = 21 – 12 = 9　　　　　　　_____

2. 4(3 + 6) = 4 • 3 + 4 • 6 = 12 + 24 = 36　　　　　　_____

3. 8(3 • 2) = 8 • 3 • 8 • 2 = 24 • 8 • 2 = 192 • 2 = 384　_____

4. (12 – 6) ÷ 3 = 12 ÷ 3 – 6 ÷ 3 = 4 – 2 = 2　　　　　_____

5. (12 – 6) ÷ 3 = 6 ÷ 3 = 2　　　　　　　　　　　　_____

6. 3 – (4 • 5) = 3 – 4 • 3 – 5　　　　　　　　　　　_____

7. 16 ÷ (8 – 4) = 2 – 4 = ⁻2　　　　　　　　　　　　_____

8. (9 + 5) • 4 = 36 + 20 = 56　　　　　　　　　　　_____

For #9 – 11, answer each question after discussing it with your partner.

9. List 3 things you have learned today.
　　1.

　　2.

　　3.

10. What do you think "distribute" means? Give a real world example of this definition.

11. What do you think the Distributive Property says?

AlgebraicThinking • Foundations   Homework 17

Name _____

Subtract.

1. 74 − 39 =

2. 46 − 12 =

3. 379 − 81 =

4. 106 − 87 =

5. 92 − 29 =

6. 240 − 156 =

7. 408 − 240 =

8. 79 − 68 =

9. 526 − 379 =

10. 86 − 38 =

Warm Up 18: Mystery Squares

Directions: *Solve each problem below. Next, cut apart all of the 16 squares. Rearrange the squares so all solutions match up and form a new 4 x 4 square. Then, glue or tape the new 4 x 4 square pieces on a blank sheet of paper.*

64 E 4•4 72 27	7•6 O 12 100 56	47 S 6•4 49 6•8	81 M 24 6•2 9•6
48 O 7•10 45 9•9	8•4 K 7•3 36 7•3	17 J 3•3 3•2 8•8	16 R 7• 4•7 8•3
20 F 7•5 70 6•3	4•9 A 5•9 16 42	6•3 T 7•7 9 36	63 L 7•8 24 4•5
9•3 H 10•10 8•9 32	54 I 28 5•5 27	8•7 W 25 21 24	18 Y 36 8•3 2•8

Algebraic Thinking • Foundations　　　　　　　　　　　　　　　　Lesson 18

Directions: *For #1 – 7, tell which property, if any, is illustrated by each example. (Be careful, #7 is a "toughy".)*

1. 5 + (3 + 9) = (5 + 3) + 9　　　　　　　　　_____

2. 8 + 4 = 4 + 8　　　　　　　　　　　　　　_____

3. 2(9 − 4) = 18 − 8　　　　　　　　　　　　_____

4. (8 + 4) ÷ 2 = 8 ÷ 2 + 4 ÷ 2　　　　　　　　_____

5. 3 • 4 • 5 = 4 • 3 • 5　　　　　　　　　　　_____

6. 9 • (2 • 7) = (9 • 2) • 7　　　　　　　　　_____

7. 12 − 8 = 4(3 − 2)　　　　　　　　　　　　_____

For #8 – 11, state whether each statement is True or False. Then, write an example of your own, to support your answer.

8. The Associative Property holds true for subtraction.　　_____

9. The Commutative Property holds true for addition.　　_____

10. The Distributive Property says that you can "give out" a factor to both numbers in a sum, then add them together afterwards.　　_____

11. The Associative Property holds true for multiplication.　　_____

Warm Up 19: SOLVE — You owe me money!

Directions: *Leah has used SOLVE to solve her problem. Look over her work and decide if her answer makes sense. Explain why or why not.*

Leah has $28. Tomorrow she has to give 3 friends back $6 that she owes each of them. How much money will she have left after she pays back her friends?

S. — How much money she will have left

O. — She has $28. She has to give 3 friends $6 each.

L. — Write and evaluate a numerical expression.

V. — Estimate - less than 28

$$28 - 3 \cdot 6$$
$$25 \cdot 6 = 150$$

E. — She will have $150 left after she pays back her friends.

Algebraic Thinking • Foundations

Lesson 19

Let's Bring Some Order to This!

"I hate rules!" "I wish there were no rules!" "Why do we have rules anyway?"

How many times have you heard those types of questions? All of us have rules that we don't like, but if we are honest with ourselves, we know that they bring order to life. Math must also have rules, or it would be very confusing. In today's lesson, you should learn some rules for math. Not only should you learn them, but you should also learn why they are the rules. These rules put the operations of math (+, −, •, ÷) in order. Consider the following problems.

Directions: *S-O-L-V-E each problem with your teacher.*

1. Mrs. Johnson took her son, Lewis, out for his 9th birthday. They ordered 5 large pizzas and had them cut into 12 pieces each. Only 52 pieces were eaten. How many did Lewis get to take home?

   S. _____

   _____

   O. _____

   _____

   L. _____

   _____

   V. _____

   _____

   E. _____

   _____

Lesson 19   **AlgebraicThinking** • Foundations

2. Mrs. Fields has a lot of kids. She has one son. She has two sets of triplets that are all girls. During the summer, four of her children stay with their grandparents for 3 weeks. How many of the children stay at home?

S. _____

O. _____

L. _____

V. _____

E. _____

Algebraic Thinking • **Foundations** Lesson 19

You may have solved problems 1 and 2 by using a two-step problem. Did you know that they could be solved with only one numerical expression?

Directions: *Complete the following problems with your teacher.* (**NOTE:** When you add an equals sign and an answer to the expression, it becomes an equation.)

> ## Wait a Minute!
> **What is a numerical expression?**
> A numerical expression is a grouping of numbers and operations.
> For example, 1 + 2 • 3

3. 4 + 3 • 5	**4.** 7 + 2 • 6	**5.** 4 • 3 − 2
6. 12 − 5 • 2	**7.** 10 ÷ 5 − 2	**8.** 12 − 8 ÷ 2
9. 3 • 2 + 4 • 5	**10.** 4 • 4 + 8 ÷ 2	**11.** 8 − 2 + 6 ÷ 2

Lesson 19   Algebraic**Thinking** • Foundations

Order of Operations
(For problems with +, –, •, ÷ only.)

1. Work all multiplication and division in order from left to right.
2. Work all addition and subtraction in order from left to right.

Directions: *Evaluate each expression.*

12. 12 – 8 + 3   **13.** 3 • 6 + 9 ÷ 3   **14.** 16 ÷ 4 + 8 – 3 • 2

15. 29 – 3 • 8   **16.** 48 ÷ 12 • 4   **17.** 23 • 2 – 40 + 2

18. 14 ÷ 2 • 3   **19.** 36 ÷ 9 • 3 ÷ 6   **20.** 28 + 5 – 10 • 2

21. 55 ÷ 5 – 3 • 3   **22.** 15 + 5 – 20 ÷ 4   **23.** 8 • 7 – 28 • 2

Algebraic Thinking • Foundations

Lesson 19

Directions: Use S-O-L-V-E to solve this problem. Try to solve it by using a numerical expression.

24. Adam gets to eat pizza slices from two different pizzas. The first one has 12 pieces and is shared between 6 people (including Adam). The second one has 10 pieces and is shared between 5 people (including Adam). How many pieces of pizza will Adam eat in all?

S. _____

_____

O. _____

_____

L. _____

_____

V. _____

_____

E. _____

_____

Homework 19   **AlgebraicThinking • Foundations**

Name _____

Multiply.

1.   9
      × 8

2.   7
      × 6

3.   4
      × 8

4.   12
      × 5

5.   26
      × 4

6.   32
      × 3

7.   48
      × 2

8.   55
      × 6

9.   47
      × 9

AlgebraicThinking • Foundations

Warm Up 20

Warm Up 20: Fast Track

Directions: *Follow the track from top to bottom. Use the answer as the first number in the next problem.*

2,625 ÷ 7 = _____

+ 25

_____ • 10 = _____

− 4

_____ ÷ 9 = _____

− 150

_____ ÷ 2 = _____

_____ − 47 = _____

÷ 5 = _____

• 13 = _____

Lesson 20

AlgebraicThinking • Foundations

More Order

Yesterday, we learned to evaluate numerical expressions with the four basic operations (+, –, •, ÷). In some situations, those rules don't make sense. For instance, read the following problem:

⇨ Adam was a member of a video club for three years. In the first year of membership he received 12 videos for only a dollar! In the last two years of the membership, he bought 9 more videos for $14 each. After he watched the movies, he decided to give them to his friends. He gave the same amount to each of his three friends. How many videos did each friend get?

S.

O.

L.

V.

E.

This problem illustrates that we should do all work within grouping symbols first. Also, we have to deal with expressions that have exponents in them.

AlgebraicThinking • Foundations Lesson 20

Just for Practice

$5^2 =$

$2^4 =$

$3^5 =$

$10^3 =$

$10^4 =$

What is an exponent?

An exponent is a number that tells how many times a base is a factor.

For example, in the expression 4^3, 4 is the base and 3 is the exponent. So, 4 is a factor 3 times.

$4^3 = 4 \cdot 4 \cdot 4 = 64$

$5^4 = 5 \cdot 5 \cdot 5 \cdot 5 = 625$

Lesson 20 **AlgebraicThinking • Foundations**

Order of Operations

> 1. Do all work within grouping symbols.
> 2. Evaluate all exponents.
> 3. Work all multiplication and division in order from left to right.
> 4. Work all addition and subtraction in order from left to right.

An easy way to remember this is the following phrase:

"**P**lease **E**xcuse **M**y **D**ear **A**unt **S**ally."

Directions: *Evaluate the following numerical expressions with your teacher.*

1. $5 + 3 \cdot 2 + 6$

2. $32 \div (10 - 6)$

3. $(3 + 2) - (4 + 1)$

4. $10 \cdot (5 - 2) + 1$

5. $7 \cdot 3 + 3^2$

6. $45 \div (11 - 2) \cdot 6$

7. $3 \cdot 2^5 - 84$

8. $\dfrac{3^2 + 6}{7 - (10 \div 5)}$

AlgebraicThinking • Foundations Lesson 20

Directions: *Use the numbers 0 – 9 to fill in the boxes to make the entire worksheet correct.*

1. ☐ • (6 − 1) + ☐ = 23

2. ☐ − 5 + ☐ = 11

3. 6 + (☐ − ☐) = 9

4. ☐ − (☐ + 4) = 2

5. 7 + ☐ − ☐ = 10

Lesson 20 Algebraic**Thinking** • Foundations

Directions: *Evaluate each numerical expression.*

1. $5 \cdot 7 - 6 \div 2 + 3^2$

2. $3 + 2 \cdot 3 + 5$

3. $12(20 - 17) - 3 \cdot 7$

4. $29 - 3(9 - 5)$

5. $15 \div 3 \cdot 5 - 4^2$

6. $(8 - 3) \cdot (12 \div 4) - 1$

7. $3(2^3 + 4^3)$

8. $5^3 - 8 \cdot 5 + 6$

9. $20 \div 4 \cdot 5 \cdot 2 \div 10$

10. $64 \div (10 - 6)^2 \cdot 10$

AlgebraicThinking • Foundations

Homework 20

Name _____

Solve each problem.

1. 706
    32
    + 496

2. 9)‾36‾

3. 92
    − 78

4. 27
    × 8

5. 10)‾400‾

6. 78 + 56 + 39 =

7. 36
    × 7

8. 147 − 27 =

Warm Up 21

Warm Up 21: "Sum" Estimate

Fill in the boxes below with the numbers 3 through 8, to get a sum close to 1,500 without going over.

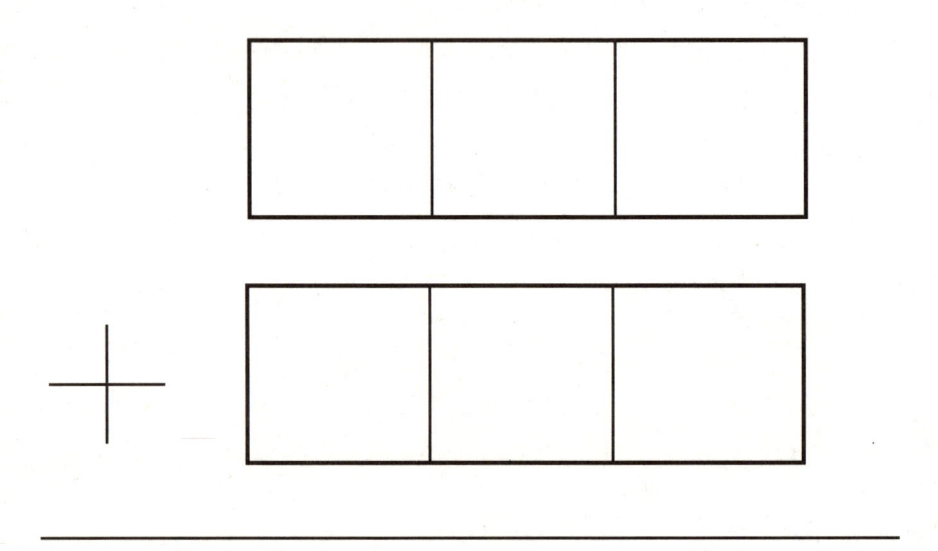

```
     ☐☐☐
  + ☐☐☐
  ─────────
```

88

AlgebraicThinking • Foundations Lesson 21

Scavenger Hunt

Directions:
1. Begin at the poster that the teacher instructs.
2. Evaluate the expression on the poster.
3. Find another poster that has the value of your expression at the bottom of the poster.
4. Keep going through each of the posters, always moving to the one that has the value to the expression you just evaluated.
5. Be sure to show all work and record the order in which you traveled from one poster to the next.

1. Poster _____

2. Poster _____

3. Poster _____

4. Poster _____

5. Poster _____

6. Poster _____

7. Poster _____

8. Poster _____

Lesson 21 AlgebraicThinking • Foundations

9. Poster _____ **10.** Poster _____

11. Poster _____ **12.** Poster _____

13. Poster _____ **14.** Poster _____

15. Poster _____

AlgebraicThinking • Foundations

Warm Up 22: SOLVE the Problem

Use the SOLVE method to answer the problem. Be sure to complete all of the steps.

Hector bags groceries at Food City. He has decided that there is a system of bagging groceries based on how many items a customer buys. If the customer buys 4 items, he can put them in 1 bag. A purchase of 9 items will take 2 bags. 14 items will require 3 bags, and 19 items will take 4 bags. How many items can Hector put in 5 bags at this rate?

S

O

L

V

E

Warm Up 23: "Tri" It

Put each number, 1 through 9, in the blank boxes below to get a sum of 20 along each side of the triangle. Each number may only be used once.

Algebraic Thinking • Foundations   Lesson 23

Points, Lines, and Planes (oh, my!)

A point is a location.
It is represented by a dot

• M

A line is a set of points that extends without end in opposite directions.

It is represented with arrowheads on each end of a segment.

⟵————⟶ m

A plane is a set of points that extends without end in all directions along a flat surface.

It is represented by a parallelogram.

M

Points, lines, and planes are the three most basic ideas of geometry. Each of these cannot be drawn. However, they can be represented by simple drawings shown at the left.

Keep in mind, they are only representations!

Today, you will learn how to name points, lines, and planes. We will also learn about parts of lines.

EXPLORE! Points, Lines, and Planes

Materials: 1) three small flat objects, such as coins; 2) a yard stick

1. Drop two of the objects on a flat surface. Can a yardstick be placed so that it touches both objects at the same time?

2. Drop the objects three more times. Is there ever a time when the yardstick doesn't touch both objects? If so, when?

3. If the yardstick were unlimited in length, would there ever be a time when the yardstick wouldn't touch both objects?

Lesson 23   Algebraic Thinking • Foundations

Keep goin'!

4. This time, drop three of your objects on a flat surface. Can a yardstick be placed so that it touches all three objects at the same time?

5. Name something (physical) that would cover all three objects at the same time.

6. Is there ever a time when the three objects can't be covered by what you choose?

7. What would you have to do to your "cover" so that it will always cover your objects?

8. What if you only drop one object? In how many ways can you place the yardstick so that it touches the object?

Fill in the blanks.

9. In the exploration, the "yardstick" that extends in all directions represents a _____. The flat objects represent a _____.

10. It took _____ objects to make the yardstick only cover them in one way. _____ points determine a line.

11. The "cover" represented a _____. _____ points determine a plane.

AlgebraicThinking • Foundations   Lesson 23

Directions: *Fill in the chart with your teacher.*

Figure	Properties	Example	Symbol	Read as
Point				
Line				
Plane				
Line Segment				
Ray				
Angle				

Did you know?
* Two lines are **parallel** if they lie in the same plane and never intersect.
* **Skew** lines are lines which do not lie in the same plane and do not intersect.

Lesson 23 Algebraic Thinking • Foundations

Directions: *Fill in the blank.*

1. A _____ continues without end in opposite directions.

2. A _____ is a part of a line and contains two endpoints.

3. A _____ represents a location.

4. A _____ is a flat surface which extends forever in all directions.

5. A _____ is part of a line and has one endpoint.

Directions: *Indicate true or false. If it is false, replace the underlined word with a word which will make the statement true.*

6. Skew lines are <u>always</u> parallel.

7. Parallel lines are <u>always</u> in the same plane.

8. A line has <u>no</u> endpoints.

9. A ray has <u>two</u> endpoints.

10. A segment has <u>two</u> endpoints.

11. Name a ray on line *m* with endpoint D.

12. What is another name for line *n*?

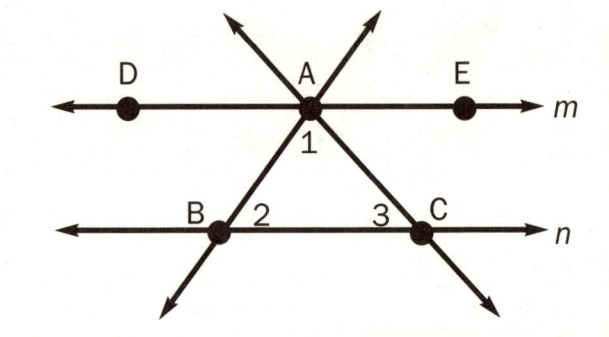

13. Which lines are parallel?

14. Give another name for angle 1.

15. Give another name for angle 2.

16. Name three segments on line *m*.

17. Name two rays on line *m*.

AlgebraicThinking • Foundations　　　　　Homework 23

Name _____

Find the mean for each set of data.

1.　17, 18, 21, 31, 25, 20

mean _____

2.　98, 76, 82, 95, 79, 85, 80, 93

mean _____

3.　42, 50, 36, 52, 45

mean _____

Warm Up 24   AlgebraicThinking • Foundations

Warm Up 24: SOLVE the Problem

Use the SOLVE method to answer the word problem. Remember to go through all of the steps.

The butcher at Food City had to cut 285 pounds of beef before his shift was over. He cut 25 pounds of steak, 30 pounds of beef ribs, and 55 pounds of roast beef. He ground 85 pounds of hamburger before he took his break. After his 10-minute break, he put out 35 pounds of chicken for sale. How many pounds of beef will he have to cut after he returns from his break, so that he can go home?

S

O

L

V

E

AlgebraicThinking • **Foundations**   Lesson 24

Angles

Hey, man, what's your angle?

Do you recall what a **ray** is? A ray is part of a **line**. It has one endpoint and continues without end in one direction.

Draw two rays beginning from the same point.

The figure you just drew is an **angle.** The point that the rays start from is called the **vertex.** Yours may not look like your neighbor's, but they are all angles. Today, we will look at the different types of angles.

But FIRST! Write a definition for the word *angle*. (**HINT:** Look back at your picture.)

_____

Lesson 24   **AlgebraicThinking** • Foundations

> **A circle has 360 degrees!**

1. Cut out the circle your teacher gave you. (Be very careful!)

2. Fold the circle in half. Trace the fold. What is the shape of the fold? _____ Since it is half of the circle, how many degrees does it have? _____

3. Fold the half circle *(semicircle)* in half. It is now $\frac{1}{4}$ of the circle. Trace the fold. What is the shape of the fold? _____ How many degrees does it have? _____

4. Fold the $\frac{1}{4}$ circle in half. It is now $\frac{1}{8}$ of the circle. Trace the fold. What is the shape of the fold? _____ How many degrees does it have? _____

2.	3.	4.

AlgebraicThinking • Foundations Lesson 24

Let's Classify Some Angles!

We are going to figure out three classifications for angles. The classifications are **right, acute, and obtuse.** Look at the following groups of angles and see if you can write a definition for the classifications.

Hey, that's a cute angle!

1. Write a definition for *right angles.*

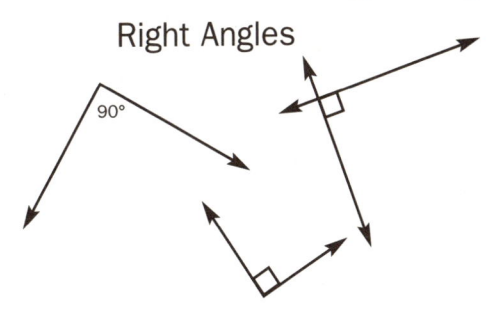

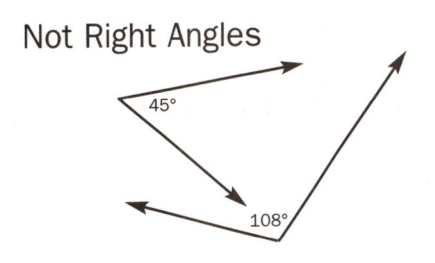

Right Angles — 90°, □

Not Right Angles — 45°, 108°

2. Write a definition for *acute angles.*

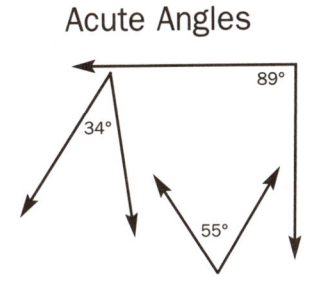

Acute Angles — 89°, 34°, 55°

Not Acute Angles — □, 102°, 91°

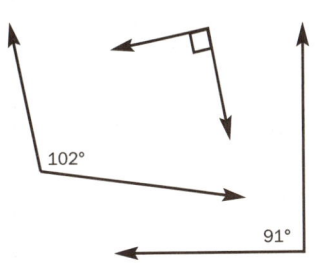

3. Write a definition for *obtuse angles.*

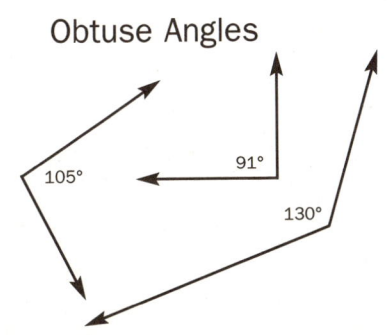

Obtuse Angles — 105°, 91°, 130°

Not Obtuse Angles — 39°, 89.9°, □

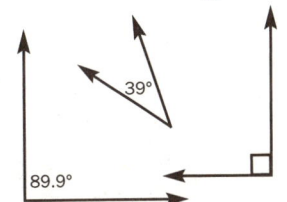

101

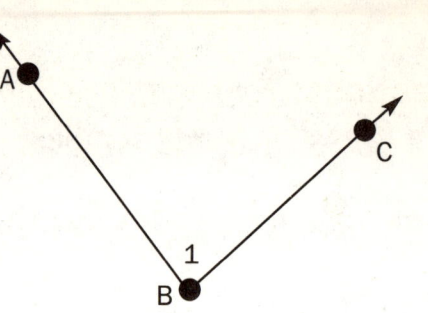

Lesson 24   **AlgebraicThinking • Foundations**

4. Give four names for the angle at the right.

5. Use a protractor to measure the angle to the right. Your teacher will help you with this.

Directions: *Use a protractor to draw angles with each of the following measures.*

6. 65°   **7.** 150°   **8.** 30°

Directions: *Measure each angle. Also, classify it as right, acute, or obtuse.*

9.   **10.**   **11.**

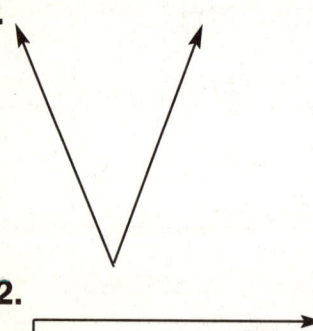

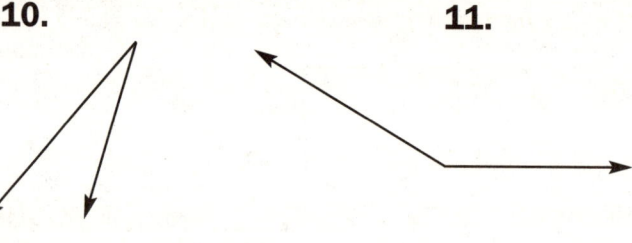

12. 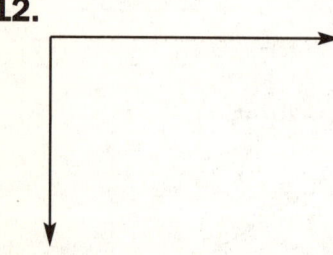   **13.**   **14.**

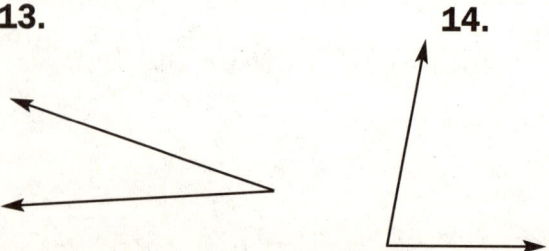

102

Algebraic Thinking • Foundations Lesson 24

Directions: For each angle, list the sides, and the vertex of each angle.

15.

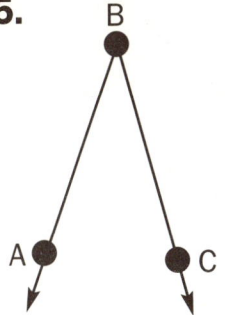

16.

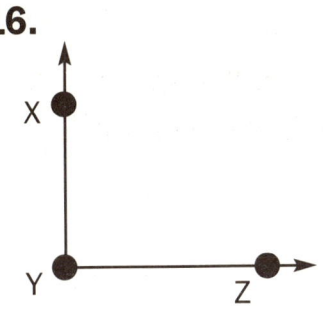

17.

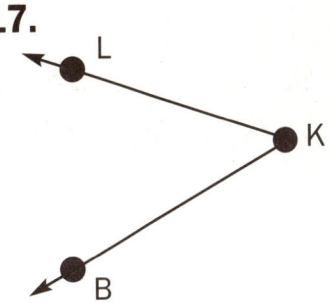

Did you know?
- Lines that form right angles are said to be **perpendicular**.
- If the sum of the measures of two angles is 90°, they are **complementary**.
- If the sum of the measures of two angles is 180°, they are **supplementary.**

Directions: Tell whether each angle is acute, right, or obtuse. Also, indicate what its complement or supplement is. (**HINT:** There may not be a complement.)

18. 45°

Complement _____

Supplement _____

19. 87°

Complement _____

Supplement _____

103

Lesson 24 AlgebraicThinking • Foundations

20. 130°

Complement _____

Supplement _____

21. 95°

Complement _____

Supplement _____

22. 90°

Complement _____

Supplement _____

23. 70°

Complement _____

Supplement _____

24. 89°

Complement _____

Supplement _____

25. 1°

Complement _____

Supplement _____

26. 100°

Complement _____

Supplement _____

27. 120°

Complement _____

Supplement _____

28. What kind of angle doesn't have a complement?

AlgebraicThinking • Foundations

Homework 24

Name _____

Draw a model for each multiplication problem.

1. 7 • 3

2. 4 • 5

3. 6 • 9

4. 3 • 7

5. 2 • 1

6. 8 • 4

Warm Up 25: Missing Squares

Fill in the missing squares with numbers so that each row, column, and diagonal will have the same sum.

635	47	467
		551
299		

Algebraic Thinking • Foundations

Lesson 25

Fraction Strips

Directions: *Today, you will make a fraction kit. Follow all instructions given by your teacher. It is very important that you work carefully. Don't hurry through this. When you finish, fill in the blanks below.*

1 blue = _____

1 brown = _____   2 browns = _____

1 green = _____   2 greens = _____   3 greens = _____

1 yellow = _____   2 yellows = _____   3 yellows = _____
4 yellows = _____

1 orange = _____   2 oranges = _____   3 oranges = _____
4 oranges = _____   5 oranges = _____   6 oranges = _____

1 red = _____   2 reds = _____   3 reds = _____
4 reds = _____   5 reds = _____   6 reds = _____
7 reds = _____   8 reds = _____

1 purple = _____   2 purples = _____   3 purples = _____
4 purples = _____   5 purples = _____   6 purples = _____
7 purples = _____   8 purples = _____   9 purples = _____

1 pink = _____   2 pinks = _____   3 pinks = _____
4 pinks = _____   5 pinks = _____   6 pinks = _____
7 pinks = _____   8 pinks = _____   9 pinks = _____
10 pinks = _____   11 pinks = _____   12 pinks = _____

Lesson 25 **AlgebraicThinking** • Foundations

Legal Trades

Record the legal trades you discovered.

AlgebraicThinking • Foundations

Homework 25

Name _____

Directions: *Shade a model for each fraction.*

1. $\frac{2}{3}$

2. $\frac{3}{5}$

3. $\frac{3}{8}$

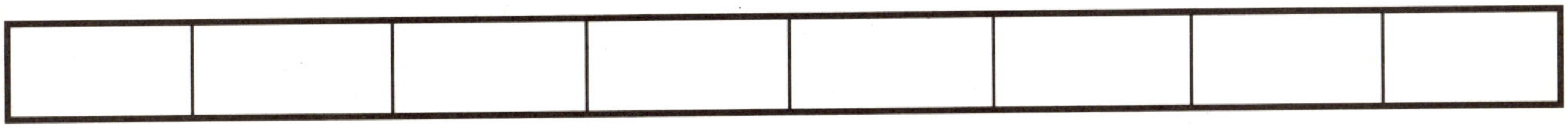

4. $\frac{3}{4}$

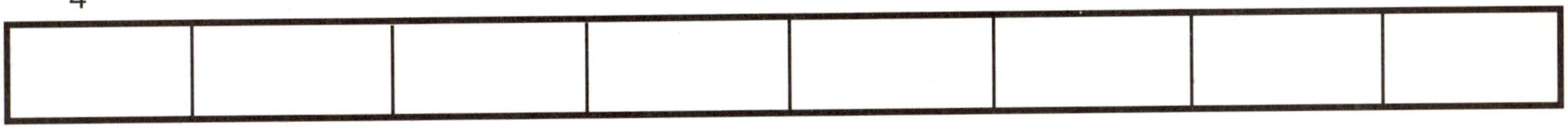

Directions: *Write the fraction for each model.*

5.

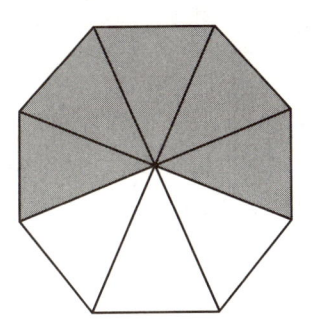

6.

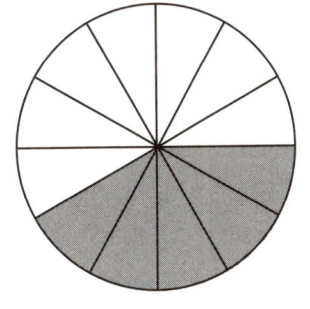

7.

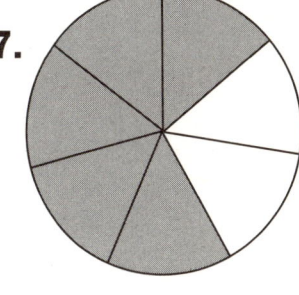

8.

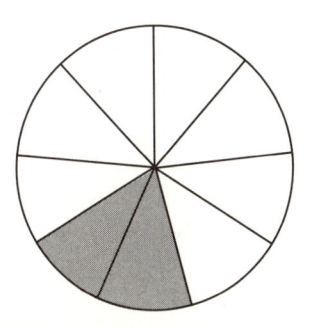

9.

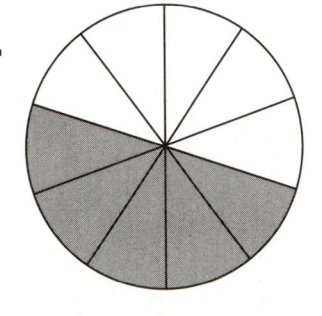

10.

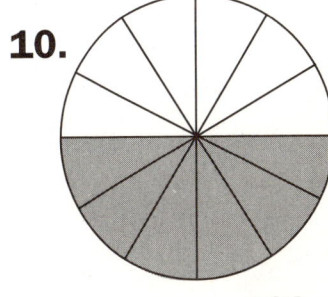

109

Warm Up 26: Place the Parentheses

For each problem, place the parentheses in the correct place, so that when you simplify the expression, you get the answer written to the right.

1. 50 − 6 • 2 + 5   Answer: 8

2. 14 + 6 ÷ 3 − 2 • 4   Answer: 38

3. 8 • 5 − 4 + 10 ÷ 2   Answer: 33

AlgebraicThinking • Foundations Lesson 26

Equivalent Fractions

Directions: *Complete the following table with your teacher.*

Model	Shaded Fraction	Unshaded Fraction	Whole Fraction
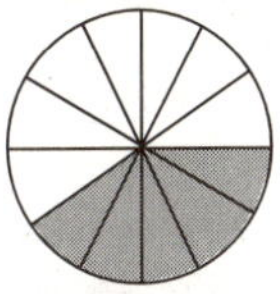			
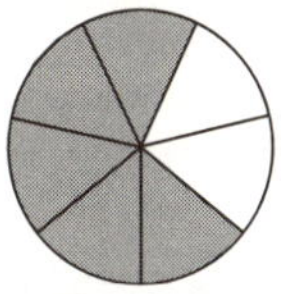			
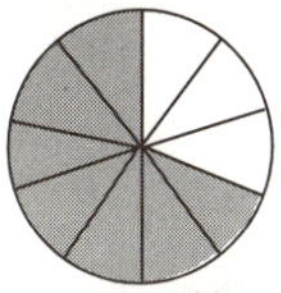			
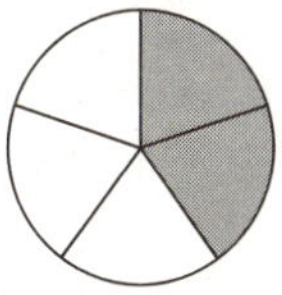			
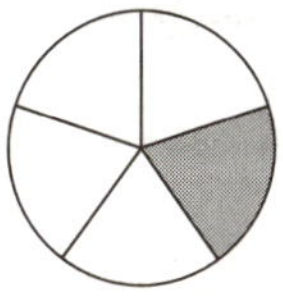			

☞ What do you notice about the fractions that represent one whole unit?

☞ Each of the fractions that have the same numerator and denominator has a value of 1. Fractions that have different names but the same value are called **equivalent fractions.**

☞ Look at the following models. Is the shaded portion more than, less than, or equal to $\frac{1}{2}$?

☞ Since these fractions do not have the same value, they are not equivalent.

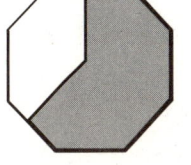

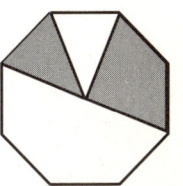

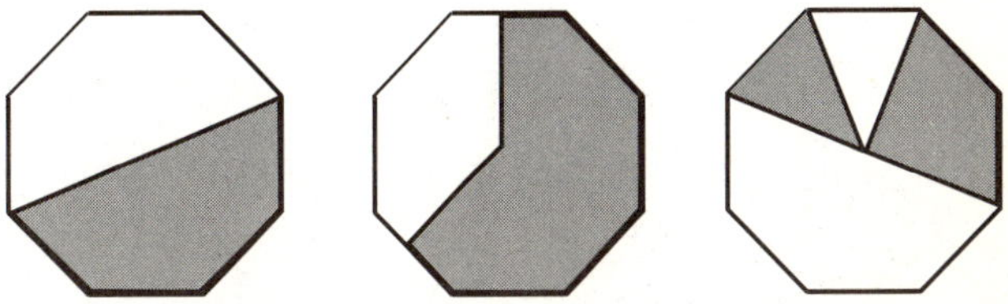

111

Lesson 26   **AlgebraicThinking • Foundations**

Directions: *Look at the following models. In each problem three fractions are modeled. They have different names, but they have the same value. They are equivalent! Write the fraction for each model in the left margin. Then write an expression that says all three fractions are equal.*

1.

2.

3.

4. Look at the fractions from problems 1 – 3. Compare the second and third fraction with the first one in each problem. Describe any patterns you see.

Algebraic Thinking • Foundations

Lesson 26

The fractions modeled in problems 1 – 3 are equivalent fractions. What are equivalent fractions? _____

_____

☞ Two equivalent fractions form a **proportion.**

☞ Circle the pairs of fractions that are proportions.
(Equivalent fractions are proportions.)

$\frac{2}{3}, \frac{4}{6}$ $\frac{3}{4}, \frac{6}{8}$ $\frac{2}{5}, \frac{1}{2}$

☞ One way to compare fractions is by using models as we have been doing. Another way is to find decimal equivalents for the fractions. Most calculators don't show fractions. However, they do show decimal equivalents for fractions. For example, find the decimal equivalent for $\frac{3}{5}$.

  ↪ $\frac{3}{5}$ means 3 ÷ 5, so press 3 ÷ 5 on your calculator. $\frac{3}{5}$ = _____
  ↪ What is the decimal equivalent for $\frac{6}{10}$? $\frac{6}{10}$ = _____
  ↪ Since the decimals for $\frac{3}{5}$ and $\frac{6}{10}$ are equal, the fractions are also equal.

☞ What is the decimal equivalent for $\frac{4}{9}$? _____

☞ What is the decimal equivalent for $\frac{5}{8}$? _____

☞ Which fraction is larger $\frac{4}{9}$ or $\frac{5}{8}$? _____

Directions: *Look at each pair of fractions. Shade the model for each fraction. Then decide if they are equal or not. If they are, write equivalent. If not, circle the fraction with the greater value.*

$\frac{5}{6}$ $\frac{19}{24}$

$\frac{5}{9}$ $\frac{5}{24}$

113

Lesson 26　　　　　　　　　　　　　　Algebraic Thinking • Foundations

Model each fraction by shading. Compare all four of these fractions with each other.

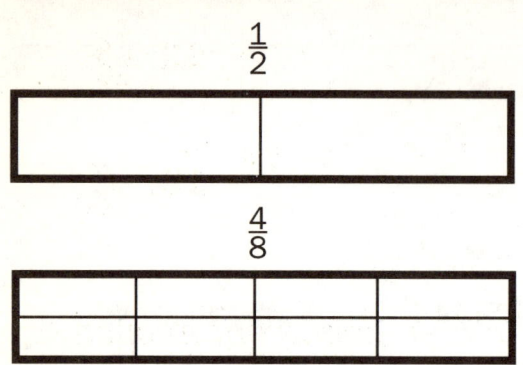

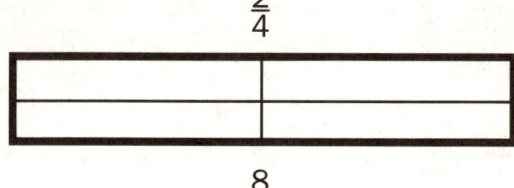

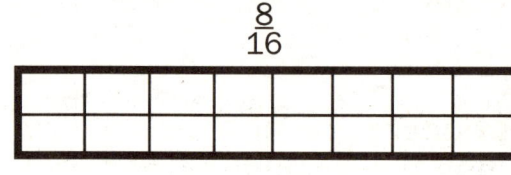

$\frac{1}{2}$

$\frac{2}{4}$

$\frac{4}{8}$

$\frac{8}{16}$

Are these fractions equivalent? _____

You can find equivalent fractions by multiplying or dividing both the numerator and denominator by the same number. Look at the following examples.

Example 1: $\frac{1}{2} = \frac{1 \cdot 2}{2 \cdot 2} = \frac{2}{4}$	Example 2: $\frac{1}{2} = \frac{1 \cdot 4}{2 \cdot 4} = \frac{4}{8}$
Example 3: $\frac{8}{16} = \frac{8 \div 4}{16 \div 4} = \frac{2}{4}$	Example 4: $\frac{6}{12} = \frac{6 \div 6}{12 \div 6} = \frac{1}{2}$

Practice it!

Directions: For problems 1 – 9, write two fractions that are equivalent to the given fraction.

1. $\frac{3}{4}$ 　　　　　2. $\frac{2}{3}$ 　　　　　3. $\frac{7}{8}$

4. $\frac{3}{5}$ 　　　　　5. $\frac{17}{20}$ 　　　　6. $\frac{5}{8}$

7. $\frac{7}{10}$ 　　　　8. $\frac{9}{20}$ 　　　　9. $\frac{1}{4}$

Algebraic Thinking • Foundations Lesson 26

Directions: *Look at the given fraction. Write an equivalent fraction that has a denominator of 10.*

10. $\frac{2}{5}$ 　　　　　　11. $\frac{1}{5}$ 　　　　　　12. $\frac{14}{20}$

13. $\frac{1}{2}$ 　　　　　　14. $\frac{3}{30}$ 　　　　　15. $\frac{70}{100}$

Directions: *Look at the given fraction. Write an equivalent fraction that has a denominator of 100.*

16. $\frac{2}{5}$ 　　　　　　17. $\frac{9}{10}$ 　　　　　18. $\frac{21}{25}$

19. $\frac{3}{50}$ 　　　　　20. $\frac{75}{500}$ 　　　　21. $\frac{3}{4}$

22. **Write in complete sentences.** *Explain how to find equivalent fractions.*

Directions: *Choose the best answer. Circle the letter of your choice.*

23. Equivalent fractions have the same _____ .
    A. denominator
    B. value
    C. numerator

24. Which of the following fractions is not equivalent to $\frac{2}{5}$?
    A. $\frac{4}{10}$
    B. $\frac{12}{30}$
    C. $\frac{8}{25}$
    D. $\frac{20}{50}$

25. A large pizza is cut into 12 pieces. Thomas ate 6 of them. Which pair of equivalent fractions represents the amount of pizza that was eaten?
    A. $\frac{1}{4}, \frac{3}{12}$ 　　B. $\frac{3}{4}, \frac{9}{12}$ 　　C. $\frac{1}{3}, \frac{4}{12}$ 　　D. $\frac{1}{2}, \frac{6}{12}$

Lesson 26　　　　　　　　　　Algebraic Thinking • Foundations

Writing Fractions in Simplest Form

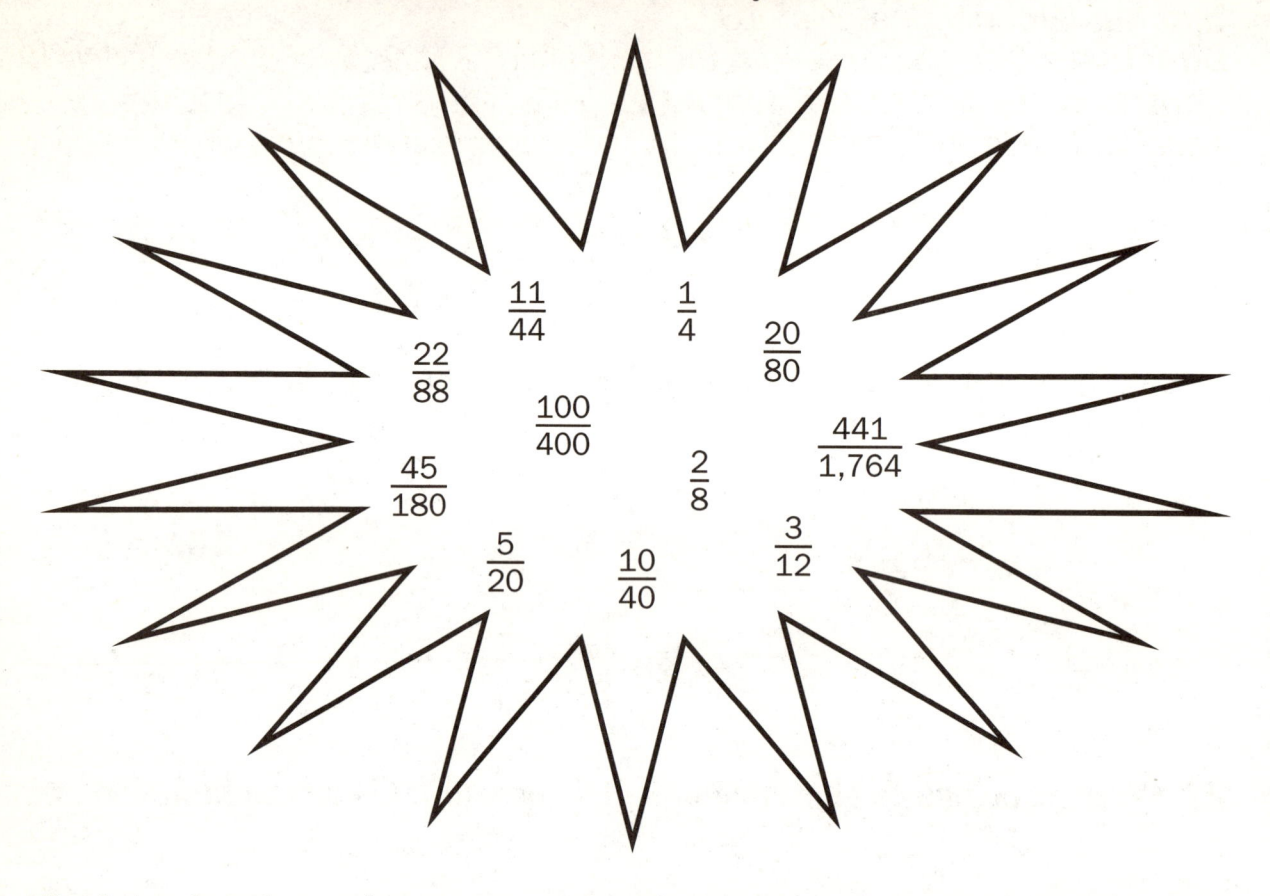

$\frac{11}{44}$　　$\frac{1}{4}$

$\frac{22}{88}$　　　　　　$\frac{20}{80}$

　　$\frac{100}{400}$

　　　　　　　$\frac{441}{1,764}$

$\frac{45}{180}$　　$\frac{2}{8}$

　$\frac{5}{20}$　$\frac{10}{40}$　$\frac{3}{12}$

All of the fractions above are equivalent. Which of these would you say is in simplest form? Why?

AlgebraicThinking • Foundations   Lesson 26

To learn more about simplest form complete the following activity.

Directions: *Use grid paper (on the next page) and a straight edge (ruler) to draw as many different rectangles as you can that have 36 of the small squares inside them. When you finish, write the dimensions in the space below.*

Algebraic Thinking • Foundations

Lesson 26

A number is a factor of another number if it will divide into the number without any remainder. The dimensions listed on the previous page are all factors of 36. You will use factors when simplifying fractions. Consider the following fraction.

$\frac{24}{36}$ → The numerator is 24 and the denominator is 36. List the factors of each of these numbers.

1. The factors of 24 are _____ .

2. The factors of 36 are _____ .

3. What are the common factors? _____

4. Which of the common factors has the greatest value? _____
   (This number is called the **Greatest Common Factor** or **GCF.**)

5. Divide the numerator and the denominator by the GCF.

6. $\frac{24}{36} = \frac{24 \div 12}{36 \div 12} = \frac{2}{3}$ When you divide the numerator and the denominator of a fraction by the GCF, you get an equivalent fraction in simplest form. We know that $\frac{2}{3}$ is the simplest form because 2 and 3 have no common factors other than 1.

7. What if you divide the fraction by a common factor that is not the GCF? Try dividing the numerator and the denominator of $\frac{24}{36}$ by 4, one of the other common factors.

8. $\frac{24}{36} = \frac{24 \div 4}{36 \div 4} = \frac{6}{9}$ The fraction $\frac{6}{9}$ is not in simplest form. However, 6 and 9 have a common factor. What is it? _____ So, when you divide the numerator and denominator by 3, you get $\frac{2}{3}$ (the fraction in simplest form).

119

Lesson 26 **AlgebraicThinking • Foundations**

9. The second method took 2 steps. What two numbers did we divide by in those steps?

10. What is the product of those two numbers? _____
So, we really divided by 12. We just did it in two steps.

11. Write a letter telling a new student how to find a fraction in simplest form. (Include two ways to find the simplest form of a fraction and how to know when a fraction is in simplest form.)

_____
_____
_____
_____
_____
_____
_____
_____
_____
_____
_____
_____

Directions: *Find the simplest form of these fractions with your teacher.*

1. $\frac{30}{40}$ **2.** $\frac{8}{20}$ **3.** $\frac{27}{33}$

4. $\frac{5}{40}$ **5.** $\frac{60}{96}$ **6.** $\frac{32}{36}$

AlgebraicThinking • Foundations   Lesson 26

Practice it!

Directions: Write the fraction in simplest form. Show all your work.

1. $\frac{8}{10}$ 2. $\frac{28}{40}$ 3. $\frac{54}{63}$

4. $\frac{110}{160}$ 5. $\frac{85}{100}$ 6. $\frac{36}{48}$

7. $\frac{8}{16}$ 8. $\frac{6}{21}$ 9. $\frac{12}{52}$

10. $\frac{55}{80}$ 11. $\frac{48}{66}$ 12. $\frac{28}{49}$

Directions: Use S-O-L-V-E to solve each problem.

13. It took Sammy 40 minutes to finish his homework last night. What fraction of an hour is this? Write your answer in simplest form.

S. _____

O. _____

L. _____

V. _____

E. _____

Lesson 26   **AlgebraicThinking** • Foundations

14. Terra surveyed her friends about the type of food they like the best. The results are in the table to the right. What fraction of the people liked pizza the best? Write your answer in simplest form.

Favorite Food	Number
Pizza	45
Hamburger	28
French Fries	20
Ice Cream	7

S. _____

O. _____

L. _____

V. _____

E. _____

15. What fraction of Terra's friends like french fries the best? Write your answer in simplest form.

S. _____

O. _____

L. _____

V. _____

E. _____

AlgebraicThinking • Foundations

Homework 26

Name _____

Use the correct order of operations to find each answer.

1. $(3 + 7) \cdot 6 =$

2. $14 - 2 + 7 =$

3. $4^2 + 9 =$

4. $5 \cdot 6 + 3 \cdot 9 =$

5. $24 - 12 \div 6 =$

6. $4 + 7 - 3 + 2 =$

7. $7 \cdot 2^3 =$

8. $4 \cdot 9 + (6 - 4) =$

9. $15 \div 3 + 7 - 6 \cdot 2 =$

Warm Up 27: Just Dessert

Use the SOLVE method to get an answer for each problem below.

Tailor Made, a men's clothing store, was having a great weekly special. They had dress shirts on sale for $19. Slacks were going for the low price of $25. Socks were selling for $3 a pair. Norman bought 3 shirts and 2 pairs of slacks. How much did he spend at the sale?

S

O

L

V

E

Algebraic Thinking • Foundations   Lesson 27

Classroom Data

Write the number of students:

1. Who are female?
2. Who are male?
3. Who are enrolled in the class?
4. Who are absent?
5. Who are present?
6. Who are right handed?
7. Who are left handed?
8. Who have a driver's license?
9. Who play a school sport?
10. Whose favorite food is pizza?
11. Whose favorite food is steamed cabbage?
12. Who want to make an A?
13. Who are wearing jeans?
14. Who are wearing tennis shoes?
15. Who are not wearing tennis shoes?
16. Who are wearing the color green?
17. Who are wearing the color yellow?
18. Who have black hair?
19. Who take a foreign language?
20. Who play a musical instrument?
21. Who were born in Texas?
22. Who were not born in the United States?
23. Who don't like chocolate?
24. Who have a pet?
25. Who have a birthday in a month that begins with a J?
26. Who have a brother or sister?
27. Who have a job?

Lesson 27   AlgebraicThinking • Foundations

Ratio Worksheet

Directions: *Use the CLASSROOM DATA form (p. 125) to write the ratio of:*

1. females to male
2. females to students
3. students absent to students present
4. right-handed students to left-handed students
5. students with a driver's license to students present
6. students with a job to students who play a school sport
7. students who want to make an "A" to students present
8. students wearing green to students present
9. students who take a foreign language class to students enrolled in this class
10. students wearing jeans to students wearing tennis shoes

Directions: *Use the CLASSROOM DATA form (p. 125) to write in words three ratios not listed above. Express each ratio as a fraction, using a colon, and using to:*

Words	Fraction	Colon	To
11.			
12.			
13.			

14. Write an example of a ratio that compares three things in words and using a colon.

AlgebraicThinking • **Foundations**   Lesson 27

Candy Ratios

Directions: *Answer questions 1 – 3 on the chart below.*

1. Open your bag of candy and count the number of pieces of candy in the bag. How many pieces of candy do you have? _____
2. Sort the candy by color. How many of each color is in your bag? (record on chart)
3. Write the ratio of each color to the total number of pieces per bag as a fraction.

COLOR	No. of Pieces	Ratio of Color to Total
Brown		
Red		
Yellow		
Green		
Orange		
Blue		
Purple		

4. Which color represented the most? _____
5. Which color represented the least? _____
6. Express each of the following as a ratio:
    a. green to red _____
    b. blue to brown _____
    c. orange to yellow _____
    d. blue to red _____
    e. yellow to brown _____
    f. yellow and brown to whole bag _____
    g. green to red to orange _____
    h. purple to total _____

127

Lesson 27 Algebraic**Thinking** • Foundations

Writing Ratios

Directions: *Write the ratio in three ways for each of the following comparisons:*

1. baseballs to basketballs

2. footballs to basketballs

3. basketballs to all balls

4. cars to pick-ups

5. cars to vehicles

Directions: *Draw a picture to represent the following ratios.*

6. 4 boys to 5 girls

7. 2 trees to 5 flowers

8. 3 triangles to 4 squares

9. 2 books to 3 pencils

10. 3 shirts to 2 pairs of pants

AlgebraicThinking • Foundations   Lesson 27

11. At Jefferson Middle School, there are 568 girls and 498 boys.
   a. What is the ratio of girls to students?

   b. What is the ratio of boys to students?

12. S-O-L-V-E: Of the 1,066 students at Jefferson Middle School, 375 are in the 6th grade. 330 of them are going on a field trip with 30 adults. The school requires a ratio of 1 adult sponsor to 12 students. The buses will hold up to 60 people. What is the ratio of students to adults? Are there enough adult sponsors?

S. _____

_____

O. _____

_____

L. _____

_____

V. _____

_____

E. _____

_____

129

13. S-O-L-V-E: Use the information from number 12 to answer, how many buses will be needed?

S. _____

O. _____

L. _____

V. _____

E. _____

AlgebraicThinking • Foundations　　　　　　　　　　Homework 27

Name _____

Directions: *Simplify each expression by performing each operation in the correct order.*

1.　$4 + 8 \div 2 - 1 =$

2.　$10 - 3 \cdot 2 =$

3.　$3 \cdot 5 - 2 =$

4.　$(4 \cdot 3 - 2) \div (1 + 4) =$

5.　$2^2 \cdot 4 - 3 =$

6.　$6 + 8 \div 2 =$

7.　$28 \div 2 \cdot 7 =$

8.　$24 \div 4 \cdot 2 =$

9.　$9 + 5 \cdot 3 =$

10.　$25 - 4 \cdot 6 =$

Warm Up 28   Algebraic Thinking • Foundations

Warm Up 28: SOLVE the Problem

Use the SOLVE method to answer the following word problem.

Candy Corner, the mall's new candy store, has a lot of great treats to purchase. Chocolate fudge is $4 a pound, and butter toffee candies are $2 per pound. Peppermint twists are $3 per dozen. Janice went in and bought her 3 children candy. She bought 2 pounds of fudge, and 12 peppermint twists. How much did she spend at Candy Corner?

S

O

L

V

E

AlgebraicThinking • Foundations   Lesson 28

Comparing and Ordering Fractions

One way to compare fractions is by constructing models for the fractions. The easiest fractions to compare are those that have the same denominator. For example, compare the following fractions.

$\frac{3}{5}$ and $\frac{4}{5}$ $\frac{3}{8}$ and $\frac{4}{8}$

Directions: *In each pair of fractions, circle the bigger of the two. Use the models above.*

1. $\frac{3}{5}$ or $\frac{4}{5}$ 2. $\frac{3}{8}$ or $\frac{3}{5}$

3. $\frac{3}{8}$ or $\frac{4}{8}$ 4. $\frac{4}{5}$ or $\frac{4}{8}$

5. When two fractions have the same denominator, how do you tell which fraction is bigger?

6. When two fractions have the same numerator, how do you tell which fraction is bigger?

Lesson 28   **Algebraic Thinking • Foundations**

What about fractions with different denominators? When the fractions have different denominators, the process is a little more complicated. However, you can still use models to compare the fractions. Compare the pairs of fractions below by modeling them. Circle the bigger of the two fractions.

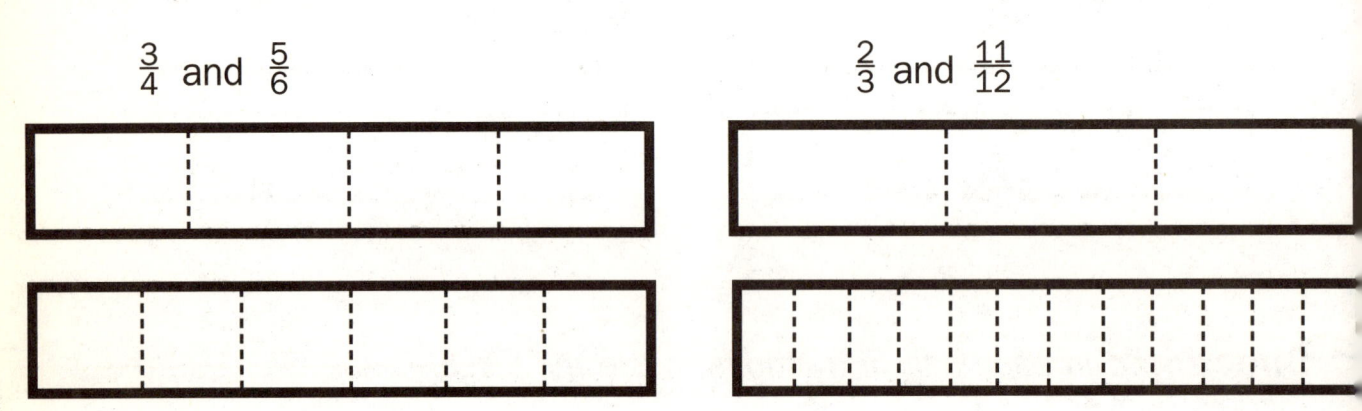

$\frac{3}{4}$ and $\frac{5}{6}$ $\frac{2}{3}$ and $\frac{11}{12}$

A second way of comparing fractions is by finding equivalent fractions with a **common denominator**. A common denominator is a number that is a multiple of two or more denominators. For example, consider the fractions $\frac{4}{9}$ and $\frac{7}{12}$.

✳ What are their denominators? _____

✳ List some multiples of 9. _____

✳ List some multiples of 12. _____

The common multiples are those that both numbers have. A common denominator for the two fractions could be 36, 72, or 108. There are infinitely many more!

✳ Write an equivalent fraction for $\frac{4}{9}$ with a denominator of 36. _____

✳ Write an equivalent fraction for $\frac{7}{12}$ with a denominator of 36. _____

✳ Which of the two fractions is bigger? _____

AlgebraicThinking • Foundations Lesson 28

Directions: *Work these example problems with your teacher. Compare each pair of the fractions by using one of the following math verbs: <, >, =.*

7. $\dfrac{3}{8}$ $\dfrac{5}{8}$ 8. $\dfrac{2}{3}$ $\dfrac{2}{9}$ 9. $\dfrac{3}{4}$ $\dfrac{7}{12}$

10. $\dfrac{5}{6}$ $\dfrac{6}{8}$ 11. $\dfrac{7}{10}$ $\dfrac{3}{4}$ 12. $\dfrac{3}{10}$ $\dfrac{4}{12}$

Directions: *Work these example problems with your teacher. Put the fractions in order from least to greatest.*

13. $\dfrac{2}{3}, \dfrac{3}{4}, \dfrac{5}{8}$ 14. $\dfrac{5}{9}, \dfrac{5}{6}, \dfrac{1}{3}$ 15. $\dfrac{2}{3}, \dfrac{3}{10}, \dfrac{7}{15}$

Lesson 28   **AlgebraicThinking • Foundations**

Practice it!

Directions: Use the fraction bars to construct models for each pair of fractions. Then use the models to compare the fractions with a <, >, or =.

1. $\frac{2}{3}$ and $\frac{3}{4}$

2. $\frac{3}{8}$ and $\frac{5}{12}$

3. $\frac{3}{8}$ and $\frac{3}{4}$

Directions: Compare each pair of fractions with a >, <, or =.

4. $\frac{1}{3}$ $\frac{2}{3}$
5. $\frac{3}{7}$ $\frac{2}{3}$
6. $\frac{7}{9}$ $\frac{3}{4}$
7. $\frac{3}{10}$ $\frac{2}{5}$
8. $\frac{5}{6}$ $\frac{3}{4}$
9. $\frac{4}{10}$ $\frac{6}{15}$
10. $\frac{9}{12}$ $\frac{15}{20}$
11. $\frac{2}{5}$ $\frac{3}{8}$
12. $\frac{5}{12}$ $\frac{7}{20}$

Directions: Write each set of fractions in order from least to greatest.

13. $\frac{2}{3}, \frac{1}{2}, \frac{3}{4}$
14. $\frac{2}{3}, \frac{8}{15}, \frac{7}{10}$
15. $\frac{1}{3}, \frac{3}{8}, \frac{5}{12}$

16. $\frac{2}{5}, \frac{3}{10}, \frac{1}{2}$
17. $\frac{4}{7}, \frac{5}{6}, \frac{2}{3}$
18. $\frac{2}{3}, \frac{4}{5}, \frac{9}{15}$

AlgebraicThinking • Foundations Homework 28

Name _____

Name the property shown in each problem.

1. 7 + 5 = 5 + 7 _____

2. 3 • (4 + 6) = 12 + 18 _____

3. (42 + 6) + 11 = 42 + (6 + 11) _____

4. 12 + 8 + 9 = 8 + 12 + 9 _____

5. 56 + 40 = 8 • (7 + 5) _____

Which operations do not work with the commutative or associative property? Give an example to support your answer.

Warm Up 29: Fast Track

Directions: *Follow the track from top to bottom. Use the answer as the first number in the next problem.*

34 • 3 = _____

_____ ÷ 6 = _____

_____ − 12 = _____

_____ • 12 = _____

_____ + 45 = _____

_____ − 33 = _____

_____ ÷ 4 = _____

_____ − 8 = _____

_____ • 4 = _____

_____ ÷ 8 = _____

_____ + 18 = _____

_____ • 25 = _____

AlgebraicThinking • **Foundations** Lesson 29

Decimal Fractions - Models

Did you know? The prefix, *deci*, means one-tenth. Decimal fractions are those fractions that have powers of 10 as their denominator. Look at the following fraction models. They are all decimal fractions. Write the fraction for each model with your teacher. Then your teacher will show you how to write the fraction using a decimal point instead of a fraction bar.

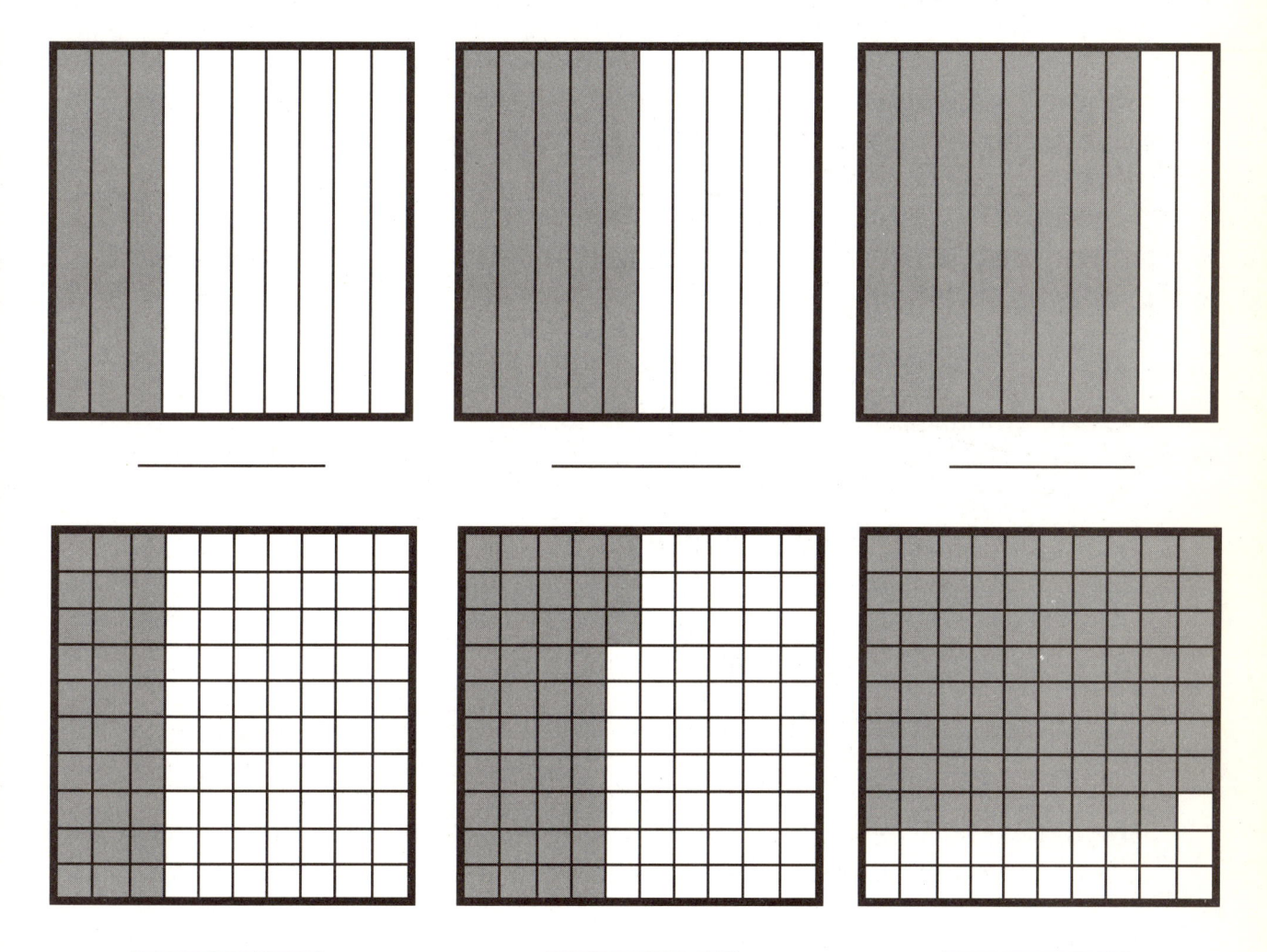

Directions: *Use the grid to model the following decimals.*

0.45   0.87   0.12

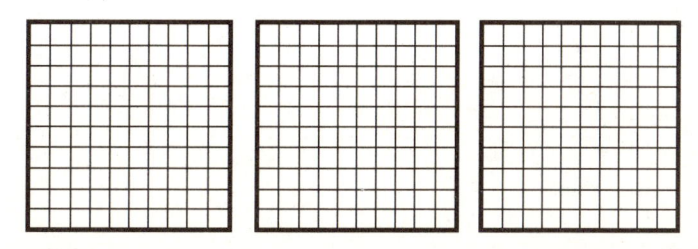

139

Lesson 29   AlgebraicThinking • Foundations

Place Value

Millions	Hundred-Thousands	Ten-Thousands	Thousands	Hundreds	Tens	Ones	.	Tenths	Hundredths	Thousandths	Ten-Thousandths	Hundred-Thousandths
	3	1	9	2	5	4	.	6	3	7	8	

In the number 319,254.6378, the 6 is in the tenths place. It has a value of six tenths. What decimal place is the 7 in and what is its value? _____

Directions: *Write each of the following numbers in fraction notation and in decimal notation.*

1. Two hundred fifty-six and thirteen hundredths
2. Thirty-four and two hundred fifty-four thousandths
3. Five and seven tenths
4. Eighty-four and eleven hundredths
5. One thousand twenty-four and eighteen thousandths
6. Seventy-five and three ten-thousandths
7. Forty-one hundredths

Directions: *Write each of the following numbers with words. Then write them in fraction notation.*

8. 27.2
9. 10.08
10. 13.74
11. 128.087
12. 0.27

AlgebraicThinking • Foundations   Lesson 29

Decimal Fractions - Comparing and Ordering

One way to compare decimals is to construct models for them. Model the following decimal fractions and then write them in order from least to greatest.

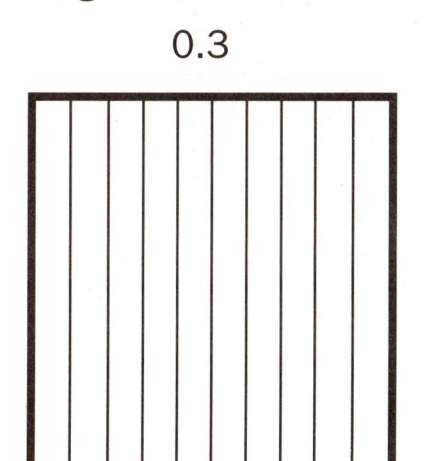

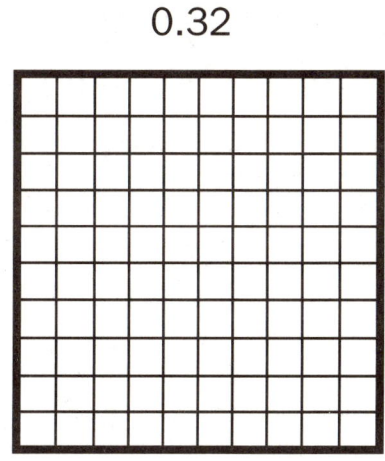

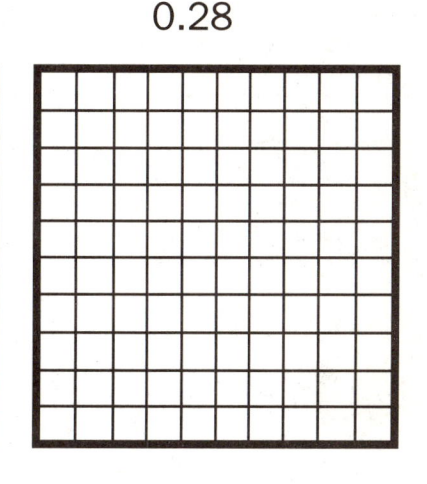

　　　0.3　　　　　　　　0.32　　　　　　　　0.28

Write in the order from least to greatest. _____, _____, _____

You can also compare decimal fractions by looking at the place value of the digits. Start at the decimal point and move to the right one place at a time. For example, order these decimals from least to greatest. (Your teacher will show you how to do this.)

13. 12.34, 12.3, 12.4　　　　　**14.** 0.8, 0.805, 0.85

15. 9.25, 9.2, 9.025, 9.3　　　**16.** 2.5, 2.6, 2.49, 2.51

17. 0.502, 0.51, 0.53, 0.601　　**18.** 4.253, 4.245, 3.256, 3.2

Lesson 29 AlgebraicThinking • Foundations

Practice it!

Directions: Write the fraction for each model. Then write it in decimal notation.

1.

2.

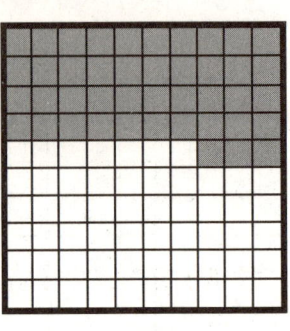

3.

_____   _____   _____

Directions: Write each fraction as a decimal.

4. $\frac{3}{10}$

5. $\frac{4}{10}$

6. $\frac{24}{100}$

7. $\frac{3}{100}$

8. $\frac{348}{1,000}$

9. $\frac{27}{1,000}$

Directions: Compare each pair of decimals by writing a <, >, or = between them.

10. 0.1   0.2

11. 0.14   0.2

12. 0.34   0.342

13. 6.8   6.75

14. 3.1   3

15. 4.6   3.6

16. 2.7   2.70

17. 10.71   10.701

18. 3.90   39.0

19. 0.247   0.246

20. 0.24   0.239

21. 0.25   0.100

142

AlgebraicThinking • Foundations Lesson 29

Directions: *Write each set of decimals in order from least to greatest.*

22. 0.24, 0.25, 0.201 **23.** 0.17, 0.1, 0.23 **24.** 3.07, 3.71, 3.241

25. 0.04, 0.40, 0.44 **26.** 8.45, 8.44, 8.4 **27.** 6.7, 7.6, 6.75

28. 10.05, 10.5, 10.005 **29.** 7.84, 7.841, 7.8 **30.** 3.15, 3.14, 3.2

Homework 29　　　　　　　　　　**AlgebraicThinking** • Foundations

Name _____

Directions: *Use the above pictures to find each ratio.*

1. Pears to apples　　　　　　　2. Apples to pears

3. Pears to bananas　　　　　　4. Bananas to fruit

5. Apples to fruit　　　　　　　6. Bananas to apples

7. Apples and pears to fruit　　　8. Pears to pear stems

144

Algebraic Thinking • Foundations

Warm Up 30

Warm Up 30: Missing Pieces

Put each number 0 through 9 in the boxes so that every line is true. Use each number exactly once.

1. _____ + (8 − _____) = 9

2. 3 + _____ • 4 + _____ = 11

3. 2 + (_____ − 5) ÷ _____ = 4

4. _____ • 3 − (_____ • 2) = 6

5. _____ + (8 − _____) = 7

145

Lesson 30   AlgebraicThinking • Foundations

Converting Between Fractions and Decimals

In the last lesson, you learned about decimal fractions. Today, you will learn how to write them in fraction bar notation and decimal point notation.

Write a Decimal as a Fraction
To write a decimal as a fraction, first consider how you would say the decimal and write the fraction that way. Consider the following examples.

1. 0.25 ➔ This decimal is pronounced "25 hundredths" since the 5 is in the hundredths place. The fraction is $\frac{25}{100}$, which simplifies to $\frac{1}{4}$.

2. 0.8 ➔ How do you say this decimal? _____

   How do you write the fraction? _____

3. 0.45 ➔ How do you say this decimal? _____

   How do you write the fraction? _____

4. 0.125 ➔ How do you say this decimal? _____

   How do you write the fraction? _____

5. 10.75 ➔ How do you say this decimal? _____

   How do you write the fraction? _____

Write a Fraction as a Decimal
One way to write a fraction as a decimal is to find an equivalent fraction that has a denominator that is a power of 10. Why does this work?

_____

_____

Consider these examples.

6. $\frac{3}{4} = \frac{3 \cdot 25}{4 \cdot 25} = \frac{75}{100} = 0.75$ 7. $\frac{16}{20} = \frac{16 \div 2}{20 \div 2} = \frac{8}{10} = 0.8$

8. $\frac{13}{20}$ 9. $\frac{9}{30}$

Algebraic Thinking • Foundations Lesson 30

A second way to convert a fraction to a decimal is to simply divide the numerator by the denominator. Consider the following examples.

10. $\frac{3}{8} = 3 \div 8 = 8\overline{)3}$

$$\frac{3}{8} = 8\overline{)3.000} \quad \begin{array}{r} 0.375 \\ \underline{-24} \\ 60 \\ \underline{-56} \\ 40 \\ \underline{-40} \\ 0 \end{array}$$

11. $\frac{2}{5} = 2 \div 5 = 5\overline{)2}$

$$5\overline{)2.0} \quad \begin{array}{r} 0.4 \\ \underline{-20} \\ 0 \end{array}$$

12. $\frac{21}{25}$

13. $\frac{2}{9}$

In problem #13, the 2's just kept on going. This is called a **repeating decimal.** Repeating decimals are written with a bar over the digits that repeat. When they do not repeat they are called **terminating decimals.** The other three examples are terminating decimals.

Directions: *Complete the following chart by converting each fraction to a decimal.*

Fraction	Decimal	Fraction	Decimal
$\frac{1}{9}$		$\frac{5}{9}$	
$\frac{2}{9}$		$\frac{6}{9} = \frac{2}{3}$	
$\frac{3}{9} = \frac{1}{3}$		$\frac{7}{9}$	
$\frac{4}{9}$		$\frac{8}{9}$	

147

Lesson 30 **Algebraic Thinking • Foundations**

Practice it!

Directions: Write each decimal as a fraction in simplest form.

1. 0.3   **2.** 0.6   **3.** 0.45

4. 0.5   **5.** 0.375   **6.** 0.4

7. 0.78   **8.** 0.48   **9.** 0.75

Directions: Use long division to convert these fractions to decimals. Show your work.

10. $\frac{4}{5}$ **11.** $\frac{5}{6}$

12. $\frac{9}{11}$ **13.** $\frac{13}{20}$

14. $\frac{2}{3}$ **15.** $\frac{3}{20}$

Directions: Use a calculator to convert these fractions to decimals.

16. $\frac{1}{3}$ **17.** $\frac{29}{30}$ **18.** $\frac{7}{8}$

19. $\frac{77}{200}$ **20.** $\frac{1}{16}$ **21.** $\frac{497}{2,000}$

22. $\frac{2}{15}$ **23.** $\frac{1,997}{2,000}$ **24.** $\frac{57}{200}$

AlgebraicThinking • Foundations Homework 30

Name _____

Name the fraction of the shaded part of each model.

1. _____

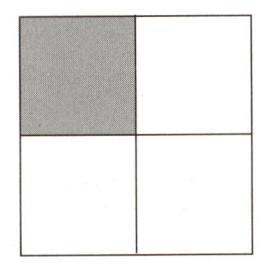

2. _____

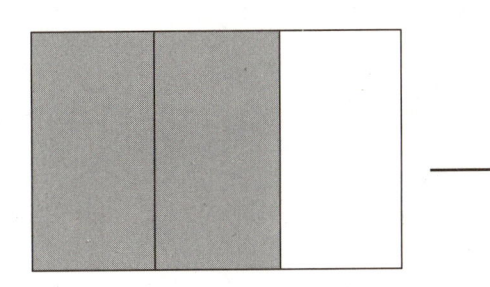

3. _____

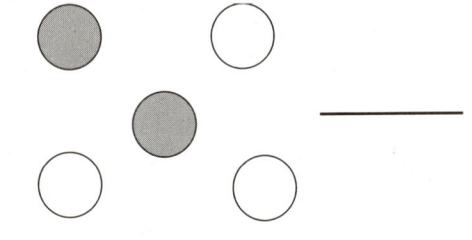

4. _____

5. Draw a model for $\frac{1}{3}$.

6. Draw a model for $\frac{7}{11}$.

149

Warm Up 31: Tic-Tac-Toe

Dion and Samantha played a game of tic-tac-toe. Find out who won the game by matching each answer on the board to the correct problem. Put the appropriate letter on the board.

Dion played the X
1,020 ÷ 12 =
1,035 ÷ 45 =
2,526 ÷ 6 =
2,286 ÷ 9 =

Samantha played the 0
475 ÷ 25 =
910 ÷ 35 =
2,544 ÷ 8 =
1,460 ÷ 4 =

421	23	19
480	85	365
254	26	318

Who won the game? _____

Algebraic Thinking • Foundations

Lesson 31

Percent Fractions

You have learned that decimal fractions are fractions that have a denominator that is a power of 10. Percent fractions are those fractions that have a denominator of 100. In fact, the word *percent* comes from the Latin term *per centum* which means "by the hundred." The fraction $\frac{25}{100}$ is a percent fraction. It can be written like this: 25%.

Look at the following fraction models. Write the fraction with a denominator of 100. Then write it in simplest form. Next, write it with the percent symbol.

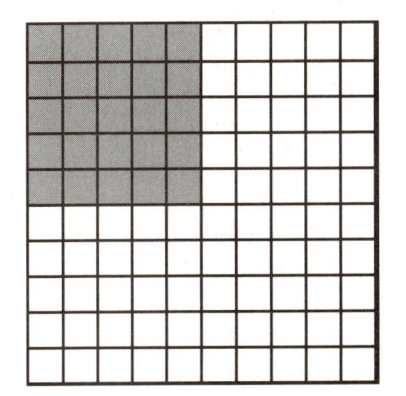

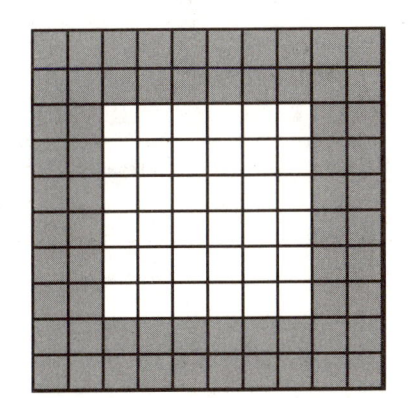

To write a **decimal as a percent,** simply move the decimal point to the right of the digit in the hundredths place. Write the following decimals as percents.

1. 0.25
2. 0.4
3. 0.257

To write a **fraction as a percent,** find an equivalent fraction that has a denominator of 100 or first write the fraction as a decimal and follow the method for writing a decimal as a percent. Write the following fractions as percents.

4. $\frac{4}{5}$
5. $\frac{36}{40}$
6. $\frac{5}{8}$

Lesson 31 **AlgebraicThinking • Foundations**

Model the following percents. Then write them as a decimal and as a fraction in simplest form.

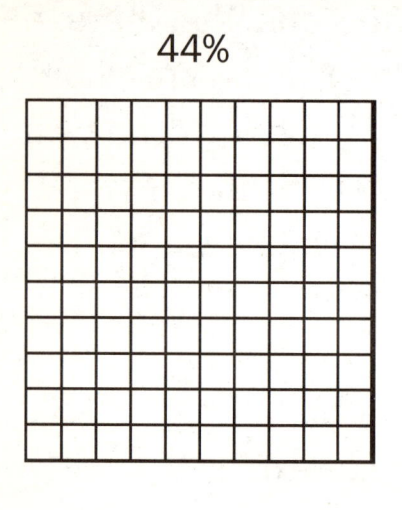

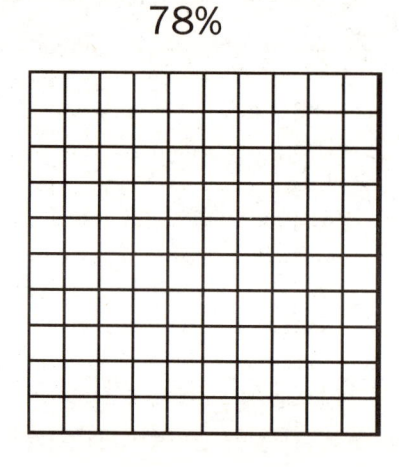

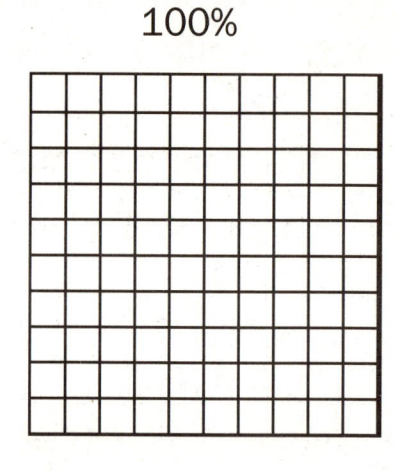

44%   78%   100%

_____   _____   _____   _____   _____   _____

To convert a **percent to a fraction,** write the number in front of the % symbol as a numerator over a denominator of 100. Then simplify. Convert these percents to fractions.

7. 70%   **8.** 85%   **9.** 25%

To convert a **percent to a decimal,** first write it as a fraction. Then convert the fraction to a decimal, by dividing. Convert these percents to decimals.

10. 45%   **11.** 60%   **12.** 25.5%

AlgebraicThinking • Foundations

Lesson 31

Practice it!

Directions: Model each number on the 10 x 10 grid. Then write each as a fraction, decimal, and percent.

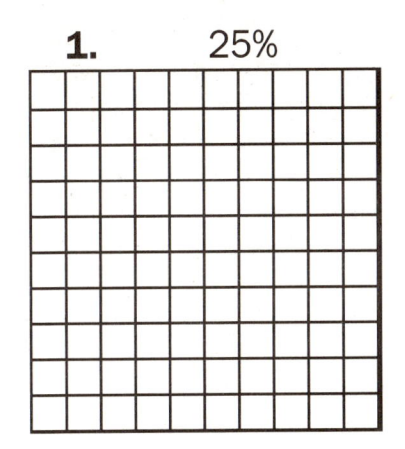

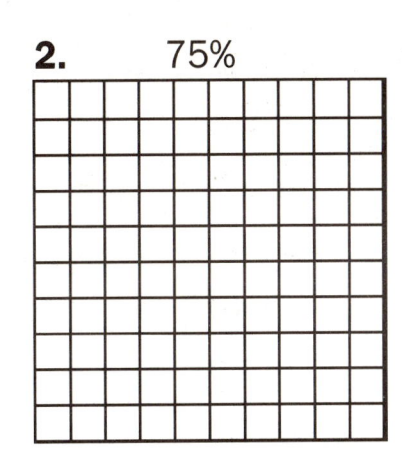

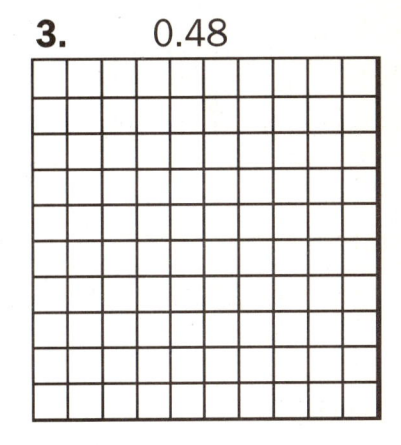

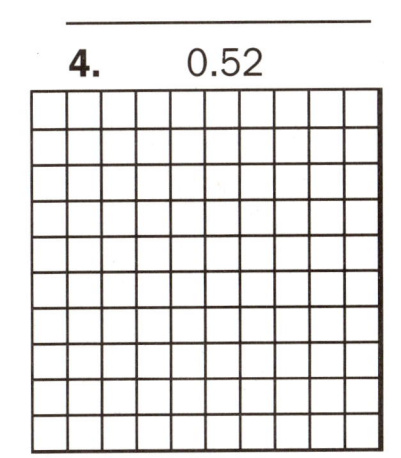

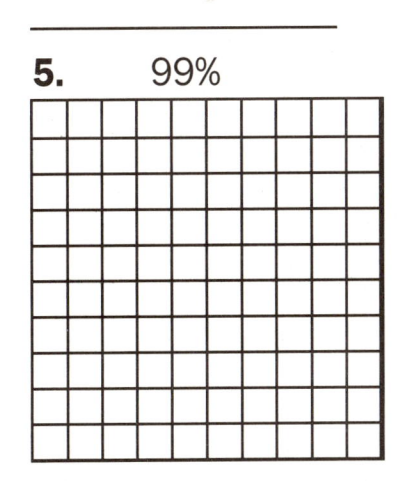

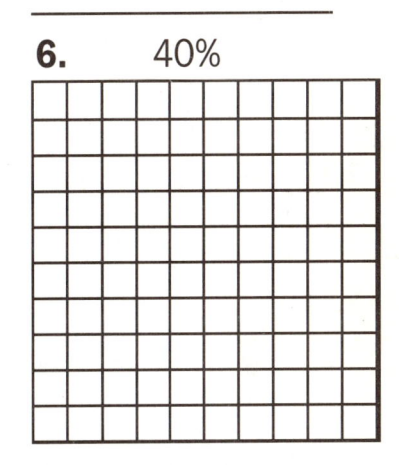

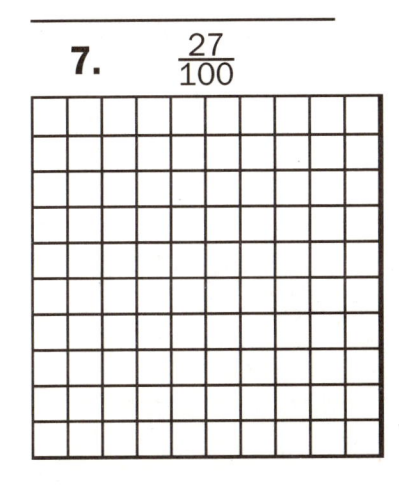

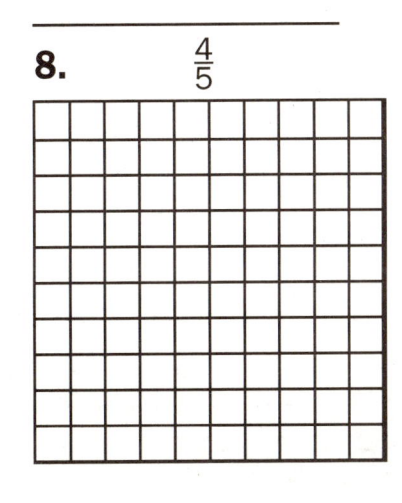

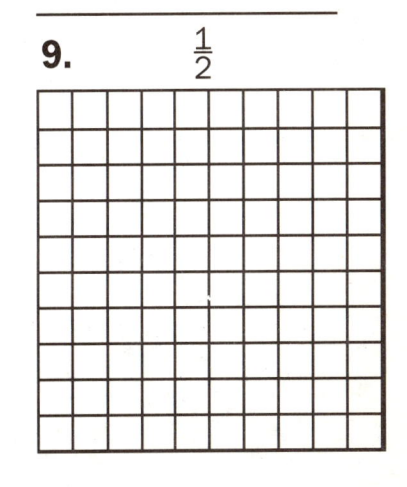

1. 25%

2. 75%

3. 0.48

4. 0.52

5. 99%

6. 40%

7. $\frac{27}{100}$

8. $\frac{4}{5}$

9. $\frac{1}{2}$

153

Lesson 31   Algebraic Thinking • Foundations

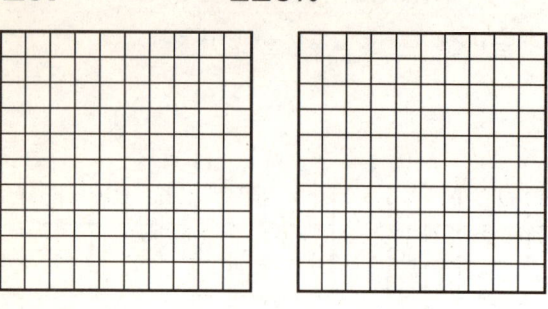

10.   125%   **11.**   1.25

_____ _____   _____ _____

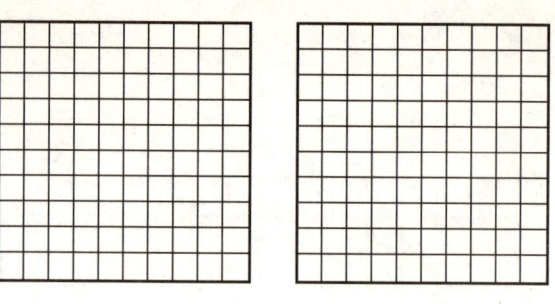

Directions: Write each percent as a decimal and as a fraction in simplest form.

12. 27%   **13.** 25%   **14.** 75%
_____ _____ _____

15. 55%   **16.** 95%   **17.** 30%
_____ _____ _____

18. 24%   **19.** 50%   **20.** 96%
_____ _____ _____

21. 48%   **22.** 20%   **23.** 70%
_____ _____ _____

Directions: Write each fraction as a decimal and a percent. Write each decimal as a fraction in simplest form and a percent.

24. $\frac{4}{5}$ **25.** $\frac{2}{5}$ **26.** $\frac{1}{4}$
_____ _____ _____

27. 0.45   **28.** 0.6   **29.** $\frac{3}{20}$
_____ _____ _____

30. $\frac{67}{100}$ **31.** 0.375   **32.** 0.4975
_____ _____ _____

33. $\frac{17}{100}$ **34.** $\frac{7}{8}$ **35.** $\frac{4}{9}$
_____ _____ _____

AlgebraicThinking • Foundations   Homework 31

Name _____

Write a story problem that would use addition to S-O-L-V-E it. Try to include unnecessary facts. S-O-L-V-E your problem below the dotted line.

Problem:

S

O

L

V

E

Warm Up 32: You Make the Call

1. Using the correct order of operations, simplify this expression:

$$3^2 \cdot 6 - 8 \div 4 =$$

2. Pearl simplified the expression below and got 7 for her answer. Charlie simplified the same expression and got 17 for his answer.

$$15 + 2 \cdot 9 \div 3 - 4 =$$

    a. Tell which one is correct.

    b. Explain what the other person's mistake was.

Algebraic Thinking • Foundations

Lesson 32

Fractions, Decimals, Percents

Write each fraction as a decimal and percent.

			decimal	percent
1.	$\frac{25}{100}$	=	_____	_____
2.	$\frac{48}{50}$	=	_____	_____
3.	$\frac{3}{5}$	=	_____	_____
4.	$\frac{4}{9}$	=	_____	_____
5.	$\frac{3}{8}$	=	_____	_____

Write each decimal as a fraction in simplest form and as a percent.

			fraction	percent
6.	0.4	=	_____	_____
7.	0.64	=	_____	_____
8.	0.875	=	_____	_____
9.	0.84	=	_____	_____
10.	0.3	=	_____	_____

Write each percent as a fraction in simplest form and as a decimal.

			fraction	decimal
11.	25%	=	_____	_____
12.	34%	=	_____	_____
13.	95%	=	_____	_____
14.	44%	=	_____	_____
15.	26.5%	=	_____	_____

Warm Up 33: What's Missing?

Directions: *Fill in the missing digits in the addition and subtraction problems below.*

```
      4 __ 6 8
         5 __ 6
  + __ 9 4 __
  ─────────────
    1 1, 1 1 1
```

```
      5 3, __ 6 7
  -   __ 5, 8 9 __
  ─────────────────
      2 7, 3 __ 5
```

Algebraic Thinking • Foundations

Warm Up 34: Division Tower

Follow the division problems from top to bottom. Use the answer for each problem as the dividend in the next problem.

48,960 ÷ 5 = ____

____ ÷ 2 = ____

____ ÷ 6 = ____

____ ÷ 3 = ____

____ ÷ 8 = ____

Lesson 34   Algebraic Thinking • Foundations

Adding Fractions

One model for fractions can be constructed from a circle. We relate fractions to things that are common because it makes them easier to work with. For instance, consider a pizza. The one at the left was cut into eight pieces. What fraction of the pizza is missing? _____ What fraction of the pizza remains? _____ If you add those two fractions together, you should get the original size. That is, 1 eighth plus 7 eighths is 8 eighths or 1 whole. In numbers, $\frac{1}{8} + \frac{7}{8} = \frac{8}{8} = 1$.

S-O-L-V-E: Samantha ate $\frac{3}{8}$ of a pizza. Alec ate $\frac{4}{8}$ of the same pizza. What fraction of the pizza was eaten?

What fraction of the pizza is left?

If there were eight pieces in the pizza to begin with, how many are left?

How many pieces are left if there were 16 pieces in the original pizza?

Algebraic Thinking • Foundations

Lesson 34

Directions: Use the fraction bars below to model the addition problems. Use the first two bars to model the addends and the third bar for the sum. Be sure to use a different color for each addend. The first one has been done for you. (On the next page, you'll have to divide the fraction bars yourself.)

1. $\frac{4}{8} + \frac{3}{8} = \frac{7}{8}$

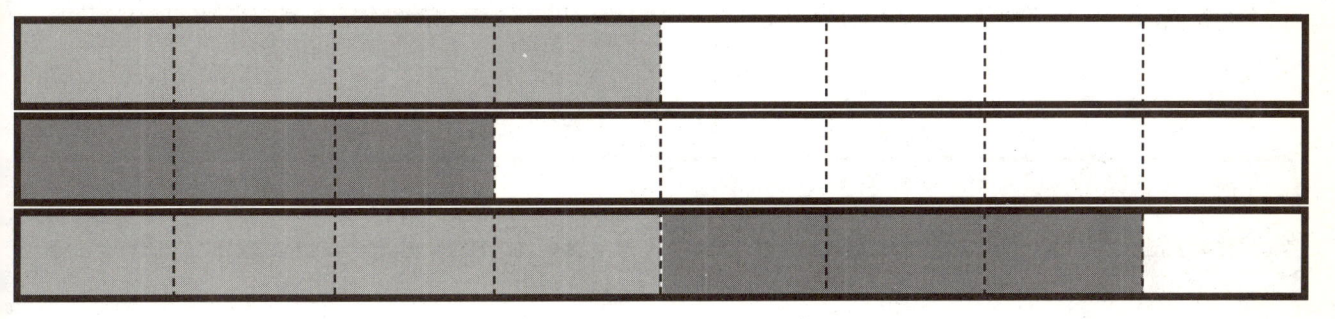

2. $\frac{3}{12} + \frac{5}{12} =$

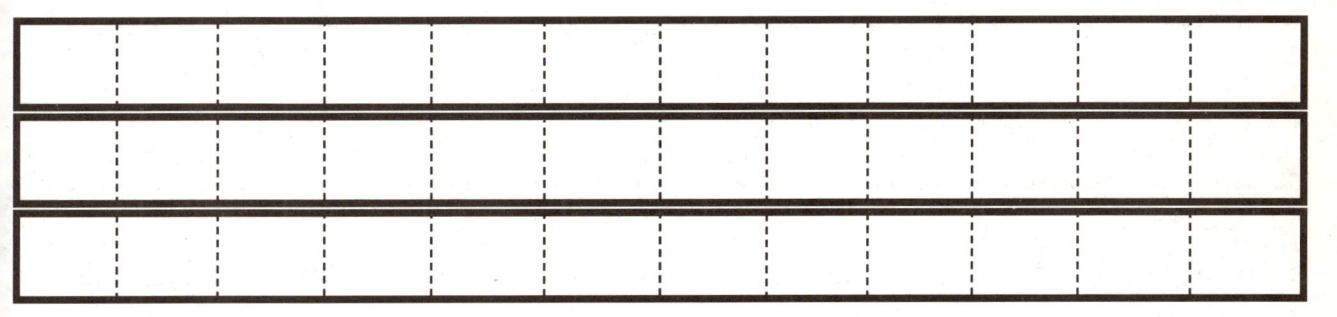

3. $\frac{4}{9} + \frac{2}{9} =$

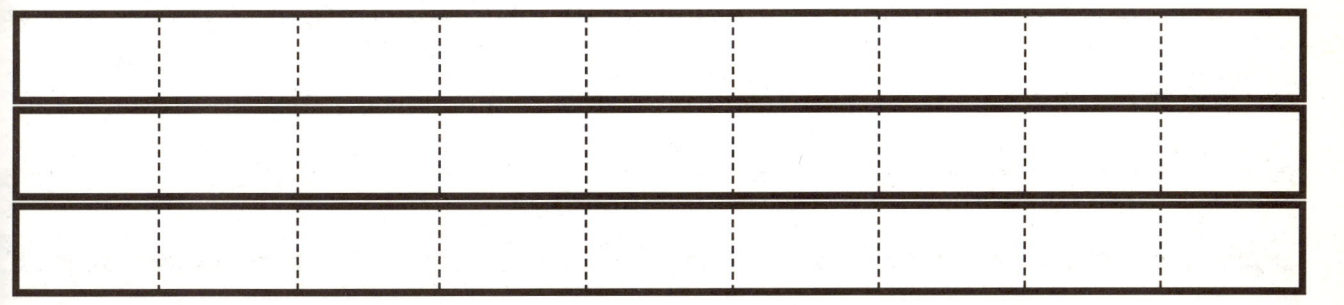

161

Lesson 34 **AlgebraicThinking • Foundations**

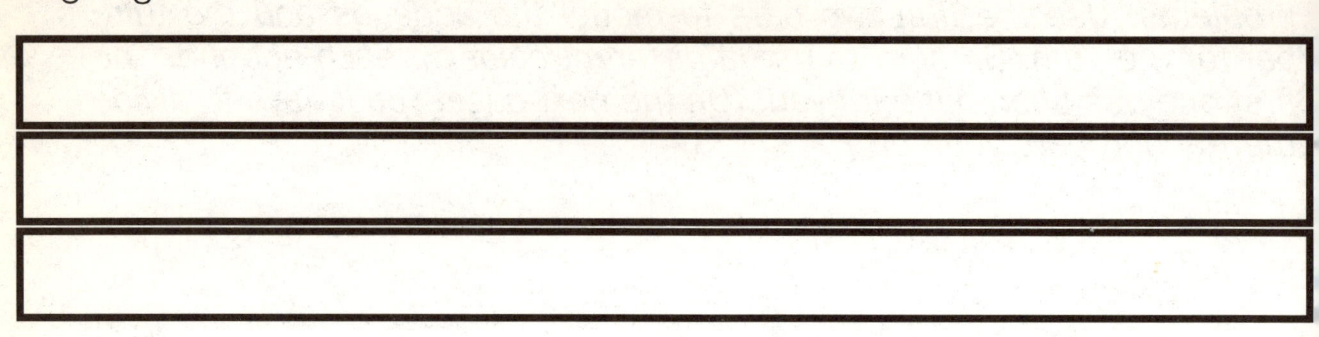

4. $\frac{1}{8} + \frac{5}{8} =$

5. $\frac{3}{5} + \frac{1}{5} =$

6. $\frac{2}{6} + \frac{2}{6} =$

7. $\frac{2}{12} + \frac{3}{12} =$

AlgebraicThinking • Foundations

Homework 34

Name _____

Write a ratio in 3 ways for each problem.

1. 7 girls to 6 boys _____

2. 14 dogs to 4 hamsters _____

3. 5 red cars to 9 blue cars _____

4. 16 baseballs to 24 basketballs _____

Draw a model for each ratio.

5. 7 squares to 5 circles

6. 6 people : 12 trees

163

Warm Up 35: S-O-L-V-E

S-O-L-V-E: The largest freshwater lake in the world is Lake Superior. It covers 31,800 square miles. (20,700 square miles in the U.S. and 11,100 square miles in Canada.) The largest lake completely within the U.S. is Lake Michigan with a surface area of 22,300 square miles. How much larger is Lake Superior than Lake Michigan?

S. _____

_____

O. _____

_____

L. _____

_____

V. _____

_____

E. _____

_____

Algebraic Thinking • Foundations Lesson 35

Directions: Use the following fraction circles to model adding fractions. When you shade the circles use a different color for each addend.

1. $\frac{1}{4} + \frac{2}{4} =$

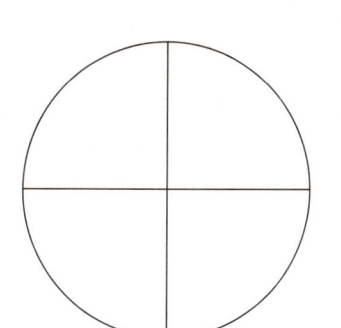

2. $\frac{3}{8} + \frac{2}{8} =$

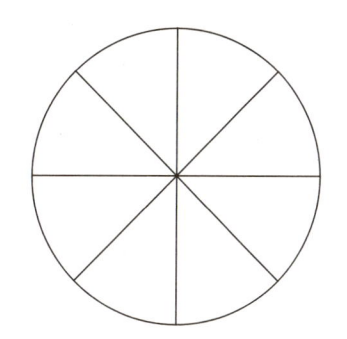

3. $\frac{1}{3} + \frac{2}{3} =$

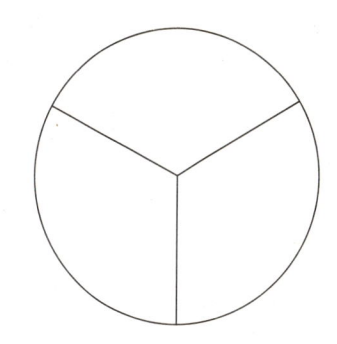

4. $\frac{1}{5} + \frac{2}{5} =$

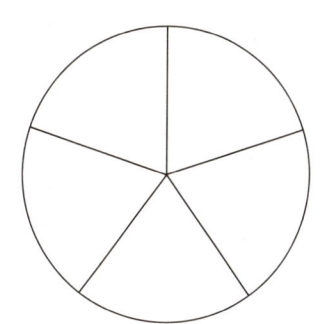

5. $\frac{5}{12} + \frac{6}{12} =$

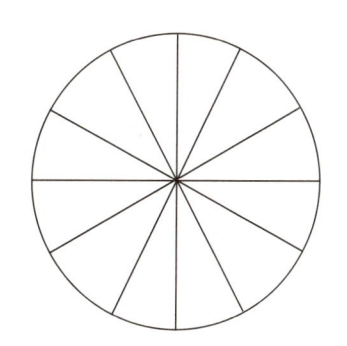

6. $\frac{3}{10} + \frac{6}{10} =$

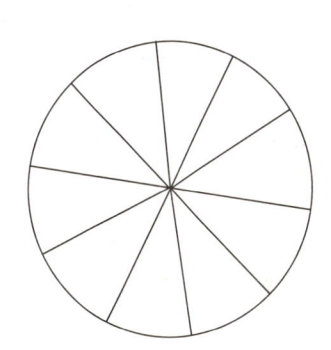

7. $\frac{4}{9} + \frac{5}{9} =$

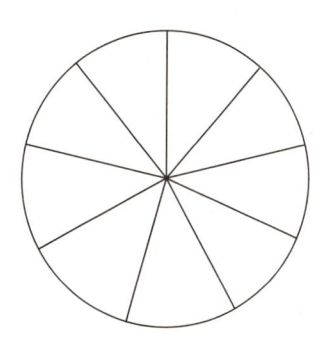

8. $\frac{7}{12} + \frac{10}{12} =$

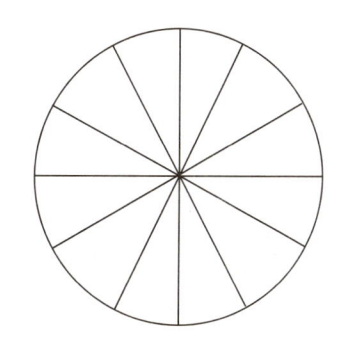

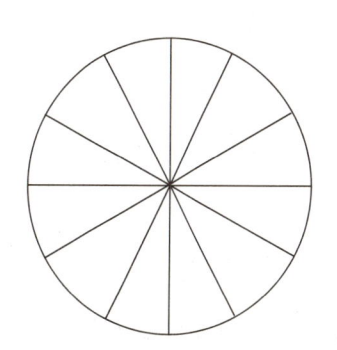

In problem #8, the fraction parts of the circle add up to more than one whole circle. When this happens, the sum is an improper fraction, a mixed number, or just a whole number.

165

Lesson 35 AlgebraicThinking • Foundations

Adding Fractions

Another way to make the adding of fractions easier is to write the problems in words. When you use this method, you only need to write out the denominator. For example, consider the problem from #1. It was $\frac{1}{4} + \frac{2}{4} = \frac{3}{4}$. The problem can be written like this: 1 fourth + 2 fourths = 3 fourths.

Directions: *Write these problems with words.*

9. $\frac{3}{8} + \frac{2}{8} =$
10. $\frac{1}{3} + \frac{2}{3} =$
11. $\frac{1}{5} + \frac{2}{5} =$
12. $\frac{5}{12} + \frac{6}{12} =$
13. $\frac{3}{10} + \frac{6}{10} =$
14. $\frac{4}{9} + \frac{5}{9} =$
15. $\frac{7}{12} + \frac{10}{12} =$

16. Write a rule for adding fractions that have denominators that are alike. _____

_____

_____

Algebraic Thinking • Foundations

Lesson 35

Practice it!

Directions: Write an addition sentence for each model.

1. _____

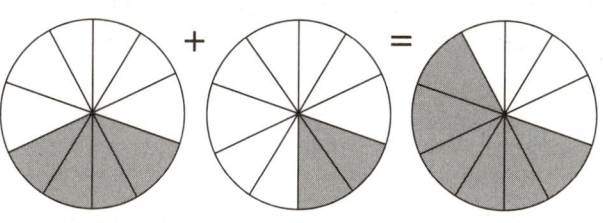

2. _____

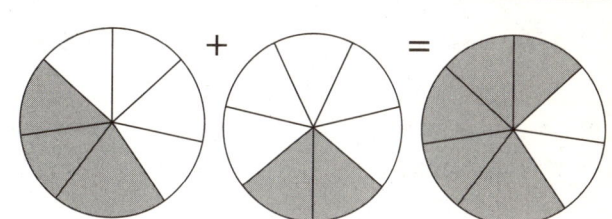

3. _____

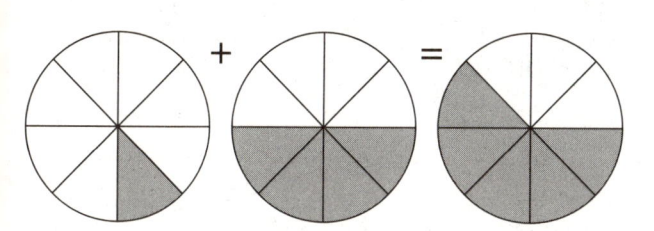

4. _____

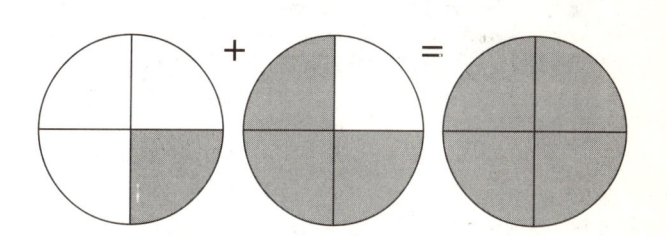

Directions: Find the sum. Write each answer in simplest form.

5. $\frac{3}{20} + \frac{5}{20} =$

6. $\frac{3}{9} + \frac{2}{9} =$

7. $\frac{1}{25} + \frac{4}{25} =$

8. $\frac{2}{14} + \frac{5}{14} =$

9. $\frac{4}{15} + \frac{6}{15} =$

10. $\frac{1}{3} + \frac{1}{3} =$

11. $\frac{2}{8} + \frac{5}{8} =$

12. $\frac{25}{100} + \frac{26}{100} =$

13. $\frac{1}{2} + \frac{1}{2} =$

167

Lesson 35 Algebraic Thinking • Foundations

14. $\frac{4}{5} + \frac{3}{5} =$ **15.** $\frac{7}{10} + \frac{6}{10} =$ **16.** $\frac{5}{6} + \frac{3}{6} =$

17. $\frac{1}{12} + \frac{3}{12} + \frac{4}{12} =$ **18.** $\frac{11}{20} + \frac{3}{20} + \frac{5}{20} =$ **19.** $\frac{8}{25} + \frac{7}{25} + \frac{5}{25} =$

20. S-O-L-V-E: Sammy ate $\frac{3}{8}$ of a pie. His sister ate $\frac{4}{8}$ of it. They both got a bellyache. What fraction of the pie was eaten?

S

O

L

V

E

AlgebraicThinking • Foundations   Lesson 35

21. S-O-L-V-E: Stephanie is making frosting for a cake. The recipe calls for $\frac{1}{4}$ cup of powdered sugar, $\frac{2}{4}$ cup of regular sugar, 2 eggs, and $\frac{3}{4}$ cup of canned milk. How much sugar is needed for the frosting?

S

O

L

V

E

22. S-O-L-V-E: Ruben attached $\frac{2}{8}$ foot of a board to another board that was $\frac{4}{8}$ foot long. How long is the board now?

S

O

L

V

E

Homework 35   Algebraic Thinking • Foundations

Name _____

Multiply or divide.

1.   72
   × 26

2.   48
   × 39

3.   51
   × 17

4.   136
   × 94

5. 12)̄384

6. 7)̄602

7. 24)̄360

8. 9)̄567

170

AlgebraicThinking • Foundations

Warm Up 36: What Are the Questions?

Read the information below. Then write questions for the answers that are given below.

The largest animal ever recorded is the blue whale. The largest female ever caught weighed 190 tons and was 90 feet 6 inches long. A longer female that was 110 feet long weighed a little less. The blue whales are 20 – 26 feet long and weigh 6,600 pounds when they are born. (1 ton = 2,000 pounds)

1. 19 feet 6 inches

2. 380,000 pounds

3. over 3 tons

4. approximately 90 feet

Lesson 36

AlgebraicThinking • Foundations

Adding Fractions

I'm searching for the method for adding fractions with different denominators.

Yesterday, when you added fractions, all of the problems had denominators that were the same. They are called **common denominators.** Today you will learn how to add fractions that have different denominators by finding common denominators. It involves the skill of finding equivalent fractions.

1. Find the sum. $\frac{3}{8} + \frac{7}{16} =$

   a. Use one color to shade $\frac{3}{8}$ of the rectangle.

   b. Use a second color to shade $\frac{7}{16}$ of the other rectangle.

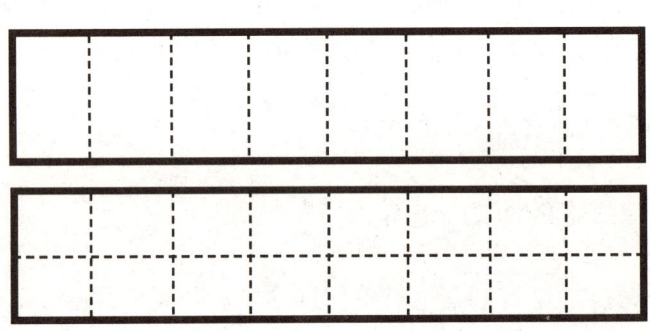

   c. Draw a line through the first rectangle so that it will be divided into 16 parts.

   d. How many sixteenths are shaded in the first rectangle?

   e. Using the rectangles find the sum.

   f. What is the common denominator for the two addends?

2. Find the sum. $\frac{3}{7} + \frac{5}{14} =$

   a. This time, use the same rectangle for both addends. To do so, you will have to write a fraction equivalent to $\frac{3}{7}$ with a denominator of 14.
   $\frac{3}{7} = \frac{?}{14}$

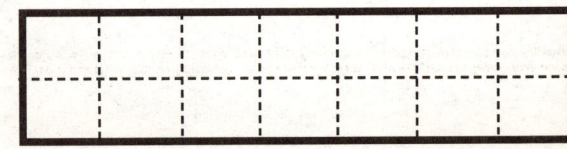

   b. What is the sum?

Algebraic Thinking • Foundations Lesson 36

3. What must you do to fractions with different denominators before you add them? _____

_____

4. Add $\frac{1}{4} + \frac{7}{20}$ using the following steps.
   a. First decide what the common denominator is. To do that, find the least common multiple (LCM) of the denominators, 4 and 20. Since 20 is a multiple of 4, it is the LCM. (So, the common denominator is 20.)
   b. Now find a fraction that is equivalent to $\frac{1}{4}$ that has a denominator of 20.
   c. Find the sum.

Directions: *Use the fraction bars to model the addition of fractions with different denominators. Use a different color for each addend. Don't forget to write the sum!*

5. $\frac{1}{3} + \frac{1}{6} =$

6. $\frac{1}{2} + \frac{1}{6} =$

173

Lesson 36 **AlgebraicThinking • Foundations**

7. $\frac{1}{2} + \frac{1}{4} =$

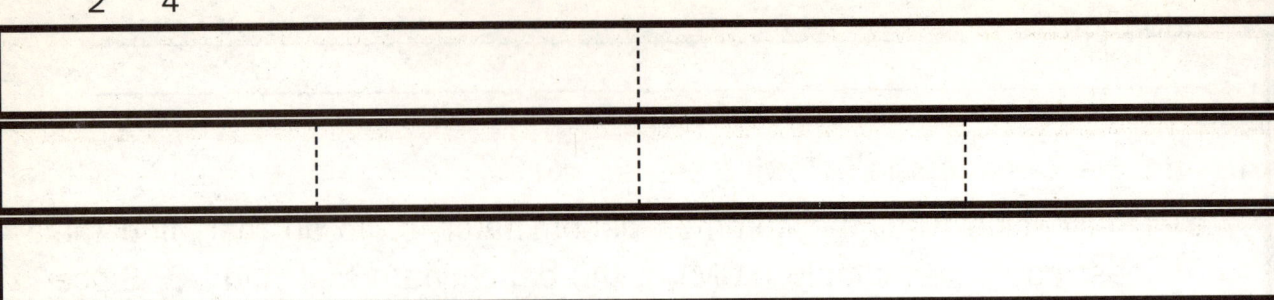

8. $\frac{2}{3} + \frac{1}{6} =$

9. $\frac{1}{3} + \frac{5}{12} =$

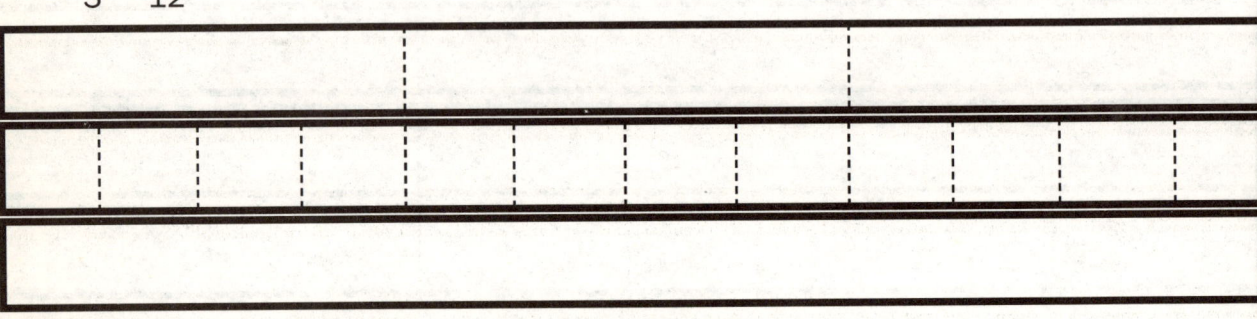

10. $\frac{1}{3} + \frac{3}{12} =$

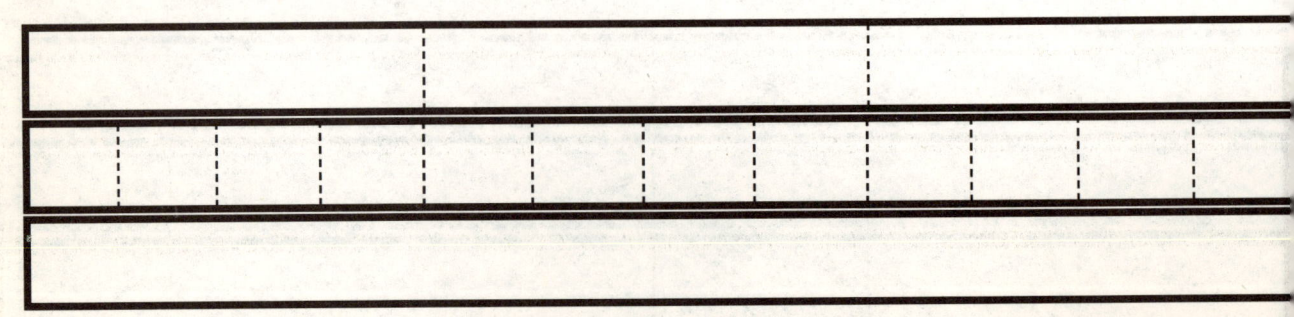

Algebraic Thinking • Foundations
Lesson 36

11. $\frac{1}{8} + \frac{2}{4} =$

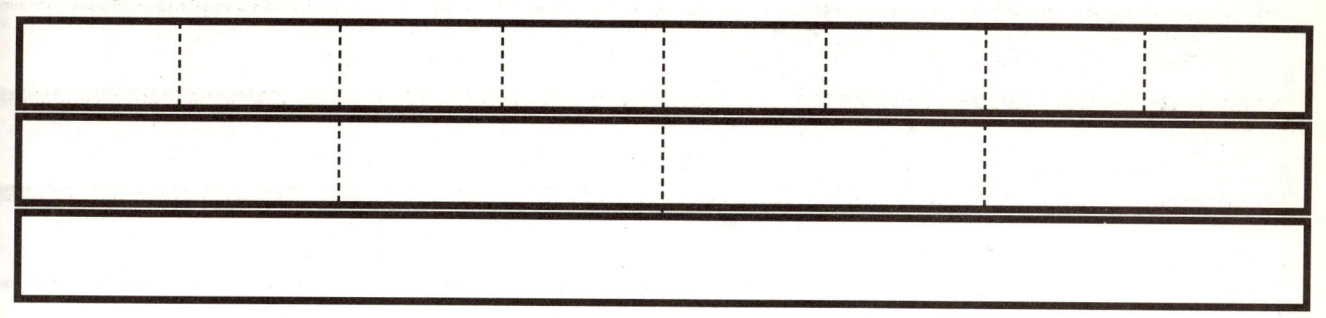

12. $\frac{3}{16} + \frac{1}{8} =$

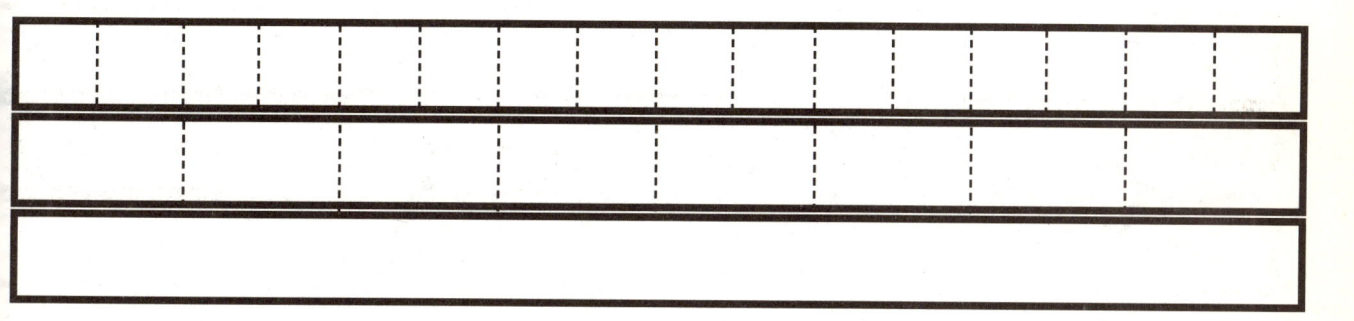

13. $\frac{1}{8} + \frac{3}{4} =$

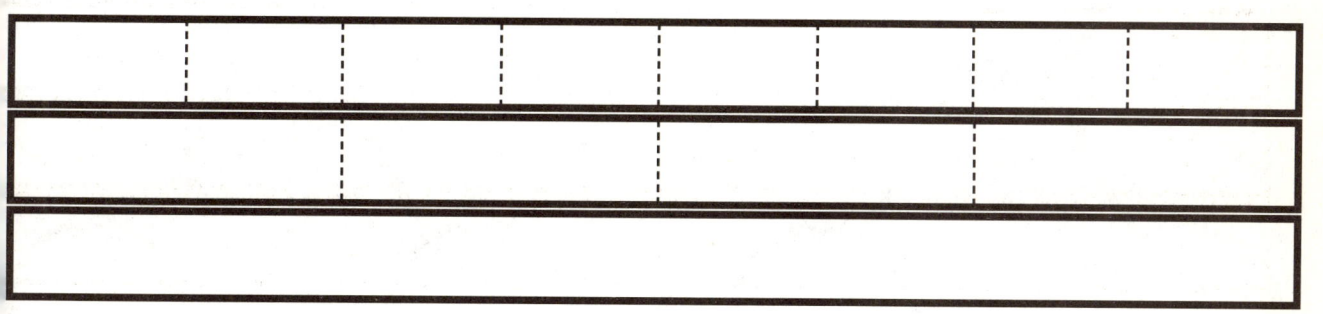

14. $\frac{1}{2} + \frac{3}{16} =$

Warm Up 37: "Sum" Star

Place the integers 1 through 12 in the circles so that the sum of the numbers in each row is the same.

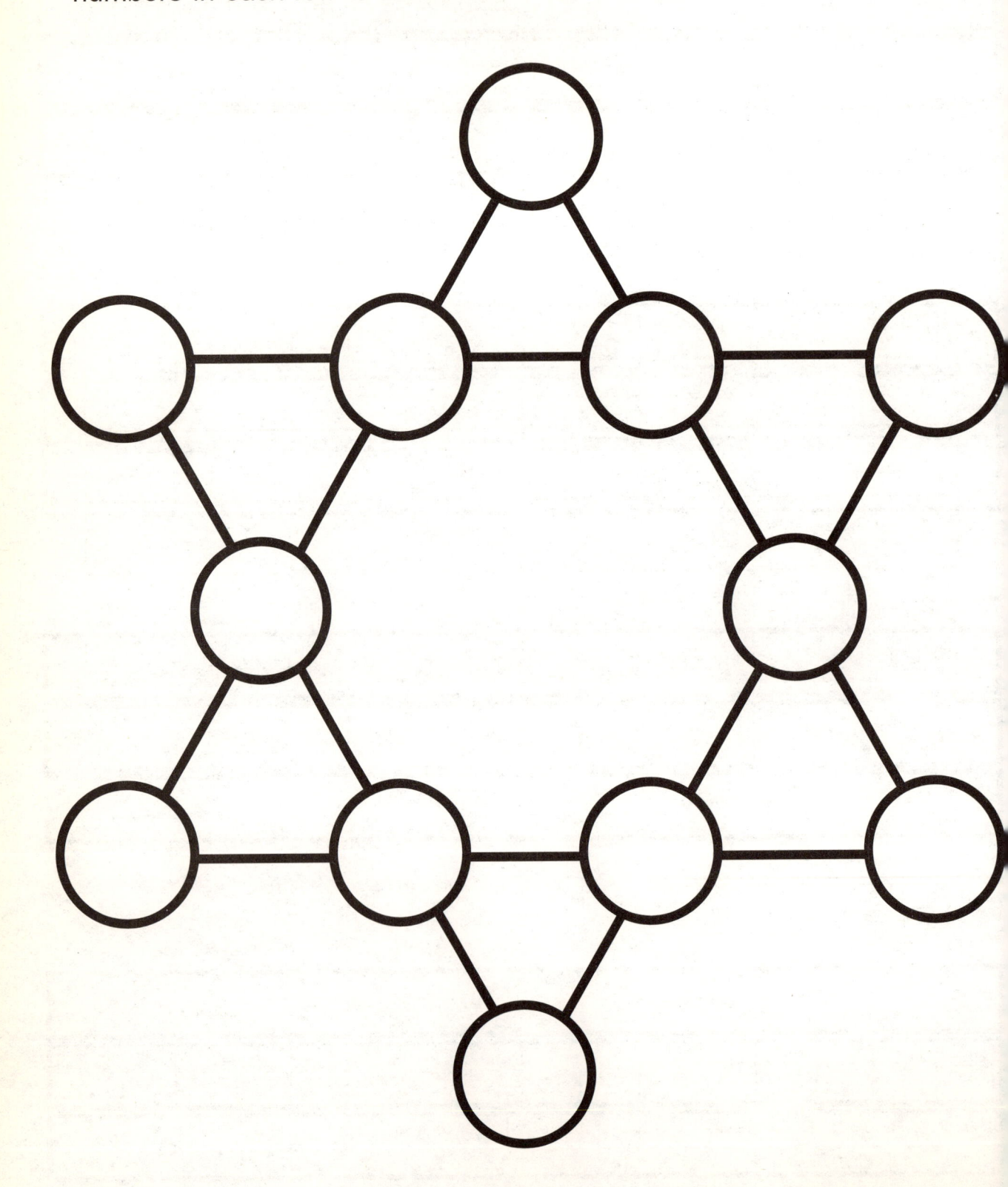

AlgebraicThinking • Foundations   Lesson 37

Try it this way.

Directions: Find the sum by writing the fractions in words. Just like in the last lesson, you only have to write the denominator in words.

Example: $\frac{1}{4} + \frac{5}{12} =$
a. 1 fourth + 5 twelfths =
b. Think, how many twelfths is 1 fourth?
c. So, the problem is 3 twelfths + 5 twelfths = 8 twelfths.
d. $\frac{1}{4} + \frac{5}{12} = \frac{3}{12} + \frac{5}{12} = \frac{8}{12}$

1. $\frac{1}{4} + \frac{1}{2} =$

2. $\frac{3}{8} + \frac{1}{4} =$

3. $\frac{2}{3} + \frac{3}{15} =$

4. $\frac{1}{5} + \frac{3}{10} =$

Directions: Add these fractions with your teacher. Write your answer in simplest form.

5. $\frac{1}{4}$
$+ \frac{5}{8}$

6. $\frac{1}{6}$
$+ \frac{2}{3}$

7. $\frac{1}{2}$
$+ \frac{5}{12}$

8. $\frac{1}{4}$
$+ \frac{3}{8}$

9. $\frac{3}{10}$
$+ \frac{2}{5}$

10. $\frac{3}{10}$
$+ \frac{6}{30}$

Lesson 37   Algebraic Thinking • Foundations

Practice it!

Directions: Write an addition sentence to match each fractional model.

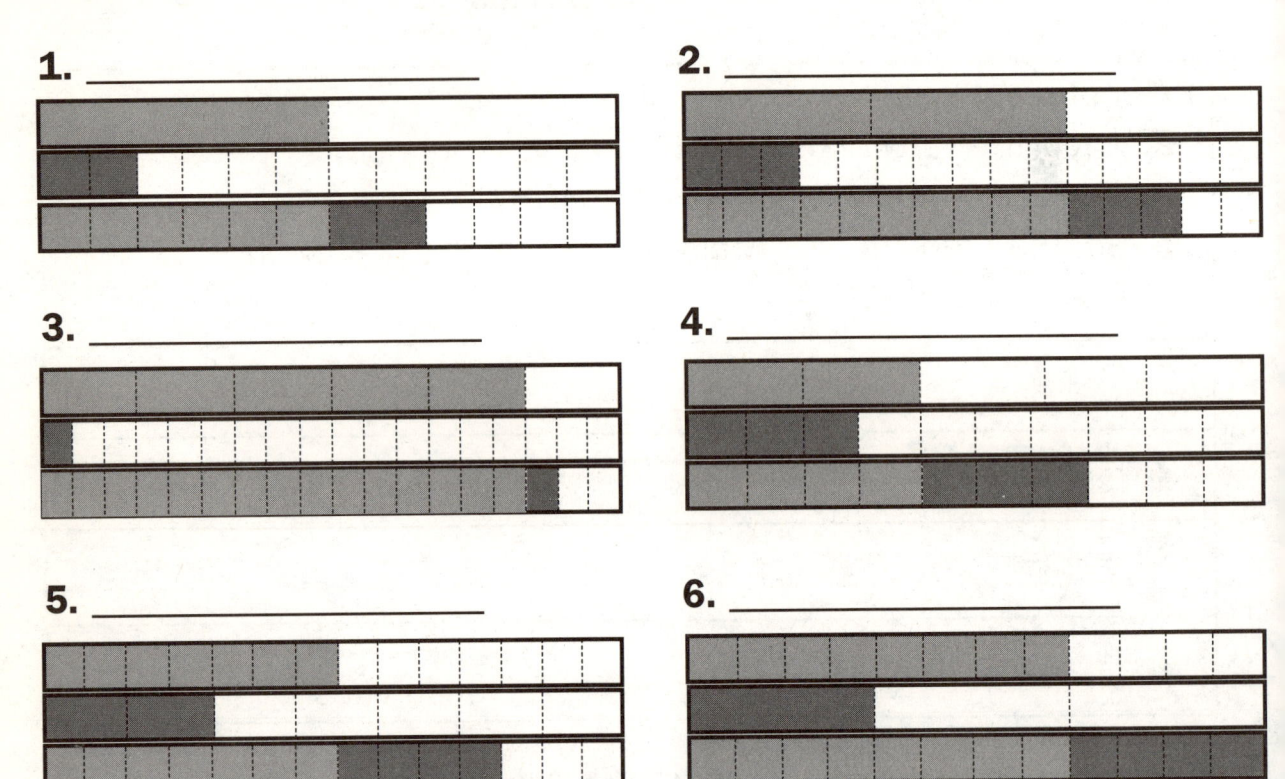

1. _____

2. _____

3. _____

4. _____

5. _____

6. _____

Directions: Find the sum after you find a common denominator. Leave your answer in simplest form. You may get an improper fraction.

7. $\dfrac{5}{12}$
   $+\dfrac{1}{6}$

8. $\dfrac{2}{3}$
   $+\dfrac{1}{6}$

9. $\dfrac{1}{2}$
   $+\dfrac{3}{6}$

10. $\dfrac{5}{7}$
    $+\dfrac{3}{14}$

11. $\dfrac{5}{8}$
    $+\dfrac{1}{16}$

12. $\dfrac{5}{12}$
    $+\dfrac{5}{24}$

Algebraic Thinking • Foundations Lesson 37

13. $\dfrac{1}{2} + \dfrac{3}{4}$

14. $\dfrac{4}{5} + \dfrac{3}{10}$

15. $\dfrac{2}{3} + \dfrac{7}{15}$

16. $\dfrac{1}{8} + \dfrac{2}{4}$

17. $\dfrac{2}{5} + \dfrac{4}{15}$

18. $\dfrac{7}{10} + \dfrac{23}{100}$

19. $\dfrac{6}{25} + \dfrac{2}{5}$

20. $\dfrac{5}{6} + \dfrac{2}{3}$

21. $\dfrac{5}{9} + \dfrac{1}{3}$

22. **S-O-L-V-E**: As a part of a fractions unit, Mrs. Johnson's class polled the students at their school. They asked their schoolmates what their favorite fast food is. They recorded the results in the table to the right. What fraction of the students liked french fries or corn dogs?

Favorite Fast Food	Fraction
Pizza	$\dfrac{3}{8}$
Hamburgers	$\dfrac{1}{4}$
French Fries	$\dfrac{1}{6}$
Tacos	$\dfrac{1}{8}$
Corn Dogs	$\dfrac{1}{12}$

S
O
L
V
E

23. **S-O-L-V-E**: The two most popular choices were pizza and hamburgers. What fraction of the students chose these two items?

S
O
L
V
E

Warm Up 38: Find the Symbol

Directions: *Shade ALL of the squares that fit the descriptions.*

1. Shade all squares that are equivalent to $\frac{5}{8}$.
2. Shade all squares that are equivalent to 80%.
3. Shade all squares that are equivalent to 0.35.
4. Shade all squares that are equivalent to $\frac{15}{25}$.
5. Shade all squares that are equivalent to 4%.
6. Shade all squares that are equivalent to 0.055.

$\frac{40}{100}$	62.5%	$\frac{1}{25}$	0.7	12.5%	$\frac{1}{2}$	0.0125	$\frac{14}{40}$
$\frac{35}{100}$	0.5	$\frac{55}{1,000}$	$\frac{1}{40}$	0.375	$\frac{7}{8}$	35%	$\frac{3}{4}$
0.08	$\frac{4}{100}$	$\frac{25}{40}$	$\frac{4}{32}$	50%	0.625	$\frac{3}{60}$	$\frac{40}{100}$
1.25%	37.5%	0.4	$\frac{7}{10}$	$\frac{80}{100}$	5%	$\frac{25}{100}$	$\frac{25}{50}$
$\frac{1}{4}$	0.025	$\frac{3}{8}$	60%	0.75	$\frac{14}{20}$	0.125	$\frac{6}{16}$
0.875	75%	$\frac{7}{20}$	0.05	2.5%	$\frac{4}{5}$	$\frac{60}{100}$	0.04
$\frac{1}{20}$	0.6	$\frac{20}{50}$	$\frac{21}{24}$	25%	5.5%	87.5%	$\frac{125}{200}$
$\frac{2}{50}$	$\frac{1}{8}$	$\frac{2}{5}$	70%	$\frac{1}{80}$	$\frac{11}{200}$	0.80	$\frac{3}{5}$

Algebraic Thinking • Foundations Lesson 38

Adding Fractions Again!

In the last lesson you added fractions by finding common denominators. You will do the same, today. The difference is that you may have to find different denominators for both fractions.

S-O-L-V-E: Kelly was going to use $\frac{1}{2}$ of an ounce of gold to make a pendant. But she decided to add another $\frac{1}{3}$ ounce before she made it. How much gold was used to make the pendant?

S

O

L

V

E

Directions: *Use the fraction bars to model the addition sentences. After the model has been drawn, rewrite the problem and answer with common denominators.*

1. $\frac{1}{2} + \frac{1}{3} =$

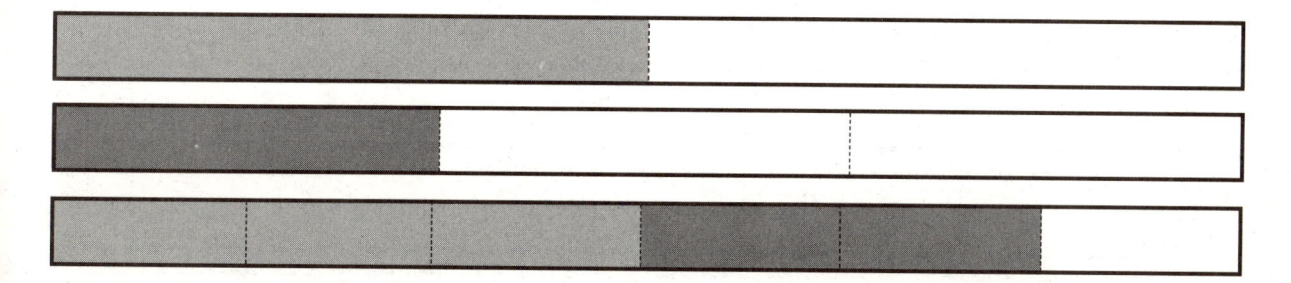

The common denominator in this problem is 6. How do you think it was found?

181

Lesson 38 **AlgebraicThinking** • Foundations

2. $\frac{1}{4} + \frac{1}{3} =$

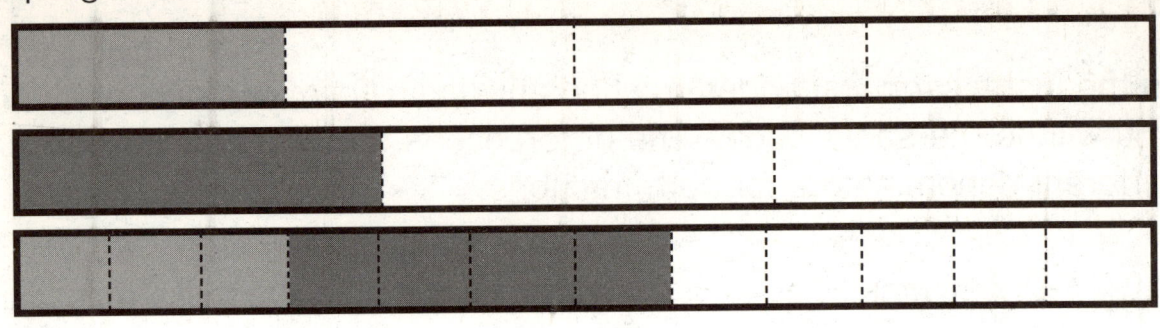

3. $\frac{3}{8} + \frac{1}{3} =$

4. $\frac{3}{4} + \frac{1}{6} =$

5. $\frac{1}{2} + \frac{2}{5} =$

Algebraic Thinking • Foundations   Lesson 38

On the other problems, you found the common denominator by multiplying the denominators together. You can always find a common denominator by doing that. Sometimes, you can find a smaller denominator. For instance on #4 the denominator was shown to be 24 since 6 • 4 = 24. The common denominator can also be 12 because 12 is a multiple of both 6 and 4.

6. $\frac{3}{4} + \frac{1}{6} =$

Keep it up! This time, you'll have to divide the models yourself.

7. $\frac{3}{8} + \frac{1}{6} =$

8. $\frac{4}{9} + \frac{1}{6} =$

Lesson 38

9. $\frac{3}{4} + \frac{1}{5} =$

10. $\frac{1}{3} + \frac{2}{5} =$

11. $\frac{1}{6} + \frac{1}{4} =$

12. $\frac{3}{8} + \frac{5}{12} =$

Algebraic Thinking • Foundations

Lesson 38

One way to find the common denominator is to list several multiples of the larger denominator. Then check to see if they are multiples of the smaller denominator. Try that with your teacher.

Directions: *Do these problems with your teacher. Find the sum after you find a common denominator.*

13. $\begin{array}{r} \frac{3}{8} \\ + \frac{2}{3} \\ \hline \end{array}$	14. $\begin{array}{r} \frac{5}{6} \\ + \frac{1}{9} \\ \hline \end{array}$
15. $\begin{array}{r} \frac{1}{4} \\ + \frac{3}{5} \\ \hline \end{array}$	16. $\begin{array}{r} \frac{5}{8} \\ + \frac{3}{10} \\ \hline \end{array}$
17. $\begin{array}{r} \frac{2}{5} \\ + \frac{13}{20} \\ \hline \end{array}$	18. $\begin{array}{r} \frac{2}{9} \\ + \frac{5}{12} \\ \hline \end{array}$
19. $\begin{array}{r} \frac{3}{10} \\ + \frac{7}{15} \\ \hline \end{array}$	20. $\begin{array}{r} \frac{3}{10} \\ + \frac{7}{25} \\ \hline \end{array}$

Warm Up 39: Tic-Tac-Toe

Lindsay and Angela played a game of tic-tac-toe. Find out who won by matching each answer on the board to the correct problem. Put the appropriate letter over that space on the board.

Lindsay played the X
267 ÷ 3 =
5,835 ÷ 15 =
1,668 ÷ 6 =
1,644 ÷ 12 =

Angela played the O
1,488 ÷ 12 =
1,143 ÷ 9 =
2,032 ÷ 8 =

89	132	127
137	124	264
278	254	389

Who won the game? _____

Algebraic Thinking • Foundations

Lesson 39

Practice it!

Directions: Write an addition sentence to match each fractional model.

1. _____

2. _____

3. _____

4. _____

5. _____

6. _____

187

Lesson 39 AlgebraicThinking • Foundations

Directions: *Find the sum after you find a common denominator. Leave your answer in simplest form.*

7. $\dfrac{5}{8}$
   $+\dfrac{1}{3}$

8. $\dfrac{4}{9}$
   $+\dfrac{1}{12}$

9. $\dfrac{7}{10}$
   $+\dfrac{2}{5}$

10. $\dfrac{1}{2}$
    $+\dfrac{2}{5}$

11. $\dfrac{1}{4}$
    $+\dfrac{2}{3}$

12. $\dfrac{4}{15}$
    $+\dfrac{11}{20}$

13. $\dfrac{5}{6}$
    $+\dfrac{1}{2}$

14. $\dfrac{3}{8}$
    $+\dfrac{1}{8}$

15. $\dfrac{2}{7}$
    $+\dfrac{5}{14}$

16. $\dfrac{1}{6}$
    $+\dfrac{3}{4}$

17. $\dfrac{3}{8}$
    $+\dfrac{5}{6}$

18. $\dfrac{2}{5}$
    $+\dfrac{3}{20}$

AlgebraicThinking • Foundations Lesson 39

19. $\frac{7}{10}$
  $+\frac{2}{25}$

20. $\frac{4}{6}$
  $+\frac{1}{3}$

21. $\frac{4}{9}$
  $+\frac{1}{6}$

22. $\frac{7}{9}$
  $+\frac{1}{12}$

23. $\frac{2}{4}$
  $+\frac{2}{3}$

24. $\frac{1}{5}$
  $+\frac{3}{4}$

25. **S-O-L-V-E:** As a part of a community service project, three students agreed to pick up trash along a rural highway. Michelle walked $\frac{1}{3}$ of a mile. Jenny walked $\frac{3}{4}$ of a mile and Scott walked $\frac{1}{6}$ of a mile. How many miles of highway did they walk?

S

O

L

V

E

Warm Up 40

Warm Up 40: "Sum" Estimate

Fill in the boxes below with the numbers 3 through 8, to get a sum close to 1,750 without going over.

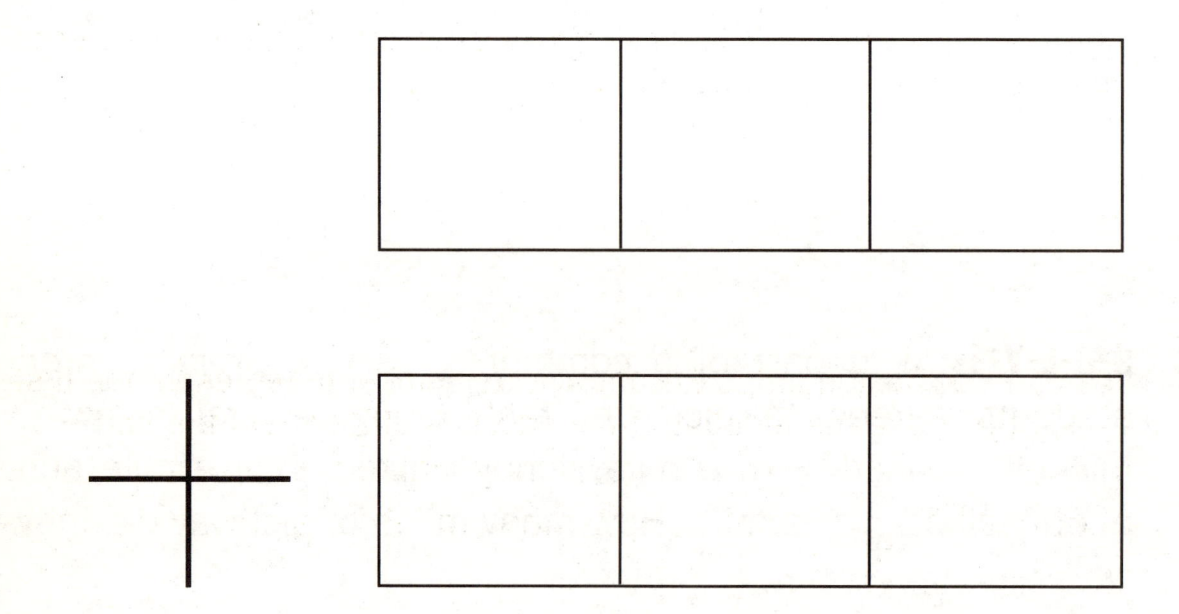

```
      ☐☐☐
  +   ☐☐☐
  ─────────
```

AlgebraicThinking • Foundations   Lesson 40

Subtracting Fractions

Today we are going to move from adding fractions to subtracting fractions. When you add, you take two groups and push them together. When you subtract, you represent the first group and then take the amount in the second group from the first group. Just to make this clear, look at the following example.

Five apples – two apples = 3 apples. Draw a picture with your teacher to model this subtraction problem.

Now let's use our fraction strips to subtract. Remember to represent the first number and then take the amount of the second number from the first.

1. $\frac{3}{4} - \frac{1}{4} =$

2. $\frac{7}{12} - \frac{6}{12} =$

3. $\frac{5}{6} - \frac{1}{6} =$

4. $\frac{5}{8} - \frac{3}{8} =$

Lesson 40

Algebraic Thinking • Foundations

Use your fraction strips to model the answer to the following problems with your teacher.

1. $\frac{1}{2} - \frac{1}{4} =$

2. $\frac{2}{3} - \frac{1}{6} =$

3. $\frac{5}{8} - \frac{1}{4} =$

4. $\frac{11}{12} - \frac{5}{12} =$

5. $\frac{11}{12} - \frac{5}{6} =$

6. $\frac{1}{3} - \frac{1}{12} =$

7. $\frac{1}{2} - \frac{1}{6} =$

AlgebraicThinking • **Foundations** Lesson 40

Now write three subtraction problems with your partner which can be modeled with your fraction strips. Make the key for your problems below.

1.

2.

3.

Key

1.

2.

3.

Homework 40 — Algebraic Thinking • Foundations

Name _____

Directions: *Find each sum.*

1. $\dfrac{1}{2}$
   $+\dfrac{1}{3}$

2. $\dfrac{2}{17}$
   $+\dfrac{2}{3}$

3. $\dfrac{3}{4}$
   $+\dfrac{2}{5}$

4. $\dfrac{5}{6}$
   $+\dfrac{3}{10}$

5. $\dfrac{3}{8}$
   $+\dfrac{5}{12}$

6. $\dfrac{7}{10}$
   $+\dfrac{2}{3}$

AlgebraicThinking • Foundations Warm Up 41

Warm Up 41: Monthly Math

Directions: *Follow the instructions below to get the correct final value.*

Write the number of days in February (not leap year).

Divide it by the number of months ending in "y."

Add the number of days in a week.

Multiply by the number of months that begin with "M."

Subtract the number of months with 32 days.

Divide by the number of months that have 5 letters in them.

Add the number of months that end in "r."

Subtract the number of days with more than 6 letters.

Multiply by the number of years in a decade.

195

Lesson 41   Algebraic Thinking • Foundations

Subtracting Fractions

In the last lesson you subtracted fractions by finding common denominators. You will do the same, today. The difference is that you may have to find different denominators for both fractions.

S-O-L-V-E: Brad has a board that is $\frac{7}{8}$ ft long. To finish his toy box project, he needs to cut a board $\frac{1}{3}$ ft long. How much of the board will not be used for the toy box?

S

O

L

V

E

Directions: *Practice these subtraction problems with your teacher.*

1. $\frac{5}{8} - \frac{1}{2} =$ 2. $\frac{1}{3} - \frac{1}{4} =$

3. $\frac{5}{6} - \frac{1}{3} =$ 4. $\frac{11}{12} - \frac{1}{4} =$

5. $\frac{2}{3} - \frac{1}{4} =$ 6. $\frac{7}{10} - \frac{1}{5} =$

AlgebraicThinking • Foundations Lesson 41

Directions: *Find the difference after you find a common denominator. Write your answer in simplest form.*

1. $\frac{3}{7} - \frac{1}{3} =$

2. $\frac{4}{5} - \frac{2}{3} =$

3. $\frac{7}{9} - \frac{1}{4} =$

4. $\frac{5}{6} - \frac{3}{8} =$

5. $\frac{11}{13} - \frac{7}{13} =$

6. $\frac{7}{8} - \frac{3}{4} =$

S-O-L-V-E: Jennifer walks $\frac{9}{10}$ mi to school. Brett walks $\frac{4}{5}$ mi to school. How much farther does Jennifer have to walk than Brett?

S

O

L

V

E

Homework 41   **AlgebraicThinking** • Foundations

Name _____

Directions: *Write each decimal as a percent and as a fraction.*

1. 0.25   **2.** 0.65

3. 0.88   **4.** 0.1

5. 0.48   **6.** 0.22

7. 5.45   **8.** 2.38

9. 0.40   **10.** 0.200

Algebraic Thinking • Foundations

Warm Up 42

Warm Up 42: Cross Number Puzzle

Directions: Solve the problems and complete the puzzle, placing one digit in each square.

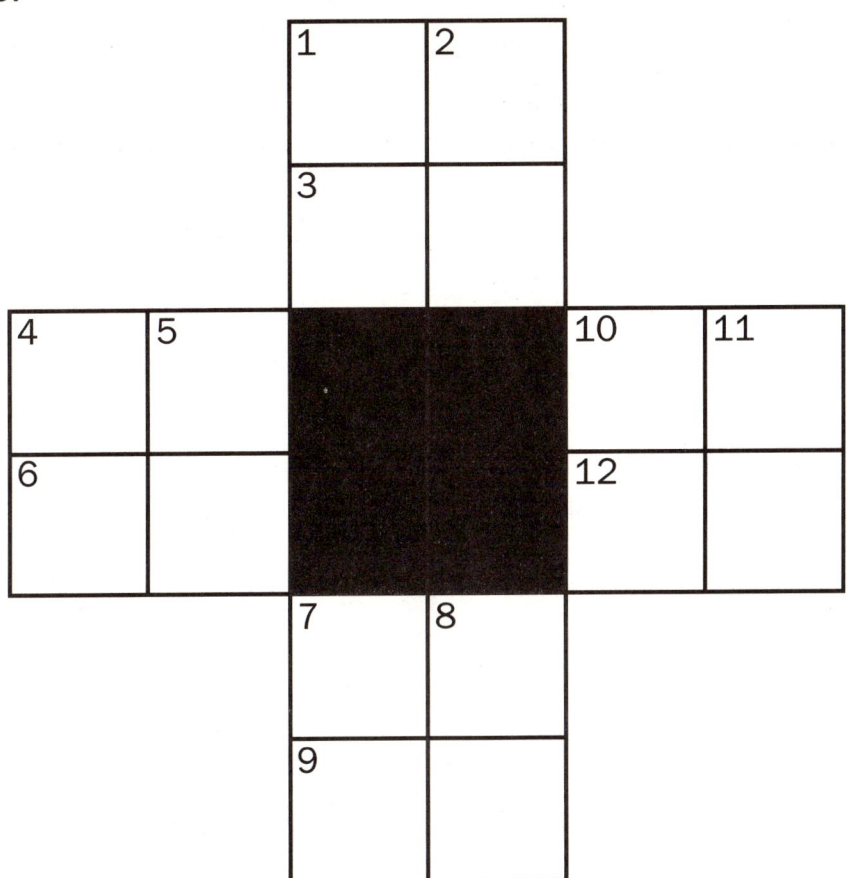

ACROSS

1. 32 • 3
3. (2 • 2) + 8
4. 22 • 4
6. 12 • 3
7. (23 + 2) • 3
9. (100 ÷ 5) + 14
10. 2 • 6
12. 35 + 36

DOWN

1. 13 • 7
2. 124 ÷ 2
4. 65 + 23 – 5
5. 43 • 2
7. 96 – 23
8. (11 • 4) + 10
10. 45 – 28
11. 11 + 10

199

Lesson 42 AlgebraicThinking • Foundations

Directions: Work together to add and subtract the fractions below. Be sure to simplify all answers to lowest terms.

1. $\dfrac{1}{2} + \dfrac{1}{4} =$

2. $\dfrac{5}{8} - \dfrac{1}{4} =$

3. $\dfrac{5}{6} + \dfrac{1}{3} =$

4. $\dfrac{1}{2} + \dfrac{3}{5} =$

5. $\dfrac{5}{6} - \dfrac{1}{5} =$

6. $\dfrac{3}{10} + \dfrac{3}{4} =$

7. $\dfrac{7}{8} - \dfrac{1}{12} =$

8. $\dfrac{5}{6} + \dfrac{7}{8} =$

Algebraic Thinking • Foundations

Lesson 42

Directions: Use each digit only once above each problem to make a true statement. The first one has been done for you.

1.

| 1 | 2 | 3 | 8 |

$$\frac{1}{2} + \frac{3}{8} = \frac{7}{8}$$

2.

| 1 | 1 | 2 | 4 |

$$\frac{}{} + \frac{}{} = \frac{3}{4}$$

3.

| 1 | 2 | 4 | 5 |

$$\frac{}{} - \frac{}{} = \frac{3}{10}$$

4.

| 1 | 4 | 4 | 5 |

$$\frac{}{} - \frac{}{} = \frac{11}{20}$$

Warm Up 43: Missing Squares

In each large square, fill in the missing squares with numbers so that each row, column, and diagonal will have the same sum.

1.

27	31	11
	23	

2.

33	12	
	24	30
	36	

Algebraic Thinking • Foundations   Lesson 43

Mixed Numbers and Improper Fractions

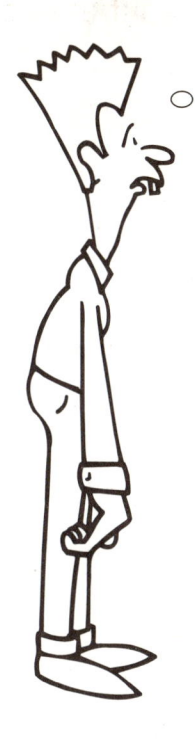

What in the world do toothpicks have to do with fractions?

We are going to measure several things today. And we are going to use our own unit. We are going to measure things in toothpicks! Each one of you will make a measuring tape marked off in toothpicks. The measuring tape will be divided into wholes, halves, and fourths of toothpicks. Your teacher will show you how to make it. When you have made your measuring tape, your teacher will assign several objects to be measured. Fill in the table with your data.

Object	Length (in toothpicks)	Object	Length (in toothpicks)

A **mixed number** is the sum of a whole number and a fraction. Another way to describe a mixed number is "the mixture of a whole number and a fraction." Make a list of the mixed numbers you found while measuring.

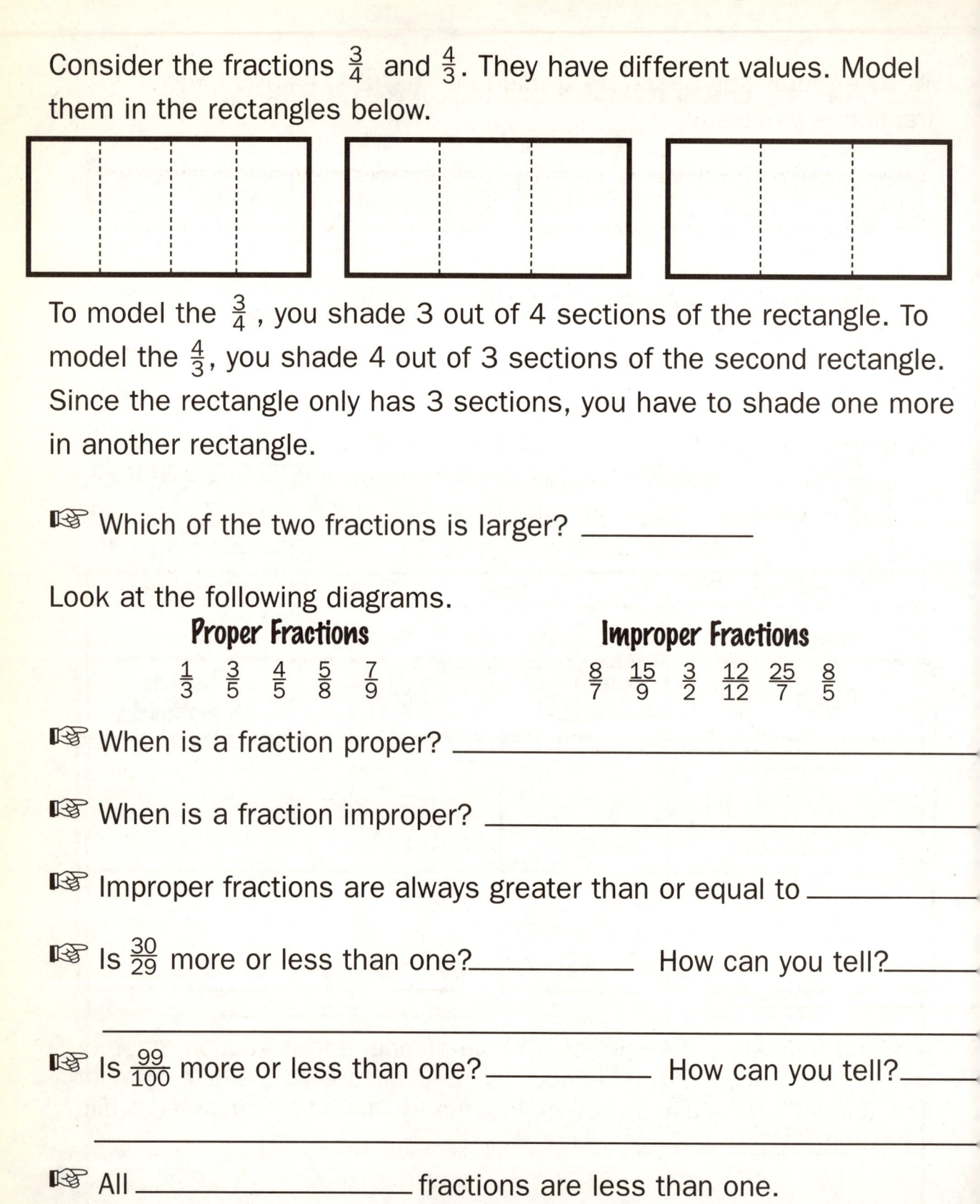

Lesson 43   **AlgebraicThinking • Foundations**

Consider the fractions $\frac{3}{4}$ and $\frac{4}{3}$. They have different values. Model them in the rectangles below.

To model the $\frac{3}{4}$, you shade 3 out of 4 sections of the rectangle. To model the $\frac{4}{3}$, you shade 4 out of 3 sections of the second rectangle. Since the rectangle only has 3 sections, you have to shade one more in another rectangle.

☞ Which of the two fractions is larger? _____

Look at the following diagrams.

Proper Fractions   **Improper Fractions**

$\frac{1}{3}$ $\frac{3}{5}$ $\frac{4}{5}$ $\frac{5}{8}$ $\frac{7}{9}$ $\frac{8}{7}$ $\frac{15}{9}$ $\frac{3}{2}$ $\frac{12}{12}$ $\frac{25}{7}$ $\frac{8}{5}$

☞ When is a fraction proper? _____

☞ When is a fraction improper? _____

☞ Improper fractions are always greater than or equal to _____

☞ Is $\frac{30}{29}$ more or less than one? _____   How can you tell? _____
_____

☞ Is $\frac{99}{100}$ more or less than one? _____   How can you tell? _____
_____

☞ All _____ fractions are less than one.

☞ All _____ fractions are greater than or equal to one.

Algebraic Thinking • Foundations

Lesson 43

★ The rectangles below are divided into eighths. What improper fraction is modeled? _____

★ How would you write this as a mixed number? _____

Directions: *Fill in the chart below with your teacher. Decide if more or less than one is shaded. Then write the fraction that is shaded. If it is improper, write the mixed number, also.*

Whole Unit	Model	Fraction/Mixed Number
	More, Less, or Equal	
	More, Less, or Equal	
	More, Less, or Equal	
	More, Less, or Equal	
		$\dfrac{11}{4} =$

205

Lesson 43 Algebraic**Thinking** • Foundations

Directions: *Model the given mixed number.*
(NOTE: There may be extra circles.)

1.	$3\frac{1}{4}$	○ ○ ○ ○ ○ ○ (circles divided into fourths)
2.	$2\frac{3}{5}$	○ ○ ○ ○ ○ ○ (circles divided into fifths)
3.	$4\frac{3}{8}$	○ ○ ○ ○ ○ ○ (circles divided into eighths)
4.	$2\frac{7}{10}$	○ ○ ○ ○ ○ ○ (circles divided into tenths)
5.	$5\frac{1}{2}$	○ ○ ○ ○ ○ ○ (circles divided into halves)

6. In problem #1, you should have shaded 3 whole circles. How many fourths is that? _____ Add on the other one-fourth. Now how many fourths are there? _____ Write that as an improper fraction. _____

7. In problem #2, how many whole circles did you shade? _____ How many fifths is that? _____ Add on the other three-fifths. Now how many fifths are there? _____ Write that as an improper fraction. _____

8. In problem #3, how many whole circles did you shade? _____ How many eighths is that? _____ Add on the other three-eighths. Now how many eighths are there? _____ Write that as an improper fraction. _____

Algebraic Thinking • Foundations   Lesson 43

9. In problem #4, how many whole circles did you shade? _____ How many tenths is that? _____ Add on the other seven-tenths. Now how many tenths are there? _____ Write that as an improper fraction. _____

10. In problem #5, how many whole circles did you shade? _____ How many halves is that? _____ Add on the other one-half. Now how many halves are there? _____ Write that as an improper fraction. _____

When writing a mixed number as an improper fraction, you may continue to draw a model for as long as you want. However, it may be quicker for you to think how many "parts" there are in the whole. Look at the following examples.

EXAMPLES – Convert a mixed number to an improper fraction.

11. $2\frac{3}{4} = 2 + \frac{3}{4}$ → <u>2 whole units</u> + 3 fourths = <u>8 fourths</u> + 3 fourths = 11 fourths = $\frac{11}{4}$

12. $4\frac{5}{6} = 4 + \frac{5}{6}$ → <u>4 whole units</u> + 5 sixths = <u>24 sixths</u> + 5 sixths = 29 sixths = $\frac{29}{6}$

EXAMPLES – Write an improper fraction as a mixed number.

13. $\frac{27}{4}$ → 27 fourths. Think, *"It takes 4 fourths to make a whole unit."* How many groups of 4 fourths are in 27 fourths? __6__ How many are left over? __3__ So, there are 6 whole units and 3 fourths. → $6\frac{3}{4}$

14. $\frac{32}{3}$ → 32 thirds. Think, *"It takes 3 thirds to make a whole unit."* How many groups of 3 thirds are in 32 thirds? __10__ How many are left over? __2__ So, there are 10 whole units and 2 thirds. → $10\frac{2}{3}$

TRY THESE!

15. $5\frac{2}{3} =$

16. $\frac{24}{10} =$

Lesson 43 — Algebraic Thinking • Foundations

Practice it!

Directions: Practice converting between improper fractions and mixed numbers. Take your time and think through each problem. In problems 1 – 8, write the mixed number as an improper fraction.

1. $2\frac{3}{8}$

2. $4\frac{3}{5}$

3. $1\frac{2}{3}$

4. $10\frac{1}{4}$

5. $7\frac{5}{9}$

6. $6\frac{1}{2}$

7. $8\frac{7}{10}$

8. $3\frac{2}{11}$

Directions: In problems 9 – 16, convert the improper fractions to a mixed number.

9. $\frac{13}{4}$

10. $\frac{19}{5}$

11. $\frac{20}{8}$

12. $\frac{12}{4}$

13. $\frac{7}{2}$

14. $\frac{8}{5}$

15. $\frac{21}{4}$

16. $\frac{17}{6}$

AlgebraicThinking • Foundations Lesson 43

17. S-O-L-V-E! Mr. Johnson told 6 students that they could have all the candy that he had as long as each student got the same amount. He had 27 pieces of candy. How much candy will each student get? Write your answer as a mixed number.

S. _____

O. _____

L. _____

V. _____

E. _____

Homework 43

AlgebraicThinking • Foundations

Name _____

Directions: *Model the given fraction and write it in simplest form.*

1. $\frac{8}{12}$

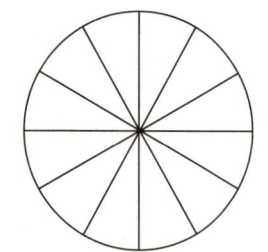

2. $\frac{4}{12}$

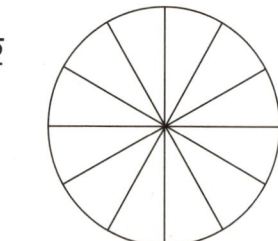

3. $\frac{5}{20}$

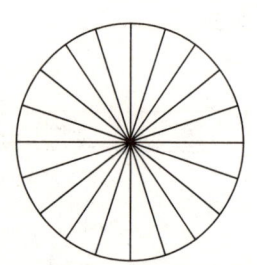

4. $\frac{10}{20}$

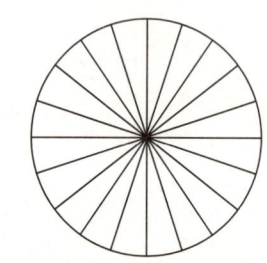

5. $\frac{2}{6}$

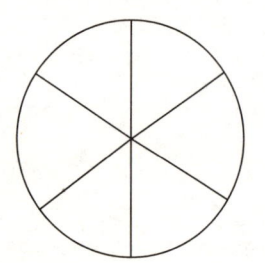

6. $\frac{4}{6}$

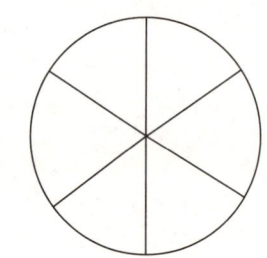

7. $\frac{3}{9}$

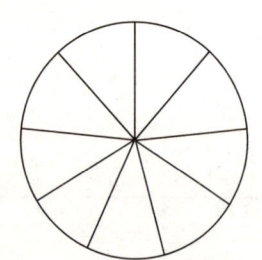

8. $\frac{6}{9}$

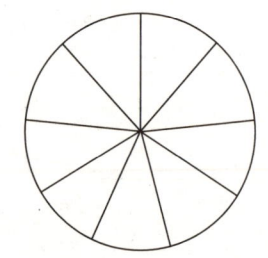

9. $\frac{4}{10}$

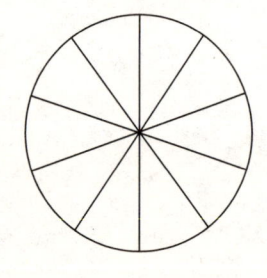

10. $\frac{8}{10}$

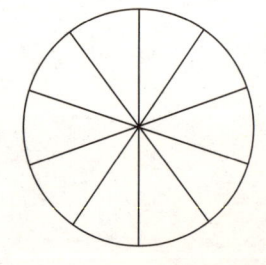

210

AlgebraicThinking • **Foundations**

Warm Up 44

Warm Up 44: Division Tower

Follow the division problems from top to bottom. Use the answer for each problem as the dividend in the next problem.

12,240 ÷ 5 = _____

           _____ ÷ 3 = _____

                     _____ ÷ 6 = _____

                               _____ ÷ 4 = _____

                                       _____ ÷ 2 = _____

Lesson 44 — Algebraic Thinking • Foundations

Adding Mixed Numbers

Do you REMEMBER When . . .

We had a lesson about toothpicks. In the lesson, we made a measuring tape. Our unit of measure was a toothpick. The lesson was about mixed numbers. Today we will learn how to add those mixed numbers. But first, take a minute to explain what a mixed number is.

S-O-L-V-E: Christine, Jessica, Nick, and Steve were in a group on the day of the "Toothpicks" lesson. They were assigned to measure the perimeter of a book. (That is the length of all four sides added together.) They decided as a group that each person would measure one of the sides and then they would add them together. Christine measured one side of the book $4\frac{3}{4}$ toothpicks long. Jessica measured another side $5\frac{1}{2}$ toothpicks long. Nick said, "Hey that's strange. Steve and I got those exact same measures for the other two sides." What is the perimeter of the book in toothpicks?

Algebraic Thinking • Foundations

Lesson 44

Nick decided to solve the problem by drawing models. First he was going to try to draw toothpicks to represent the fractions. They were easy to draw, but he couldn't use them to model fractions very well. So he decided to use circles since they are easy to divide into fractions. Here is the model he constructed.

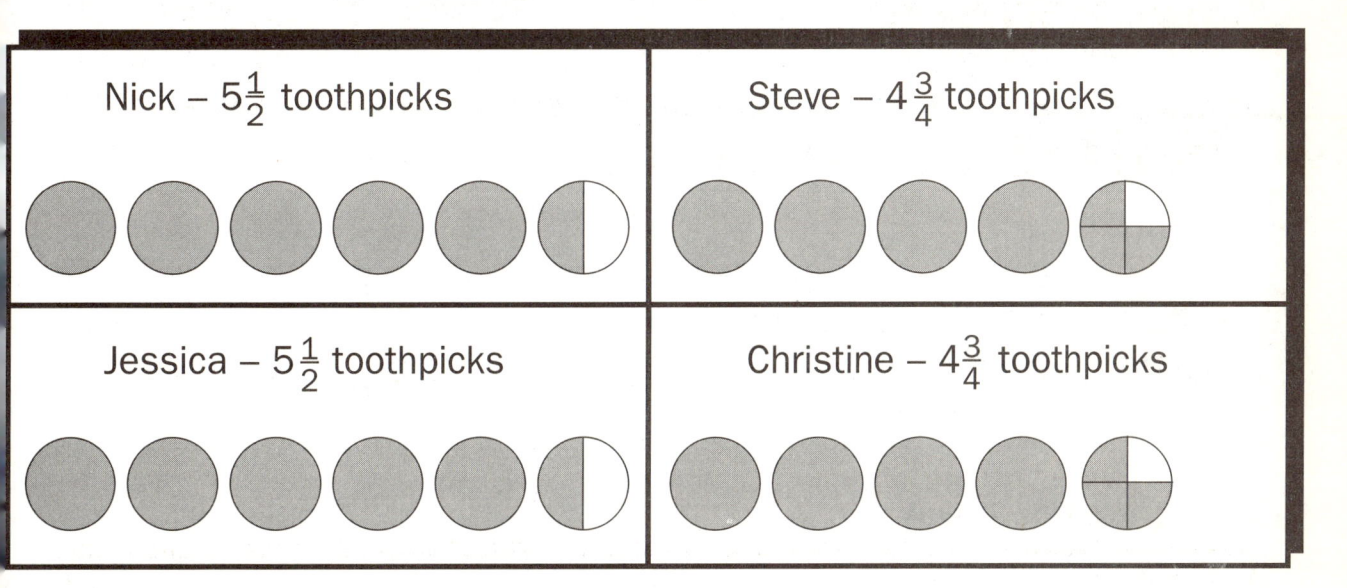

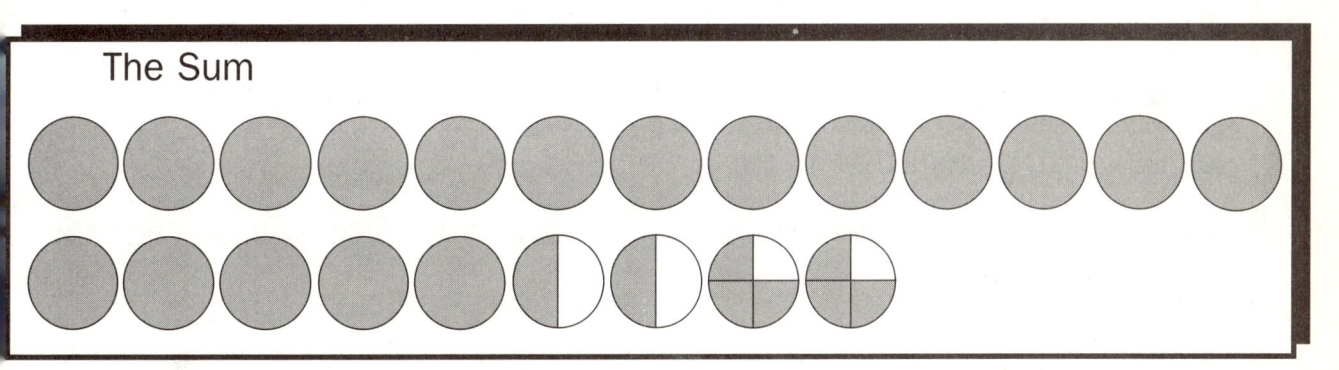

Nick – $5\frac{1}{2}$ toothpicks

Steve – $4\frac{3}{4}$ toothpicks

Jessica – $5\frac{1}{2}$ toothpicks

Christine – $4\frac{3}{4}$ toothpicks

The Sum

Nick says the sum is 18 whole toothpicks, 2 half toothpicks, and 6 fourths of toothpicks.

Jessica says that the 2 halves make another whole and the 6 fourths make another whole with a half left over. Jessica says the answer is $20\frac{1}{2}$ toothpicks.

Lesson 44 Algebraic Thinking • Foundations

Steve says, "just convert all the mixed numbers to improper fractions and add them with a common denominator." Here is how he does it.

$4\frac{3}{4} = \frac{19}{4}$ and $5\frac{1}{2} = \frac{11}{2}$. So the problem is $\frac{19}{4} + \frac{19}{4} + \frac{11}{2} + \frac{11}{2}$. To do the problem, Steve found the common denominator of 4.

Rewrite the problem for Steve and add the fractions. Then convert the fraction back to the mixed number.

Christine says, "There is another way. Why not just do it like two separate problems. First add the whole numbers. Then add the fractions. Then add the two numbers together."

Try it Christine's way.

Directions: *Add these mixed numbers with your teacher. Find the sum after you find a common denominator.*

1. $4\frac{1}{3} + 6\frac{1}{4} =$ **2.** $8\frac{3}{5} + 4\frac{7}{10} =$ **3.** $1\frac{2}{3} + 4\frac{5}{6} =$

4. $1 + 3\frac{1}{2} =$ **5.** $7\frac{3}{8} + 5\frac{3}{4} =$ **6.** $2\frac{1}{2} + 2\frac{1}{2} =$

Algebraic Thinking • Foundations   Lesson 44

Directions: Find the sum after you find a common denominator. Leave your answer in simplest form.

1. 7
   $+\ 3\frac{3}{10}$

2. 5
   $+\ 4\frac{3}{8}$

3. $7\frac{1}{2}$
   $+\ 8\frac{5}{12}$

4. $10\frac{1}{5}$
   $+\ 4\frac{5}{6}$

5. $1\frac{1}{3}$
   $+\ 6\frac{7}{12}$

6. $2\frac{2}{5}$
   $+\ 3\frac{9}{10}$

7. $5\frac{1}{6}$
   $+\ 4\frac{3}{4}$

8. $6\frac{1}{8}$
   $+\ 3\frac{2}{5}$

9. $11\frac{13}{24}$
   $+\ 2\frac{1}{3}$

10. $9\frac{3}{8}$
    $+\ 2\frac{3}{4}$

11. $7\frac{15}{16}$
    $+\ 1\frac{3}{8}$

12. $2\frac{2}{15}$
    $+\ 8\frac{9}{10}$

Lesson 44   AlgebraicThinking • Foundations

13. $7\frac{4}{5}$
     $+\,9\frac{7}{10}$

14. $5\frac{5}{6}$
     $+\,8\frac{7}{12}$

15. $3\frac{3}{5}$
     $+\,9\frac{2}{3}$

16. $2\frac{5}{12}$
     $+10\frac{1}{3}$

17. $4\frac{7}{10}$
     $+\,2\frac{3}{4}$

18. $1\frac{9}{10}$
     $+\,3\frac{7}{12}$

19. **S-O-L-V-E:** Charles sells carnations to florists. A case of carnations has 400 flowers in it and sells for $140. On Monday, Charles sold $2\frac{1}{2}$ cases to a school for a fundraiser. He also sold $10\frac{3}{4}$ cases to a large florist and 2 cases to a hospital gift shop. How many cases did he sell in all?

S

O

L

V

E

AlgebraicThinking • **Foundations** Lesson 44

20. **S-O-L-V-E:** Jonathon is conducting an experiment with fruit juice. In order to be precise, he must measure the orange juice very carefully. In one container, he has $2\frac{3}{8}$ cups of orange juice. In another container, he has $1\frac{3}{4}$ cups of apple juice. How much juice does he have in all?

S

O

L

V

E

21. **Write a problem.** Write a problem that can be solved by adding mixed numbers.

Warm Up 45: Concentrate on Fractions

Cover up each fraction with counters or with pieces of paper. Uncover them two at a time. When you uncover equivalent fractions, keep the counters. The person with the most counters wins.

(**HINT:** Matches will be on opposite sides of the center line.)

$\frac{70}{100}$	$\frac{6}{16}$	$\frac{9}{10}$	$\frac{7}{8}$
$\frac{2}{5}$	$\frac{1}{5}$	$\frac{5}{25}$	$\frac{8}{20}$
$\frac{1}{2}$	$\frac{27}{30}$	$\frac{2}{3}$	$\frac{4}{5}$
$\frac{12}{15}$	$\frac{4}{6}$	$\frac{7}{10}$	$\frac{4}{8}$
$\frac{21}{24}$	$\frac{5}{6}$	$\frac{9}{12}$	$\frac{3}{12}$
$\frac{3}{4}$	$\frac{1}{4}$	$\frac{3}{8}$	$\frac{10}{12}$

Algebraic Thinking • Foundations

Lesson 45

Subtracting Fractions and Mixed Numbers

Directions: *Work through the following activity to learn about subtracting fractions.*

1. The following rectangle is divided into eight equal pieces.

   ★ Lightly shade 5 pieces with a pencil.
   ★ What fraction is shaded?
   ★ Erase 2 of the pieces you shaded.
   ★ What fraction did you erase?
   ★ What fraction is left?
   ★ What subtraction problem did you just model?

S-O-L-V-E: Thomas is home-schooled. His parents told him to do an evaporation experiment by putting water in a 55-gallon drum in the backyard. (A drum is a type of barrel.) Because of a crack in the drum, it would only hold $47\frac{5}{8}$ gallons of water. When Thomas checked it 2 weeks later, he found that it only had $46\frac{1}{4}$ gallons of water still in it. How much water had evaporated?

S

O

L

V

E

219

Lesson 45 AlgebraicThinking • Foundations

Directions: *Practice these subtraction problems with your teacher.*

1. $5\frac{7}{8}$
   $-2\frac{3}{8}$

2. $\frac{11}{12}$
   $-\frac{1}{6}$

3. $5\frac{2}{3}$
   $-2\frac{1}{6}$

4. $12\frac{4}{5}$
   $-7\frac{7}{15}$

5. $7\frac{3}{8}$
   $-3\frac{1}{4}$

6. $17\frac{7}{10}$
   $-11\frac{1}{2}$

7. $6\frac{2}{3}$
   $-3\frac{1}{4}$

8. $12\frac{5}{8}$
   $-1\frac{1}{3}$

Writing: Explain the difference between adding fractions and subtracting fractions. Also, explain how they are alike.

_____
_____
_____
_____

Algebraic Thinking • Foundations Lesson 45

9. **S-O-L-V-E:** Before Kathy loaned Gina $3\frac{1}{2}$ cups of flour, she had $5\frac{1}{4}$ cups. How much does she have now?

S

O

L

V

E

Just like all addition or subtraction problems, you must find a common denominator. So, this is the problem to be solved:

$$\begin{array}{r} 5\frac{1}{4} = 5\frac{1}{4} \\ -3\frac{1}{2} = 3\frac{2}{4} \\ \hline \end{array}$$ There's a difficulty with doing this subtraction problem. What is it?

When subtracting a larger fraction from a smaller fraction in mixed numbers, it is necessary to rename the mixed number with the smaller fraction. Consider the model for this problem.

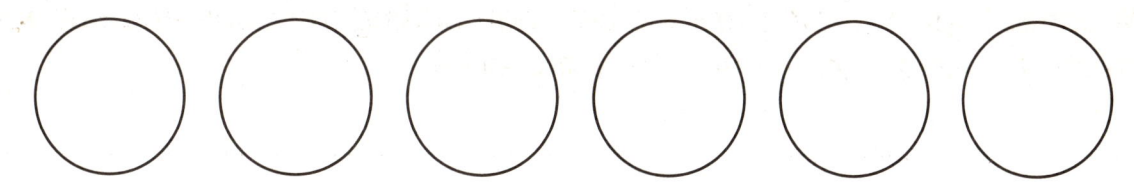

◯ ◯ ◯ ◯ ◯ ◯

10. Start off by lightly shading $5\frac{1}{4}$ circles with a pencil.
    ◆ Then erase $3\frac{2}{4}$ of them.
    ◆ What must you do to one of the circles before you can subtract the $\frac{2}{4}$?
    ◆ Show that process with numbers. (Your teacher will help you.)

221

Lesson 45 — Algebraic Thinking • Foundations

Example Problems

Directions: *Find the difference in the following problems as your teacher works through these.*

11. $\quad 3\frac{4}{5}$
    $-1\frac{2}{5}$
    ───────

12. $\quad 7\frac{7}{8}$
    $-2\frac{1}{4}$
    ───────

13. $\quad 4\frac{7}{20}$
    $-3\frac{2}{5}$
    ───────

14. $\quad 1\frac{1}{6}$
    $-\frac{2}{3}$
    ───────

15. $\quad 10\frac{3}{8}$
    $-2\frac{7}{8}$
    ───────

16. $\quad 12$
    $-3\frac{1}{4}$
    ───────

17. $\quad 4\frac{1}{8}$
    $-1\frac{3}{4}$
    ───────

18. $\quad 4\frac{2}{3}$
    $-1\frac{5}{6}$
    ───────

Algebraic Thinking • Foundations — Lesson 45

Practice it!

Directions: Find the difference in each problem after you find the common denominator.

1. $5\frac{1}{2} - 2\frac{3}{8}$

2. $5\frac{9}{10} - 4\frac{2}{5}$

3. $\frac{3}{4} - \frac{5}{12}$

4. $3\frac{9}{15} - \frac{2}{5}$

5. $3\frac{1}{6} - 1\frac{2}{3}$

6. $\frac{7}{8} - \frac{2}{3}$

7. $4\frac{7}{8} - 2\frac{3}{4}$

8. $10\frac{2}{9} - 5\frac{1}{2}$

9. $2\frac{5}{12} - 1\frac{1}{6}$

10. $\frac{3}{10} - \frac{1}{5}$

11. $5\frac{3}{8} - 4\frac{1}{4}$

12. $8\frac{2}{3} - 5\frac{1}{9}$

13. $5\frac{11}{12} - 2\frac{5}{8}$

14. $11\frac{3}{5} - 8\frac{7}{10}$

15. $\frac{5}{6} - \frac{4}{9}$

16. $4\frac{3}{4} - 2\frac{1}{8}$

17. $7\frac{5}{6} - 2\frac{7}{12}$

18. $9\frac{2}{3} - 5\frac{1}{9}$

19. $5\frac{11}{12} - 1\frac{5}{8}$

20. $3\frac{7}{10} - 2\frac{3}{5}$

21. $6\frac{8}{9} - 2\frac{2}{3}$

Lesson 45   **AlgebraicThinking** • **Foundations**

22. **S-O-L-V-E:** Greg was asked to repair a fence for his neighbor as a community service project. The nails that he bought are $2\frac{3}{4}$ inches long. The boards that he needs to nail them through are $2\frac{1}{2}$ inches long. At the least, how much shorter should the nails be?

S

O

L

V

E

23. **Writing:** Write a story problem that can be solved by subtracting mixed numbers. (Remember, subtraction involves "take away" or "difference.")

AlgebraicThinking • Foundations   Homework 45

Name _____

Directions: *In problems 1 – 4, write each mixed number as an improper fraction. In problems 5 – 10, write each improper fraction as a mixed number.*

1. $6\frac{2}{3}$

2. $5\frac{4}{9}$

3. $2\frac{1}{5}$

4. $10\frac{5}{12}$

5. $\frac{17}{3}$

6. $\frac{24}{7}$

7. $\frac{11}{2}$

8. $\frac{33}{10}$

9. $\frac{17}{12}$

10. $\frac{25}{10}$

Warm Up 46: Equal Partners

Directions: *Put the fractions below into groups of equivalent fractions. Then, unscramble the letters in each group to get a word. Arrange the words to get a message for you.*

O $\frac{8}{9}$

G $\frac{14}{49}$

A $\frac{5}{6}$

Y $\frac{10}{35}$

O $\frac{2}{3}$

A $\frac{8}{28}$

N $\frac{2}{7}$

D $\frac{32}{36}$

C $\frac{40}{48}$

Y $\frac{8}{12}$

H $\frac{16}{56}$

T $\frac{18}{63}$

U $\frac{16}{24}$

N $\frac{20}{24}$

I $\frac{12}{42}$

N $\frac{4}{14}$

AlgebraicThinking • Foundations   Warm Up 47

Warm Up 47: Pyramids

Perform the operations from left to right. Put the answer for each pair of fractions above and between them.

Addition

$\frac{1}{5}$ $\frac{1}{10}$ $\frac{7}{20}$ $\frac{2}{5}$ $\frac{1}{2}$

Addition

$\frac{1}{3}$ $\frac{1}{6}$ $\frac{2}{9}$ $\frac{5}{12}$ $\frac{2}{3}$

Lesson 47   Algebraic Thinking • Foundations

Multiplying Fractions and Whole Numbers

Did you know that 2 • 3 and 3 • 2 mean two different things? Well, they do! They have the same value, but they mean different things. 2 • 3 means "2 groups of 3." 3 • 2 means" 3 groups of 2." Draw a picture to represent those two problems.

So, what does $\frac{1}{4}$ • 40 mean?

S-O-L-V-E: A farmer gave this information about his cows. One-fourth of them are for milking. If he has 40 cows, how many of them are for milking? Use the model to find one-fourth of 40 cows.

This problem is solved by this multiplication problem: $\frac{1}{4}$ • 40.

This problem, 40 • $\frac{1}{4}$, gets the correct answer, but it is not the correct multiplication sentence for the problem. It means 40 groups of one-fourth cows. I think the farmer would be mad if we cut his cows into fourths!

Algebraic Thinking • Foundations   Lesson 47

S-O-L-V-E: A teacher let his students correct the multiple-choice questions on a test for half a point apiece. One student corrected 9 problems. How many points did she get? (Use the circles to create a model.)

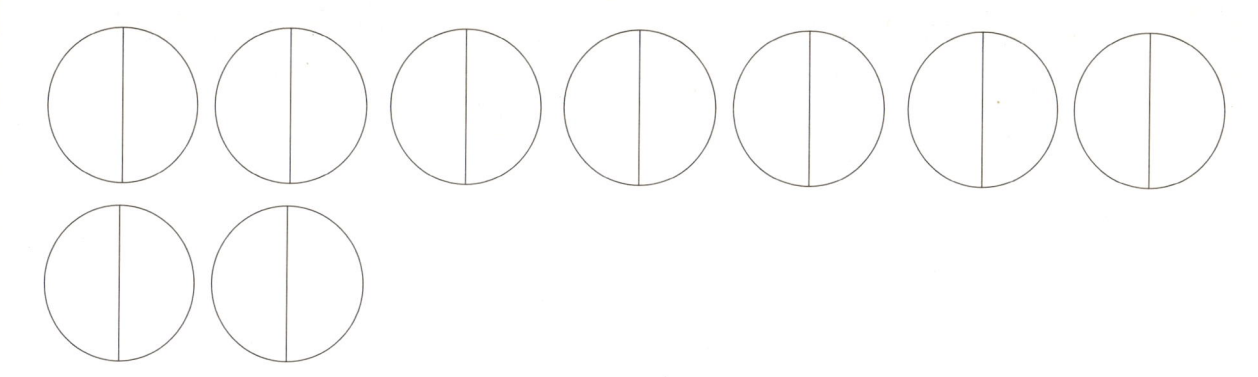

Is this problem correctly written as $\frac{1}{2} \cdot 9$ or $9 \cdot \frac{1}{2}$?

Writing the problem in words also helps to simplify it.

$9 \cdot \frac{1}{2}$ ➡ 9 groups of 1 half = 9 halves or $\frac{9}{2}$ = _____ .

Directions: *Write the meaning of each problem. Then model the problem with your fraction strips. Then write the product. (Your teacher will help you.)*

Problem	Meaning	Model
1. $3 \cdot \frac{1}{4}$ =		
2. $2 \cdot \frac{2}{3}$ =		
3. $4 \cdot \frac{2}{5}$ =		
4. $\frac{2}{3} \cdot 9$ =		
5. $\frac{3}{8} \cdot 16$ =		

NOTE: Problems 4 and 5 may not be suited for the fraction strips. Consider a model like the cows earlier in the lesson.

229

Lesson 47 **AlgebraicThinking • Foundations**

Practice it!

Directions: *For each problem, write the meaning and find the product. If necessary, you may use your fraction strips or create a model.*

1. $4 \cdot \frac{1}{8} =$

2. $\frac{1}{2} \cdot 2 =$

3. $3 \cdot \frac{9}{10} =$

4. $\frac{2}{5} \cdot 10 =$

5. $8 \cdot \frac{3}{4} =$

6. $\frac{5}{6} \cdot 18 =$

7. $2 \cdot \frac{1}{5} =$

8. $\frac{3}{10} \cdot 20 =$

9. $5 \cdot \frac{7}{12} =$

10. $\frac{3}{4} \cdot 4 =$

11. $3 \cdot \frac{1}{2} =$

12. $\frac{2}{9} \cdot 3 =$

Algebraic Thinking • Foundations Lesson 47

13. $6 \cdot \frac{4}{9} =$

14. $\frac{1}{8} \cdot 2 =$

15. $2 \cdot \frac{2}{3} =$

16. $\frac{2}{3} \cdot 6 =$

17. $7 \cdot \frac{5}{6} =$

18. $\frac{1}{2} \cdot 7 =$

19. $4 \cdot \frac{5}{9} =$

20. $\frac{1}{6} \cdot 8 =$

21. Mr. Johnson's Algebra Preparatory class surveyed family members to find out what their favorite TV show is. One hundred twenty people responded. One-fourth of the people said that their favorite show was Program A. How many people said their favorite show was Program A?

S

O

L

V

E

Lesson 47　　　　　　　　　　　　**Algebraic**Thinking • Foundations

Directions: *Find the product by modeling these fraction problems with your teacher.*

Problem	Meaning	Model
1. $\frac{1}{2} \cdot \frac{1}{4} =$		
2. $\frac{1}{2} \cdot \frac{2}{3} =$		
3. $\frac{1}{2} \cdot \frac{3}{4} =$		
4. $\frac{2}{3} \cdot \frac{1}{2} =$		
5. $\frac{3}{4} \cdot \frac{1}{2} =$		
6. $\frac{2}{5} \cdot \frac{1}{2} =$		

Algebraic Thinking • Foundations

Lesson 47

It's another fraction model!

The more models we have, the smarter we are! Try this one.

Pretend that you are building a tree house. While trying to make the floor you realize that the piece of plywood you have is too big. You need it to be cut so that its width is $\frac{2}{3}$ of the original width and the length is $\frac{3}{4}$ of the original length. What fraction of the original sheet of plywood will you cut? Use the model below to solve this problem.

★ Shade $\frac{3}{4}$ of the rows with one color. (horizontal)

★ Shade $\frac{2}{3}$ of the columns with another color. (vertical)

★ What fraction of the whole model is the area shaded by both colors?

★ What multiplication problem is modeled?

You can also multiply fractions using pencil and paper without models. Just multiply the numerators together and the denominators together. Then simplify. Look at the example.

$$\frac{3}{4} \cdot \frac{2}{3} = \frac{3 \cdot 2}{4 \cdot 3} = \frac{6}{12} = \frac{1}{2}$$

Lesson 47   **AlgebraicThinking • Foundations**

Directions: *Find the product by modeling these fraction problems with your teacher.*

Problem	Meaning	Model
7. $\frac{1}{2} \cdot \frac{3}{8} =$		
8. $\frac{3}{4} \cdot \frac{1}{3} =$		
9. $\frac{5}{6} \cdot \frac{2}{5} =$		
10. $\frac{2}{3} \cdot \frac{1}{4} =$		
11. $\frac{1}{2} \cdot \frac{1}{2} =$		
12. $\frac{1}{4} \cdot \frac{1}{4} =$		

Algebraic Thinking • Foundations   Lesson 47

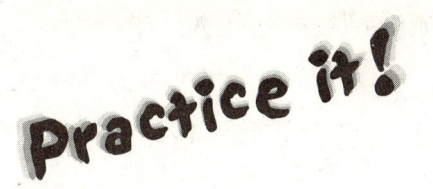

Practice it!

Directions: *For each problem, write the meaning and then find the product.*

1. $\frac{1}{3} \cdot \frac{3}{5} =$	2. $\frac{1}{4} \cdot \frac{4}{5} =$
3. $\frac{1}{7} \cdot \frac{7}{8} =$	4. $\frac{1}{4} \cdot \frac{8}{10} =$
5. $\frac{3}{4} \cdot \frac{8}{9} =$	6. $\frac{3}{4} \cdot \frac{4}{5} =$
7. $\frac{2}{5} \cdot \frac{10}{12} =$	8. $\frac{1}{4} \cdot \frac{2}{5} =$
9. $\frac{3}{8} \cdot \frac{4}{9} =$	10. $\frac{5}{6} \cdot \frac{2}{5} =$
11. $\frac{7}{12} \cdot \frac{3}{4} =$	12. $\frac{4}{9} \cdot \frac{3}{8} =$
13. $\frac{5}{6} \cdot \frac{12}{15} =$	14. $\frac{9}{10} \cdot \frac{5}{12} =$
15. $\frac{1}{2} \cdot \frac{8}{9} =$	16. $\frac{3}{4} \cdot \frac{8}{9} =$

Lesson 47 **AlgebraicThinking • Foundations**

17. S-O-L-V-E: One-half of a new park will be devoted to sports fields. One-third of that area will be used to build a softball field. What fraction of the total field will be used for a softball field?

S
O
L
V
E

18. S-O-L-V-E: Mrs. McDonald ate half of an apple and then gave each of 4 students $\frac{1}{4}$ of the other half. What fraction of the whole apple did each student get?

S
O
L
V
E

19. S-O-L-V-E: Lewis asked for their pizza to be cut into 12 pieces. He ate 4 pieces. David ate $\frac{1}{4}$ of the remaining $\frac{8}{12}$. What fraction of the total pizza did David eat?

S
O
L
V
E

Algebraic Thinking • Foundations   Homework 47

Name _____

Directions: *In problems 1 – 4, put the fractions in order from least to greatest. In problems 5 – 10, put <, >, or = between the two fractions to make a true sentence.*

1. $\frac{1}{2}, \frac{2}{9}, \frac{4}{6}$

2. $\frac{1}{2}, \frac{3}{8}, \frac{2}{3}$

3. $\frac{3}{4}, \frac{7}{12}, \frac{5}{6}$

4. $\frac{3}{10}, \frac{2}{5}, \frac{17}{20}$

5. $\frac{3}{4}$? $\frac{5}{12}$

6. $\frac{2}{3}$? $\frac{4}{9}$

7. $\frac{4}{7}$? $\frac{6}{7}$

8. $\frac{5}{6}$? $\frac{20}{30}$

9. $\frac{3}{8}$? $\frac{15}{40}$

10. $\frac{2}{3}$? $\frac{5}{8}$

Warm Up 48: Concentrate on Fractions and Decimals

Cover up each square with counters or with pieces of paper. Uncover them two at a time. When you uncover a fraction and its equivalent decimal, keep the counters. The person with the most counters wins. (**HINT:** Matches will be on opposite sides of the center line.)

$\frac{1}{2}$	$\frac{4}{5}$	0.7	0.125
$\frac{3}{8}$	$\frac{1}{4}$	0.3	0.6
$\frac{1}{3}$	$\frac{2}{3}$	0.5	$0.\overline{3}$
$\frac{3}{5}$	$\frac{3}{10}$	0.8	0.375
$\frac{1}{8}$	$\frac{7}{10}$	0.25	$0.\overline{6}$

AlgebraicThinking • Foundations Lesson 48

Dividing Fractions

In order to be successful at division, you need to understand the different models for division. Use the groups of dogs below to show two models for the division problem, 6 ÷ 2.

It can mean, "How many groups of two can be made from 6 items?"

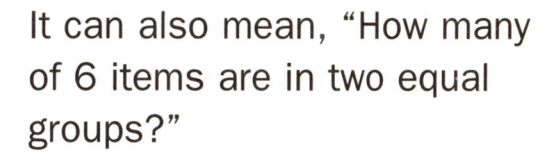

It can also mean, "How many of 6 items are in two equal groups?"

Consider the division problem $6 \div \frac{1}{2} =$

It means, "How many groups of $\frac{1}{2}$ are in 6?" Now, we can't use dogs as a model this time, but we can use pizza as a model. Think, **"How many $\frac{1}{2}$ pizzas can be made from 6 whole pizzas?"** Use the circles below to represent the pizzas.

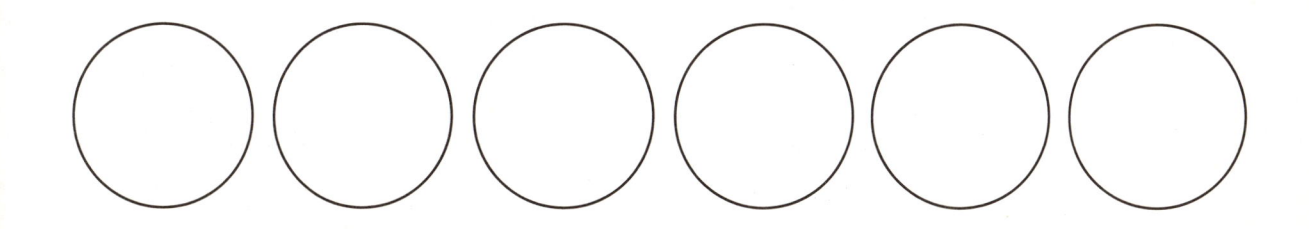

Lesson 48 Algebraic Thinking • Foundations

Try this one! $6 \div \frac{1}{3} =$

It means, how many $\frac{1}{3}$'s are in 6?
Think, **"How many pieces of pizza can be made from 6 pizzas if each piece is $\frac{1}{3}$ of the whole?"** Use the circles below as pizzas.

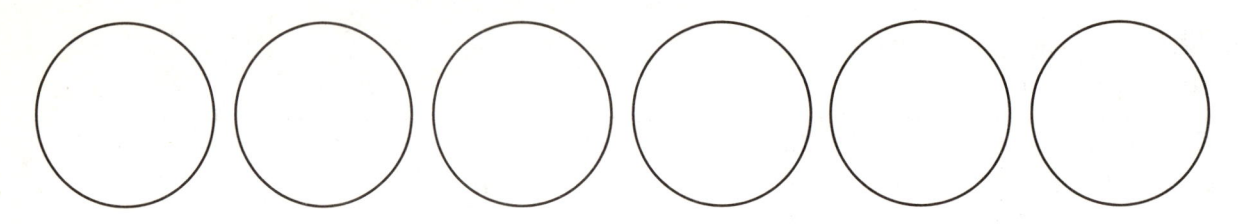

◯ ◯ ◯ ◯ ◯ ◯

Can you do this one? $6 \div \frac{1}{4} =$

It means, how many $\frac{1}{4}$'s are in 6?
Think, **"How many pieces of pizza can be made from 6 pizzas if each piece is $\frac{1}{4}$ of the whole?"** Use the circles below as pizzas.

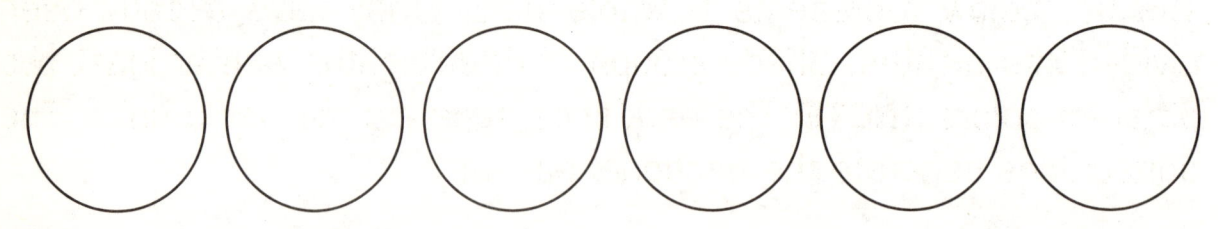

◯ ◯ ◯ ◯ ◯ ◯

Try this for a challenge! $6 \div \frac{3}{4} =$

It means, how many $\frac{3}{4}$ are in 6?
Think, **"How many hungry teenagers can be fed from 6 pizzas if each person is promised $\frac{3}{4}$?"** Use the circles below as pizzas.

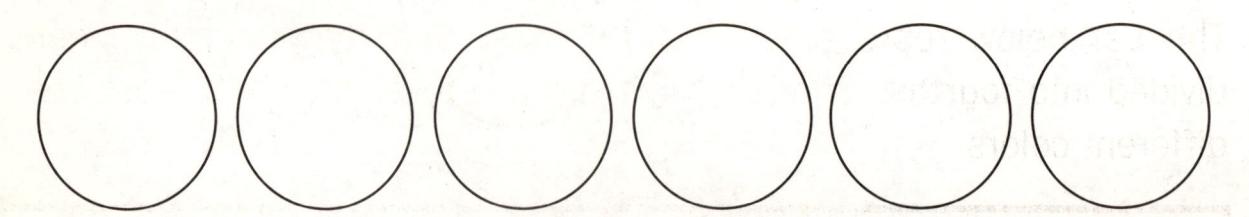

◯ ◯ ◯ ◯ ◯ ◯

HINT: Divide the circles into fourths. Then shade groups of three.

Algebraic Thinking • Foundations   Lesson 48

You can also use bars to model division of fractions.

Try this problem! $5 \div \frac{1}{2} =$

What does this mean? _____

_____

The bar below represents 5 whole units. Divide each unit into halves.

1	1	1	1	1

Try another one! $6 \div \frac{3}{8} =$

What does this mean? _____

_____

The bar below represents 6 whole units. They have already been divided into eighths. Shade groups of three-eighths with at least two different colors. (**NOTE:** The dark lines separate the whole units. The dotted lines separate the fractional parts.)

Can you do this one? $3 \div \frac{3}{4} =$

What does this mean? _____

_____

The bar below represents 3 whole units. They have already been divided into fourths. Shade groups of three-fourths with at least two different colors.

Lesson 48   Algebraic Thinking • Foundations

Try this one!   10 ÷ $\frac{2}{5}$ =

What does this mean? _____
_____

The bar below represents 10 whole units. They have already been divided into fifths. Shade groups of two-fifths with at least two different colors.

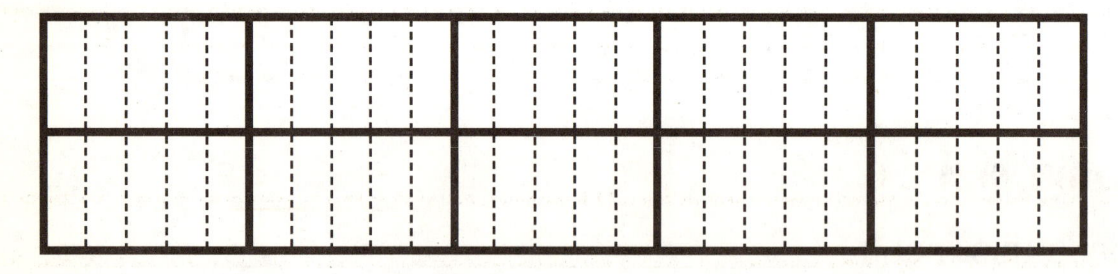

This one is a little harder!   10 ÷ $\frac{4}{5}$ =

What does this mean? _____
_____

The bar below represents 10 whole units. They have already been divided into fifths. Shade groups of four-fifths with at least two different colors.

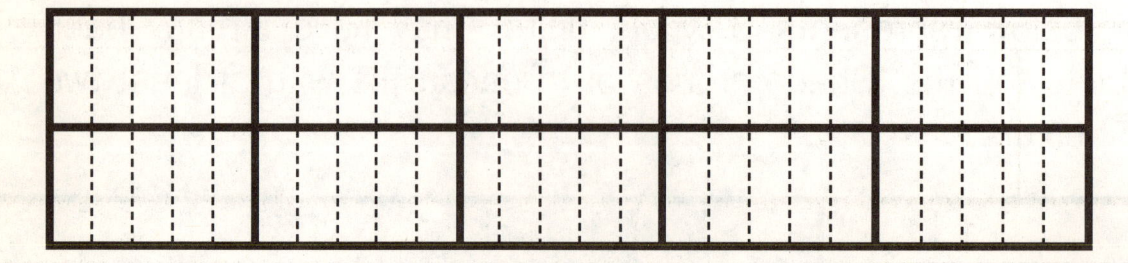

Algebraic Thinking • Foundations

Lesson 48

Practice it!

Directions: Translate each division problem into an equivalent question. Then find the quotient using the models. The first one has been done for you.

Problem	Question (Meaning)	Quotient
1. $2 \div \frac{1}{4} = 8$	How many $\frac{1}{4}$'s are in 2 whole units?	There are 8 one-fourths in 2 whole units.

| $\frac{1}{4}$ | $\frac{1}{4}$ | $\frac{1}{4}$ | $\frac{1}{4}$ | $\frac{1}{4}$ | $\frac{1}{4}$ | $\frac{1}{4}$ | $\frac{1}{4}$ |

2. $3 \div \frac{1}{2} =$

| 1 | 1 |
| 1 | |

3. $4 \div \frac{1}{3} =$

| 1 | 1 |
| 1 | 1 |

4. $6 \div \frac{3}{4} =$

1	1
1	1
1	1

5. $4 \div \frac{4}{5} =$

| 1 | 1 |
| 1 | 1 |

Lesson 48   **AlgebraicThinking** • Foundations

Directions: *Translate each division problem to an equivalent question. Then use mental math to find the quotient. Write your answer in a complete sentence. The first one has been done for you.*

6. $2 \div \frac{1}{5} =$ How many $\frac{1}{5}$'s are in 2? There are 10 one-fifths in 2.	**7.** $3 \div \frac{1}{5} =$
8. $5 \div \frac{1}{2} =$	**9.** $8 \div \frac{1}{2} =$
10. $3 \div \frac{1}{4} =$	**11.** $5 \div \frac{1}{4} =$
12. $2 \div \frac{1}{3} =$	**13.** $7 \div \frac{1}{3} =$
14. $1 \div \frac{1}{9} =$	**15.** $3 \div \frac{1}{9} =$

AlgebraicThinking • Foundations   Lesson 48

Dividing Fractions

This is a story about 4 apple-loving friends. No one in the world loves apples more than these 4 friends. Every day, each of the 4 apple-loving friends eats 4 apples. One apple is eaten for breakfast, one for lunch, one for dinner, and one for a bedtime snack.

Every Thursday the 4 apple-loving friends go to the market to buy apples. One Thursday, however, they arrive at the market and their worst nightmare is realized: there are no apples. The 4 apple-loving friends search all the markets they can find, but no apples are to be found. As they walk wearily toward home, they find an elderly woman eating an apple. So, they tell the woman, we'll give you $25 for the half of the apple you haven't eaten yet. (That was all the money they had between them.) The woman agreed and the 4 apple-loving friends now have half an apple to share between them. What fraction of the whole apple will each of the friends get to eat? Draw a model to answer the question.

One of the four friends decided he was going to keep his routine and eat equal parts of his share of the half-apple at breakfast, lunch, dinner, and bedtime snack. What fraction of a whole apple will he eat each time? Draw a model to answer the question.

Lesson 48

AlgebraicThinking • Foundations

S-O-L-V-E: Mr. Thompson's Dalmatians eat $\frac{1}{2}$ pound of dog food per day. He buys the food in 4 pound bags. How long does a bag last?

S

O

L

V

E

Directions: *Write a sentence that means the same as the division problem. Then model each division problem.*

Problem	Question (Meaning)	Quotient
1. $\frac{1}{2} \div \frac{1}{4} =$		

$\frac{1}{2}$	$\frac{1}{2}$

Problem	Question (Meaning)	Quotient
2. $\frac{3}{4} \div \frac{1}{4} =$		

$\frac{1}{4}$	$\frac{1}{4}$	$\frac{1}{4}$	$\frac{1}{4}$

Problem	Question (Meaning)	Quotient
3. $\frac{3}{4} \div \frac{1}{8} =$		

$\frac{1}{4}$	$\frac{1}{4}$	$\frac{1}{4}$	$\frac{1}{4}$

AlgebraicThinking • Foundations

Lesson 48

4. $\frac{1}{3} \div \frac{1}{9} =$

| $\frac{1}{3}$ | $\frac{1}{3}$ | $\frac{1}{3}$ |

5. $\frac{2}{3} \div \frac{1}{9} =$

| $\frac{1}{3}$ | $\frac{1}{3}$ | $\frac{1}{3}$ |

6. $\frac{2}{3} \div \frac{2}{9} =$

| $\frac{1}{3}$ | $\frac{1}{3}$ | $\frac{1}{3}$ |

7. $\frac{1}{3} \div \frac{2}{9} =$

| $\frac{1}{3}$ | $\frac{1}{3}$ | $\frac{1}{3}$ |

8. $\frac{2}{3} \div \frac{1}{6} =$

| $\frac{1}{3}$ | $\frac{1}{3}$ | $\frac{1}{3}$ |

Lesson 48   **AlgebraicThinking** • Foundations

Practice it!

Directions: Write a sentence that means the same as the division problem. Then find the quotient.

1. $\frac{2}{5} \div \frac{1}{10} =$	**2.** $\frac{3}{5} \div \frac{1}{10} =$
3. $\frac{5}{12} \div \frac{1}{12} =$	**4.** $\frac{3}{4} \div \frac{1}{8} =$
5. $\frac{5}{6} \div \frac{1}{12} =$	**6.** $\frac{2}{3} \div \frac{1}{12} =$
7. $\frac{2}{3} \div \frac{1}{3} =$	**8.** $\frac{7}{8} \div \frac{1}{16} =$
9. $\frac{2}{5} \div \frac{1}{10} =$	**10.** $\frac{3}{5} \div \frac{3}{10} =$

AlgebraicThinking • **Foundations**　　　　　　　　　　　　Lesson 48

11. S-O-L-V-E: Only half of a banana pie is left from a party. It was promised to three boys. If it is shared equally, what fraction of the whole pie will each boy get?

S

O

L

V

E

12. S-O-L-V-E: Sharon wants pieces of ribbon that are no more than $\frac{1}{8}$ of an inch long for confetti for her party. How many of those pieces of ribbon can she make from a piece that is $\frac{3}{4}$ of an inch long?

S

O

L

V

E

Homework 48 — AlgebraicThinking • Foundations

Name _____

Directions: *Choose the fraction that is equivalent to the given fraction.*

1. $\frac{1}{2}$
   A. $\frac{3}{8}$
   B. $\frac{4}{8}$
   C. $\frac{5}{8}$

2. $\frac{3}{10}$
   A. $\frac{3}{20}$
   B. $\frac{6}{30}$
   C. $\frac{9}{30}$

3. $\frac{3}{4}$
   A. $\frac{4}{8}$
   B. $\frac{5}{8}$
   C. $\frac{6}{8}$

4. $\frac{2}{5}$
   A. $\frac{4}{5}$
   B. $\frac{4}{10}$
   C. $\frac{2}{10}$

5. $\frac{6}{10}$
   A. $\frac{30}{50}$
   B. $\frac{18}{20}$
   C. $\frac{27}{30}$

6. $\frac{8}{16}$
   A. $\frac{16}{30}$
   B. $\frac{1}{2}$
   C. $\frac{4}{9}$

7. $\frac{3}{12}$
   A. $\frac{6}{22}$
   B. $\frac{9}{38}$
   C. $\frac{1}{4}$

8. $\frac{1}{3}$
   A. $\frac{33}{100}$
   B. $\frac{9}{27}$
   C. $\frac{2}{9}$

9. $\frac{15}{20}$
   A. $\frac{5}{8}$
   B. $\frac{3}{4}$
   C. $\frac{5}{6}$

10. $\frac{5}{8}$
    A. $\frac{22}{33}$
    B. $\frac{15}{16}$
    C. $\frac{25}{40}$

AlgebraicThinking • Foundations

Warm Up 49

Warm Up 49: Tic-Tac-Toe

Allison and Alex played a game of tic-tac-toe. Find out who won the game by matching each answer on the board to the correct problem. Put the appropriate letter on the board.

Allison played the X
$\frac{1}{2} + \frac{1}{4} =$
$\frac{2}{5} + \frac{3}{10} =$
$\frac{1}{2} + \frac{1}{8} =$
$\frac{2}{3} + \frac{1}{6} =$

Alex played the O
$\frac{1}{3} + \frac{1}{6} =$
$\frac{3}{4} + \frac{1}{8} =$
$\frac{1}{4} + \frac{3}{16} =$
$\frac{3}{5} + \frac{2}{15} =$

$\frac{7}{16}$	$\frac{11}{15}$	$\frac{1}{2}$
$\frac{7}{8}$	$\frac{3}{4}$	$\frac{7}{10}$
$\frac{5}{6}$	$\frac{2}{3}$	$\frac{5}{8}$

Who won the game? _____

251

Lesson 49   Algebraic Thinking • Foundations

The Easiest Number to Divide By

I wish all division problems were "divided by 1."

What is the easiest number to divide by? Did you know that every division problem can be converted to "divide by 1"?

That's what we're going to learn to do, today. Look at the table below and see if you can figure out what a **reciprocal** is. Then complete the chart.

What is a **reciprocal**?

_____

_____

_____

_____

Reciprocals	
2 and $\frac{1}{2}$	5 and $\frac{1}{5}$
8 and $\frac{1}{8}$	10 and $\frac{1}{10}$
$\frac{2}{3}$ and $\frac{3}{2}$	$\frac{5}{8}$ and $\frac{8}{5}$
$\frac{4}{5}$ and $\frac{5}{4}$	$\frac{7}{9}$ and $\frac{9}{7}$
$\frac{3}{4}$ and ?	4 and ?

Example: *Find the product.*

1. $\frac{2}{5} \cdot \frac{5}{2} =$ 2. $\frac{3}{4} \cdot \frac{4}{3} =$ 3. $\frac{7}{8} \cdot \frac{8}{7} =$

4. $\frac{5}{12} \cdot \frac{12}{5} =$ 5. $\frac{2}{3} \cdot \frac{3}{2} =$ 6. $\frac{5}{6} \cdot \frac{6}{5} =$

7. What is the product of two reciprocals?

Now, since the easiest number to divide by is 1, we'll change every division problem to "divide by 1." Look at the example on the next page.

Algebraic Thinking • Foundations

Lesson 49

$\frac{1}{2} \div \frac{1}{4}$ can be written, $\dfrac{\frac{1}{2}}{\frac{1}{4}}$

Then you can change it to "divide by one" by multiplying the denominator by its reciprocal. (Remember that whatever you do to the denominator, you have to do to the numerator.)

$$\dfrac{\frac{1}{2}}{\frac{1}{4}} = \dfrac{\frac{1}{2} \cdot \frac{4}{1}}{\frac{1}{4} \cdot \frac{4}{1}} = \dfrac{\frac{4}{2}}{1} = \dfrac{2}{1} = 2$$

Directions: *Use the method described above to find the quotient with your teacher.*

8. $\frac{3}{5} \div \frac{3}{10} =$	9. $\frac{1}{6} \div \frac{1}{18} =$
10. $\frac{2}{3} \div \frac{4}{5} =$	11. $\frac{9}{10} \div \frac{1}{2} =$
12. $\frac{5}{6} \div \frac{2}{3} =$	13. $\frac{5}{8} \div \frac{1}{4} =$
14. $\frac{1}{2} \div \frac{3}{4} =$	15. $\frac{3}{4} \div \frac{1}{2} =$

Lesson 49 — Algebraic Thinking • Foundations

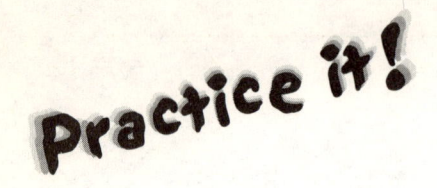

Practice it!

Directions: *Find the quotient. Write your answer in simplest form.*

1. $\frac{3}{8} \div \frac{1}{2} =$

2. $\frac{1}{2} \div \frac{3}{8} =$

3. $\frac{5}{8} \div \frac{1}{2} =$

4. $\frac{1}{2} \div \frac{5}{8} =$

5. $\frac{7}{8} \div \frac{1}{4} =$

6. $\frac{1}{4} \div \frac{7}{8} =$

7. $\frac{1}{2} \div \frac{2}{3} =$

8. $\frac{5}{9} \div \frac{2}{9} =$

9. $\frac{7}{12} \div \frac{2}{3} =$

10. $\frac{3}{5} \div \frac{3}{10} =$

11. $\frac{4}{5} \div \frac{1}{20} =$

12. $\frac{7}{8} \div \frac{2}{5} =$

13. $\frac{4}{15} \div \frac{2}{5} =$

14. $\frac{7}{12} \div \frac{1}{3} =$

15. $\frac{11}{12} \div \frac{1}{2} =$

16. $\frac{1}{2} \div \frac{1}{12} =$

17. $\frac{7}{10} \div \frac{3}{8} =$

18. $\frac{1}{8} \div \frac{2}{9} =$

AlgebraicThinking • Foundations Homework 49

Name _____

Directions: *Convert the decimals to fractions. Convert the fractions to decimals.*

1. 0.2

2. 0.65

3. 0.55

4. 0.38

5. 0.4

6. $\frac{3}{4}$

7. $\frac{7}{10}$

8. $\frac{17}{20}$

9. $\frac{3}{8}$

10. $\frac{2}{3}$

Warm Up 50: Tic-Tac-Toe

Katie and Kevin played a game of tic-tac-toe. Find out who won the game by matching each fraction with a percent. Put the appropriate letter on the board.

Katie played the X

$\frac{3}{4}$

$\frac{2}{5}$

$\frac{24}{25}$

$\frac{11}{20}$

Kevin played the O

$\frac{3}{8}$

$\frac{4}{5}$

$\frac{7}{25}$

$\frac{6}{12}$

50%	80%	40%
75%	55%	96%
37.5%	45%	28%

Who won the game? _____

Algebraic Thinking • Foundations

Lesson 50

Multiplying and Dividing with Mixed Numbers

S-O-L-V-E: Kathy has $10\frac{1}{2}$ yards of some fabric that she is using to make costumes for a class play. Each of the costumes that she makes requires $2\frac{1}{4}$ yards of the fabric. How many costumes can she make from the fabric?

S

O

L

V

E

S-O-L-V-E: Last Halloween, there were $5\frac{1}{2}$ bags of candy left. Joey's mother said that she would give it to him and his two brothers if each of the three boys got equal amounts of the candy. (She told them that they couldn't eat it all at once!) How many bags should each boy get?

S

O

L

V

E

Lesson 50   **AlgebraicThinking** • Foundations

S-O-L-V-E: Alex is dog-sitting for a man who owns 5 large dogs. Every day each dog eats $2\frac{1}{3}$ cans of dog food. How many cans will the dogs eat in all for one week (7 days)?

S

O

L

V

E

Each of the problems above involves multiplication or division of mixed numbers. We can continue to learn how to do division by constructing models or we can use what we've learned in previous lessons. Multiplying and dividing mixed numbers becomes easier when you convert the mixed numbers to an improper fraction.

Directions: Practice multiplying these mixed numbers with your teacher.

1. $2\frac{1}{2} \cdot 5 =$

2. $3\frac{1}{4} \cdot 4 =$

3. $4\frac{4}{5} \cdot 2\frac{3}{4} =$

4. $10\frac{5}{8} \cdot 2\frac{2}{5} =$

5. $2\frac{5}{6} \cdot \frac{3}{4} =$

6. $2\frac{1}{2} \cdot 5\frac{1}{6} =$

AlgebraicThinking • Foundations Lesson 50

Write a problem: Write a problem that can be solved by multiplying $8 \cdot 1\frac{1}{4}$. You can use the beginning of this problem or write your own.

Jill was making baby dresses for 8 dolls. _____

_____

_____

_____

_____

_____

Directions: *Complete each division problem with your teacher.*

7. $4\frac{4}{5} \div 1\frac{1}{6} =$ 　　　　　8. $2\frac{3}{4} \div \frac{3}{8} =$

9. $4\frac{2}{3} \div 1\frac{5}{6} =$ 　　　　　10. $1\frac{7}{8} \div 1\frac{1}{2} =$

11. $2\frac{5}{8} \div \frac{3}{4} =$ 　　　　　12. $2\frac{7}{10} \div 1\frac{4}{5} =$

259

Lesson 50

Algebraic Thinking • Foundations

Write a problem: Write a problem that can be solved with the following division problem: $20 \div 3\frac{3}{4}$. Use the beginning of this problem or write your own.

Jonathon has a piece of pipe that is 20 feet long.

Algebraic Thinking • Foundations — Lesson 50

Practice it!

Directions: Write a sentence that means the same as the problem. Then find the product or quotient. Be careful. There are multiplication and division problems mixed throughout the exercises.

1. $1\frac{1}{2} \cdot \frac{4}{5} =$

2. $\frac{3}{8} \cdot 3\frac{5}{9} =$

3. $3\frac{2}{3} \div \frac{2}{3} =$

4. $4\frac{1}{2} \div \frac{3}{4} =$

5. $6 \div 1\frac{1}{5} =$

6. $6\frac{2}{3} \div 1\frac{1}{4} =$

7. $3\frac{5}{9} \cdot \frac{3}{8} =$

8. $\frac{7}{10} \cdot 2\frac{3}{7} =$

9. $4\frac{2}{11} \div 2\frac{3}{4} =$

10. $5\frac{1}{5} \div 1\frac{2}{3} =$

11. $4\frac{2}{3} \div 1\frac{7}{9} =$

12. $1\frac{1}{4} \div 1\frac{1}{2} =$

13. $9 \div 2\frac{1}{2} =$

14. $7 \div 2\frac{3}{4} =$

15. $3\frac{1}{3} \cdot \frac{3}{5} =$

16. $4\frac{1}{2} \cdot 2\frac{1}{4} =$

17. $8\frac{1}{4} \cdot \frac{2}{3} =$

18. $6\frac{1}{2} \cdot 1\frac{3}{7} =$

19. $4\frac{2}{3} \div \frac{2}{3} =$

20. $\frac{2}{5} \div 4\frac{2}{5} =$

Algebraic Thinking • Foundations					Lesson 50

21. **S-O-L-V-E:** Kevin wants to put a decorative fence around his mother's flower garden for her birthday. It is in the shape of a regular hexagon in the middle of a bigger garden. (A regular hexagon has six equal sides.) He measures one of the sides and finds out that it is $5\frac{1}{4}$ feet long. How many feet of fencing will he need?

S

O

L

V

E

Homework 50 **AlgebraicThinking • Foundations**

Name _____

Directions: *Find each product.*

1. $\dfrac{5}{7} \cdot \dfrac{1}{2} =$ 2. $\dfrac{1}{5} \cdot \dfrac{2}{3} =$

3. $\dfrac{5}{8} \cdot \dfrac{1}{12} =$ 4. $\dfrac{1}{4} \cdot \dfrac{5}{6} =$

5. $\dfrac{5}{8} \cdot \dfrac{3}{4} =$ 6. $\dfrac{4}{5} \cdot \dfrac{3}{8} =$

7. $\dfrac{1}{6} \cdot \dfrac{7}{8} =$ 8. $\dfrac{3}{4} \cdot \dfrac{2}{3} =$

9. $\dfrac{2}{9} \cdot \dfrac{1}{3} =$ 10. $\dfrac{3}{5} \cdot \dfrac{7}{10} =$

Algebraic Thinking • Foundations

Warm Up 51: Concentrate on Fractions and Percents

Cover up each fraction with counters or with pieces of paper. Uncover them two at a time. When you uncover equivalent fractions, keep the counters. The most counters wins.
(**HINT:** Matches will be on opposite sides of the center line.)

$\frac{70}{100}$	$\frac{1}{2}$	25%	40%
$\frac{2}{5}$	$\frac{1}{5}$	30%	75%
$\frac{23}{100}$	$\frac{3}{10}$	23%	20%
$\frac{21}{25}$	$\frac{9}{10}$	70%	8%
$\frac{11}{20}$	$\frac{2}{25}$	84%	90%
$\frac{3}{4}$	$\frac{1}{4}$	50%	55%

Warm Up 52: Let's Guess?

Directions: *Estimate each answer before you actually find it. How close did you get for each one?*

Problem	Estimate	Actual #	How Close?
36 • 14			
275 + 326			
837 − 249			
274 • 6			
73 + 432			
2,124 ÷ 36			
931 − 286			
969 ÷ 51			

AlgebraicThinking • Foundations Lesson 52

Directions: *Perform the operation indicated. Simplify all answers to lowest terms. Change any improper fractions to mixed numbers.*

1. $\dfrac{3}{4} + \dfrac{5}{8} =$

2. $\dfrac{6}{7} - \dfrac{1}{3} =$

3. $\dfrac{2}{5} \cdot \dfrac{3}{5} =$

4. $5 \div \dfrac{2}{3} =$

5. $\dfrac{3}{8} \cdot \dfrac{2}{7} =$

6. $\dfrac{4}{9} \div \dfrac{1}{2} =$

7. $\dfrac{5}{11} + \dfrac{4}{5} =$

8. $2\dfrac{1}{5} - 1\dfrac{5}{7} =$

9. $6 + 1\dfrac{8}{9} =$

10. $\dfrac{7}{10} \cdot \dfrac{6}{5} =$

11. $\dfrac{7}{9} - \dfrac{2}{9} =$

12. $3\dfrac{1}{2} \div \dfrac{3}{4} =$

Warm Up 53: Small Change

1. Gerry has an equal number of dimes and quarters. If she has a total of $2.45, how many of each coin does she have?

2. Use 20 coins to make a dollar.

AlgebraicThinking • Foundations   Lesson 53

Scavenger Hunt

Directions:
1. Begin at the poster that the teacher instructs.
2. Solve the problem on the poster.
3. Find another poster that has the solution to your problem at the bottom of the poster.
4. Keep going through each of the posters, always moving to the one which has the answer to the problem you just worked.
5. Be sure to show all work and record the order in which you traveled from one poster to the next.

1. Poster _____   2. Poster _____

3. Poster _____   4. Poster _____

5. Poster _____   6. Poster _____

7. Poster _____   8. Poster _____

Lesson 53 **AlgebraicThinking** • Foundations

9. Poster _____ **10.** Poster _____

11. Poster _____ **12.** Poster _____

13. Poster _____ **14.** Poster _____

15. Poster _____

AlgebraicThinking • **Foundations**   Warm Up 54

Warm Up 54: Find the Fractions

Directions: *Find the missing numbers so that each row, column, and diagonal has the same sum.*

A	B	$5\frac{1}{4}$
C	$4\frac{1}{2}$	D
$3\frac{3}{4}$	E	$2\frac{1}{4}$

A = _____

B = _____

C = _____

D = _____

E = _____

Warm Up 55: Fraction Pyramid

Add the fractions to get to the top.

$\frac{2}{3}$ $\frac{1}{2}$ $\frac{3}{4}$ $\frac{1}{6}$ $\frac{2}{9}$

AlgebraicThinking • Foundations Lesson 55

Simple Probability

Probability is a measure of how probable it is that an event will occur. Probability is measured from 0 to 1. A probability of 0 means that it is impossible for an event to occur. A probability of 1 means that it is definite that the event will occur. What do you think a probability of 0.5 means?

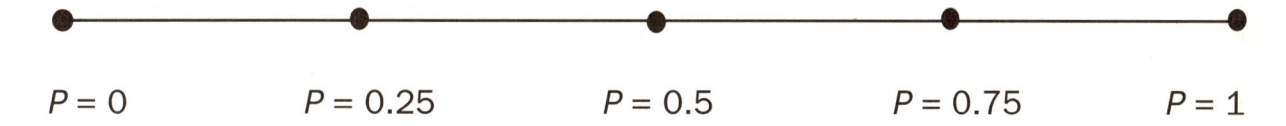

●————————●————————●————————●————————●

$P = 0$ $P = 0.25$ $P = 0.5$ $P = 0.75$ $P = 1$

There are two types of probability. Write them in the spaces below.

1. _____
2. _____

In experimental probability, data is collected through observations or trials. Each result of a trial is called an event. The probability of an event is equal to the number of times an event occurs divided by the total number of trials.

Experimental Probability

$$P(\text{event}) = \frac{\text{number of times an event occurs}}{\text{total number of trials}}$$

When all possible events or **outcomes** are equally likely to occur, the theoretical probability can be found without collecting data from an experiment.

Theoretical Probability

$$P(\text{event}) = \frac{\text{number of favorable outcomes}}{\text{total number possible outcomes}}$$

Lesson 55   **AlgebraicThinking • Foundations**

1. When flipping a coin, how many possible outcomes are there?

2. What is the **theoretical probability** that you will get "heads" when flipping a coin?

3. Flip a coin 50 times and record the results with tally marks in the table below.

Heads	Tails

4. What did you get for the **experimental probability** of getting heads?

5. This time, try flipping a coin and rolling a number cube. Make a list of the possible outcomes.

6. Find the theoretical probability of each of the following.
   a. P(heads and 2)
   b. P(heads and even number)
   c. P(tails and 7)
   d. P(tails and number greater than 4)

7. Now find the experimental probability of each of the same events. *(Flip a coin and roll a number cube 50 times. Record your data in the table below.)*
   a. P(heads and 2)
   b. P(heads and even number)
   c. P(tails and 7)
   d. P(tails and number greater than 4)

H1	H2	H3	H4	H5	H6	T1	T2	T3	T4	T5	T6

Algebraic Thinking • Foundations Lesson 55

Practice it!

Directions: In problems 1 – 4, determine whether the situation is theoretical probability or experimental probability.

1. A number cube is rolled 100 times. Fifteen outcomes are 4. The probability of a 4 is $\frac{15}{100}$ or $\frac{3}{20}$.

2. A red number cube and a green number cube will be rolled. There are 36 possible outcomes. The probability of rolling "doubles" is $\frac{6}{36}$ or $\frac{1}{6}$.

3. The spinner to the right has 12 sections. Each section is equally likely to occur. The probability that the spinner will land in the shaded portion is $\frac{8}{12}$ or $\frac{2}{3}$.

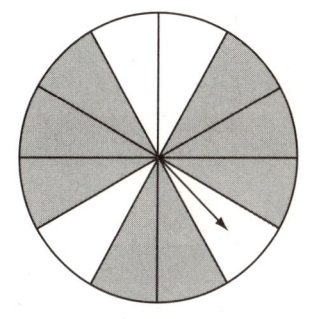

4. A quarter, a dime, and a nickel are flipped 50 times. All three coins come up "heads" 12 times. The probability of all heads is $\frac{12}{50}$ or $\frac{6}{25}$.

If a baby is equally likely to be born on each day of the week, the theoretical probability that a baby will be born on Sunday is $\frac{1}{7}$. Some students collected data on 100 babies to find out how many babies were born on each day. The results are in the table below.

Day of the Week	Sunday	Monday	Tuesday	Wednesday	Thursday	Friday	Saturday
Number of babies born	10	20	15	12	25	8	10

Directions: Find each <u>experimental probability</u> in the problems below. Write your answer as a fraction, decimal, and percent.

5. P(Monday) _____

6. P(Thursday) _____

7. P(Weekend) _____

8. P(Weekday) _____

9. P(Saturday) _____

10. P(Friday) _____

275

Lesson 55   **AlgebraicThinking** • Foundations

11. A coin is flipped 50 times. Thirty-two of the outcomes are "heads."

     a. What is the experimental probability of heads?

     b. What is the experimental probability of tails?

Directions: *A number cube is rolled. Find the theoretical probability.*

12. P(5)   **13.** P(even number)   **14.** P(7)

15. P(number greater than 4)   **16.** P(2 or 3)   **17.** P(number greater than 0)

Directions: *The spinner at the right is spun. Write each probability as a fraction, percent, and a decimal.*

18. P(5)   **19.** P(multiple of 5)

20. P(odd number)   **21.** P(number less than 21)

22. P(not 20)   **23.** P(1)

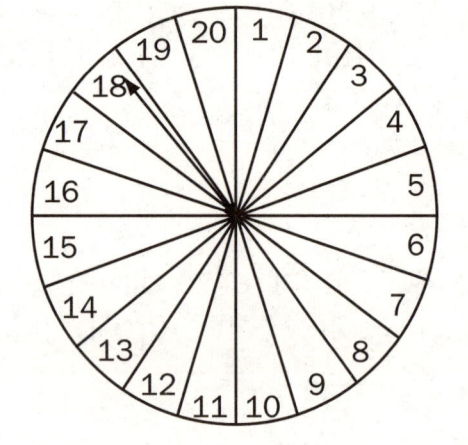

24. On a ski mountain in Colorado, there is a 75% chance of snow. Which of the following is an appropriate conclusion?

     a. It will snow 3 out of the next 4 days.

     b. On similar days in the past, 3 of 4 have had snow.

     c. Seventy-five percent of the mountain will have snow.

Algebraic Thinking • Foundations

Homework 55

Name _____

Directions: *Find each sum or difference. Remember that you may need to find a common denominator.*

1. $\frac{7}{8}$
   $+ \frac{3}{4}$

2. $\frac{7}{8}$
   $- \frac{3}{4}$

3. $2\frac{3}{5}$
   $+ 5\frac{1}{4}$

4. $10\frac{2}{3}$
   $+ 4\frac{1}{3}$

5. $8\frac{7}{10}$
   $- 2\frac{1}{5}$

6. $5\frac{2}{5}$
   $- 1\frac{4}{5}$

7. $12\frac{2}{6}$
   $- 5\frac{5}{9}$

8. $\frac{7}{15}$
   $+ \frac{1}{2}$

9. $4\frac{5}{8}$
   $+ 2\frac{2}{3}$

10. $\frac{1}{2}$
    $+ \frac{5}{10}$

Warm Up 56 — AlgebraicThinking • Foundations

Warm Up 56: The Average Sixth Grader

How would you describe the average sixth grader? One class tried to do just that. They tried to describe the weight and height of the average 6th grader at their middle school. Here are the results from the survey. Find the mean and the median for each data set.

1. How tall are you? (inches)

61, 59, 64, 73, 58, 62, 61, 63, 62, 61, 70, 62, 58, 59, 62, 68, 64, 65, 66, 67, 55, 65, 64, 61, 65

2. How much do you weigh? (pounds)

121, 89, 125, 148, 98, 110, 120, 115, 145, 155, 125, 98, 147, 156, 130, 115, 110, 175, 140, 150, 85, 147, 135, 130, 106

Algebraic Thinking • Foundations   Lesson 56

How to Count - Sample Spaces

When dealing with situations involving probability, it is helpful to know the **sample space** for the situation. A sample space is the set of all possible outcomes. Consider the following: If you choose the two lucky letters from A, B, C, D, E, F, you will win $10 million. List the sample space (the set of all possible outcomes).

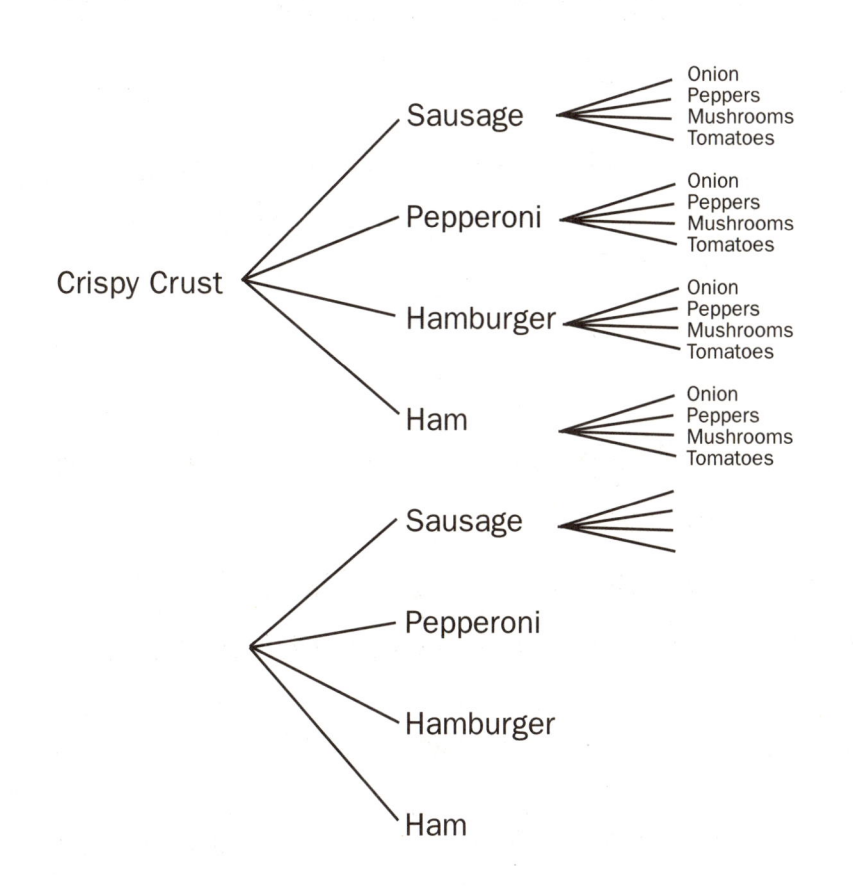

One way to construct a sample space is drawing a **tree diagram.** Consider this situation: A local pizza parlor is offering a special price on two-topping pizzas. You can choose between two crust types: crispy crust or pan crust. You can choose between the following four meat toppings: sausage, pepperoni, hamburger, or ham; and the following four vegetable toppings: onions, peppers, mushrooms, or tomatoes. Only these toppings are included in the special price. Complete the tree diagram above to show the sample space for the special price.

279

Lesson 56   AlgebraicThinking • Foundations

1. How many different pizzas can be made?

2. If you tell the manager to pick the pizza for you, what is each probability?

    a. *P*(crispy crust, sausage, tomatoes)

    b. *P*(peppers)

    c. *P*(pan crust)

When there are lots of outcomes, drawing a tree diagram can be difficult. When this happens, you can use the **counting principle** to determine the number of outcomes. *Just multiply the number of choices at each stage of the tree diagram.*

2 crust choices • 4 meat choices • 4 vegetable choices = 32 possible pizzas

Be CAREFUL! If you toss three coins many people might think that there are six possible outcomes because they think 3 coins times 2 choices for each coin equals 6. However, there are 8 possible outcomes when you toss three coins. Explain why 3 x 2 is not the correct multiplication problem.

(HINT: Try using three different coins-quarter, dime, and nickel-to make the sample space. Or you may want to use the space below to draw a tree diagram.)

Algebraic Thinking • Foundations

Lesson 56

Practice it!

Directions: Make a tree diagram and then a list to show all possible outcomes for each sample space. You may have to use separate paper.

1. Toss a coin and roll a standard number cube.

2. Toss four different coins.

3. Make a sandwich with (1) wheat or white bread; with (2) mayonnaise or mustard; and (3) roast beef, turkey, ham, or pastrami.

4. Toss a coin and spin a spinner with numbers 1 to 5 on it.

Directions: Find the number of outcomes for each situation.

5. Roll three number cubes.

6. Toss two coins and roll a number cube.

7. Choose three letters from A, B, C, D, or E – You may use the same letter more than once.

8. Choose three letters from A, B, C, D, or E – You may use each letter only once.

9. When looking for the phone number of a friend, you discover that the page in the phonebook is ripped. The number that shows is 808-37 and the last two digits are missing. How many possible phone numbers could that be?

10. The five officers for the Music Club are having their picture taken for the yearbook. In how many ways can they line up in a row?

11. A state lottery requires participants to choose 6 numbers from the numbers 1 – 50. A number cannot be used more than once. How many outcomes are there?

12. What is the probability of winning the lottery from #11?

Homework 56 — **AlgebraicThinking** • Foundations

Name _____

Directions: *Find each sum.*

1. $3\frac{1}{2}$
  $+\ 9\frac{2}{5}$

2. $5\frac{2}{3}$
  $+\ 7\frac{7}{8}$

3. $2\frac{7}{10}$
  $+\ 5\frac{1}{12}$

4. $6\frac{5}{6}$
  $+\ 5\frac{7}{9}$

5. $4\frac{3}{8}$
  $+\ 2\frac{1}{4}$

6. $2\frac{5}{12}$
  $+\ 3\frac{7}{12}$

7. $1\frac{1}{6}$
  $+\ 2\frac{2}{3}$

8. $3\frac{7}{10}$
  $+\ 4\frac{2}{3}$

9. $10\frac{5}{6}$
  $+\ 2\frac{1}{3}$

10. $5\frac{3}{4}$
  $+\ 3\frac{7}{16}$

Algebraic Thinking • Foundations

Warm Up 57

Warm Up 57: Name that Month

For #1 – 4, find the month of the year that is described.

1. $\frac{3}{8}$ of the letters in this 8-letter month are e's.

2. $\frac{2}{7}$ of the letters in this 7-letter month are o's.

3. $\frac{1}{4}$ of the letters in this 4-letter month are y's.

4. $\frac{1}{2}$ of the letters in this 4-letter month are vowels.

5. Describe the month that you were born using fractions.

6. Describe your first name using fractions.

Lesson 57 AlgebraicThinking • Foundations

Compound Probability

⊃ Compound probability refers to probability that two or more events will occur.

⊃ In compound probability, you will deal with **independent** events and **dependent** events.

⊃ Two events are <u>independent</u> if the outcome of the first event does not affect the outcome of the second event.

⊃ Two events are <u>dependent</u> if the outcome of the first event affects the outcome of the second event.

Explore! Compound Probability

Directions: *Complete this activity to learn about independent probability and dependent probability.*

1. Pretend that your teacher has a bag of pencils to give away. There are 10 blue pencils, 8 green pencils, 4 yellow pencils, and 2 white pencils. Your teacher will choose pencils from the bag at random.

2. How many pencils are there in all?

3. If your teacher gives you the first pencil what is the probability that you will get a blue pencil?

4. Pretend that you are the fifth student to get a pencil. Your teacher has already handed out 2 blue pencils and 2 green pencils. How many pencils are left in the bag? How many are blue? How many are green?

5. What is the probability that you will get a blue pencil, now?

6. Each time a pencil is given away, the probabilities change. We can say that the probability **depends** on previous events. These events are called _____ events.

Algebraic Thinking • Foundations — Lesson 57

To find the probability of dependent events, find the probability of each event and multiply them together.

PROBABILITY OF DEPENDENT EVENTS

If A and B are dependent events, then the probability of both events occurring is

$$P(A, \text{ then } B) = P(A) \cdot P(B \text{ after } A)$$

7. What is the probability that the first student will get a green pencil and the second student a blue?

8. What is the probability that the first student will get a blue pencil and the second student a green?

9. In the situation described above, what is the probability that the first two students will get a white pencil?

10. What is the probability that the first three students will get a white pencil?

11. Now pretend that you are playing a game in which you draw 2 marbles from a paper bag that has 5 marbles in it. Each marble has a number (1 to 5) on it to indicate the number of spaces you get to move on the game board. You draw the marbles one at a time and after you see the marble, you return it to the bag.

12. How many possible outcomes are there for the first choice? Since you return the marble to the bag, how many possible outcomes are there for the second choice?

13. What is the probability of drawing a 5 on the first choice?

14. What is the probability of drawing a 5 on the second choice?

15. If you had to draw a third time, what would the probability of drawing a 5 be?

16. In this situation, the first event (choosing the first marble) doesn't affect the second event (choosing the second marble). Since one event doesn't affect the second event, they are called _____ events.

285

Lesson 57 AlgebraicThinking • Foundations

To find the probability of independent events find the probability of each event and multiply the probabilities together.

PROBABILITY OF INDEPENDENT EVENTS

If A and B are independent events, then the probability of both events occurring is

$$P(A \text{ and } B) = P(A) \cdot P(B)$$

17. In the situation described in #11, what is the probability of drawing a 4 and then a 2?

18. What is the probability of drawing two fives?

19. If you had to draw three times what would be the probability of drawing three fives?

20. If you had to draw three times what would be the probability of drawing a 1, 2, 3, and a 4?

Directions: *Complete these problems in pairs. Determine whether or not the situations are independent or dependent.*

21. You flip a quarter and then you flip a nickel.

22. Draw a card and without replacing it draw another card.

23. You have won two prizes from a "grab bag." You choose one and then the second.

24. You spin a spinner and roll a number cube.

AlgebraicThinking • Foundations   Lesson 57

Directions: *Work with a partner. Find each probability.*

25. The numbers 1 to 20 are placed on a deck of 20 cards. What is the probability of drawing a 4 and then a 7? (The cards are not replaced after drawing them.)

26. What is the probability of drawing two double-digit numbers?

27. If the cards are replaced what is the probability of drawing a 4 and then a 7?

28. If the cards are replaced what is the probability of drawing two double-digit numbers?

29. Suppose you have cards with the letters A, B, and C on them.

   a. Make a tree diagram to show the sample space for selecting a card, *replacing it*, and selecting a second card.

   b. Make a tree diagram to show the sample space for selecting a card, *not replacing it*, and selecting a second card.

   c. Which tree diagram represents independent events and which one represents dependent events?

   d. For the independent probability, find *P*(A and B). For the dependent probability, find *P*(A, then B).

287

Lesson 57　　　　　　　　　　　　AlgebraicThinking • Foundations

Practice it!

Directions: A number cube is rolled two times. Find each probability.

1. P(3 and 5)
2. P(even and odd)
3. P(2 evens)
4. P(5 and even)
5. P(6 and 7)
6. P(1 and 1)

7. If the number cube is rolled three times, what is the probability of rolling two fives and an even number?

Directions: You draw a card from those at the right and then replace it. Then you draw a second card. Find each probability.

8. P(2 red cards)　　9. P(2 black cards)

10. P(10 and black)　　11. P(ace and ace)

12. P(red, then black)　　13. P(black, then red)

Hearts and Diamonds are red.
Spades and Clubs are black.

Directions: Using the same cards, you draw a card and without replacing it, you draw a second card.

14. P(2 red cards)　　15. P(2 black cards)　　16. P(10 and black)

17. P(ace and ace)　　18. P(red, then black)　　19. P(black, then red)

288

AlgebraicThinking • Foundations   Homework 57

Name _____

Directions: *Find each quotient.*

1. $\frac{3}{4} \div \frac{3}{8} =$

2. $\frac{4}{5} \div \frac{1}{5} =$

3. $\frac{1}{2} \div \frac{1}{8} =$

4. $\frac{2}{3} \div \frac{2}{9} =$

5. $\frac{2}{3} \div \frac{1}{6} =$

6. $\frac{2}{5} \div \frac{1}{10} =$

7. $\frac{3}{8} \div \frac{1}{16} =$

8. $\frac{4}{5} \div \frac{1}{10} =$

9. $\frac{1}{3} \div \frac{1}{12} =$

10. $\frac{3}{5} \div \frac{3}{10} =$

Warm Up 58: Uniquely You

Directions: *Answer each question below to show your uniqueness.*

1. What are your hobbies?

2. What qualities do you possess that make you a good friend?

3. Describe your best friend. (3 sentences or more)

4. What is the one thing about yourself that you are most proud of?

5. If you could be an animal at the zoo, which one would you choose to be? Why?

Algebraic Thinking • Foundations　　　　　　　　　　Lesson 58

Arranging Objects – Combinations and Permutations

There are two types of arrangements that we will study. A **permutation** is an arrangement of objects or numbers in which the order is important. A **combination** is an arrangement in which the order does not matter.

Directions: *Determine whether or not the order is important in each arrangement.*

1. First, second, and third place will be selected from the class.

2. Five people will be selected to serve on a committee.

3. Five finalists will be selected in random order for a talent contest.

4. A 5-digit code should be entered to disable the alarm.

5. Locks like the one in the picture are called combination locks. What would be a better name for these locks and why?

Explore! Permutations

6. Write the letters A – D on 4 index cards or pieces of paper. Arrange them in order and record the result. Then rearrange them in a different order and record that result. For example, two results are A, B, C, D, or D, C, B, A. These two arrangements are of the same letters. They are the same combination, but different permutations.

7. Make a tree diagram showing all of the results.

8. How many permutations of three of the cards are there? Draw a tree diagram to show the results.

9. How many permutations do you think there would be with 5 cards?

AlgebraicThinking • Foundations   Lesson 58

10. As you can see from the table at the right, the number of permutations increases rapidly as the number of objects increases. Study the table and see if you can discover the pattern.

Number of Objects	Number of Permutations
1	1
2	2
3	6
4	24
5	120
6	720
7	5,040
8	40,320
9	362,880
10	3,628,800
n	

11. The pattern is called a _____.

PERMUTATION OF n OBJECTS

The number of permutations of n objects is

$n \cdot (n-1) \cdot (n-2) \cdot (n-3) \cdot \ldots 3 \cdot 2 \cdot 1$

This number is represented by the expression $n!$, which is pronounced **n factorial.**

Directions: *Evaluate each of these expressions. Show how to get your answer. Compare your answers with the person next to you.*

12. 4!   **13.** 3!   **14.** 6!

In many arrangements, the order doesn't matter. If the order doesn't matter then 1, 2, 3 is the same arrangement as 3, 2, 1. Pretend that you are buying some markers. You buy a blue, red, green, and yellow marker. That's the same as buying a yellow, green, red, and blue marker. The order in which you buy them is not important. They are the same **combination.**

293

15. Pretend you are going to buy some markers. The colors that you can choose from are black, blue, red, green, and yellow. You only have enough money to buy 2 markers. How many possible combinations of markers are there?

16. The track coach must select a relay team with 4 people on it. Seven people have tried out for the team. How many ways can the coach pick the team? (Make a list of the combinations.)

17. Use the letters A, B, C, and D.

- Find the number of 2-letter combinations.

- Find the number of 2-letter permutations.

- Which is greater, the number of 2-letter combinations or the number of 2-letter permutations?

AlgebraicThinking • Foundations — Lesson 58

Practice it!

Directions: *Find the number of permutations in each situation. (Use the counting principle.)*

1. Put 5 people in a line.

2. Arrange 4 trophies in a case.

3. Put 6 books on a shelf.

4. Award first, second, and third place to the first three students from a group of 5.

5. How many different outcomes can be made from the letters A, B, C, D, and E by choosing three letters at a time?

6. Consider the letters O, P, S, T. List all of the permutations of those letters. How many of those permutations are words?

7. When dialing a long-distance phone number, you use a three-digit area code. Use the counting principle to determine how many possible area codes there are. (The first number cannot be 0 or 1. The other digits can be anything.)

8. The Young Historians Club will select three officers from their membership of 6 students. They will select a president first, then a vice president, and a secretary. How many different outcomes are possible?

Lesson 58 AlgebraicThinking • Foundations

Directions: *Find the number of combinations.*

9. Select 4 students from a group of 6 to ride a roller coaster together.

10. Join a music club by selecting 3 CDs from a list of 5.

11. Choose three athletes from a group of 7 to run the 100-meter dash.

12. Pick two events from five to participate in during a field day at your school.

13. Buy two video games from a shelf with 10 games on it.

14. Check out 6 books from a shelf that holds 8 books.

Writing: *In your own words, explain the difference between a permutation and a combination. Give an example for each.*

_____
_____
_____
_____
_____
_____
_____
_____
_____
_____

AlgebraicThinking • Foundations

Homework 58

Name _____

Directions: *Find each product or quotient.*

1. $4 \cdot 3\frac{1}{5} =$

2. $2\frac{1}{2} \cdot \frac{5}{8} =$

3. $4\frac{1}{5} \div 3\frac{1}{2} =$

4. $4\frac{2}{3} \cdot 1\frac{1}{7} =$

5. $3\frac{3}{16} \div \frac{1}{8} =$

6. $6\frac{1}{3} \div 3\frac{2}{3} =$

7. $8 \cdot 5\frac{4}{5} =$

8. $2\frac{5}{8} \cdot 6 =$

9. $3\frac{2}{3} \div \frac{5}{6} =$

10. $4\frac{1}{4} \div 2\frac{3}{8} =$

Warm Up 59

Warm Up 59: Add Another

Put a third number in each box to get the sum of 92 in each one.

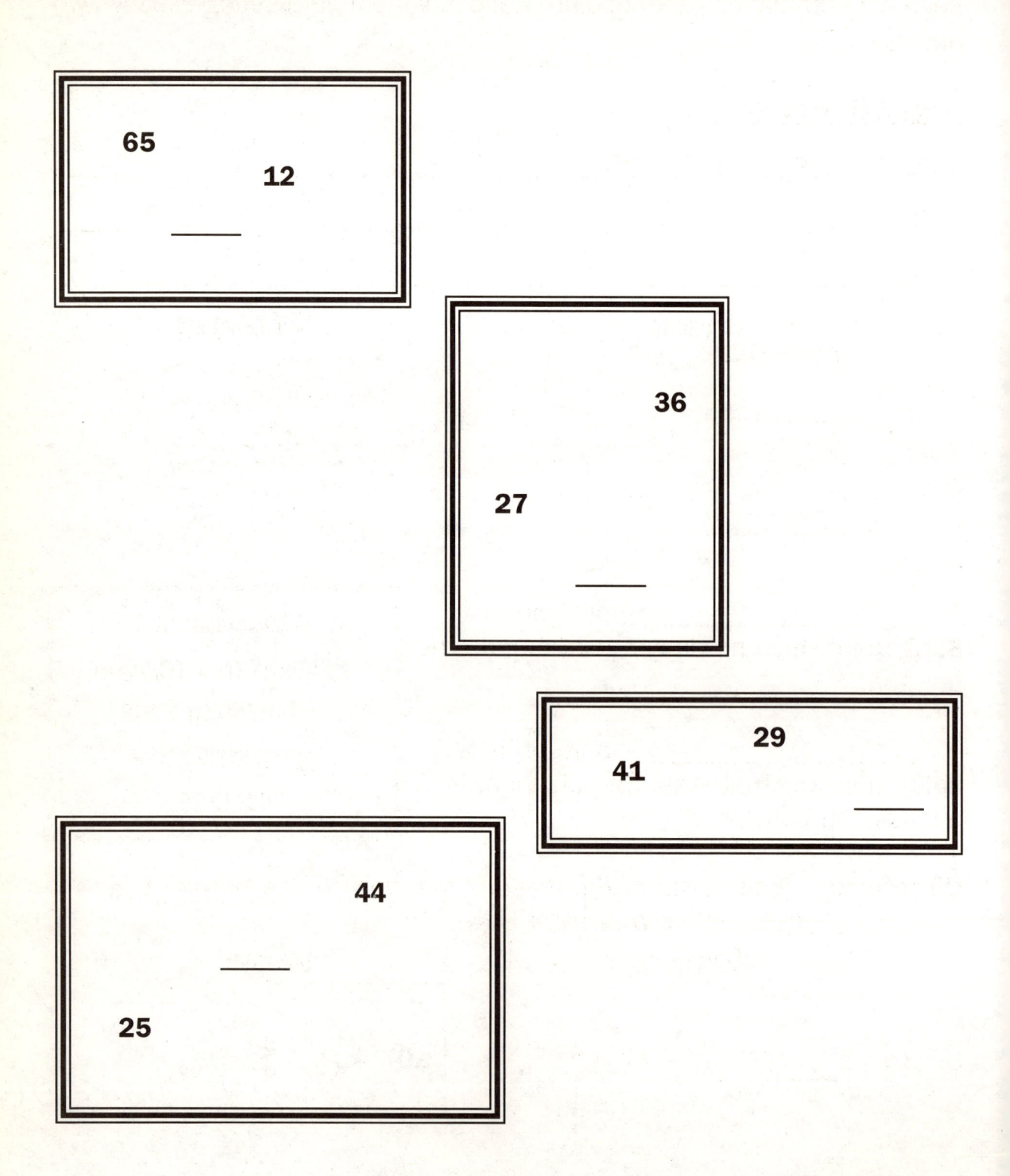

```
┌─────────────────────┐
│  65                 │
│           12        │
│     ____            │
└─────────────────────┘
```

```
┌───────────────┐
│               │
│          36   │
│               │
│  27           │
│               │
│        ____   │
└───────────────┘
```

```
┌───────────────────────┐
│              29       │
│     41                │
│                 ____  │
└───────────────────────┘
```

```
┌─────────────────────┐
│          44         │
│      ____           │
│  25                 │
└─────────────────────┘
```

298

Algebraic Thinking • Foundations Lesson 59

Polygons

A **polygon** is a closed geometric figure in one plane formed by connecting segments endpoint to endpoint. Each segment intersects exactly two others.

Break it Down!

1. _____
2. _____
3. _____

Polygons

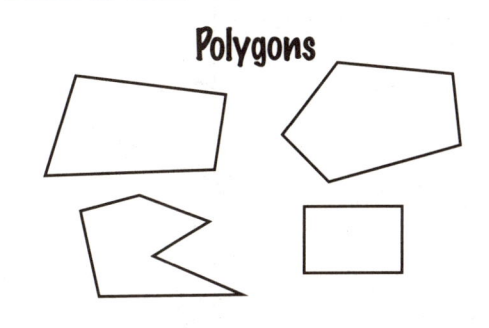

Not Polygons

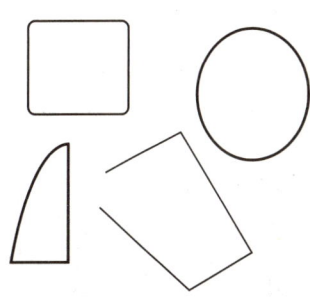

A _____ polygon is a polygon in which no diagonal is outside the polygon.

A _____ polygon is a polygon in which at least one diagonal is outside the polygon.

> **A diagonal is a segment in a polygon connecting two nonconsecutive vertices.**

Directions: Draw some of the diagonals in each of the polygons below. (Use a straight edge.)

Convex

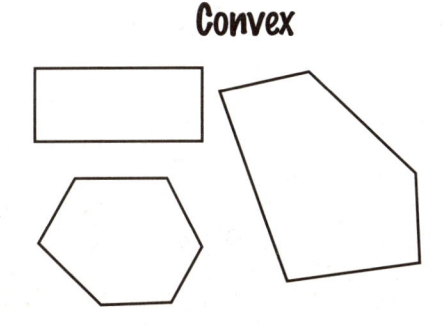

Concave

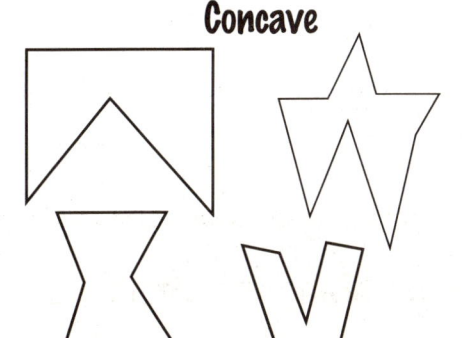

Lesson 59 **AlgebraicThinking • Foundations**

Let's Classify Some Polygons!

Polygons are classified according to the number of sides they have. If all the sides have the same length, it is called **equilateral.** Fill in the names of polygons in the following chart.

No. of Sides	Name of Polygon
3	
4	
5	
6	
7	
8	
9	
10	
11	
12	
n	

I say "polygon" when my bird is missing.

Many polygons, as well as other shapes, are symmetric.

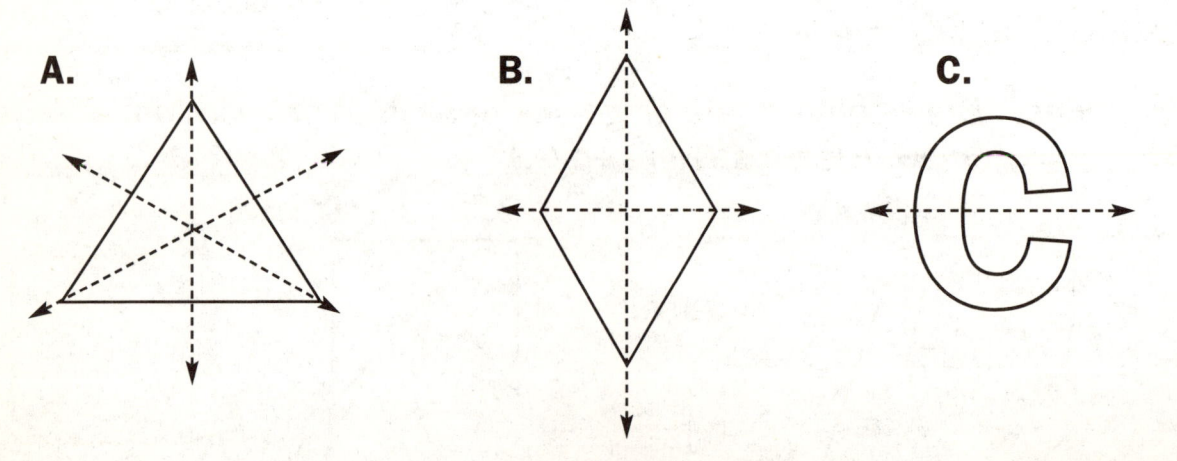

A.   B.   C.

Each side of the dotted line is a reflection of the other. The dotted lines are line(s) of reflection or line(s) of **symmetry.**

300

Algebraic Thinking • Foundations

Lesson 59

Directions: *Look at each figure.* **(1)** *If it is a polygon, write the name of the polygon. If it is not, write "not a polygon."* **(2)** *If it is regular, circle the polygon. You may use a ruler and protractor to check if it's regular. Draw all lines of symmetry.*

1. _____

2. _____

3. _____

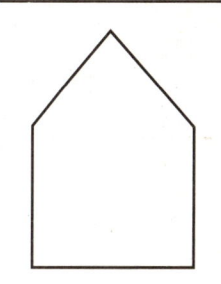

4. _____

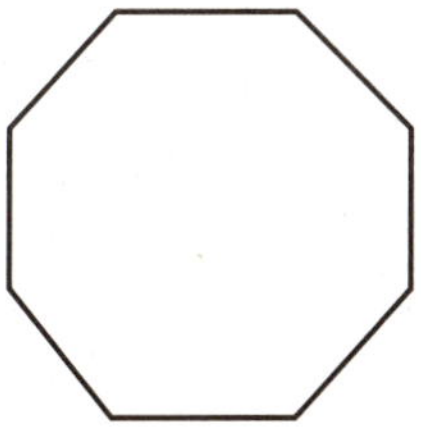

5. _____

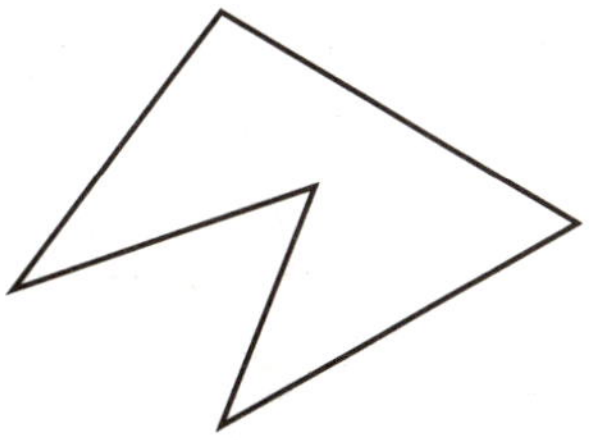

6. _____

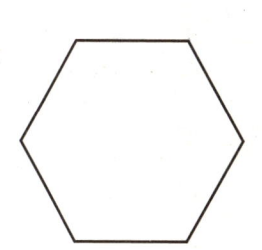

7. _____

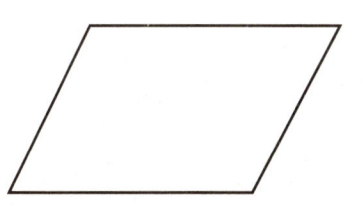

8. _____

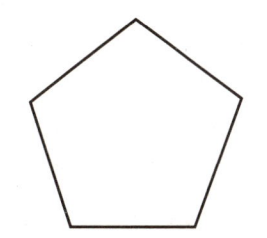

9. _____

10. _____

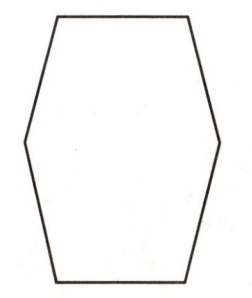

11. _____

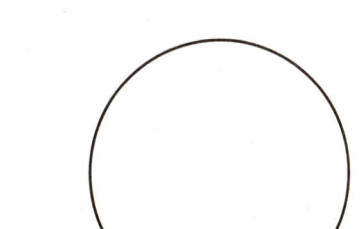

12. _____

301

Homework 59 — **AlgebraicThinking** • Foundations

Name _____

Directions: *Find each quotient.*

1. $\dfrac{1}{3} \div \dfrac{2}{5} =$

2. $\dfrac{3}{4} \div \dfrac{5}{6} =$

3. $\dfrac{4}{5} \div \dfrac{1}{8} =$

4. $\dfrac{5}{6} \div \dfrac{7}{8} =$

5. $\dfrac{1}{3} \div \dfrac{4}{5} =$

6. $\dfrac{3}{4} \div \dfrac{5}{8} =$

7. $\dfrac{2}{3} \div \dfrac{5}{6} =$

8. $\dfrac{3}{8} \div \dfrac{4}{9} =$

9. $\dfrac{2}{5} \div \dfrac{3}{7} =$

10. $\dfrac{8}{9} \div \dfrac{1}{3} =$

AlgebraicThinking • Foundations

Warm Up 60

Warm Up 60: Division Tower

Follow the division problems from top to bottom. Use the answer for each problem as the dividend in the next problem.

20,160 ÷ 10 = _____

_____ ÷ 9 = _____

_____ ÷ 4 = _____

_____ ÷ 8 = _____

_____ ÷ 7 = _____

Lesson 60   AlgebraicThinking • Foundations

Triangles

Triangles are polygons that have three sides and three angles.

Classify!

Sometimes triangles are classified according to the size of the largest angle. Another way to classify triangles is by the number of congruent sides.

EXPLORE! Triangles

1. Cut out the triangles on the paper your teacher will give you.

2. Separate them into the following three groups:
   a) no congruent sides
   b) two congruent sides
   c) all three sides congruent

3. Write the word **scalene** on the triangles with no congruent sides.

4. Write the word **isosceles** on the triangles with two congruent sides.

5. Write the word **equilateral** on the triangles with three congruent sides.

6. Now arrange the triangles in the following three groups:
   a) largest angle is acute
   b) largest angle is right
   c) largest angle is obtuse

7. Write the word **acute** on those with the largest angle being acute.

8. Write the word **right** on those with the largest angle being right.

9. Write the word **obtuse** on those with the largest angle being obtuse.

10. Do any of the triangles have more than one acute angle? _____

11. Do any of the triangles have more than one right angle? _____

12. Do any of the triangles have more than one obtuse angle? _____

Algebraic Thinking • Foundations

Lesson 60

Directions: Fill in the following chart.
(Example: For the box with the star in it: Can a triangle be both acute and scalene?)

	Scalene	Isosceles	Equilateral
Acute	★		
Right			
Obtuse			

13. Use a colored pencil to color the angles of a triangle.

14. Tear off the angles like in the figure at the right.

15. Tape the angles together on the line below so that the vertices touch, the angles do not overlap, and there is no space between the angles.

_____

16. The figure you formed is a picture of the **sum** of the angles of a triangle. Together the angles form a straight angle. What is the sum of the measure of the angles of a triangle?
    (Answer in a complete sentence.)

_____

_____

Lesson 60 **AlgebraicThinking • Foundations**

Directions: *Find the value of each variable in each triangle. Then classify the triangle according to its sides and angles.*

1. _____

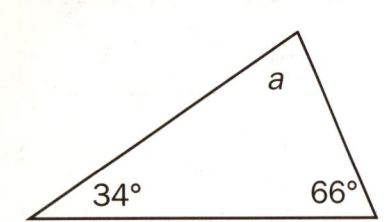

a, 34°, 66°

2. _____

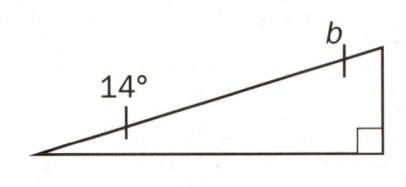

b, 14°

3. _____

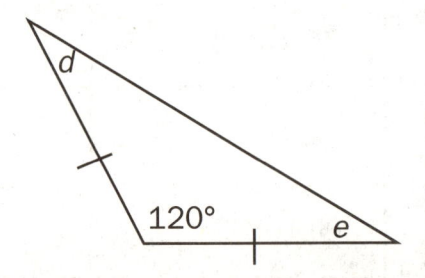

d, 120°, e

4. _____

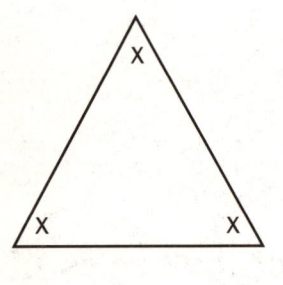

x, x, x

5. _____

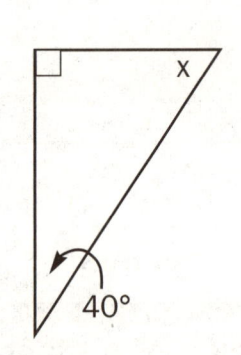

x, 40°

6. _____

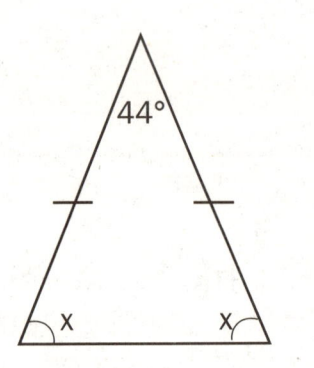

44°, x, x

AlgebraicThinking • Foundations Homework 60

Name _____

Directions: *Convert each fraction and decimal to a percent.*

1. 0.35

2. $\frac{1}{2}$

3. $\frac{3}{5}$

4. $\frac{7}{25}$

5. 0.70

6. 0.7

7. $\frac{13}{20}$

8. 0.375

9. $\frac{3}{10}$

10. 0.625

Warm Up 61: Tic-Tac-Toe

David and Alec played a game of tic-tac-toe. Find out who won by matching each answer on the board to the correct problem. Put the appropriate letter over that space on the board.

David played the X
$2\frac{1}{2} + 3\frac{3}{4} =$
$\frac{4}{5} \cdot \frac{2}{3} =$
$4\frac{3}{5} \div \frac{3}{10} =$
$8\frac{9}{16} - 3\frac{3}{8} =$

Alec played the O
$1\frac{3}{8} + 4\frac{2}{3} =$
$\frac{5}{6} \cdot 12 =$
$\frac{7}{16} \div 2\frac{1}{2} =$
$3\frac{4}{5} - 2\frac{1}{3} =$

$15\frac{1}{3}$	$6\frac{1}{4}$	$6\frac{1}{24}$
$\frac{7}{40}$	$\frac{8}{15}$	10
$5\frac{3}{16}$	$1\frac{7}{15}$	$\frac{2}{13}$

Who won the game? _____

Algebraic Thinking • Foundations Lesson 61

Quadrilaterals

A **quadrilateral** is any **polygon** with four sides. In the space below, draw several quadrilaterals. Can you draw a **concave** quadrilateral?

Your teacher will give you a sheet of paper with several quadrilaterals on it. Cut them out. We are going to sort them based on characteristics of their sides and angles.

1. Find all the quadrilaterals with one pair of opposite sides parallel. These are called **trapezoids.** Draw several trapezoids in the space below.

Write a definition for *trapezoid*. A trapezoid is a quadrilateral with

Lesson 61 **Algebraic**Thinking • Foundations

2. Find all the quadrilaterals with both pairs of opposite sides parallel. These are called **parallelograms.** Draw several parallelograms in the space below.

Write a definition for *parallelogram*. A parallelogram is a quadrilateral with

_____

3. Find all the *parallelograms* that have four right angles. These are called **rectangles.** Draw several rectangles in the space below.

Write a definition for *rectangle*. A rectangle is a parallelogram with

_____

AlgebraicThinking • Foundations   Lesson 61

4. Find all the parallelograms that have four congruent sides. These are called **rhombi.** The singular form is rhombus. Draw several rhombi in the space below.

Write a definition for *rhombus*. A rhombus is a parallelogram with

_____

5. Find all the parallelograms that have four right angles and four congruent sides. These are called **squares.** Draw several squares in the space below.

Write a definition for *square*. A square is a parallelogram with

Lesson 61 **AlgebraicThinking** • Foundations

Directions: *Fill in the properties of the quadrilaterals with your teacher.*

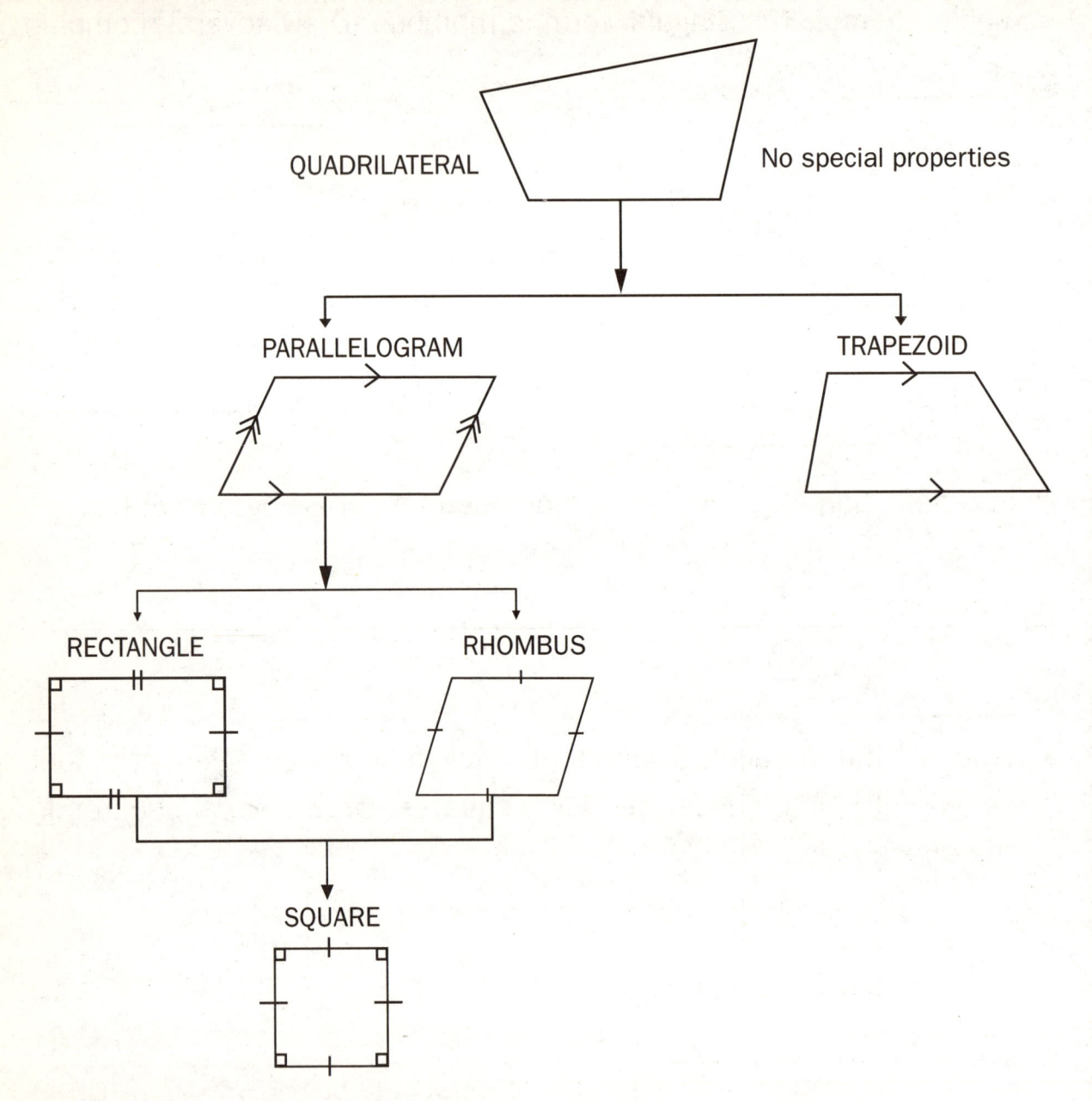

QUADRILATERAL   No special properties

PARALLELOGRAM   TRAPEZOID

RECTANGLE   RHOMBUS

SQUARE

Directions: *Answer true or false to the following questions.*

1. All squares are rectangles.
2. All squares are rhombi.
3. All squares are parallelograms.
4. All rectangles are squares.
5. All rhombi are squares.
6. All parallelograms are squares.
7. A square is a rhombus and a rectangle.
8. A rhombus is never a rectangle.

Algebraic Thinking • Foundations   Lesson 61

Directions: *Classify each quadrilateral. Use the most specific name.*

1. _____

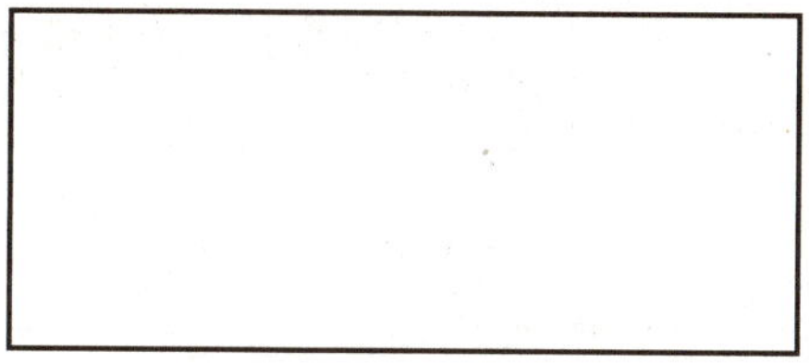

2. _____

3. _____

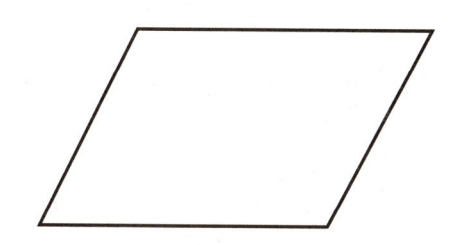

4. _____

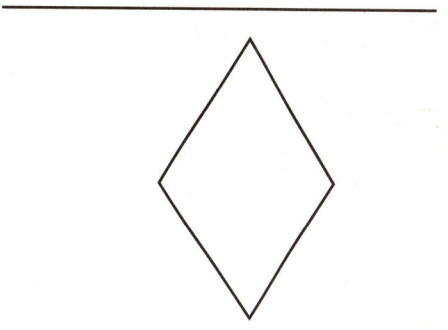

5. _____

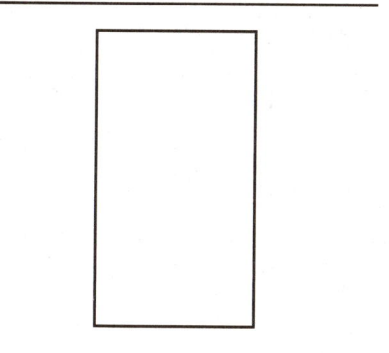

6. _____

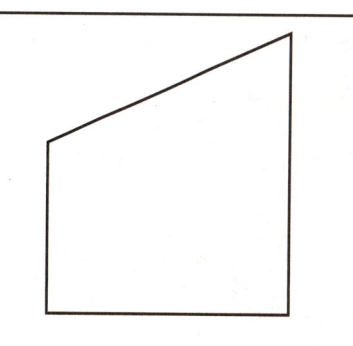

7. _____

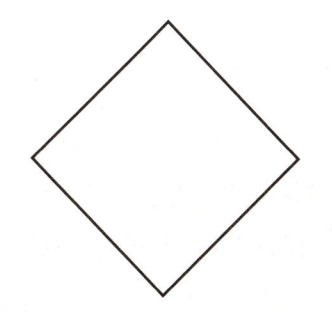

8. _____

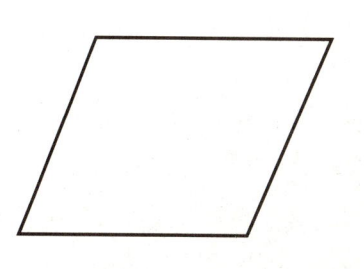

Directions: *Draw the lines of symmetry in the above quadrilaterals.*

313

Homework 61 — AlgebraicThinking • Foundations

Name _____

Directions: *Find each quotient.*

1. $3 \div \frac{1}{4} =$

2. $5 \div \frac{1}{10} =$

3. $2 \div \frac{1}{9} =$

4. $6 \div \frac{2}{5} =$

5. $4 \div \frac{1}{5} =$

6. $9 \div \frac{3}{4} =$

7. $7 \div \frac{1}{2} =$

8. $1 \div \frac{1}{6} =$

9. $8 \div \frac{1}{3} =$

10. $2 \div \frac{2}{5} =$

AlgebraicThinking • Foundations

Warm Up 62: Hmmm...

How can you arrange eight congruent toothpicks to make a square and four equilateral triangles?

Lesson 62

Algebraic Thinking • Foundations

Area and Perimeter

Let's talk measurement! Earlier in this unit, we practiced **linear measurement** as well as some non-linear measurement. Today we are going to talk about measurements that are not linear. List some of the previous non-linear measurement units we talked about.

Measurement! OH YEAH!!!!!!

Give this a try!

1. Draw each of the following figures on centimeter grid paper.

	Perimeter	Area
a rectangle with length 8 and width 4		
a rectangle with length 18 and width 2		
a rectangle with length 6 and width 6		

2. Record the **perimeter** of each rectangle.

3. Are the rectangles with the same perimeter congruent, similar, or neither?

4. To find the area, count the number of squares in the interior of each rectangle. Record each area.

5. Are the rectangles with the same area congruent, similar, or neither?

6. Do rectangles with the same perimeter have the same area?

7. Can a rectangle have a larger number for its perimeter than for its area?

Algebraic Thinking • Foundations

Lesson 62

We will use **square units** to measure the area of a **polygon.** The area of a polygon is the number of square units enclosed by the polygon. Earlier, when you found the area of the rectangles, you did it by counting. Is there a way to find the square units without counting them?

> The area of a rectangle is equal to the length of the base times the height. (A = bh)

You have 36 yards of fencing. You need to make a rectangular pen for your pet pig, Peachy. Draw some possible pens and find their area.

What are the dimensions that will result in the maximum area?

What is the maximum area?

317

Lesson 62 **AlgebraicThinking** • Foundations

Try these!

1. A rectangle has a base with a length of 10 cm and a width of 5 cm. What is its area?

2. What is the perimeter of the rectangle in question 1?

3. A rectangle has a perimeter of 24 inches. The length of its base is 4 inches. What is its area? (**Problem Solver's Hint:** Draw a picture of the rectangle.)

4. A square and a rectangle have the same area. The rectangle is 4 cm long and 16 cm wide. What are the dimensions of the square?

AlgebraicThinking • Foundations   Lesson 62

Directions: *Tell whether each situation involves perimeter or area.*

5. paint a wall

6. baseboard for a room

7. tinting for a window

8. tile for the edge of a swimming pool

9. **S-O-L-V-E:** You want to build a new rectangular pen for Peachy. She deserves it, she won the grand prize at the county fair! You have 120 feet of fencing to use for the project. What are the dimensions for the pen with the greatest area?

S

O

L

V

E

Lesson 62   Algebraic Thinking • Foundations

Directions: *Find the area and perimeter of each rectangle.*

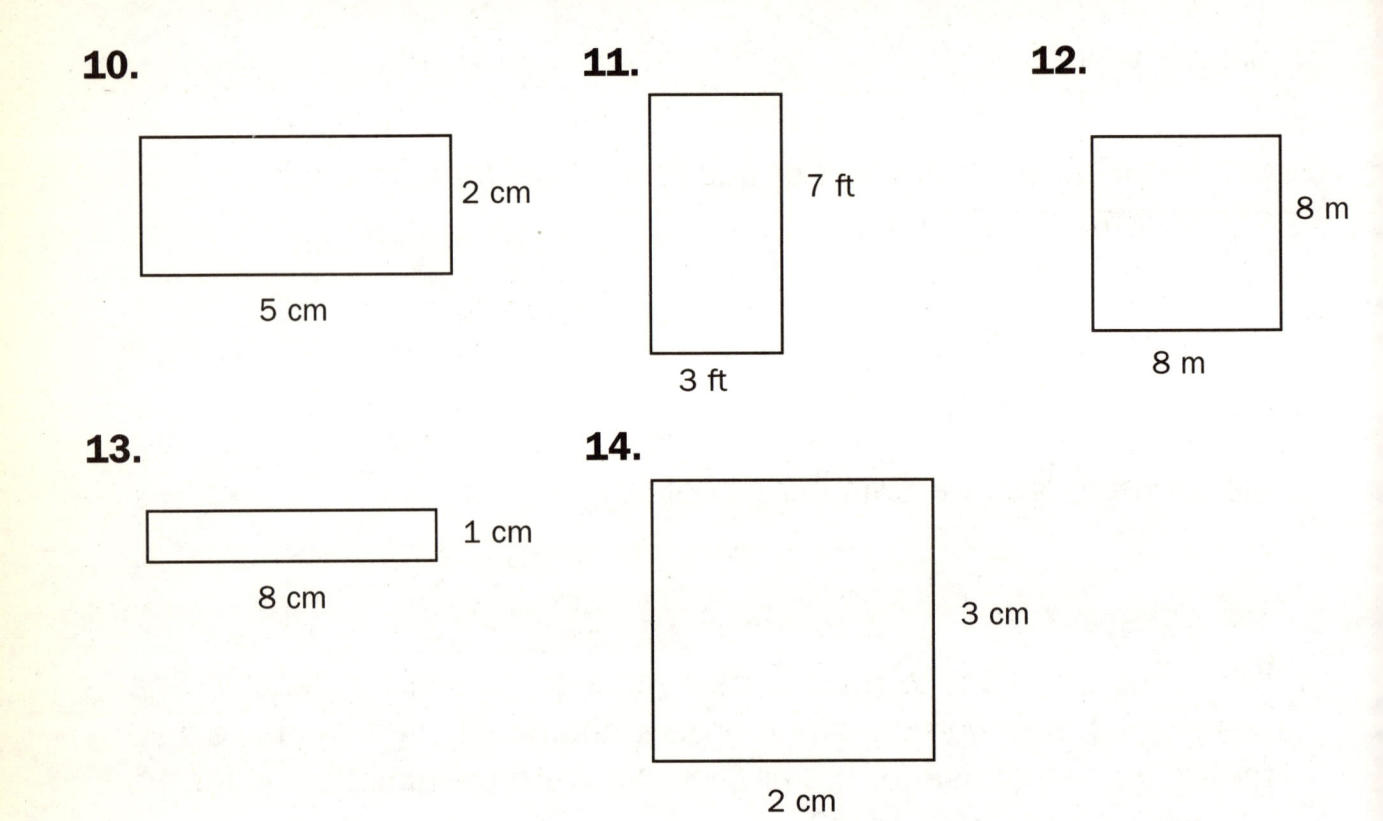

10.

2 cm
5 cm

11.

7 ft
3 ft

12.

8 m
8 m

13.

1 cm
8 cm

14.

3 cm
2 cm

15. The area of a rectangle is 120 cm². The length of the base is 10 cm. What is the height of the rectangle?

16. The area of a square is 100 m². What is the length of the sides?

AlgebraicThinking • Foundations

Homework 62

Name _____

Directions: *Find each product or quotient. Write the answer in simplest form.*

1. $\frac{1}{2} \cdot 8 =$

2. $\frac{1}{2} \cdot 9 =$

3. $\frac{1}{3} \cdot 12 =$

4. $\frac{2}{3} \cdot 12 =$

5. $5 \cdot 2\frac{1}{2} =$

6. $5 \div 2\frac{1}{2} =$

7. $\frac{3}{4} \div 3 =$

8. $\frac{4}{9} \div \frac{1}{9} =$

9. $\frac{7}{10} \div \frac{2}{5} =$

10. $\frac{11}{12} \div \frac{1}{6} =$

Warm Up 63: Empty Squares

Fill in the empty squares with numbers so that each row, column, and diagonal will have the same sum.

117	73	110
93		
	127	

AlgebraicThinking • **Foundations**   Lesson 63

Areas of Triangles and Parallelograms

Recall that the area for a rectangle is found by multiplying the length of the base times the height of the rectangle *(A = bh)*. The area formulas for triangles and parallelograms are derived from the rectangle formula. So, let's discover the formulas.

Materials: *grid paper, straight edge, tape, scissors.*

1. Each person in the class should draw and cut out any rectangle. When you draw the rectangle use different colors for the height and base. Record the length of the base, the height, and the area of the rectangle.

2. Draw a point anywhere on the base of your rectangle. (This will be easier if you use the longer side as the base.) Draw a **segment** from the point you drew to either vertex on the opposite side. Cut along that line segment.

3. What is the shape of the piece you cut off of the rectangle? _____ "Slide" it to the other side of the rectangle and tape the two segments from the original rectangle together. You did not lose any area in doing this. You just "rearranged" the shape. It is now a parallelogram.

4. Look at your parallelogram. Notice the colors you used in the rectangle. They were the base and height of the rectangle. Now the colors represent the base and height of the parallelogram! Record the length of the base, the height, and the area of the parellelogram.

5. In the space below, draw a parallelogram and label the base and height. Write the area formula for a parallelogram.

Lesson 63   Algebraic Thinking • Foundations

6. This time, each person should draw and cut out a parallelogram. What is the formula for the area of a parallelogram?

7. Draw a **diagonal** of the parallelogram. Cut along the diagonal.

8. How does the area of the triangle compare to the area of a rectangle?

9. Draw a triangle in the space below. Label the base and the height. Write the area formula for a triangle.

Area of a triangle: A = _____

Directions: *Find the area of each parallelogram or triangle.*

10.
8 cm
4 cm

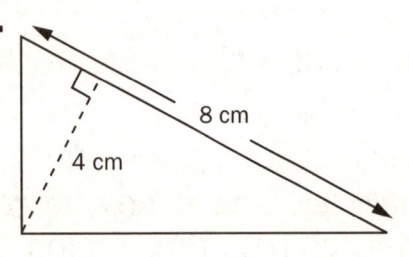

11.
65 cm
100 cm

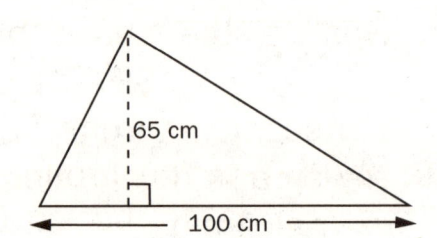

12.
7 in.
12 in.

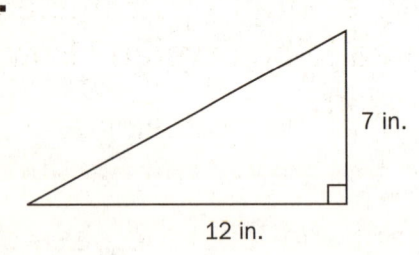

13.
5 in.
3 in.
4 in.

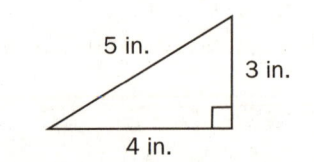

14.
8 cm
3 cm

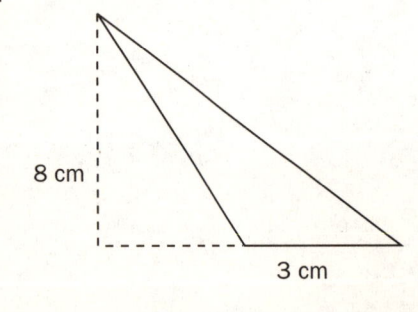

15.
8 cm
3 cm

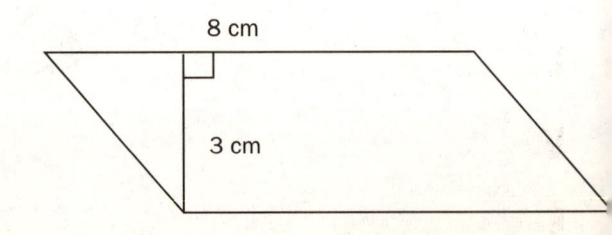

Algebraic Thinking • Foundations

Lesson 63

Directions: Find the area of each parallelogram or composite figure.

16.

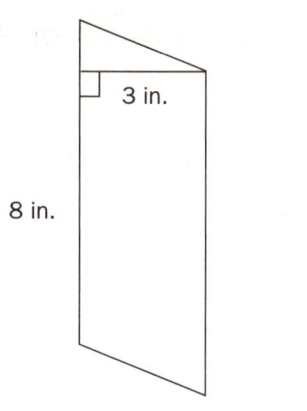

3 in.

8 in.

17.

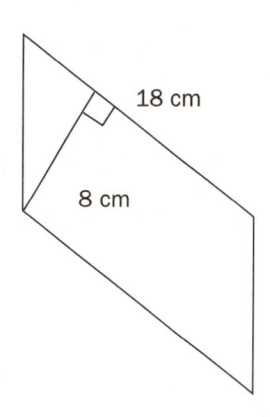

18 cm

8 cm

18.

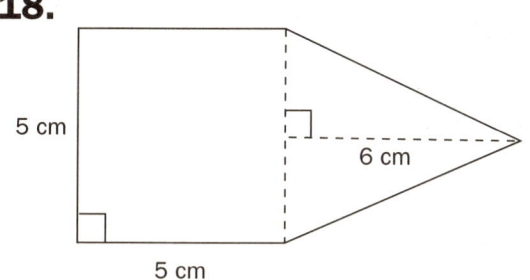

5 cm

6 cm

5 cm

19.

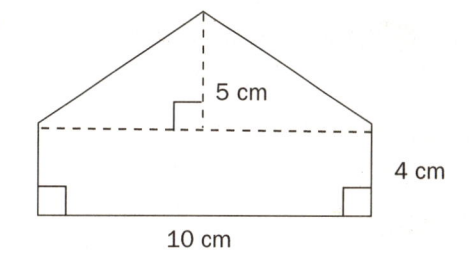

5 cm

4 cm

10 cm

20. S-O-L-V-E: The ground around a jungle gym at a new child care center is to be covered with cedar chips. The region to be covered is rectangular in shape with a width of 25 meters and a length of 35 meters. What is the area to be covered? How much fencing is needed to surround the region?

S

O

L

V

E

Homework 63   AlgebraicThinking • Foundations

Name _____

Directions: *Find each product.*

1. $12 \cdot \frac{1}{2} =$

2. $3 \cdot \frac{5}{8} =$

3. $4 \cdot \frac{3}{7} =$

4. $2 \cdot \frac{4}{9} =$

5. $5 \cdot \frac{2}{3} =$

6. $\frac{5}{6} \cdot 12 =$

7. $\frac{3}{4} \cdot 8 =$

8. $\frac{1}{8} \cdot 20 =$

9. $\frac{2}{5} \cdot 3 =$

10. $\frac{7}{9} \cdot 4 =$

AlgebraicThinking • Foundations

Warm Up 64: How Many Squares?

How many squares can you find in the figure below?

Lesson 64 **AlgebraicThinking** • Foundations

Areas of Trapezoids

We can use parallelograms to develop the formula for the area of a trapezoid.

1. Use grid paper to draw and cut out two **congruent** trapezoids.

2. Cut out the trapezoids and label the bases b_1 and b_2 on both trapezoids. Also, draw and label the height of each trapezoid.

3. Turn one of the trapezoids upside down and tape it to the other so that they form a parallelogram.

4. The area of a parallelogram is $A = bh$. Write an expression for the base of the parallelogram.

5. Write an expression for the area of the parallelogram using b_1, b_2, and h.
   $A = $ _____

6. How does the area of one of the trapezoids relate to the area of the parallelogram? Write the formula for the area of a trapezoid.

Try this!

7. **S-O-L-V-E:** The state of Nevada is almost a trapezoid. The two sides that are parallel run north-south. One is about 212 miles long and the other is about 480 miles long. The distance between the two bases is about 315 miles. What is the approximate area of Nevada?

S

O

L

V

E

Algebraic Thinking • Foundations　　　　Lesson 64

Directions: *Find the area of each trapezoid.*

8. A = _____

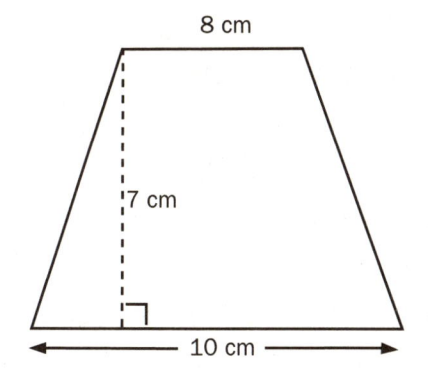

8 cm
7 cm
10 cm

9. A = _____

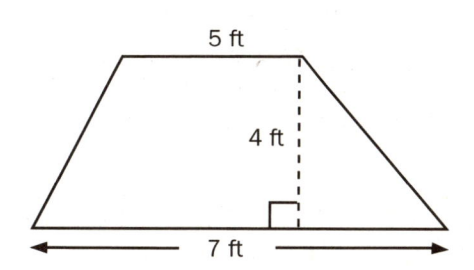

5 ft
4 ft
7 ft

10. A = _____

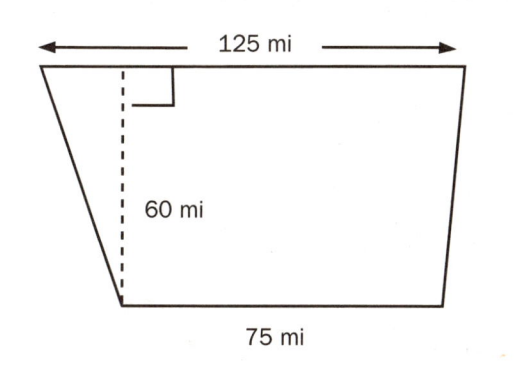

125 mi
60 mi
75 mi

11. A = _____

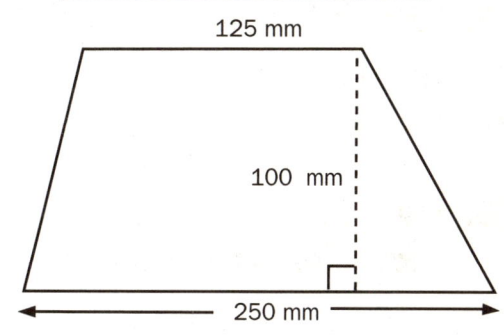

125 mm
100 mm
250 mm

12. A = _____

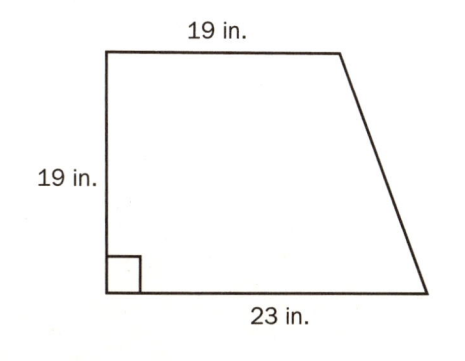

19 in.
19 in.
23 in.

13. A = _____

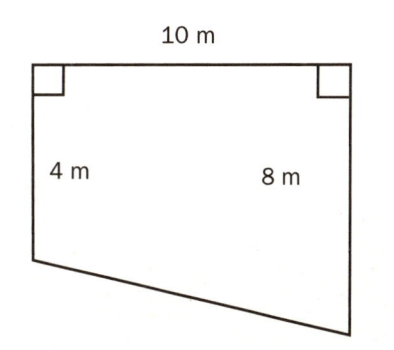

10 m
4 m
8 m

329

Lesson 64   Algebraic Thinking • Foundations

Find the area of each trapezoid given the height and bases.

14. $h = 7$ ft; $b_1 = 4$ ft; $b_2 = 5$ ft

15. $h = 20$ in.; $b_1 = 15$ in.; $b_2 = 5$ in.

16. $h = 8$ yd; $b_1 = 8$ yd; $b_2 = 6$ yd

17. $h = 28$ cm; $b_1 = 22$ cm; $b_2 = 34$ cm

18. S-O-L-V-E: The roof on a house can be formed by trapezoids. Pretend that one of the sides of your roof needs new shingles. One base is 35 feet long and the other is 25 feet long. The distance between the bases is 15 feet. You have selected shingles that will cover $1\frac{1}{2}$ ft² of area. How many shingles should you buy?

S

O

L

V

E

AlgebraicThinking • Foundations   Homework 64

Name _____

Directions: *Answer each question.*

1. Write line segment *AB* in symbolic form.

2. Write angle *XYZ* in symbolic form.

3. Draw an acute angle and label it to match #2.

4. Write ray *BA* in symbolic form.

5. Draw a ray and label it to match #4.

6. Angle *ABC* has a supplement of 150°. What is the complement of Angle *ABC*?

7. Two angles are supplementary and congruent. What are their measures?

8. What kind of angle do the hands of a clock form when it is 3:00?

9. What is the supplement of angle *XYZ* if its complement is 130°?

10. Challenge! What is the angle formed by the hands of a clock when it is 1:00?

331

Warm Up 65: Isosceles, Isosceles, Isosceles

How many isosceles triangles can you find in the figure below?

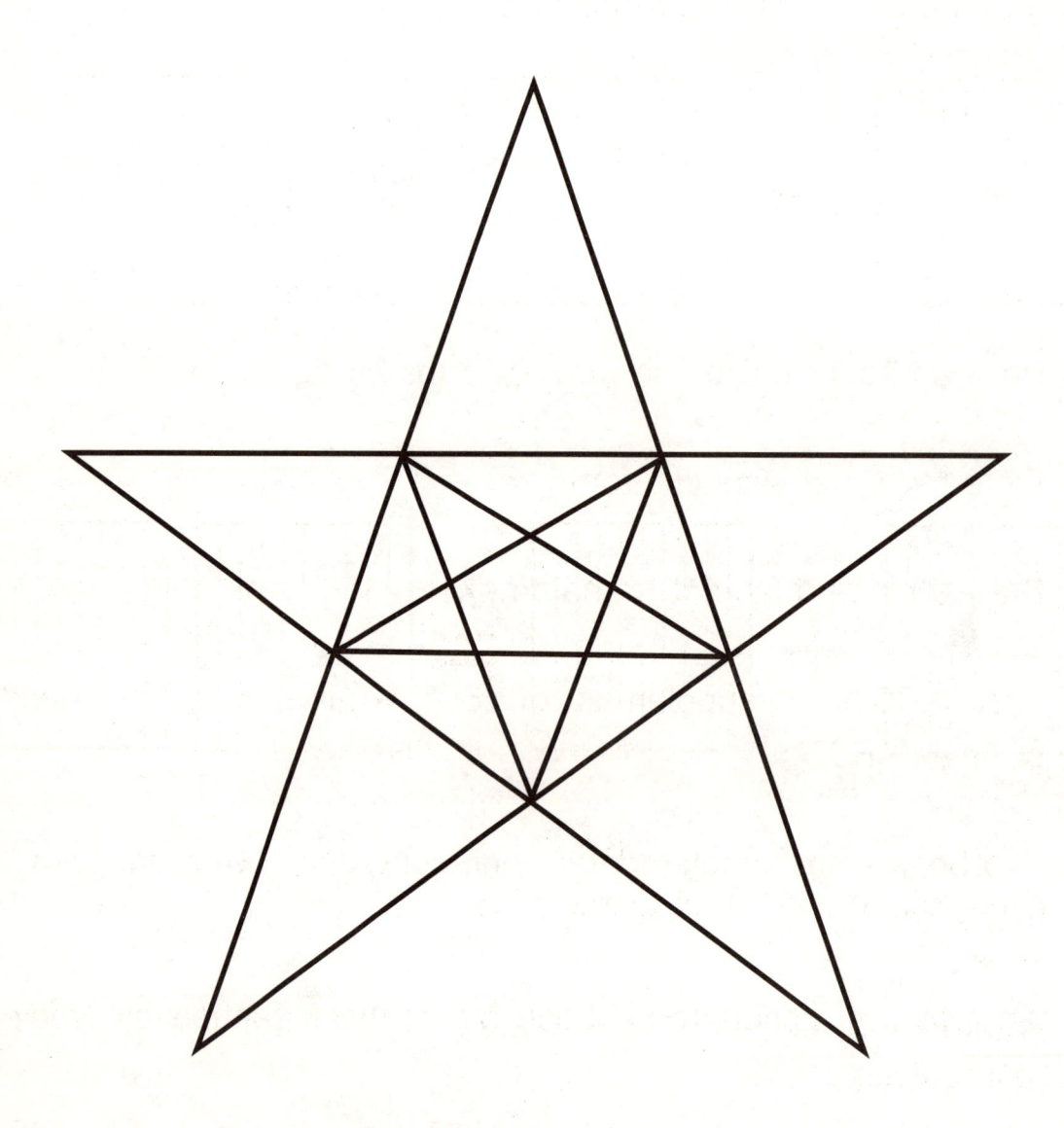

Algebraic Thinking • Foundations　　　　　　　　Lesson 65

Adding and Subtracting Decimals

Today, we will look at two methods for adding and subtracting decimals. One of them is by modeling. The other is lining up the decimal places. Model this problem with your teacher.

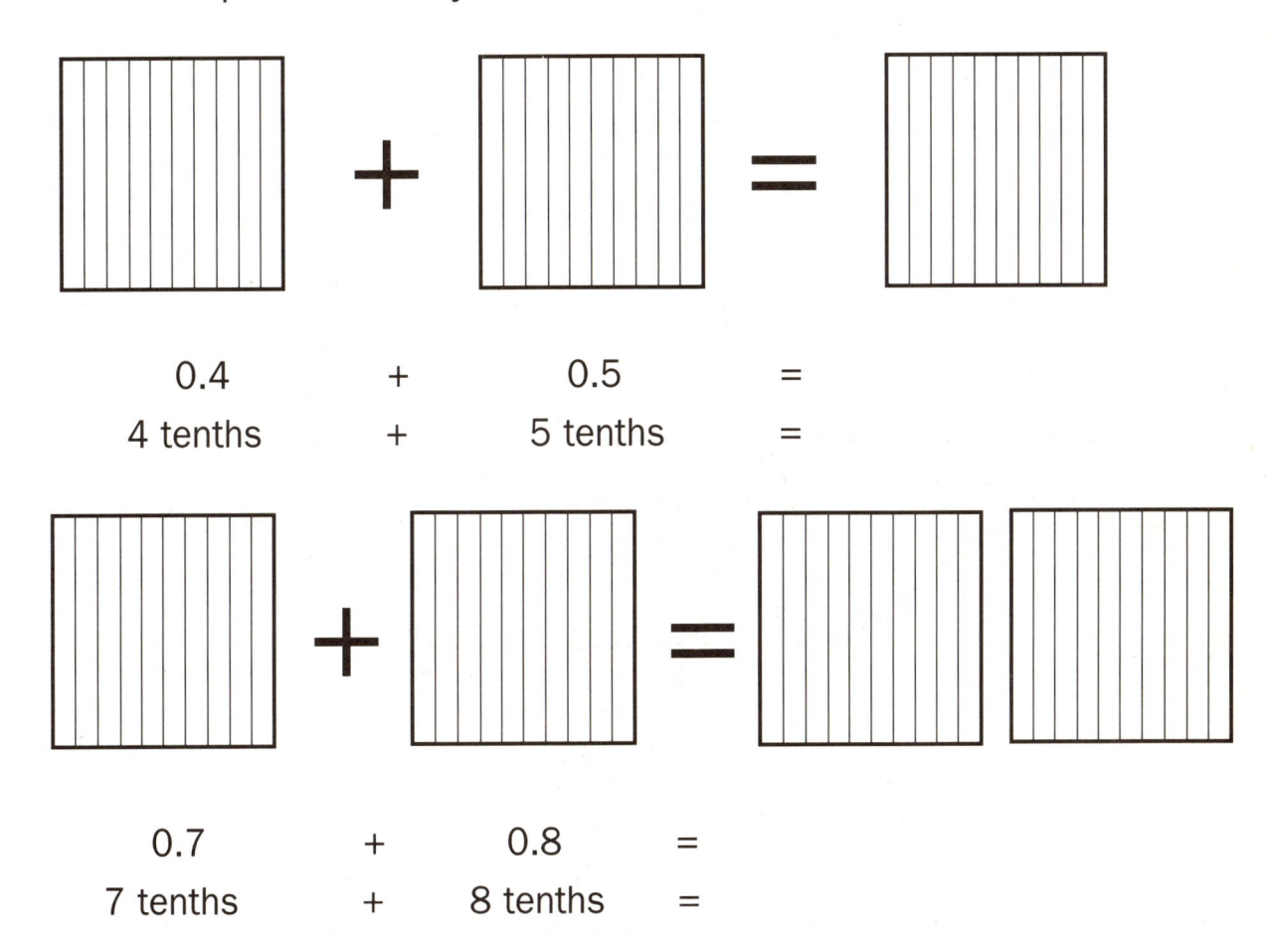

0.4　　　+　　　0.5　　　=
4 tenths　+　5 tenths　=

0.7　　　+　　　0.8　　　=
7 tenths　+　8 tenths　=

You can also use models to subtract. Model these subtraction problems with your teacher.

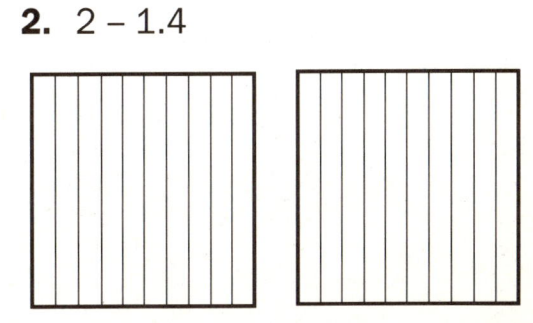

1. 2 – 0.6

2. 2 – 1.4

333

Lesson 65 AlgebraicThinking • Foundations

Another way to add and subtract decimals is by lining up the decimal places. Work these problems with your teacher.

1. 24.2 + 3.47 =

   24.20
   + 3.47
   ———

2. 13.78 + 9.2 =

3. 123.87 − 19.42

4. 10.24 − 9.715 =

Practice it!

Directions: *Work each of the problems below. Show your work.*

1. 3.4 + 5.7 =

2. 0.9 + 2.4 =

3. 3 + 6.7 =

4. 0.48 + 0.52 =

5. 3.85 + 6.8 =

6. 27.4 − 1.67 =

7. 0.25 + 3.8 =

8. 7.8 − 6.09 =

9. 12.35 − 7.05 =

AlgebraicThinking • **Foundations**   Lesson 65

10. 12.45 – 3.7 =   **11.** 15.8 – 7.05 =   **12.** 0.967 + 3.85 =

13. 10.05 + 100 =   **14.** 24 – 0.25 =   **15.** 97.4 – 2.6 =

Directions: *Use S-O-L-V-E to solve these word problems.*

16. Mr. Bowman bought a pack of pencils for $1.89. He also bought a pack of markers for $4.99 and some drawing paper for $2.49. What was the total cost (not including tax)?

S. _____

_____

O. _____

_____

L. _____

_____

V. _____

_____

E. _____

_____

Lesson 65

AlgebraicThinking • Foundations

17. The treadmill that Gina works out on has an LED read-out on it that tells her how far she has jogged. On Monday, she jogged 1.2 miles. On Wednesday, she jogged 1.37 miles and on Friday she did very well, jogging 2.14 miles. How many more miles did she jog on Friday than Monday?

S. _____

O. _____

L. _____

V. _____

E. _____

AlgebraicThinking • Foundations Homework 65

Name _____

Directions: *Find each difference.*

1. $5\frac{4}{5}$
    $- 2\frac{1}{2}$

2. $11\frac{1}{3}$
    $- 3\frac{7}{9}$

3. $10\frac{3}{4}$
    $- 5\frac{1}{5}$

4. $4\frac{5}{6}$
    $- 1\frac{1}{12}$

5. $9\frac{2}{3}$
    $- 3\frac{5}{6}$

6. $8\frac{5}{6}$
    $- 2\frac{1}{8}$

7. $6\frac{1}{2}$
    $- 2\frac{9}{10}$

8. $3\frac{2}{5}$
    $- 1\frac{3}{5}$

9. $3\frac{2}{3}$
    $- 1\frac{1}{2}$

10. $5\frac{4}{5}$
    $- 2\frac{7}{10}$

Warm Up 66 — Algebraic Thinking • Foundations

Warm Up 66: Money Sense

In how many different ways can you make $1.00 using quarters, dimes, and nickels?

AlgebraicThinking • Foundations　　　　　　　　　Lesson 66

Multiplying Decimals

Model the sum 0.7 + 0.7 + 0.7 + 0.7 in the grids below.

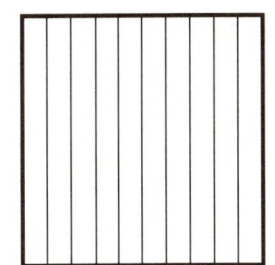

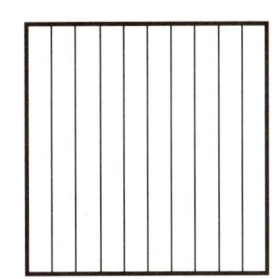

✶ How can you rewrite the problem as a multiplication problem? _____
✶ How many tenths are shaded in all? _____
✶ 4 groups of 7 tenths is _____ tenths.
✶ Write that with a decimal point. _____

Another model is useful when multiplying two decimals together. You will need two different colors for this model. Do the following things in the grid to the right.

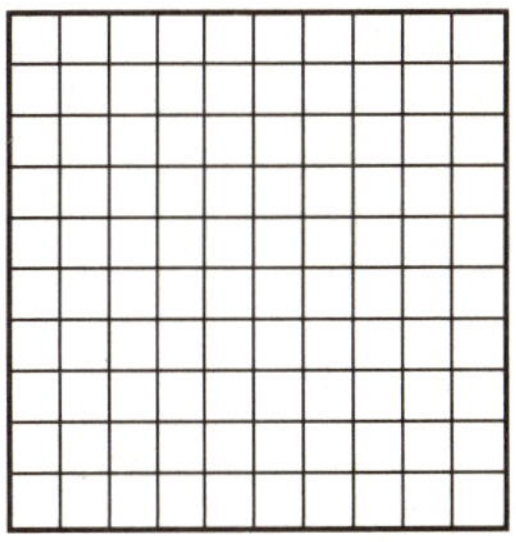

✶ Shade 7 rows with one color. What decimal does this represent? _____
✶ Shade 4 columns with another color. What decimal does this represent? _____
✶ The "overlap area" is the area shaded by both colors. It shows the product of 0.7 and 0.4. How many squares do both areas shade? _____
✶ What decimal does this represent? _____

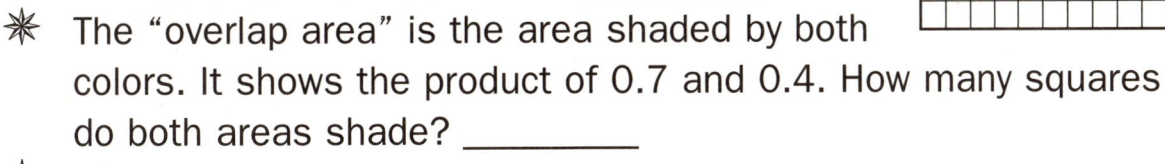

Try These!

　　　　　0.8 • 0.4　　　　　　　　　　0.8 • 1.5

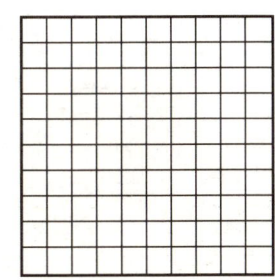

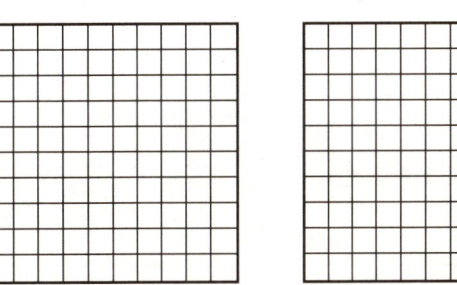

339

Lesson 66 AlgebraicThinking • Foundations

Practice it!
Directions: Use the grids to model each product.

	Problem	Model	Product
1.	4 • 0.9		
2.	2 • 0.8		
3.	6 • 0.5		
4.	4 • 0.1		
5.	3 • 0.9		
6.	2 • 0.75		
7.	3 • 0.61		
8.	5 • 0.45		
9.	3 • 0.25		

Algebraic Thinking • Foundations Lesson 66

Directions: *Use the grids to model each product.*

Problem	Model/Product
10. 0.8 • 0.7	
11. 0.6 • 0.9	
12. 0.9 • 0.9	
13. 0.4 • 0.3	
14. 0.5 • 0.7	
15. 0.1 • 0.6	

Problem	Model/Product
16. 1 • 0.6	
17. 0.7 • 1.5	
18. 0.9 • 1.1	
19. 0.5 • 2.5	
20. 0.1 • 2.3	
21. 0.2 • 2.7	

22. **Writing:** Consider the problem, 0.5 • 0.5. Since 0.5 = $\frac{1}{2}$, the problem could be written, $\frac{1}{2}$ • $\frac{1}{2}$. So, the problem means "$\frac{1}{2}$ of a group of $\frac{1}{2}$."

    a. What is 0.5 • 0.5? _____

    b. Write 0.25 as a fraction. _____

    c. That means that $\frac{1}{2}$ • $\frac{1}{2}$ = _____ .

    d. Explain the answer to "part c" using the above information. _____

_____

Homework 66 — AlgebraicThinking • Foundations

Name _____

1. What are the two ways that triangles are classified?

Directions: *Find the missing angle of the following triangles and classify them according to their angles.*

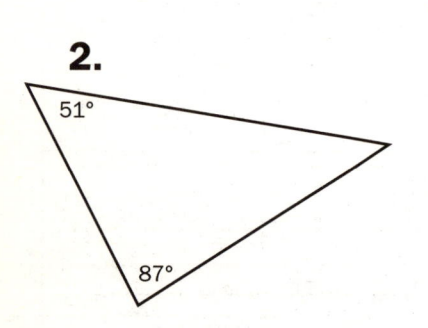

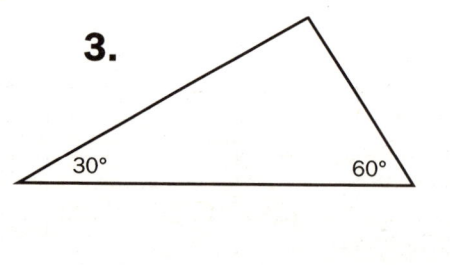

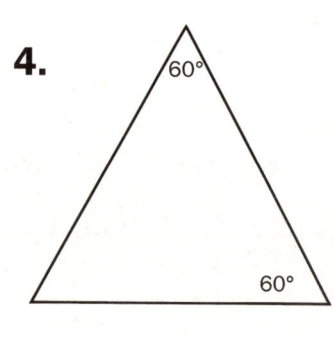

2. (triangle with angles 51°, 87°)

3. (triangle with angles 30°, 60°)

4. (triangle with angles 60°, 60°)

5. Draw an isosceles triangle.

6. Classify the triangle in #4 according to its sides.

7. Draw an obtuse triangle.

Directions: *Complete the following conversions.*
8. 4 feet = ? inches **9.** 100 yards = ? feet **10.** 18 inches = ? feet

342

AlgebraicThinking • Foundations

Warm Up 67: S-O-L-V-E

Greg won a cash prize in a contest. He donated half of the money to the Leukemia Society of America. He spent $15.31 on a used video game and $9.75 at the movies. He put the rest, $49.94, in his savings account. How much money did he win?

Lesson 67 Algebraic Thinking • Foundations

Multiplying Decimals

In today's lesson you will learn how to multiply decimals without using models. Use a calculator to multiply these decimals. When you finish, we will look for a pattern.

Problem	Product	Problem	Product
1a. 3.7 • 2.1		**1c.** 0.37 • 0.21	
1b. 0.37 • 2.1		**1d.** 3.7 • 21	
2a. 12.3 • 45		**2c.** 12.3 • 0.45	
2b. 12.3 • 4.5		**2d.** 0.123 • 0.45	
3a. 1.1 • 92		**3c.** 0.11 • 92	
3b. 11 • 9.2		**3d.** 1.1 • 0.92	
4a. 0.67 • 0.89		**4c.** 6.7 • 8.9	
4b. 6.7 • 0.89		**4d.** 6.7 • 89	
5a. 24.5 • 89		**5c.** 0.245 • 89	
5b. 2.45 • 89		**5d.** 0.245 • 8.9	

- Each set of four problems has the same digits, but different place values.

- Compare the products in each set of four problems. How are they alike? How are they different?

- Compare the number of decimal places in the problem and the number of decimal places in the product.

- Write a rule for multiplying decimals.

Algebraic Thinking • Foundations   Lesson 67

Practice it!

Directions: Find the product.

1. 1.7 • 2 =	**2.** 3.4 • 2.5 =	**3.** 2.1 • 3.5 =	**4.** 10.5 • 8 =
5. 22.8 • 3.5 =	**6.** 6 • 8.4 =	**7.** 7 • 9.2 =	**8.** 8.4 • 3.2 =
9. 0.55 • 6 =	**10.** 0.75 • 0.8 =	**11.** 0.25 • 3.7 =	**12.** 7 • 0.5 =
13. 9.9 • 3.4 =	**14.** 6.7 • 2 =	**15.** 5.5 • 2 =	**16.** 8.5 • 2 =
17. 9 • 2.5 =	**18.** 6.45 • 3.5 =	**19.** 10.2 • 0.8 =	**20.** 7.5 • 7.5 =

Lesson 67 AlgebraicThinking • Foundations

Directions: *Use a calculator to find the product. Then look for a pattern.*

21. 1.2 • 10 =   **22.** 7.98 • 100 =

23. 3.84 • 10 =   **24.** 0.4898 • 1,000 =

25. 7.8 • 100 =   **26.** 0.2 • 100 =

27. 16 • 0.1 =   **28.** 16 • 0.01 =

29. 84.3 • 0.001 =   **30.** 34.9 • 0.1 =

31. 184.9 • 0.001 =   **32.** 78.452 • 0.01 =

33. In problems 21 – 26, you multiplied by 10, 100, or 1,000. Write a shortcut rule for this.

34. In problems 27 – 32, you multiplied by 0.1, 0.01, or 0.001. Write a shortcut rule for this.

AlgebraicThinking • Foundations   Lesson 67

Directions: *Use mental math to find the product.*
35. 25.4 • 10 =   **36.** 3.78 • 1,000 =   **37.** 7.8 • 0.1 =

38. 27.3 • 0.01 =   **39.** 43.9 • 100 =   **40.** 25.4 • 0.1 =

S-O-L-V-E: *Sara bought a one-way airline ticket for $99. She will drive home in a rental car that she rented at a cost of $24.99 per day for 5 days. Her hotel costs $79.95 per night for 4 nights. What was her total cost for lodging and travel? (Ignore taxes.)*

S. _____

O. _____

L. _____

V. _____

E. _____

Homework 67 — AlgebraicThinking • Foundations

Name _____

Directions: *Find each sum or difference.*

1. 6.8 + 3.4 =

2. 15.4 − 2.57 =

3. 8.2 + 5 =

4. 28.35 − 7.6 =

5. 0.853 + 3.17 =

6. 105 + 0.235 =

7. 2.05 − 1.785 =

8. 25.4 + 7.655 =

9. 11.52 − 7.85 =

10. 23.4 − 12.32 =

AlgebraicThinking • Foundations   Warm Up 68

Warm Up 68: Tangrams!

Inside each tangram piece, write its area. What is the total area of the figure?

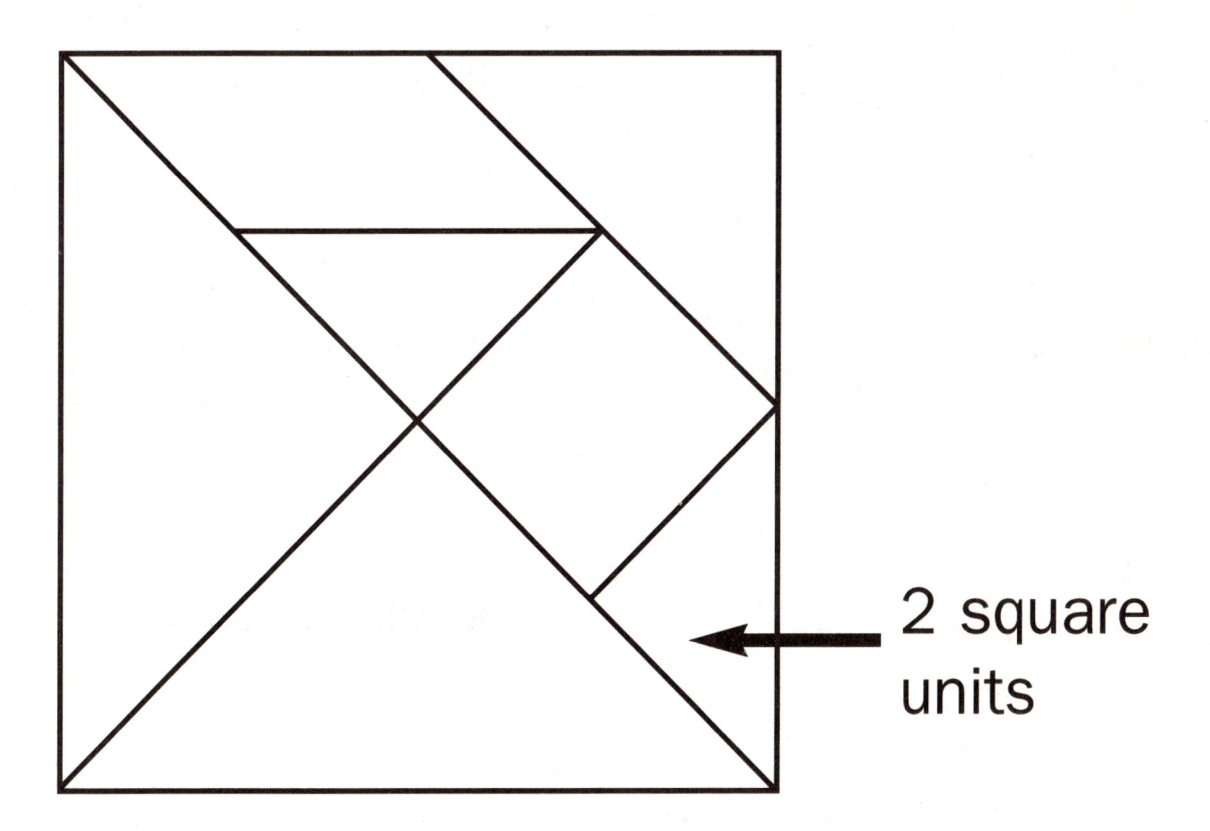

← 2 square units

Lesson 68

AlgebraicThinking • Foundations

Dividing Decimals

Today we will use models to show division by tenths and by hundredths. Complete the following models with your teacher. The first five show how to model division by tenths. Problems 6 – 10 show division by hundredths.

Problem	Model	Quotient
1. 0.8 ÷ 0.2		
2. 3.2 ÷ 0.4		
3. 0.6 ÷ 0.1		
4. 2.4 ÷ 0.8		
5. 2.4 ÷ 0.4		

AlgebraicThinking • Foundations

Lesson 68

Problem	Model	Quotient
6. 1 ÷ 0.25		
7. 1.5 ÷ 0.75		
8. 3.4 ÷ 1.7		
9. 0.75 ÷ 0.05		
10. 0.45 ÷ 0.09		

351

Lesson 68

Algebraic Thinking • Foundations

Directions: Use the model to complete each division.

Practice it!

1. 1.0 ÷ ? = 2

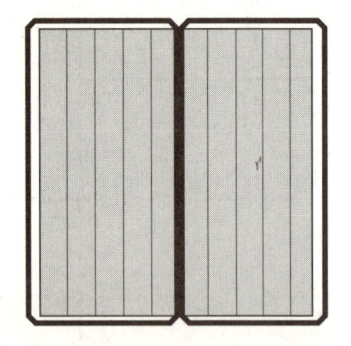

2. 0.45 ÷ 0.09 = ?

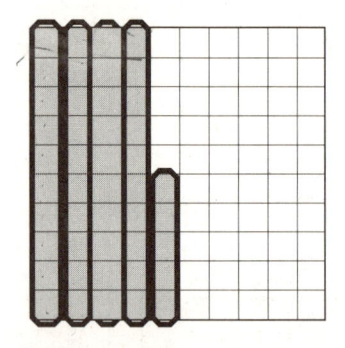

3. 1.00 ÷ 0.50 = ?

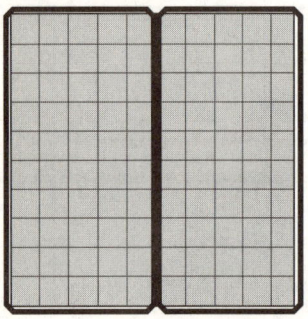

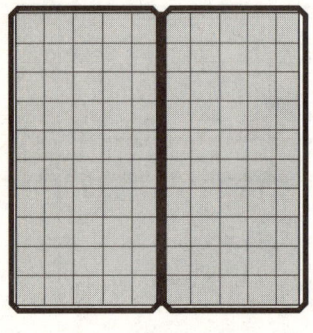

4. ? ÷ 0.25 = 3

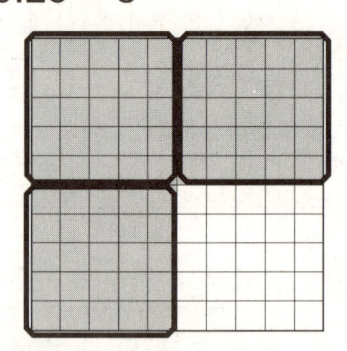

5. 2.6 ÷ 1.3 = ?

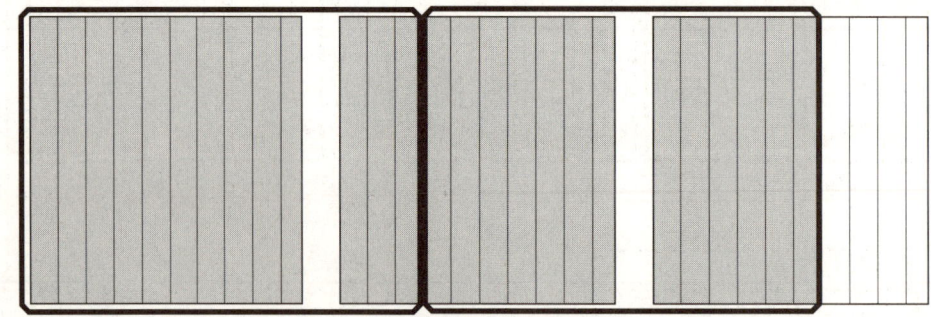

6. 4.2 ÷ ? = 7

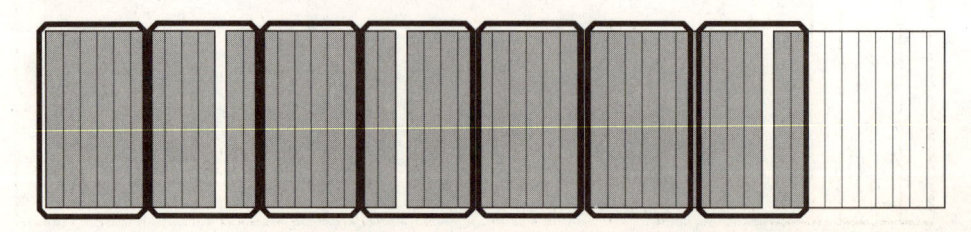

352

AlgebraicThinking • Foundations

Lesson 68

Directions: *Construct a model for each division problem. Take your time and be neat.*

7. 0.8 ÷ 0.4 =

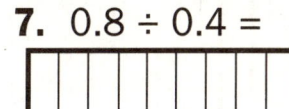

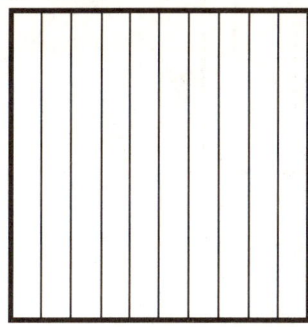

8. 1.8 ÷ 0.2 =

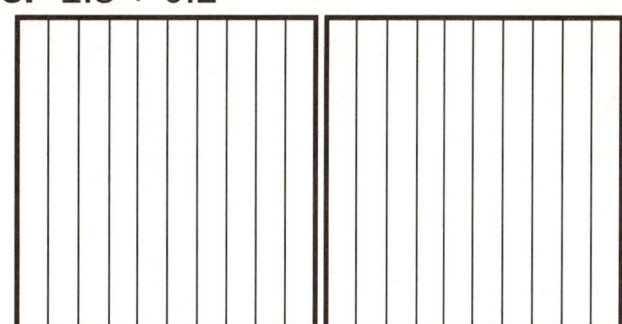

9. 3.6 ÷ 0.6 =

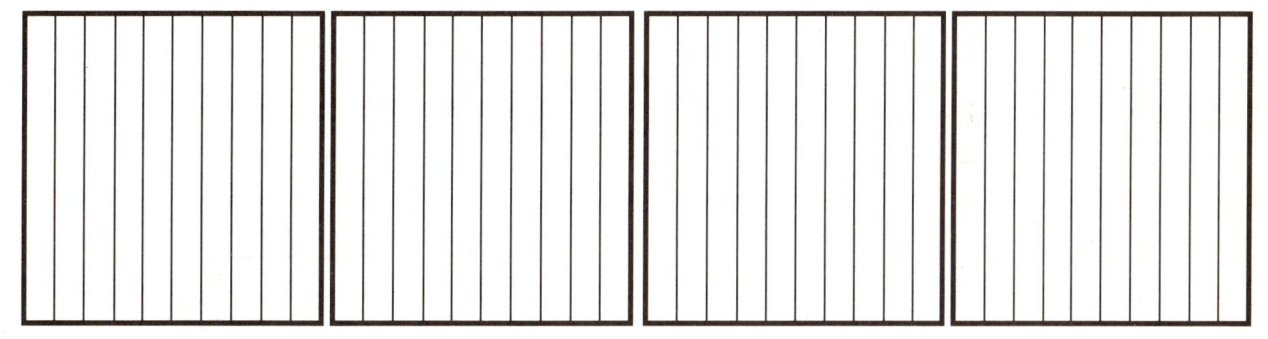

10. 2.4 ÷ 0.3 =

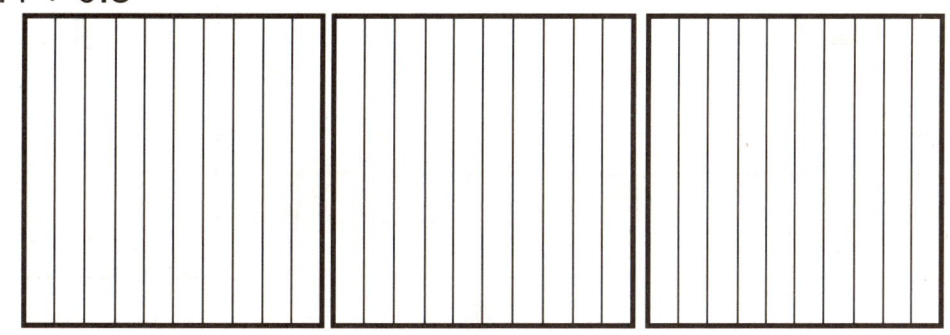

11. 2.1 ÷ 0.7 =

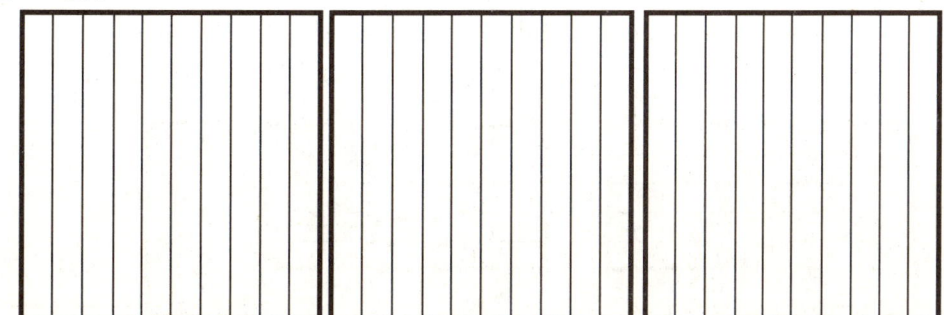

Lesson 68   Algebraic Thinking • Foundations

12. 4.8 ÷ 1.2 =

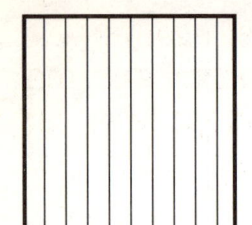

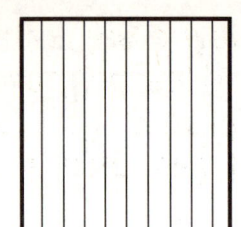

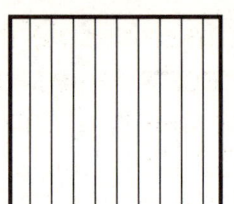

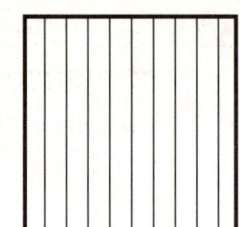

13. 0.63 ÷ 0.09 =

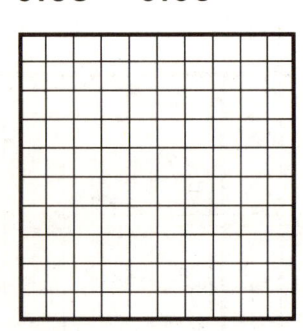

14. 0.54 ÷ 0.06 =

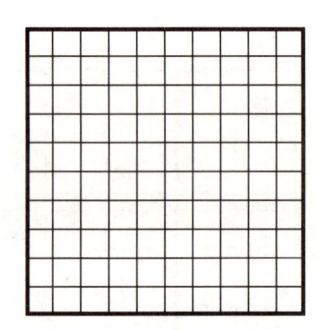

15. 2.75 ÷ 0.25 =

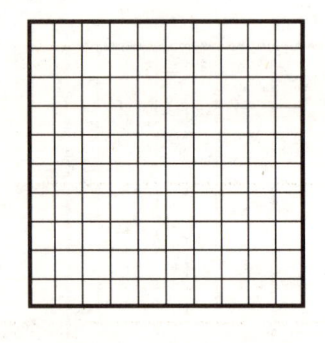

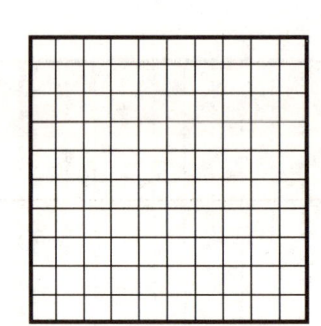

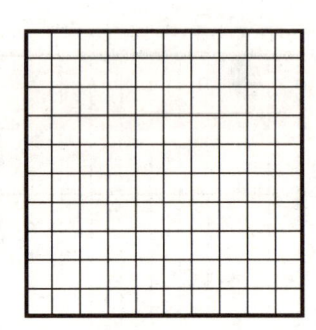

16. 1.50 ÷ 0.75 =

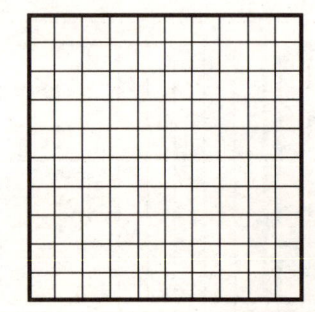

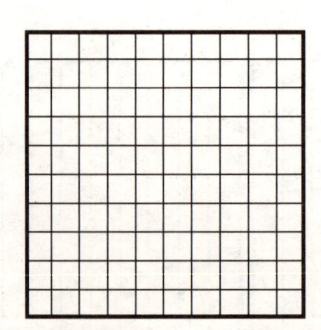

AlgebraicThinking • Foundations   Lesson 68

Directions: *Use S-O-L-V-E to solve this word problem.*

17. One thing that people consider when buying a car is fuel economy. It is measured in miles per gallon (mpg). Miles per gallon means the number of miles a car will go on one gallon of gas. Suppose a car travels 552.4 miles on 14.5 gallons of gas. How many miles per gallon did the car get?

S. _____

O. _____

L. _____

V. _____

E. _____

Homework 68 **AlgebraicThinking** • Foundations

Name _____

Directions: *Mark each statement true or false. If it is false change the underlined word to make it true.*

1. Any four-sided figure is called a(n) <u>rectangle</u>.

2. A(n) <u>scalene</u> triangle has all three sides congruent to each other.

3. A(n) <u>six</u>-sided figure is called a pentagon.

4. Any quadrilateral with opposite sides parallel can be called a(n) <u>parallelogram</u>.

5. A(n) <u>ray</u> has two endpoints.

6. Draw and label three rectangles that have an area of 24 square units.

7. Draw and label three triangles that have an area of 12 square units.

AlgebraicThinking • Foundations

Warm Up 69: Coded Message

The tallest office building in the world is in Malaysia. What is the tallest office building in the world?

N	2.3 • 4 =

O	6.1 • 10 =

A	2.5 • 0.3 =

T	12.4 – 3.5 =

W	6.1 + 2.54 =

E	0.4 • 0.9 =

S	3.2 • 7.5 =

P	27.4 + 3.8 =

R	2.5 • 4 =

$\overline{}$ $\overline{}$ $\overline{}$ $\overline{}$ $\overline{}$ $\overline{}$ $\overline{}$ $\overline{}$
31.2   0.36   8.9   10   61   9.2   0.75   24

$\overline{}$ $\overline{}$ $\overline{}$ $\overline{}$ $\overline{}$ $\overline{}$ $\overline{}$
8.9   61   8.64   0.36   10   24

Lesson 69 Algebraic Thinking • Foundations

Dividing Decimals

S-O-L-V-E: Franco's mileage check for Wednesday was $112.50. He drove 250 miles on that day. How much is he paid per mile?

S

O

L

V

E

Directions: *Practice dividing decimals by whole numbers with your teacher.*

1. 42.4 ÷ 5 =

2. 12.6 ÷ 4 =

3. 89.6 ÷ 8 =

4. 31.05 ÷ 9 =

5. 5.4 ÷ 12 =

6. 68.2 ÷ 11 =

Algebraic Thinking • Foundations   Lesson 69

Directions: Use a calculator to complete this chart and look for a pattern.

Dividend		Divisor		Quotient
12.95	÷	10	=	
12.95	÷	100	=	
12.95	÷	1,000	=	
12.95	÷	10,000	=	

✳ What happens to the quotient as the divisor increases?

✳ How is the number of zeros in the divisor related to the number of places the decimal point moves to the left?

✳ Write a shortcut rule for dividing by a multiple of 10.

✳ Use mental math to find the value of 0.98 ÷ 1,000. Explain how you got your answer.

✳ Use mental math to find the value of 3.5 ÷ 100. Explain how you got your answer.

Practice it!

Directions: Use mental math to find each quotient. Explain the method you used.

1. 7.2 ÷ 100 =

2. 127.8 ÷ 10 =

3. 13.9 ÷ 1,000 =

4. 38 ÷ 1,000 =

5. 14.95 ÷ 100 =

6. 0.024 ÷ 100 =

Lesson 69 **AlgebraicThinking • Foundations**

Directions: *Find the quotient using long division. Show your work.*

7. 27.5 ÷ 9 =   **8.** 3.85 ÷ 2 =   **9.** 27.4 ÷ 4 =

10. 16.1 ÷ 7 =   **11.** 47.4 ÷ 12 =   **12.** 37.4 ÷ 15 =

13. 206.4 ÷ 8 =   **14.** 341.1 ÷ 9 =   **15.** 64.2 ÷ 10 =

16. 157.2 ÷ 4 =   **17.** 127.35 ÷ 5 =   **18.** 224.42 ÷ 7 =

AlgebraicThinking • Foundations   Lesson 69

19. 530.4 ÷ 6 =   **20.** 39.75 ÷ 3 =   **21.** 204.8 ÷ 8 =

22. S-O-L-V-E: In March, it rained 3.3 inches. In April, it rained 2.5 inches and in May it rained 1.4 inches. What was the mean (average) rainfall for the three months?

S

O

L

V

E

Homework 69 **AlgebraicThinking** • Foundations

Name _____

Directions: *Find each sum.*

1. $\dfrac{3}{8}$
   $+\ \dfrac{1}{4}$

2. $\dfrac{4}{15}$
   $+\ \dfrac{2}{5}$

3. $\dfrac{2}{3}$
   $+\ \dfrac{3}{5}$

4. $\dfrac{7}{10}$
   $+\ \dfrac{3}{4}$

5. $\dfrac{5}{8}$
   $+\ \dfrac{3}{5}$

6. $\dfrac{2}{7}$
   $+\ \dfrac{2}{3}$

AlgebraicThinking • Foundations Warm Up 70

Warm Up 70: Composite Figure

Find the area of the composite figure.

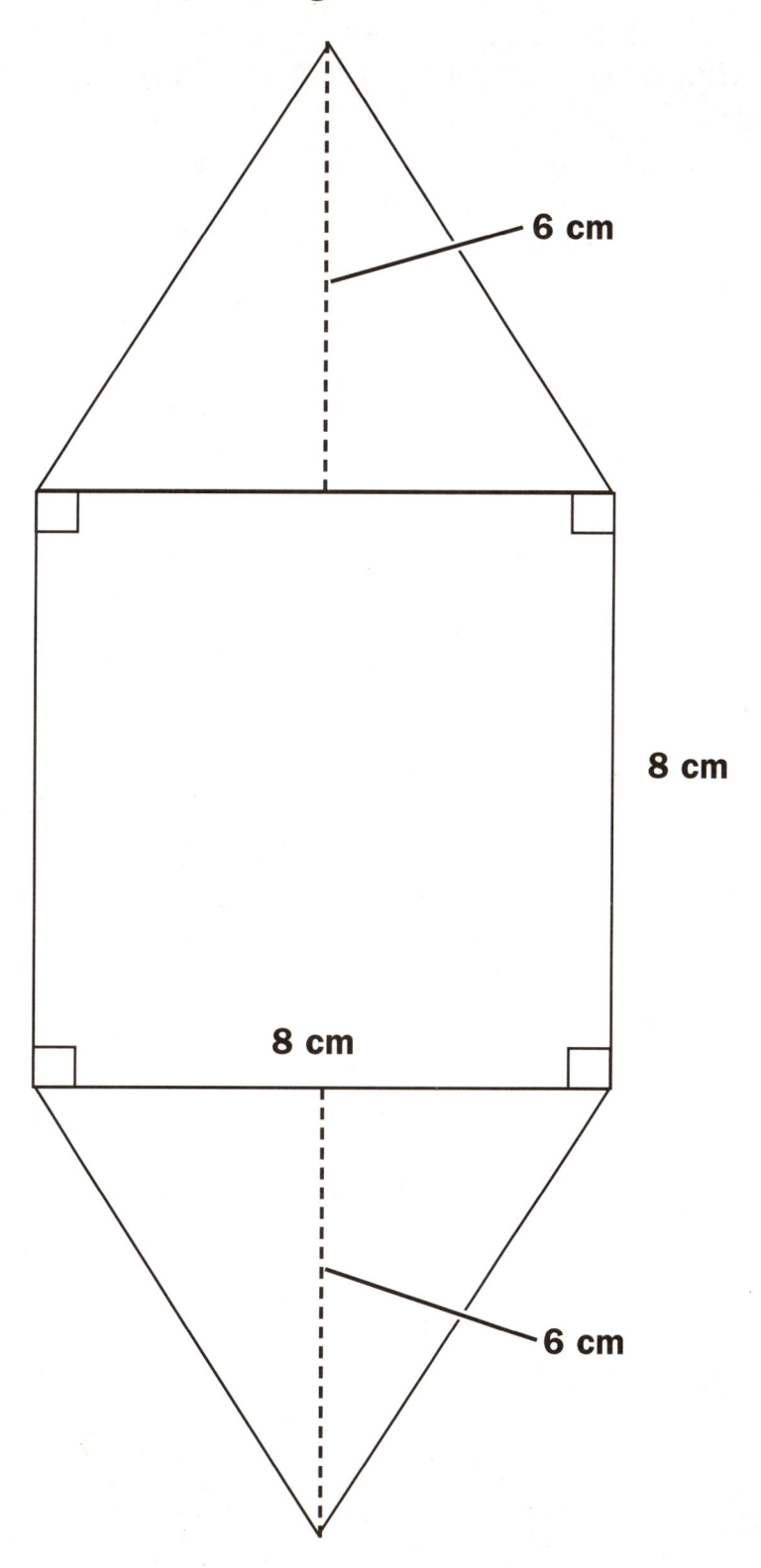

— 6 cm

8 cm

8 cm

— 6 cm

363

Dividing Decimals

S-O-L-V-E: Shannon and her family went to Grandma's house over the holidays. But, when they were about 45 miles from her house they ran out of gas. Luckily, Shannon's dad kept a gas can in the car for such emergencies. The label on the can indicates that there are 2.4 gallons of gas in it. How many miles per gallon will they have to average to make it to Grandma's house on the gas in the can?

S

O

L

V

E

Directions: *Practice dividing a decimal by a decimal with your teacher.*

1. 2.9 ÷ 0.5 =

2. 45.5 ÷ 0.25 =

3. 4.2 ÷ 1.2 =

4. 2.3 ÷ 2.3 =

AlgebraicThinking • **Foundations**　　　Lesson 70

Directions: *Use a calculator to complete this chart and look for a pattern.*

Dividend	Divisor	Quotient
12.95 ÷	0.1 =	
12.95 ÷	0.01 =	
12.95 ÷	0.001 =	
12.95 ÷	0.0001 =	

✳ What happens to the quotient as the divisor decreases?

✳ How is the number of decimal places in the divisor related to the number of places the decimal point moves to the right?

✳ Write a shortcut rule for dividing 0.1, 0.01, or 0.001.

✳ Use mental math to find the value of 0.98 ÷ 0.01. Explain how you got your answer.

✳ Use mental math to find the value of 3.5 ÷ 0.1. Explain how you got your answer.

Practice it!

Directions: *Use mental math to find each quotient. Explain the method you used.*

1. 10.45 ÷ 0.1 =　　　**2.** 10.45 ÷ 0.01 =

3. 164.2 ÷ 0.001 =　　**4.** 164.2 ÷ 0.0001 =

Lesson 70 Algebraic Thinking • Foundations

Directions: *Find the quotient using long division. Show your work*

5. 27 ÷ 0.25 =	**6.** 88 ÷ 1.1 =	**7.** 5.6 ÷ 0.8 =
8. 3.21 ÷ 0.3 =	**9.** 10.8 ÷ 0.12 =	**10.** 3 ÷ 0.05 =
11. 8.4 ÷ 0.07 =	**12.** 0.28 ÷ 0.04 =	**13.** 16 ÷ 0.2 =
14. 7 ÷ 0.8 =	**15.** 9 ÷ 0.2 =	**16.** 15.66 ÷ 9 =

Algebraic Thinking • Foundations Lesson 70

17. 135.75 ÷ 2.5 =	18. 248.96 ÷ 6.4 =	19. 2.0945 ÷ 7.1 =

20. S-O-L-V-E: Matthew bought $17.22 worth of gas. His father told him to write the number of gallons he put in the car, but he forgot. Matthew does remember that the gas cost $2.46 per gallon. How many gallons did he buy? Round your answer to the nearest tenth.

S

O

L

V

E

367

Homework 70   **AlgebraicThinking • Foundations**

Name _____

Directions: *Find each sum or difference.*

1. 18 + 0.35 =

2. 22 – 0.65 =

3. 22.09 – 3.2 =

4. 38.25 + 2.8 =

5. 3.5 + 6.55 =

6. 100 – 75.8 =

7. 10.78 + 3.32 =

8. 19.8 – 3.4 =

9. 17.2 – 3.25 =

10. 4.9 + 25.28 =

AlgebraicThinking • Foundations

Warm Up 71: Making the Grade

Shade the answers to the following problems on the chart below.

1. 6.7 + 0.06 + 2 + 0.5

2. 4.3 • 0.03

3. 8.9 − 3.27

4. 9.6 ÷ 0.6

5. 4 − 0.12

6. 5 • 0.34

7. 0.27 + 5 + 0.3

8. 0.048 ÷ 0.02

9. 3.05 • 4

10. 9.12 ÷ 6

8	0.001	0.21	2.6	0.5	26	55.7
3.2	10.3	64	3.88	8.5	69	18
0.04	0.111	0.129	12.2	9.26	87	0.563
10	1.7	2.4	5.57	1.52	16	0.24
12.2	1.22	12.9	77	0.2	92.6	5.63
6.9	0.065	35	21	15.2	1.29	0.69
0.152	15	1.6	0.17	0.122	4	0.557

Lesson 71   Algebraic Thinking • Foundations

Directions: *DECIMAL TRAIL – follow the trail by performing operations with decimals.*

6.3 ÷ 3 = ____

　　　　+ 2.7 = ____

　　　　　• 1.2 = ____

　　　　　　− 2.26 = ____

　　　　　　+ 8.7 = ____

　　　　　　　÷ 4 = ____

　　　　　　　　− 0.33 = ____

　　　　　　　　　• 3.5 = ____

　　　　　　　　　　− 2.048 = ____

　　　　　　　　　　　÷ 2 = ____

　　　　　　　　　　+ 2.004 = ____

　　　　　　　　　• 3.5 = ____

　　　　　　　− 12.58 = ____

　　　　　　÷ 2.5 = ____

　　　　　+ 2.496 = ____

　　　　• 3.2 = ____

　　　• 0.2 = ____

÷ 5.5 = ____

AlgebraicThinking • Foundations   Lesson 71

Directions: *DECIMAL CIRCUIT – get a final answer in each circuit.*

1. Start at 0.3, DOWN 3, RIGHT 5, multiply.
2. Start at 6, LEFT 4, DOWN 2, RIGHT 2, DOWN 1, divide first number into last.
3. Start at 21.3, DOWN 5, RIGHT 3, UP 2, subtract.
4. In row 6, add every second number.
5. Start at 98, RIGHT 2, UP 5, RIGHT 3, multiply.
6. Start at 0.113, RIGHT 2, DOWN 3, RIGHT 2, UP 1, subtract smaller number from larger.
7. In the third column, divide the last number by the second number.
8. In the fifth row, multiply the fifth number by the fifth number in the seventh row.
9. Start at 101, RIGHT 2, UP 4, divide the last number into the first.
10. Add all the numbers in the fifth column.

2.9	5.07	50	10	11.9	0.21	0.24	0.90
43	21.3	0.9	40	0.61	56.1	8	66
7.8	58	4.9	0.33	0.407	15	1.8	0.7
100	0.3	0.113	500	3.5	1.89	25	251
1.03	23	60	9	0.156	7	4.8	6
13	0.96	98	0.136	7.21	4	1.81	34
0.41	101	80	0.34	45	0.112	67	20
5	41	1	0.97	0.68	0.03	179	0.12

DECIMAL DICE
Rules

1. You will get three dice from your teacher. After this, each person should roll one of the die. The one who rolls the highest number is Player #1. The other will be Player #2.

2. Each player will need a piece of scratch paper to do computations. You will put a decimal in front of each number on the dice. For example, 1 is now 0.1, 2 is 0.2, 3 is 0.3, etc. The dice may be this way already. If not, don't forget that part.

3. Player #1 should roll the three dice. Choose two of them and perform any operation (addition, subtraction, multiplication, or division) with them. Record the answer.

4. Roll the one remaining die that you did not use before and perform an operation with that number and the answer from the previous operation. Record the answer in the chart below.

5. Player #2 should repeat steps 3 and 4. The highest answer wins the round. The player who wins more rounds, wins the game.

Round Number	Player #1 _____	Player #2 _____	Round Winner
1			
2			
3			
4			
5			
6			
7			
8			
		Game Winner	

AlgebraicThinking • Foundations

Warm Up 72

Warm Up 72: Finished Product

Fill in the top border of the chart with the numbers from the box and the left border with the numbers 1 – 6 so that the products inside the chart are in the correct spot. Then complete the inside of the chart.

| 0.25 | 0.5 | 0.6 | 1.5 | 2.5 | 3.5 |

X			1.5			
	5					1.2
	10				1	
			4.5		0.75	
		3		21		
		2.5				3
				3.5	0.25	

Warm Up 73: Find the Missing Angle

Find the measure of angle *x*.

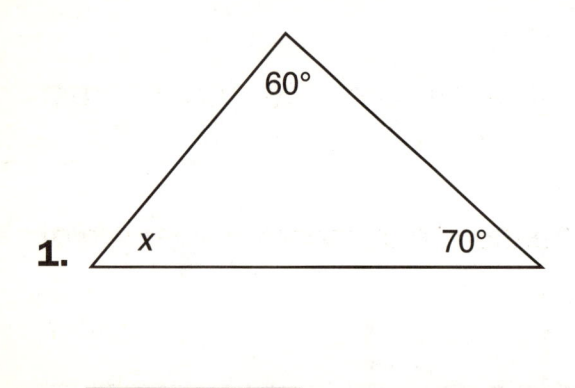

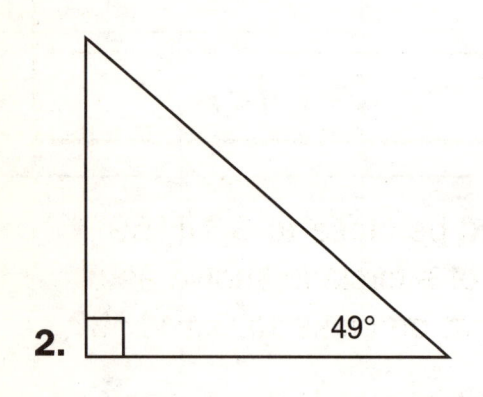

1. [Triangle with angles 60°, 70°, and *x*]

   _____

2. [Right triangle with a 90° angle and a 49° angle]

   _____

AlgebraicThinking • Foundations Lesson 73

Circles – Area and Circumference

Circumference is the **perimeter** of a circle. To complete this activity, you will need several round objects, some string, the table below, and a measuring device.

1. Measure and record the diameter of each circle to the nearest **millimeter.**

2. Wrap a string around the object and measure and record the length of the string to the nearest millimeter.

Object	Diameter (d)	Circumference (C)	$\frac{C}{d}$

Each of the numbers in the last column should be close to 3.14159. The ratio of the circumference to the diameter of a circle is known as pi (π). What are some reasons that they might not be close to 3.14159?

Circumference Formula

Since $\frac{C}{d} = \pi$, then $C = \pi d$.

Lesson 73   Algebraic Thinking • Foundations

3. With your compass, make a circle with a radius of approximately three inches. Cut out your circular region.

4. Fold your circle in half. Color each half a different color. Fold it in half a second time. Fold it in half again. Ok, last time, fold it in half again.

5. Unfold your circle and cut out the 16 sectors (wedges).

6. Arrange the sectors in a row, alternating tips up and down. What shape does the figure represent?

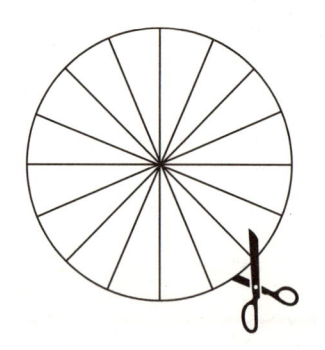

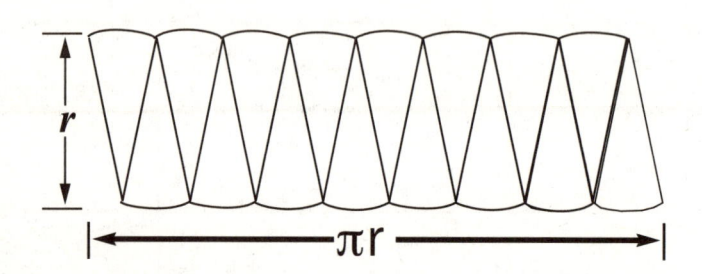

7. If we had folded the circle more, our shape would look more like a parallelogram.

8. What is the formula for the area of a parallelogram?

    $A = $ _____

9. Substitute the values for the "parallelogram" above into the formula and simplify.

    $A = $ _____

AlgebraicThinking • Foundations   Lesson 73

Directions: Try these! Find the area and circumference of each circle. Use 3.14 for pi (π).

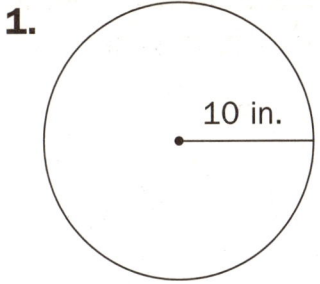

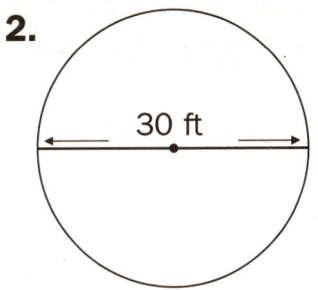

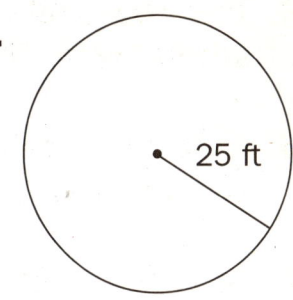

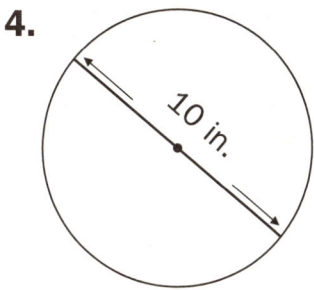

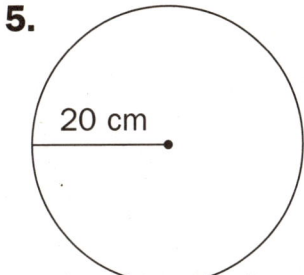

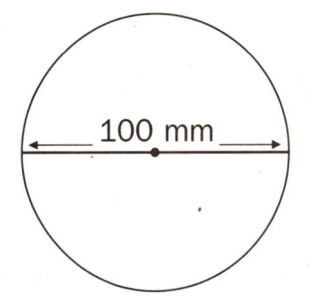

1. 10 in. (radius)

2. 30 ft (diameter)

3. 25 ft (radius)

4. 10 in. (diameter)

5. 20 cm (radius)

6. 100 mm (diameter)

7. **S-O-L-V-E:** A circular lawn sprinkler can spray water a distance of 7 feet when the water is on high. How much area can it water?

8. **S-O-L-V-E:** A fringe is to be sewn on a circular rug. The rug has a radius of 5 feet. How much fringe is needed?

Homework 73　　　　　　　　　　**AlgebraicThinking** • Foundations

Name _____

Directions: *Find each product. Write the answer in simplest form.*

1. $\frac{1}{2} \cdot \frac{4}{5} =$ 　　　　2. $\frac{2}{3} \cdot \frac{5}{8} =$ 　　　　3. $\frac{7}{16} \cdot \frac{7}{10} =$

4. $2\frac{3}{4} \cdot 2 =$ 　　　　5. $3\frac{5}{8} \cdot \frac{3}{16} =$ 　　　　6. $\frac{3}{4} \cdot \frac{8}{9} =$

Algebraic Thinking • Foundations   Warm Up 74

Warm Up 74: Toss Up

Kayla played a game of Toss Up. She threw 5 bean bags and hit the target below each time. Her final score was 60 points. Draw on the target below where the 5 bean bags hit.

20
15
11
9
8

Lesson 74 **AlgebraicThinking • Foundations**

Today we are going to start out looking at some patterns. Look at the first few lines in the chart and see if you can complete the charts using the same pattern.

10	10	10^1
100	10 • 10	10^2
1,000	10 • 10 • 10	10^3
10,000		
100,000		
1,000,000		
10,000,000		

50	5.0 • 10	5.0 • 10^1
500	5.0 • 100	5.0 • 10^2
5,000	5.0 • 1,000	5.0 • 10^3
50,000		
500,000		
5,000,000		
50,000,000		

56	5.6 • 10	5.6 • 10^1
560	5.6 • 100	5.6 • 10^2
5,600	5.6 • 1,000	5.6 • 10^3
56,000		
560,000		
5,600,000		
56,000,000		

Algebraic Thinking • Foundations

Lesson 74

Looking at the charts, what pattern do you see?

_____

Writing very large numbers as multiples of ten is called scientific notation. Using the charts to help, write the following numbers in scientific notation.

1. 4,000

2. 6,000,000

3. 12,000

4. 30,000,000

5. 420,000,000,000

To write a large number in scientific notation _____

_____.

Lesson 74 **Algebraic Thinking** • Foundations

Scientists need a way to write very small numbers as a multiple of ten as well. Look at the first few lines in the chart and see if you can complete the charts using the same pattern.

0.1	$\frac{1}{10}$	10^{-1}
0.01	$\frac{1}{100}$	10^{-2}
0.001	$\frac{1}{1,000}$	10^{-3}
0.0001		
0.00001		
0.000001		
0.0000001		

0.5	$5.0 \cdot \frac{1}{10}$	$5.0 \cdot 10^{-1}$
0.05	$5.0 \cdot \frac{1}{100}$	$5.0 \cdot 10^{-2}$
0.005	$5.0 \cdot \frac{1}{1,000}$	$5.0 \cdot 10^{-3}$
0.0005		
0.00005		
0.000005		
0.0000005		

AlgebraicThinking • Foundations

0.56	$5.6 \cdot \frac{1}{10}$	$5.6 \cdot 10^{-1}$
0.056	$5.6 \cdot \frac{1}{100}$	$5.6 \cdot 10^{-2}$
0.0056	$5.6 \cdot \frac{1}{1,000}$	$5.6 \cdot 10^{-3}$
0.00056		
0.000056		
0.0000056		
0.00000056		

Lesson 74

AlgebraicThinking • Foundations

What pattern do you see in the second set of charts? _____

_____

Using the charts to help, write the following numbers in scientific notation.

1. 0.000006

2. 0.00003

3. 0.000000000007

4. 0.0000045

5. 0.0000000063

To write a small number in scientific notation _____

_____

_____.

AlgebraicThinking • Foundations   Homework 74

Name _____

Directions: *Find each quotient.*

1. 24 ÷ 0.8 =   **2.** 3.7 ÷ 0.01 =

3. 40.5 ÷ 10 =   **4.** 84 ÷ 2.5 =

5. 15 ÷ 0.5 =   **6.** 19.95 ÷ 0.7 =

7. 151.2 ÷ 0.56 =   **8.** 12.8 ÷ 0.2 =

9. 0.32 ÷ 0.08 =   **10.** 43.2 ÷ 100 =

Warm Up 75

Warm Up 75: Decimal Trail

Directions: Follow the trail from top to bottom. Use the answer as the first number in the next problem.

20.09 ÷ 3.5 = ____

        – 2.004 = ____

                • 2 = ____

                      + 2.048 = ____

                            ÷ 3.5 = ____

                    + 0.33 = ____

                • 4 = ____

          – 8.7 = ____

+ 2.26 = ____

        ÷ 1.2 = ____

              – 2.7 = ____

                    • 3 = ____

AlgebraicThinking • Foundations

Lesson 75

Directions: *Follow along with your teacher to complete the problems below.*

1. The earth is 93,000,000 miles away from the sun.

2. The diameter of a protozoan is approximately 0.0000002 kilometers.

3. Pluto is 5,914,300,000 kilometers from the sun.

4. The weight of a molecule of oxygen is 0.000000000000000000005 gram.

5. Jupiter has a diameter of 142,700 kilometers.

6. An electron weighs 0.0000000000000000000000009 gram.

7. A light year is about 6,000,000,000,000 miles.

8. Copper wire pairs used in telephone transmissions, 0.000643 millimeter in diameter, can carry 24 simultaneous conversations.

9. A nanosecond is 0.000000001 of one second.

Lesson 75 AlgebraicThinking • Foundations

Directions: *Write each number below in scientific notation.*

Scientific Notation

1. One bacterium can produce over 16 million new bacteria in twenty-four hours.

2. The diameter of a single bacterium is about 0.00003937 of an inch.

3. 60

4. 4,000

5. 89,000

6. 0.0038

7. 0.0000125

8. 9.6 million

9. 0.0002

10. 58 billion

11. 750,000

12. 5,800

13. 267.8 million

14. 0.0712

AlgebraicThinking • Foundations Homework 75

Name _____

Directions: *Find each quotient.*

1. 20.4 ÷ 3 =

2. 12.1 ÷ 4 =

3. 8.4 ÷ 5 =

4. 25.7 ÷ 100 =

5. 56.1 ÷ 6 =

6. 337.4 ÷ 7 =

7. 10.4 ÷ 2 =

8. 31.79 ÷ 11 =

9. 7.84 ÷ 10 =

10. 143.2 ÷ 8 =

Warm Up 76: Choose a Duo

Pick two of the four numbers and create a division problem with the greatest possible quotient. Write the number sentence and solve it. Show your work.

1. 20, 4, $\frac{1}{2}$, $\frac{1}{4}$

2. 12, 6, $\frac{1}{3}$, $\frac{1}{5}$

3. 10, 2, $\frac{1}{6}$, $\frac{1}{2}$

4. 15, 5, $\frac{1}{2}$, $\frac{3}{4}$

5. 5, 7, $\frac{1}{10}$, $\frac{1}{4}$

Algebraic Thinking • Foundations

Lesson 76

Writing and Evaluating Variable Expressions

Make a list of words that have to do with each operation.

Variable
A variable is a letter or other symbol that stands for an unknown number.

Addition	Multiplication
Subtraction	Division

Directions: *Match each word phrase to the appropriate algebraic expression.*

1. The sum of a number and 2
2. A number less than 5
3. Twice a number
4. The quotient of a number and 10
5. The difference of a number and 2
6. A number divided by 3
7. 9 times a number
8. 6 less than a number
9. The product of 5 and a number
10. 8 more than a number

A. $2n$
B. $n - 2$
C. $5n$
D. $n + 2$
E. $9n$
F. $n + 8$
G. $5 - n$
H. $n - 6$
I. $n \div 10$
J. $\dfrac{n}{3}$

Lesson 76 AlgebraicThinking • Foundations

The treasurer of the school choir delivered this fundraiser report to the members of the choir. "We earned twice the money we earned last year. We sold 150 more carnations this year and 25 less roses. Because of the success, each student will have to pay $\frac{2}{5}$ of what they paid last year to go on a field trip."

11. Pick a variable for each of the following things. (A variable can be any letter or symbol.)

   a. money earned last year _____

   b. carnations sold last year _____

   c. roses sold last year _____

   d. cost of last year's field trip _____

12. Write a variable expression for the following things. (Use the variables from #11.)

   a. money earned this year _____

   b. carnations sold this year _____

   c. roses sold this year _____

   d. cost of this year's field trip _____

13. Evaluate those expressions with this information: Last year the choir raised $640. They sold 420 carnations and 60 roses. Each person that went on the trip paid $27 last year.

   a. money made this year _____

   b. carnations sold this year _____

   c. roses sold this year _____

   d. cost of this year's field trip _____

Algebraic Thinking • Foundations

Lesson 76

Practice it!

Directions: Write two phrases for each algebraic expression.

1. $n + 7$
2. $8n$
3. $n - 4$
4. $\frac{2}{3}n$
5. $12 - n$
6. $\frac{n}{5}$

Directions: Write an algebraic expression for each verbal expression.

7. 14 less than n
8. $\frac{3}{4}$ of a number
9. 4 decreased by a number
10. 3 more than n
11. the quotient of 15 and a number
12. the difference of n and 12

Directions: Evaluate each of the following expressions for the value of the variable.

13. $n + 8$ $n = 12$
14. $x - 3$ $x = 10$
15. $t - 8$ $t = 15$
16. $4y$ $y = 6$
17. $a \div 10$ $a = 25$
18. $n + 4.2$ $n = 3.1$
19. $7b$ $b = 3$
20. $9 - z$ $z = 5$
21. $\frac{5n}{3}$ $n = 6$

Homework 76 **AlgebraicThinking** • Foundations

Name _____

Directions: *Find each product.*

1. 2 • 0.7 =

2. 3 • 0.85 =

3. 4.1 • 0.5 =

4. 5 • 0.75 =

5. 3.8 • 0.4 =

6. 5.8 • 4 =

7. 0.6 • 0.5 =

8. 4.7 • 0.3 =

9. 0.5 • 0.9 =

10. 7 • 0.8 =

AlgebraicThinking • **Foundations**   Warm Up 77

Warm Up 77: Pyramid Challenge!

Directions: Add your way up the pyramid.
(**HINT:** Put all of the numbers in the same form.)

                              _____

                   _____   _____

         _____   _____   _____

_____   _____   _____   _____

0.75 $1\frac{1}{2}$ 0.3 $\frac{4}{5}$ $\frac{5}{2}$

395

Lesson 77   **AlgebraicThinking • Foundations**

Verbal and Variable Expressions

Directions: *Follow along with your teacher to complete the following problems.*

1. The number of dogs decreased by 14. _____

2. 3 • m or 3m _____

3. Seven taken from a number. _____

4. k + 5 _____

5. Six more than the number of girls. _____

6. 13 – q _____

7. The product of four and g. _____

8. r ÷ 2 _____

9. The total number of boys less than the number of boys wearing green.
   _____

10. b + k _____

AlgebraicThinking • Foundations   Homework 77

Name _____

Directions: *Answer each question. Show your work and any formulas that you use.*

1. Find the circumference of a circle that has a diameter of 18 inches.

2. What are the dimensions of a square with an area of 64 cm²?

3. Sketch and label two rectangles with an area of 100 m².

4. What is the area of a circle that has a radius of 4 feet?

5. What is the perimeter of a rectangle that has an area of 48 cm² and a height of 12 cm?

Warm Up 78: Addition Pyramid

Add your way up the pyramid!

```
                    ____
                ____    ____
            ____    ____    ____
        ____    ____    ____    ____
        0.7     2.2     3       1.1     0.02
```

AlgebraicThinking • Foundations   Lesson 78

Scavenger Hunt

Directions:
1. Begin at the poster that the teacher instructs.
2. Evaluate the expression on the poster.
3. Find another poster that has the value of your expression at the bottom of the poster.
4. Keep going through each of the posters, always moving to the one that has the value to the expression you just evaluated.
5. Be sure to show all work and record the order in which you traveled from one poster to the next.

$$a = 4 \qquad b = 6 \qquad c = 12$$

1. Poster _____   2. Poster _____

3. Poster _____   4. Poster _____

5. Poster _____   6. Poster _____

7. Poster _____   8. Poster _____

Lesson 78   **Algebraic**Thinking • Foundations

9. Poster _____   10. Poster _____

11. Poster _____   12. Poster _____

13. Poster _____   14. Poster _____

15. Poster _____

AlgebraicThinking • Foundations

Warm Up 79: Coded Message

Work through each problem below. For each problem, write the letter of the alphabet that corresponds with the answer in the blank above the number. (A = 1, B = 2, C = 3, D = 4, and so on.)

1. 45 − 37 = _____　　　　　2. 25 ÷ 5 = _____

3. 5^2 = _____　　　　　　　4. 3 • 3 = _____

5. 44 − 22 = _____　　　　　6. 35 ÷ 7 = _____

7. 11 − 4 = _____　　　　　　8. 100 − 85 = _____

9. 6 + 14 = _____　　　　　　10. 3^2 = _____

11. 5 • 4 = _____　　　　　　　12. 28 ÷ 2 = _____

13. 3 • 5 = _____　　　　　　　14. 69 ÷ 3 = _____

___ ___ ___! ___'___ ___   ___ ___ ___   ___ ___   ___ ___ ___!
 1   2   3   4 5   6   7   8   9   10 11   12 13 14

Warm Up 80: Opposites

Directions: *Write the opposite of each word in the list.*

Hot	Big
Over	Rough
Day	Loud
Old	Bright
Good	Up
North	Happy
West	Dry
Above	Color TV
In	Add
On	Multiply
Tall	High
Fast	Exciting
Destroy	Positive

Algebraic Thinking • Foundations Lesson 80

TOUCHDOWN!

Directions: Cut apart the strip of integers at the bottom of the page. Place them in a cup. Decide who will go first and put one marker for each player on the start space.

If you draw a positive integer, you move forward (right) that many spaces.
If you draw a negative integer, you move backward (left) that many spaces.

If you go off the board on the WIN end, you get 7 points. If you go off the board on the LOSE end, your opponent gets 7 points. Keep score in the box as you go.

Any time someone goes off the board, both players should return to start.

| ⁻6 | ⁻5 | ⁻4 | ⁻3 | ⁻2 | ⁻1 | 0 START | ⁺1 | ⁺2 | ⁺3 | ⁺4 | ⁺5 | ⁺6 | WIN |

SCORES

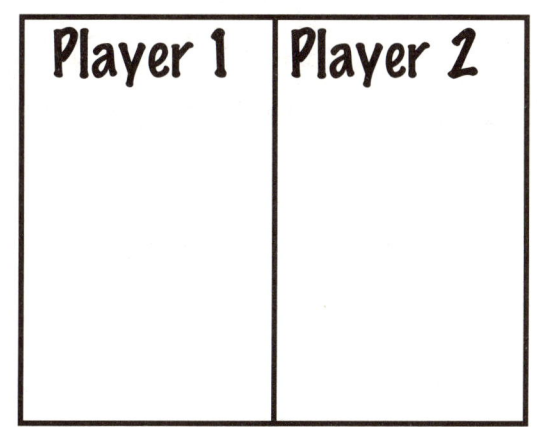

Player 1	Player 2

| ⁻3 | ⁻2 | ⁻1 | 1 | 2 | 3 |

Lesson 80   **AlgebraicThinking** • Foundations

Comparing and Ordering Integers

-7 -6 -5 -4 -3 -2 -1 0 1 2 3 4 5 6 7

Have you ever heard someone say, "It's freezing cold"? When the temperature gets below 0°C, it is considered freezing. In South Texas, the temperature rarely gets that cold. When the temperature is colder than 0°C, you have to use negative numbers. Negative numbers are less than _____.

In today's warm-up, you wrote some opposites. Here are some more. Negative 7 is the opposite of positive 7. Negative 2 is the opposite of positive 2. What is the opposite of positive 5? _____

These numbers we are talking about are called integers. Integers are _____. The numbers 5 and ⁻5 are opposites because they are both the same distances away from zero. The number 5 is 5 units away from zero and the number ⁻5 is 5 units away from zero. On a number line the distance a number is away from zero is called its _____. You write "the absolute value of negative 5" as |⁻5|.

1. Write out |⁻3| in words. Then find its value.

2. What two numbers have an absolute value of 6?

3. The absolute value cannot be ⁻7. Why not?

404

Algebraic Thinking • Foundations   Lesson 80

Directions: *For questions 4 – 5, consider the following information. Six people played golf twice a week during the summer and during the winter. Their average scores are given in the table below.*

Person	Summer Average	Winter Average
Brenda	⁺5	⁺8
Brian	⁺11	⁺7
Carol	⁺2	⁻4
Misty	⁻3	⁺1
Regina	⁺3	⁻1
Steve	⁻7	⁻6

4. Draw a number line and graph the average scores for the summer on the number line.

5. Draw a number line and graph the average scores from the winter on the number line.

6. In golf, the lower the score, the better. Who had the best score? Who had the worst score? Which person improved the most from the summer to the winter?

7. The elevators in a building let passengers off in a parking garage 20 feet below the ground. Write an integer to represent this.

8. The temperature in Gunnison, Colorado is sometimes 40 degrees below zero. Write an integer to represent this.

9. The temperature on the side of the moon facing the earth is 270°F. Write an integer to represent this.

Directions: *Make each number sentence true by using one of the following math verbs: <, >, or =. (You might want to draw a number line.)*

10. 4 ⁻4   11. 0 ⁻4   12. 1 ⁻12   13. ⁻8 ⁻10

14. |⁻8| 8   15. ⁻19 0   16. ⁻4 5   17. 4 ⁻5

405

Homework 80   **AlgebraicThinking • Foundations**

Name _____

Directions: *Translate each word phrase into an algebraic expression.*

1. Eight more points than team B

2. Three years younger than Sam

3. Nine degrees hotter than yesterday

4. Five times a number increased by eight

5. The number of pizzas divided by four

Directions: *S-O-L-V-E the following problem.*

6. A couple of painters need to know which ladder to bring to a building they are going to paint. They hope they can bring the shorter ladder that is 20 feet long. It's easier to carry around. Before they decide, they have to know how tall the building is. Rick, who thinks he is the smarter of the two painters, decides to get his yardstick out. He places it perpendicular to the ground and discovers that the yardstick's shadow is $6\frac{1}{2}$ feet long. Joseph, not wanting to be outdone, measures the length of the building's shadow. It is 50 feet long. How tall is the building? Do they have to bring the longer ladder?

Algebraic Thinking • Foundations

Warm Up 81: Coded Message

What is the hardest substance in the human body?

L   125 ÷ 5 =

O   5 • 14 =

T   123 − 78 =

A   216 ÷ 8 =

E   26 + 57 =

H   129 • 3 =

N   93 − 67 =

T   180 ÷ 12 =

M   452 + 358 =

E   255 − 209 =

O   13 • 65 =

___   ___   ___   ___   ___
15   70   845   45   387

___   ___   ___   ___   ___   ___
83   26   27   810   46   25

Adding Integers

Directions: Using 2-color counters, model each problem with your teacher. Look for some patterns that will help you when adding integers.

1. $^+6 + {}^+2 =$

2. $^+4 + {}^+3 =$

3. $^+3 + {}^+1 =$

4. $^-4 + {}^-2 =$

5. $^-7 + {}^-2 =$

6. $^-5 + {}^-2 =$

AlgebraicThinking • Foundations Lesson 81

7. $^+5 + {}^-2 =$

8. $^+4 + {}^-1 =$

9. $^-8 + {}^+10 =$

10. $^-6 + {}^+2 =$

11. $^-6 + {}^+9 =$

12. $^+5 + {}^-9 =$

13. $^+4 + {}^-7 =$

Lesson 81   Algebraic Thinking • Foundations

Practice it!   **Directions:** *Find the sum in each problem. Draw a model for each of the first 10 problems. Don't forget to take out the zero pairs!*

1. ⁻9 + 7 =	2. ⁻4 + ⁻6 =
3. 10 + ⁻8 =	4. 3 + 7 =
5. 1 + ⁻4 =	6. ⁻4 + ⁻4 =
7. ⁻3 + 3 =	8. 7 + ⁻7 =
9. ⁻2 + ⁻3 =	10. ⁻3 + 8 =

410

AlgebraicThinking • Foundations

Lesson 81

Directions: *Find the sum in each problem. You don't have to draw a model. However, you may if you want to.*

11. ⁻8 + ⁻9 =

12. ⁻4 + 7 =

13. ⁻4 + 12 =

14. 10 + ⁻3 =

15. ⁻17 + ⁻3 =

16. 12 + 5 =

17. ⁻19 + 19 =

18. ⁻12 + 0 =

19. ⁻25 + ⁻25 =

20. ⁻3 + 27 =

21. 17 + 14 =

22. 15 + ⁻22 =

Lesson 81 Algebraic Thinking • Foundations

Directions: *Use S-O-L-V-E to solve this problem. Try to use addition to solve each problem.*

23. In golf, the lower the score the better. Negative scores are the best ones to have! In some tournaments, the players play four rounds. The final score is determined by adding the scores from all four rounds. What would be the final score for a person who scored ⁺3, ⁻4, ⁻5, and ⁺2?

S. _____

_____

O. _____

_____

L. _____

_____

V. _____

_____

E. _____

_____

AlgebraicThinking • Foundations Lesson 81

24. Sammy scored ⁺4 in both the first and second rounds of a 3-round golf tournament. He scored a ⁻3 in the final round. What was his total score?

S. _____

_____

O. _____

_____

L. _____

_____

V. _____

_____

E. _____

_____

413

Lesson 81

AlgebraicThinking • Foundations

25. After Sammy finished his round of golf, he went home and decided to see how his stocks were doing. He has three different stocks. Only one of them went up. It was stock in a microchip company. It rose 2 points. The two athletic supply company stocks both dropped 3 points each. What was the overall change in Sammy's stocks?

S. _____

O. _____

L. _____

V. _____

E. _____

414

AlgebraicThinking • Foundations Homework 81

Name _____

Directions: *Find each quotient.*

1. 2.00 ÷ 0.50 =

2. 4.2 ÷ 0.7 =

3. 0.6 ÷ 0.3 =

4. 5.6 ÷ 2 =

5. 2.5 ÷ 0.05 =

6. 0.54 ÷ 0.9 =

7. 2.4 ÷ 0.8 =

8. 7.75 ÷ 0.25 =

9. 1.2 ÷ 0.4 =

10. 0.27 ÷ 0.03 =

Warm Up 82: You're the Teacher

Sasha has finished the following division quiz below. It is your job to look over her paper and explain what she did wrong. You should also show the correct solution for each problem.

Sasha's Quiz	What was her mistake?	Correct Solution

1. $36 \overline{)7{,}380}$ with quotient 25

* *

2. $25 \overline{)1{,}750}$ with quotient 7

* *

3. $3{,}040 \div 32 = 3{,}008$

* *

4. $2{,}028 \div 26 = 708$

Algebraic Thinking • Foundations   Lesson 82

Think Maximum

⁻1	9	⁻4	2	⁻5	3	12
⁻5	⁻4	⁻2	8	M	6	7
2	0	⁻9	⁻1	6	⁻8	⁻4
12	⁻4	3	⁻10	1	2	⁻7
⁻3	7	8	⁻4	0	⁻3	⁻5
5	3	⁻2	6	⁻7	1	2
⁻6	2	⁻5	6	7	⁻4	3

Homework 82 — **AlgebraicThinking** • Foundations

Name _____

Directions: *Find each product.*

1. 6.4 • 2.8 =

2. 7 • 5.3 =

3. 0.42 • 6.1 =

4. 0.92 • 0.3 =

5. 5.25 • 6.5 =

6. 9.5 • 10 =

7. 38 • 0.01 =

8. 5.5 • 0.001 =

9. 6.3 • 100 =

10. 0.748 • 1,000 =

AlgebraicThinking • Foundations Warm Up 83

Warm Up 83: Product Trap

Get the answer to each multiplication problem below. With a straight line, connect each problem at the bottom of the page to its correct answer along the left side.

175

98

144

324

384

405

325

448

  35 • 5   14 • 7   36 • 4   54 • 6   48 • 8   45 • 9   65 • 5   56 • 8

419

Lesson 83　　　Algebraic Thinking • Foundations

Subtracting Integers

Directions: *Model each problem with your teacher. Today, we will focus only on problems in which both the <u>minuend</u> and the <u>subtrahend</u> have the same sign.*

> **Wait a Minute!**
> **What is a minuend and a subtrahend?**
> In the problem 10 − 7 = 3, the 10 is the minuend. The 7 is the subtrahend.

1. ⁺5 − ⁺3 =

2. ⁺7 − ⁺4 =

3. ⁺12 − ⁺3 =

4. ⁻5 − (⁻3) =

5. ⁻7 − (⁻4) =

6. ⁻12 − (⁻3) =

AlgebraicThinking • Foundations   Lesson 83

Practice it! **Directions:** *Find the difference in each problem. Draw a model for problems 7 – 12.*

7. ⁻8 – (⁻5) =	8. ⁻7 – (⁻1) =
9. ⁺12 – ⁺3 =	10. ⁻4 – (⁻4) =
11. ⁻14 – (⁻10) =	12. ⁺7 – ⁺5 =

Directions: *Answer the following questions about the problems you just worked.*

13. In each of the problems 1 – 6, which number has a bigger absolute value, the minuend or the subtrahend? (**HINT:** The minuend is the first number. The subtrahend is the second number.) _____

14. **Fill in the blank:** When the absolute value of the minuend is greater than the absolute value of the subtrahend, the sign of the answer will be the same as the sign of the _____ .

421

Lesson 83   Algebraic Thinking • Foundations

Oh yeah? What if the subtrahend is bigger?

Directions: Model each problem with your teacher. Now, the second number in the problem will have the greater absolute value. See if you can figure out how that makes these problems different than the problems from earlier today. We will still focus only on problems in which both the <u>minuend</u> and <u>subtrahend</u> have the same sign.

15. $^+3 - {^+5} =$

16. $^+4 - {^+7} =$

17. $^+3 - {^+12} =$

18. $^-3 - (^-5) =$

19. $^-4 - (^-7) =$

20. $^-3 - (^-12) =$

Algebraic Thinking • Foundations   Lesson 83

Practice it! **Directions:** Find the difference in each problem. Draw a model for problems 21 – 26.

21. ⁻5 – (⁻8) =

22. ⁻1 – (⁻7) =

23. ⁺3 – ⁺4 =

24. ⁺5 – ⁺7 =

25. ⁻16 – (⁻20) =

26. ⁺23 – ⁺25 =

27. Fill in the blank: When the subtrahend has a bigger absolute value than the minuend, the sign is _____ of what you started with.

28. Stephanie is always borrowing money from her math teacher. She owes him $26, so he agrees to let her babysit for him two times. He will subtract $30 from her debt. (He didn't know that she only owed him $26.) Write a subtraction sentence to show how much money she will get from babysitting.

Directions: Find each difference. Take your time and think about each problem.

29. ⁻15 – (⁻10) =   **30.** ⁺10 – ⁺8 =   **31.** ⁻16 – (⁻10) =

32. ⁻3 – (⁻14) =   **33.** ⁺7 – ⁺14 =   **34.** 10 – 12 =

35. ⁻12 – (⁻12) =   **36.** ⁻6 – (⁻10) =   **37.** 8 – 15 =

Homework 83 — AlgebraicThinking • Foundations

Name _____

Directions: *Make each number sentence true by using one of the following math verbs: <, >, =.*

1. 0 ? ⁻8

2. 0 ? 8

3. ⁻9 ? ⁻8

4. 5 ? ⁻5

5. ⁻100 ? ⁻75

6. 10 ? ⁻10,000

7. ⁻300 ? ⁻250

8. 125 ? ⁻10

9. ⁻15 ? ⁻15

10. 38 ? 17

424

Warm Up 84: Missing Parentheses

Put the parentheses in the correct places, so that when you simplify the expression you get the answer at the right.

75 − 12 • 3 + 2 =	15
12 + 8 ÷ 4 − 2 • 2 =	1
80 ÷ 8 + 2 • 5 − 3 =	37
39 + 6 ÷ 3 − 3 • 4 =	3
8 + 24 ÷ 4 + 8 • 3 =	14

Lesson 84   Algebraic Thinking • Foundations

More Subtracting Integers

Yesterday, we learned how to subtract integers in which both the minuend and the subtrahend had the same sign. Today, we will learn how to subtract two numbers that have different signs.

Directions: *Model each subtraction problem with your teacher.*

1. $^+4 - (^-2) =$

2. $^+5 - (^-4) =$

3. $^+3 - (^-7) =$

4. $^-4 - {^+2} =$

5. $^-5 - {^+4} =$

AlgebraicThinking • Foundations Lesson 84

6. $^-3 - {^+7} =$

7. $^+4 - (^-8) =$

8. $^-4 - {^+8} =$

9. $^-7 - {^+10} =$

10. $7 - (^-10) =$

11. $24 - (^-21) =$

12. $^-21 - 24 =$

Lesson 84   Algebraic Thinking • Foundations

Practice it! **Directions:** *Find the difference in each problem. Draw a model for problems 13 – 18.*

13. ⁻8 – ⁺7 =	14. ⁺12 – (⁻8) =
15. ⁺5 – (⁻10) =	16. ⁻2 – ⁺5 =
17. ⁻4 – 3 =	18. ⁺3 – (⁻6) =

19. If you start with an amount of positives and *take away* negatives, you get more _____ .

20. If you start with an amount of negatives and *take away* positives, you get more _____ .

21. Subtraction is the same as _____ .

Algebraic Thinking • Foundations　　　　　　　　　　Lesson 84

Match These!

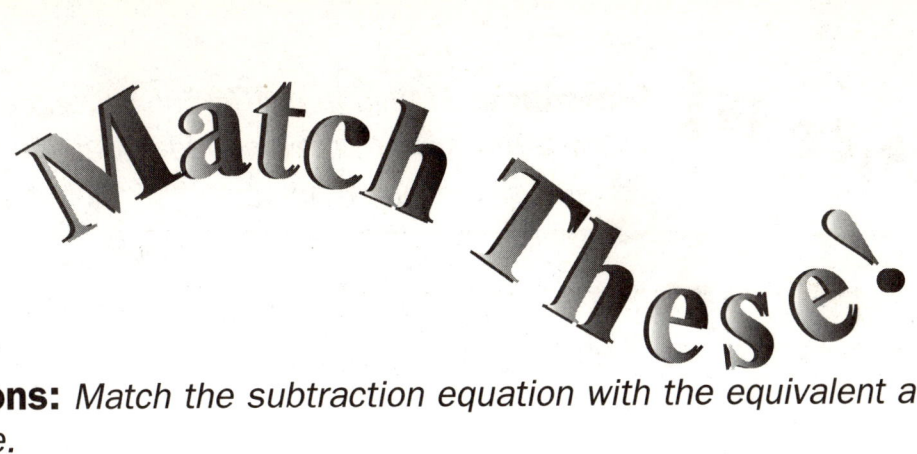

Directions: *Match the subtraction equation with the equivalent addition sentence.*

1. 8 − 7 =

2. 2 − 5 =

3. ⁻8 − (⁻12) =

4. 4 − (⁻10) =

5. ⁻3 − 22 =

6. 17 − 8 =

7. ⁻4 − (⁻5) =

8. 11 − 5 =

9. ⁻11 − 5 =

10. 8 − (⁻1) =

A. ⁻8 + 12 =

B. ⁻11 + (⁻5) =

C. 4 + 10 =

D. 8 + (⁻7) =

E. 8 + 1 =

F. 17 + (⁻8) =

G. 11 + (⁻5) =

H. 2 + (⁻5) =

I. ⁻4 + 5 =

J. ⁻3 + (⁻22) =

429

Lesson 84

AlgebraicThinking • Foundations

Practice it!

Directions: Find the difference in each problem. You don't have to draw a model, but you may if you want. Take your time and think about what each problem is asking you to do.

Hint: You may want to rewrite each problem as an addition problem. Subtraction is the same as adding the opposite.

11. ⁻4 – ⁺8 =

12. ⁻4 – ⁻8 =

13. 12 – (⁻3) =

14. ⁻8 – 10 =

15. 1 – (⁻4) =

16. ⁻10 – ⁺5 =

17. 11 – (⁻8) =

18. ⁻6 – 2 =

19. 8 – (⁻5) =

20. ⁻7 – ⁺2 =

21. 18 – (⁻10) =

22. ⁻2 – 13 =

23. 11 – (⁻9) =

24. ⁻4 – 15 =

25. 6 – (⁻5) =

AlgebraicThinking • Foundations Homework 84

Name _____

Directions: *Find the sum in each problem.*

1. ⁻6 + ⁻4 =

2. ⁻10 + 7 =

3. ⁻5 + ⁻10 =

4. 9 + ⁻8 =

5. ⁻4 + 3 =

6. 8 + ⁻12 =

7. ⁻3 + ⁻5 =

8. 2 + ⁻11 =

9. ⁻5 + 5 =

10. ⁻7 + ⁻9 =

Warm Up 85   Algebraic Thinking • Foundations

Warm Up 85: "Think Minimum"

This is a variation on the game "Think Maximum" that you have already played in class. Decide who will move left and right and who will move up and down. This time, you are trying to get the <u>smallest</u> total you can. <u>Remember</u>, you begin at the M. Add up the numbers as you go. Once a number has been chosen, it is marked off and cannot be used again.

"THINK MINIMUM"

11	⁻4	10	⁻7	12	8	13
5	⁻7	⁻1	4	9	⁻1	8
13	⁻2	3	11	⁻4	2	⁻9
⁻3	16	⁻2	M	⁻7	11	⁻1
2	⁻7	⁻3	0	⁻4	⁻9	12

Keep score below:

    <u>Player 1 (Left and Right)</u>   <u>Player 2 (Up and Down)</u>

Algebraic Thinking • Foundations

Lesson 85

Mystery Squares

Directions: Solve each problem below. Next, cut apart all of the 16 squares. Rearrange the squares so all solutions match up and form a new 4 x 4 square. Then, glue or tape the new 4 x 4 square pieces on a blank sheet of paper.

7 A ⁻3 – ⁻1 6 – 4 ⁻11	⁻4 – ⁻7 Q 36 ⁻2 8 – 3	14 K ⁻6 – ⁻10 ⁻7 – 1 ⁻1	12 – 8 V 24 ⁻5 ⁻4 – 10
8 – 7 U ⁻8 10 9 – 0	⁻2 N 5 – 10 10 – 6 18	7 S ⁻2 – 1 ⁻5 – 7 ⁻3	⁻4 – 7 J ⁻12 ⁻3 ⁻2 – 0
⁻6 – 5 D ⁻12 5 3 – 9	⁻6 Y 5 – ⁻4 10 – ⁻7 12	5 P 3 – 8 ⁻6 – 6 4	6 E 1 – 6 9 – 11 3
⁻8 – 5 M ⁻2 4 0 – ⁻7	9 R ⁻8 – 2 1 – 9 ⁻11	5 – 8 O 4 9 6 – 2	5 – 6 X 2 ⁻10 8 – 1

433

Warm Up 86: Pyramids

Perform the operations from left to right. Put the answer for each pair of numbers above and between them.

Addition

```
                        _____
                   _____     _____
              _____           _____
     _____                         _____
1.8      3.4           0.2            10.4       1.9
```

Multiplication

```
                        _____
                   _____     _____
              _____           _____
     _____                         _____
10       0.2           0.5            0.5        4
```

Subtraction

```
                        _____
                   _____     _____
              _____           _____
     _____                         _____
5        ⁻10           3              ⁻3         12
```

AlgebraicThinking • Foundations Warm Up 87

Warm Up 87: Choose a Trio

For each line below, use three of the four numbers from the box to complete a true sentence.

2   3   4   8

_____ • _____ − _____ = 2

_____ + _____ ÷ _____ = 4

_____ + _____ • _____ = 28

_____ • _____ ÷ _____ = 16

_____ • _____ ÷ _____ = 1

Lesson 87 — Algebraic Thinking • Foundations

Multiplying Integers

Directions: Write the meaning of each problem with your teacher. Then model each of the problems with your teacher. After you model all of the problems, you will go back and draw a picture of the model.

1. $^+2 \cdot {}^+3 =$

2. $^+4 \cdot {}^+2 =$

3. $^+2 \cdot {}^-5 =$

4. $^+3 \cdot {}^-4 =$

5. $^+6 \cdot {}^-2 =$

AlgebraicThinking • Foundations   Lesson 87

6. $^-2 \cdot {}^+3 =$

7. $^-4 \cdot {}^+2 =$

8. $^-2 \cdot {}^-5 =$

9. $^-3 \cdot {}^-4 =$

10. $^-6 \cdot {}^-2 =$

Lesson 87   Algebraic Thinking • Foundations

Practice it!

Directions: Write the meaning of each problem. Then draw a model for each problem. Find the product. (The product is the answer to a multiplication problem).

Problem	Meaning	Drawing of Model
⁺2 • ⁺3 = 6	Gain 2 groups of positive three	YYY YYY
1. ⁺3 • ⁺6 =		
2. ⁺4 • ⁺1 =		
3. ⁺8 • ⁻2 =		
4. ⁺5 • ⁻3 =		
5. ⁻7 • ⁺2 =		
6. ⁻2 • ⁺4 =		
7. ⁻3 • ⁺5 =		
8. ⁻4 • ⁺2 =		

438

Algebraic Thinking • Foundations Lesson 87

Directions: Find the product for each problem. You don't have to draw the model, but you may if you want.

9. 4 • ⁻8 =

10. ⁻8 • 2 =

11. ⁻7 • ⁻10 =

12. ⁻9 • ⁻4 =

13. 5 • ⁻11 =

14. ⁻1 • 6 =

15. 15 • ⁻3 =

16. ⁻6 • ⁻12 =

17. ⁻14 • 0 =

18. 3 • 8 =

19. ⁻3 • ⁻8 =

20. ⁻12 • ⁻8 =

21. 6 • 7 =

22. 20 • ⁻5 =

23. ⁻5 • 20 =

Directions: Use S-O-L-V-E to solve each word problem. Try to use a multiplication sentence to solve each problem.

24. When Ruben was on the way to the bank, he lost 4 bags of money. Each bag had $150 in it. How much money did Ruben lose?

S. _____

O. _____

L. _____

V. _____

E. _____

Lesson 87 AlgebraicThinking • Foundations

25. Marcus and Susan Ramirez are paying off the debt they have from buying a 36-inch television. The TV originally cost $1,000. They have made 3 payments of $250 each. *(Making payments on a debt can be considered a loss of debt. Debt can be considered negative money.)*

   a. Write and solve a mathematical sentence to represent how much they have paid.

   b. Write and solve a mathematical sentence to show how much they owe. (Remember that debt can be represented with a negative number.)

AlgebraicThinking • Foundations   Homework 87

Name _____

Directions: *Find the difference in each problem.*

1. 6 − (⁻4) =

2. ⁻5 − 2 =

3. ⁻7 − (⁻3) =

4. ⁻8 − (⁻8) =

5. ⁻10 − 4 =

6. ⁻6 − (⁻5) =

7. ⁻10 − (⁻7) =

8. ⁻4 − 9 =

9. ⁻6 − (⁻3) =

10. 12 − (⁻7) =

Warm Up 88: Fast Track

Directions: *Follow the truck from top to bottom. Use the answer as the first number in the next problem.*

287 + 13 = ____

÷ 10

____ • 5 = ____

− 52

____ ÷ 7 = ____

+ 6

____ ÷ 5 = ____

____ + 17 = ____

+ 9 = ____

÷ 3 = ____

+ 18

____ • 10 = ____

AlgebraicThinking • Foundations   Lesson 88

Dividing Integers

Directions: *Write the meaning of each problem with your teacher. Then model each of the problems with your teacher. After you model all of the problems, you will go back and draw a picture of the model.*

1. $10 \div 2 =$

2. $^{-}10 \div 2 =$

3. $^{-}10 \div {}^{-}2 =$

4. $10 \div {}^{-}2 =$

443

Lesson 88   **AlgebraicThinking • Foundations**

Directions: Fill in the chart by writing the division problems related to the multiplication problem. The first problem has been done for you.

Multiplication Problem	Relative Division Problems
1. ⁻5 • 4 = ⁻20	⁻20 ÷ ⁻5 = 4; ⁻20 ÷ 4 = ⁻5
2. ⁻7 • ⁻9 = 63	
3. 6 • ⁻8 = ⁻48	
4. ⁻10 • ⁻25 = 250	
5. ⁻3 • 8 = ⁻24	
6. ⁻7 • 5 = ⁻35	
7. ⁻2 • ⁻9 = 18	
8. 12 • 7 = 84	
9. ⁻5 • 8 = ⁻40	
10. ⁻3 • ⁻12 = 36	

Algebraic Thinking • Foundations Lesson 88

Directions: *Find the quotient of each set of integers. (A quotient is the answer to a division problem.)*

11. ⁻20 ÷ ⁻10 =   **12.** ⁻14 ÷ 7 =   **13.** 26 ÷ 13 =

14. ⁻56 ÷ ⁻8 =   **15.** ⁻48 ÷ 6 =   **16.** ⁻54 ÷ ⁻9 =

17. ⁻15 ÷ 3 =   **18.** ⁻27 ÷ ⁻3 =   **19.** ⁻55 ÷ 5 =

20. ⁻450 ÷ ⁻10 =   **21.** 16 ÷ 4 =   **22.** ⁻27 ÷ 3 =

Directions: *Use S-O-L-V-E to solve the word problem.*

23. While playing a card game, Jeff had scores of ⁻20, 14, ⁻10, ⁻8, 6, and ⁻12. What was his average score?

S. _____

O. _____

L. _____

V. _____

E. _____

Homework 88 — AlgebraicThinking • Foundations

Name _____

Directions: *Find the difference in each problem.*

1. 10 − (⁻8) =

2. ⁻6 − 3 =

3. 9 − (⁻5) =

4. 7 − (⁻8) =

5. ⁻5 − 12 =

6. 4 − (⁻7) =

7. 15 − (⁻11) =

8. ⁻4 − 2 =

9. 10 − (⁻15) =

10. ⁻3 − 5 =

AlgebraicThinking • Foundations   Warm Up 89

Warm Up 89: Think Minimum

Play this game like you played "Think Maximum." However, in this game, the person with the lowest score wins.

⁻1	9	⁻4	2	⁻5	12
⁻5	⁻4	⁻2	8	**M**	7
2	0	⁻9	⁻1	6	⁻4
12	⁻4	3	⁻10	1	⁻7
⁻3	7	8	⁻4	0	⁻5
⁻6	2	⁻5	6	7	3

Player 1 (Up and Down)   Player 2 (Left and Right)

Lesson 89   Algebraic Thinking • Foundations

Directions: *Draw a model for each problem with your teacher. Try to write a rule for each operation on the "Integer Rule Sheet."*

Addition

| 1. ⁻9 + ⁻10 = | 2. 12 + ⁻7 = | 3. ⁻8 + 3 = |

Subtraction

| 4. ⁻3 − (⁻5) = | 5. 5 − (⁻2) = | 6. ⁻7 − 5 = |

Multiplication

| 7. 3 • ⁻5 = | 8. ⁻4 • ⁻2 = | 9. ⁻2 • 5 = |

Division

| 10. ⁻14 ÷ ⁻7 = | 11. ⁻12 ÷ 6 = | 12. 8 ÷ ⁻2 = |

Algebraic Thinking • Foundations

Lesson 89

Integer Rule Sheet

Adding Integers

Same Signs — _____ the two numbers and use the _____ sign.

Different Signs — _____ the two numbers and use the sign of _____.

Subtracting Integers

Subtraction is the same as …

Change the _____ sign to the _____ sign and change the sign of the number after the subtraction sign.

Follow _____.

Multiplying and Dividing Integers

Multiplication and Division have the same rules.

Same Signs — When the signs are the same, the product is a _____.

Different Signs — When the signs are different, the product is a _____.

Integer Card Game

1. Read along with your teacher as he or she goes through these rules.
2. Give the score sheet to the person selected as the scorekeeper. This person should put each player's name on the score sheet.
3. The oldest person should deal first. Then, for each hand, the dealer will be the next person to the left of the previous dealer.
4. Red cards (hearts and diamonds) are negative. Black cards (spades and clubs) are positive.
5. Numbered cards carry the value of the number on them.
   Example: 4 of hearts = ⁻4   10 of clubs = ⁺10
6. Aces = 1   Queens = 12
   Jacks = 11   Kings = 0
7. The dealer decides how many cards to deal (no more than 6). The dealer also decides which operation to use (add, subtract, or multiply). Division does not lend itself to this game.

Example:

If the dealer calls 3 cards with addition, and someone gets the Jack of hearts, 2 of clubs, and 5 of diamonds, this person's hand is worth

$$^-11 + {}^+2 + {}^-5$$
$$^-9 + {}^-5 = {}^-14 \text{ points.}$$

8. The object of the game is to have the highest number of points. A player may subtract two cards in any order, which ever is better for that person.
9. At the end of each hand, the scorekeeper should record the name of the person who had the highest points for that hand.
10. At the end of the game, the players of the group are to add up all of the hands for each person to see who is the "BIG WINNER" for their group.

AlgebraicThinking • Foundations

ROUND	# of Cards	Add, Subtract, or Mult.	Player 1	Player 2	Player 3	Player 4	Winner
1							
2							
3							
4							
5							
6							
7							
8							
Game Totals							

Warm Up 90: Coded Message

What is the name of the largest ferris wheel in the United States?

T $^-8 + 5 =$

A $^-40 \div {}^-10 =$

R $^-12 - {}^-10 =$

T $^-15 - {}^-24 =$

S $6 \cdot {}^-3 =$

S $^-11 + {}^-4 =$

X $13 - 20 =$

E $^-8 \div 2 =$

A $4 - {}^-12 =$

$\overline{9}$ $\overline{{}^-4}$ $\overline{{}^-7}$ $\overline{4}$ $\overline{{}^-18}$

$\overline{{}^-15}$ $\overline{{}^-3}$ $\overline{16}$ $\overline{{}^-2}$

AlgebraicThinking • Foundations   Warm Up 91

Warm Up 91: S-O-L-V-E

At a math contest, 10 problems were given. Each participant received 5 points for each correctly solved problem and lost 2 points for each incorrectly solved problem. How many problems were correctly solved by a student who received a final score of 22?

⁻6 points?

43 points?

Lesson 91 **AlgebraicThinking** • Foundations

IN

?

OUT

454

AlgebraicThinking • Foundations

Directions: *Given the operations stated below, give the output that you would get if each number in the chart was put into your function machine.*

Operations: *Two times the input plus one.*

INPUT	OUTPUT
⁻5	
⁻4	
⁻2	
⁻1	
0	
1	
2	
3	
5	

Homework 91　　　　　　　　　　AlgebraicThinking • Foundations

Name _____

Directions: *Translate each verbal expression into an algebraic expression.*

1. A number divided by 8

2. 2 more than a number

3. The product of a number and 6

4. 5 less than a number

Directions: *Evaluate each expression.*

5. $8f$　　$f = {}^-7$

6. $11 - h$　　$h = 6$

7. $a + 7.3$　　$a = 10$

8. ${}^-4b$　　$b = 3$

9. ${}^-3x + 5$　　$x = 2$

10. $5y - 8$　　$y = {}^-2$

AlgebraicThinking • Foundations

Warm Up 92: Crossnumber

ACROSS
2. 75 • 8
4. 78 + 45
6. 25 − 100
7. 7 • ⁻2
9. 13 • 8

DOWN
1. 63 + ⁻23
2. 201 + 98 + 354
3. 132 ÷ 12
5. 23 • 9
6. 24 − 58
8. 121 + ⁻20

If the answer is negative, the negative sign will have its own square.

457

Abandon Ship
Rule Sheet

1. Each player should have a game board. Each student will have 4 ships: a two-man, a three-man, a four-man, and a five-man ship. Ships can be placed vertically, horizontally, or diagonally as long as each "man" on a ship is on a point on the graph. Each player should put their ships on the upper "My Ships" graph on the game board.

2. Once both players have placed their ships on the upper grid, the game can begin. The oldest player goes first.

3. Player One guesses a point where he or she thinks one of the other players' ships is. If Player One hits, he or she gets to guess again. If Player One misses, the next player gets a turn to guess.

4. To keep track of guesses, each player should mark them on the lower "Enemy Ships" grid. You may even want to put a dot when you guess correctly and an "X" when you miss. Use a system to keep up with all guesses.

5. The game is over when one player sinks all of the other player's ships. (Or ... if time runs out, the player who has sunk the most ships or made the most hits, wins.)

AlgebraicThinking • Foundations   Lesson 92

Abandon Ship Board Game

My Ships

Enemy Ships

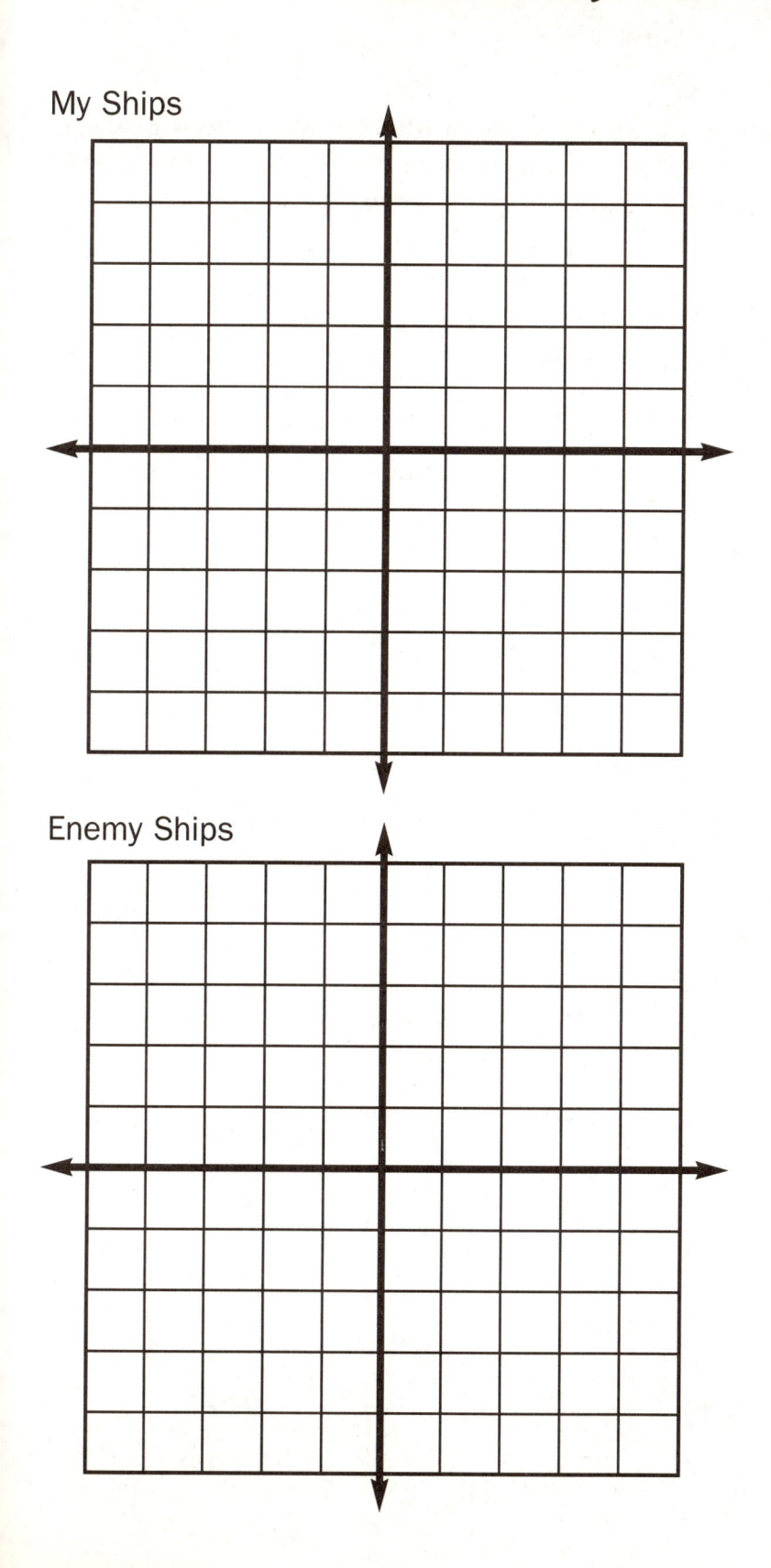

Homework 92 — Algebraic Thinking • Foundations

Name _____

Directions: *Find each product or quotient. Write the answer in simplest form.*

1. $\frac{1}{2} \cdot \frac{^-3}{8} =$

2. $\frac{^-2}{3} \cdot 4\frac{3}{8} =$

3. $\frac{^-5}{6} \cdot \frac{5}{12} =$

4. $^-3\frac{3}{8} \div \frac{^-3}{4} =$

5. $1\frac{1}{2} \cdot 8 =$

6. $1\frac{1}{3} \cdot \ ^-9 =$

7. $5\frac{1}{2} \div \frac{1}{2} =$

8. $5\frac{1}{2} \div \frac{1}{4} =$

9. $10 \div 2\frac{1}{2} =$

10. $20 \div 2\frac{1}{2} =$

AlgebraicThinking • Foundations   Warm Up 93

Warm Up 93: "Sum" Products

Find two integers that have the sum in the first column and the product in the second column.

Sum	Product	Integers
⁻8	12	
7	⁻18	
⁻2	⁻35	
⁻1	⁻56	
⁻11	24	
0	⁻9	

Lesson 93 Algebraic Thinking • Foundations

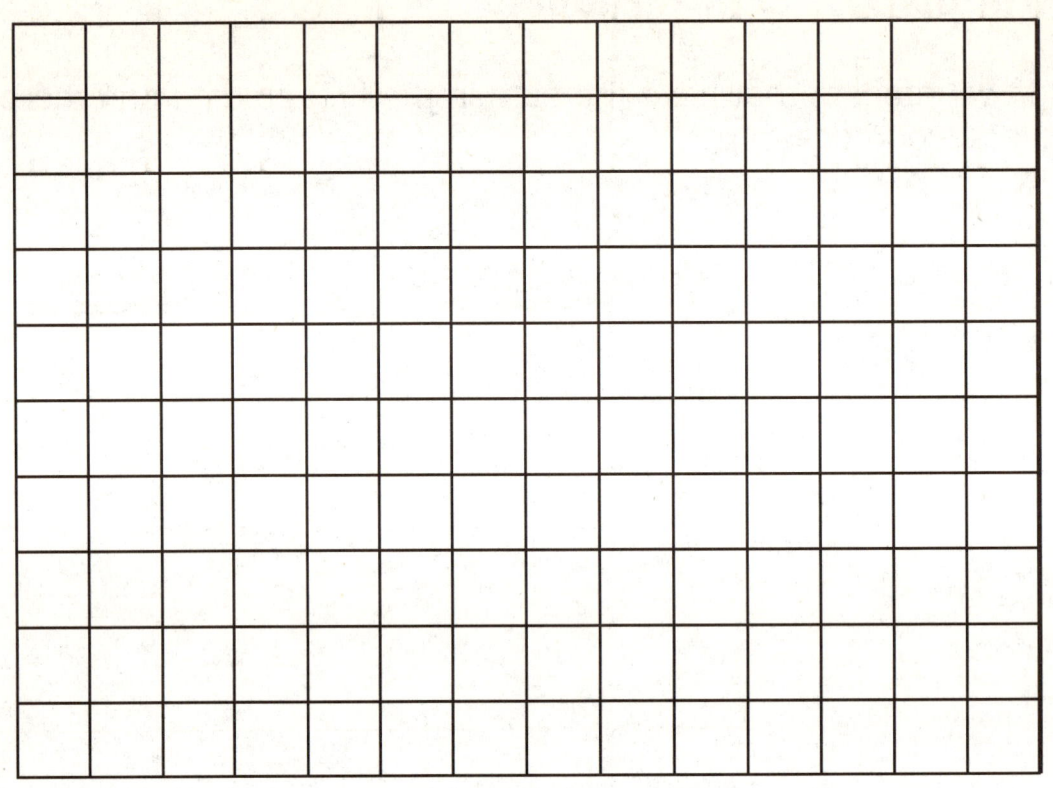

1 cm = 1 ft

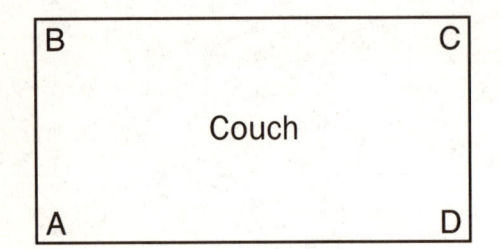

Couch (rectangle with corners B, C, A, D)

Table (trapezoid with corners J, K, M, L)

Algebraic Thinking • Foundations   Lesson 93

Find the new points with the described translation of the couch.

Original	Translation	New
A (1, 1)	<2, 3>	A' (3, 4)
B (1, 4)	<2, 3>	B' (____ , ____)
C (7, 4)	<2, 3>	C' (____ , ____)
D (7, 1)	<2, 3>	D' (____ , ____)

Use the given points to describe the translation of the couch.

Original	Translation	New
A (0, 7)	_____	A' (4, 7)
B (0, 10)	_____	B' (4, 10)
C (6, 10)	_____	C' (10, 10)
D (6, 7)	_____	D' (10, 7)

Find the new points if you are going to move the couch to the right three units and down 4 units from the original points.

Original	Translation	New
A (0, 7)	_____	A' (____ , ____)
B (0, 10)	_____	B' (____ , ____)
C (6, 10)	_____	C' (____ , ____)
D (6, 7)	_____	D' (____ , ____)

A translation could also be called a _____.

Lesson 93 — **AlgebraicThinking** • Foundations

With your partner, place the table (trapezoid) on the original points. Move the table to the right six spaces. This is your translation. Find the new coordinates for points K, L, and M.

Original	Translation	New
J (1, 3)	<6, 0>	J' (7, 3)
K (5, 3)	<6, 0>	K' (____ , ____)
L (4, 2)	<6, 0>	L' (____ , ____)
M (2, 2)	<6, 0>	M' (____ , ____)

Use the given points to describe the translation.

Original	Translation	New
J (2, 4)	_____	J' (5, 6)
K (2, 8)	_____	K' (5, 10)
L (3, 7)	_____	L' (6, 9)
M (3, 5)	_____	M' (5, 7)

Find the new points if you are going to move the table to the right one unit and up one unit from the original points.

Original	Translation	New
J (2, 4)	_____	J' (____ , ____)
K (2, 8)	_____	K' (____ , ____)
L (3, 7)	_____	L' (____ , ____)
M (3, 5)	_____	M' (____ , ____)

AlgebraicThinking • Foundations

Homework 93

Name _____

Directions: *Find the product.*

1. 4 • ⁻5 =

2. ⁻2 • ⁻6 =

3. ⁻8 • 3 =

4. ⁻12 • 0 =

5. ⁻6 • ⁻6 =

6. 7 • ⁻8 =

7. ⁻1 • ⁻8 =

8. ⁻3 • 9 =

9. 12 • ⁻7 =

10. 11 • ⁻10 =

465

Warm Up 94: Pyramids

Perform the operations from left to right. Put the answer for each pair of integers above and between them.

Addition

⁻10   ⁻12   6   1   ⁻3

Multiplication

⁻3   1   5   ⁻4   1

Subtraction

4   7   ⁻8   ⁻5   3

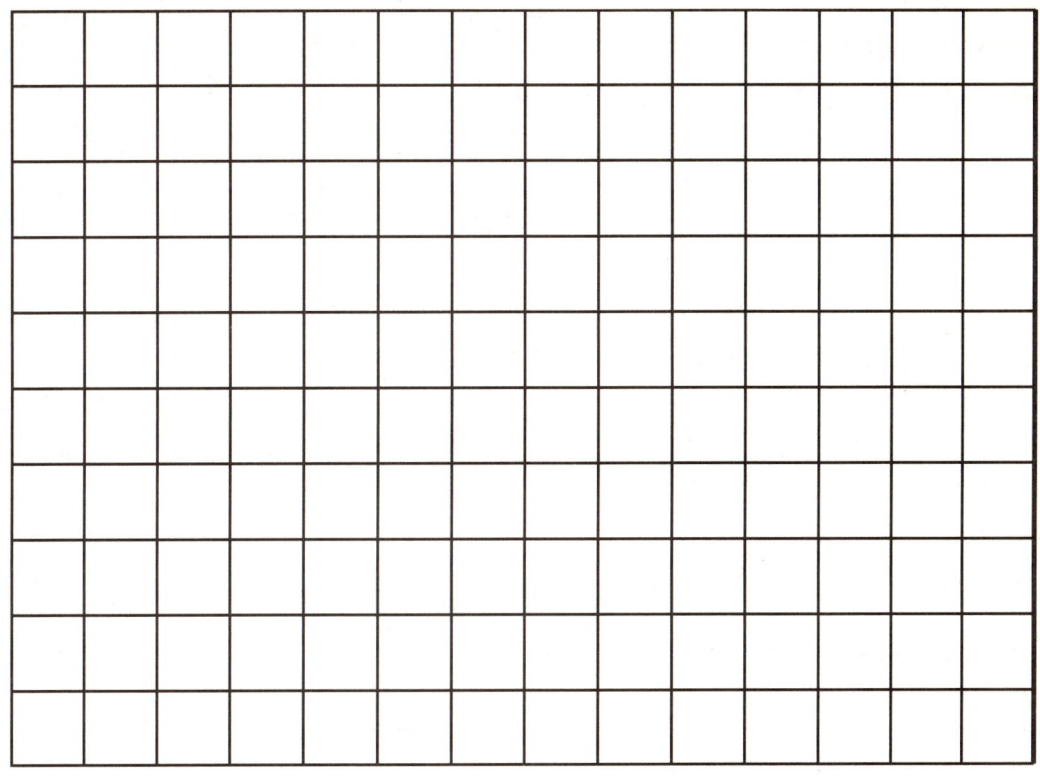

Algebraic Thinking • Foundations Lesson 94

1 cm = 1 ft

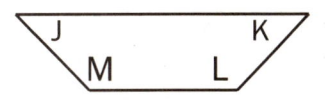

467

Lesson 94 Algebraic Thinking • Foundations

Today we are going to look at another type of transformation. In the last lesson we discussed translations which could also be described as a slide. Today we are going to discuss reflections. A reflection can be described as a flip.

Use student page **467,** which is exactly like the graph from yesterday, to discover how a polygon will move when reflected. Cut out the rectangle. Today label the back corners of the rectangle as well. In other words, on the corner of the rectangle which says A, when you look at the back of the exact same corner, it should also be labeled A.

Place your rectangle on the original points. Remember that a reflection is a flip, so in order to get your rectangle to the new points, you are going to reflect about side $\overline{AD}$. This means the points A and D are going to stay in the same place. Flip the rectangle over and make sure the points are now in the new points. This is a reflection.

Original Points   **New Points**

A (1, 4)   A' (1, 4)

B (1, 7)   B' (1, 1)

C (7, 7)   C' (7, 1)

D (7, 4)   D' (7, 4)

Now put the rectangle back in the same original points. Reflect the rectangle about side $\overline{CD}$. Remember that points C and D will stay in the same place.

Original Points   **New Points**

A (1, 4)   A' (_____ , _____)

B (1, 7)   B' (_____ , _____)

C (7, 7)   C' (_____ , _____)

D (7, 4)   D' (_____ , _____)

AlgebraicThinking • Foundations

Lesson 94

Let's try another reflection. Put your rectangle on the original points given. Reflect the rectangle about the side $\overline{BC}$. Write the new points of the reflection.

Original Points   **New Points**

A (5, 3)   A' (5 , 9)

B (5, 6)   B' (5 , 6)

C (11, 6)   C' (11 , 6)

D (11, 3)   D' (11 , 9)

Here is an example of a reflection. Write which side of the rectangle the reflection is about.

Original Points   **New Points**

A (3, 6)   A' (3, 6)

B (3, 9)   B' (3, 3)

C (9, 9)   C' (9, 3)

D (9, 6)   D' (9, 6)

The reflection above is about side $\overline{AD}$.

Now place the trapezoid on the following original points. Reflect the trapezoid about the side $\overline{JK}$. Write down the new points for each vertex.

Original Points   **New Points**

J (9, 2)   J' (9 , 2)

K (13, 2)   K' (13 , 2)

L (12, 1)   L' (12 , 3)

M (10, 1)   M' (10 , 3)

469

Homework 94 — AlgebraicThinking • Foundations

Name _____

Directions: *Find the quotient.*

1. ⁻56 ÷ 7 =

2. ⁻63 ÷ ⁻9 =

3. ⁻24 ÷ ⁻12 =

4. ⁻40 ÷ 8 =

5. ⁻18 ÷ ⁻3 =

6. ⁻84 ÷ 12 =

7. ⁻55 ÷ 11 =

8. ⁻500 ÷ ⁻25 =

9. ⁻98 ÷ 7 =

10. ⁻75 ÷ 5 =

AlgebraicThinking • Foundations

Warm Up 95: Finished Product

Fill in the borders of the chart with the integers from the box so that the products inside the chart are in the correct spot. Then complete the inside of the chart.

2	3	⁻1	3	5	⁻2
3	⁻4	1	1	2	4

x			3			
				⁻2		
		⁻16				12
3	15		9			
		4			⁻2	
				1		
			6			

471

Lesson 95   **AlgebraicThinking • Foundations**

Today you will use a spreadsheet to help answer the following problems.

The Cheap Chat long distance company offers calls for $0.15 for the first minute and $0.07 for each additional minute. The Rattle On long distance company offers calls for $0.08 per minute anywhere, any time. The following spreadsheet shows the cost for calls up to 11 minutes.

	A	B	C
1	Minutes Talked	Cheap Chat	Rattle On
2	1	$0.15	$0.08
3	2	$0.22	$0.16
4	3	$0.29	$0.24
5	4	$0.36	$0.32
6	5	$0.43	$0.40
7	6	$0.50	$0.48
8	7	$0.57	$0.56
9	8	$0.64	$0.64
10	9	$0.71	$0.72
11	10	$0.78	$0.80
12	11	$0.85	$0.88

1. What heading is in cell A1?

2. What value is in cell B11?

3. Which long distance company is listed in cell C1?

4. Which long distance company is cheaper if you only talk for 4 minutes?

5. What is the length of the call at which point it would not matter which long distance company you chose?

6. In what row does Rattle On become more expensive?

7. What would be the cost of a 12-minute call with Cheap Chat?

8. Which long distance company would you choose and why?

Algebraic Thinking • Foundations

Lesson 95

Use the following spreadsheet to answer the questions below.

Molly Brown has a new fish pond in her yard. Lately she has been having trouble with cats sneaking into the yard to get her fish. She has decided she needs to build a fence around the pond. She went to the home improvement store and bought 30 feet of fencing to enclose the pond. The following spreadsheet shows the various rectangles she could construct with the 30 feet of fencing.

	A Length	B Width	C Perimeter	D Area
1				
2				
3	1	14	30	14
4	2	13	30	26
5	3	12	30	36
6	4	11	30	44
7	5	10	30	50
8	6	9	30	54
9	7	8	30	56
10	8	7	30	56
11	9	6	30	54
12	10	5	30	50
13	11	4	30	44
14	12	3	30	36
15	13	2	30	26
16	14	1	30	14
17	15	0	30	0
18	16	-1	30	-16
19	17	-2	30	-34
20	18	-3	30	-54
21	19	-4	30	-76
22	20	-5	30	-100
23	21	-6	30	-126

Lesson 95   Algebraic Thinking • Foundations

1. What information is located in column A?

2. What information is located in column C?

3. Which column is the area of the pond listed in?

4. What would be the area of the pond if the rectangle was 7 feet by 8 feet?

5. What is the largest perimeter Molly Brown can have? Explain.

6. What is the largest area Molly Brown can have?

7. The spreadsheet has given us too much data. What types of numbers can we cross out right away? Why?

8. Which fencing option would you choose and why?

9. Could any of the fencing options create a square?

Algebraic Thinking • Foundations

Lesson 95

Write three questions for each spreadsheet that can be answered using the information provided in the spreadsheets.

Spreadsheet 1

1. _____

2. _____

3. _____

Spreadsheet 2

1. _____

2. _____

3. _____

Homework 95 **AlgebraicThinking** • Foundations

Name _____

Directions: *Find each sum or difference.*

1. 4 − ⁻10 =

2. ⁻8 + ⁻15 =

3. ⁻5 − ⁻8 =

4. 10 − ⁻6 =

5. 27 − ⁻13 =

6. ⁻18 − ⁻14 =

7. ⁻12 + 25 =

8. ⁻16 + 0 =

9. The high temperature for a town in Colorado one day during the winter was only 8°. The low temperature on that same day was ⁻22°. How much did the temperature change on that day?

AlgebraicThinking • Foundations

Warm Up 96: What Am I?

1. I am a three-digit number. My last digit is three times my first digit. My first digit is twice my middle digit. What number am I?

2. I am a two-digit number. When I am divided by 2, 3, 4, or 5, the remainder is 1. What number am I?

3. I am a four-digit number. All of my digits are different. My first digit is twice my fourth digit. My second digit is twice my first digit. The sum of my digits is 15. What number am I?

AlgebraicThinking • Foundations

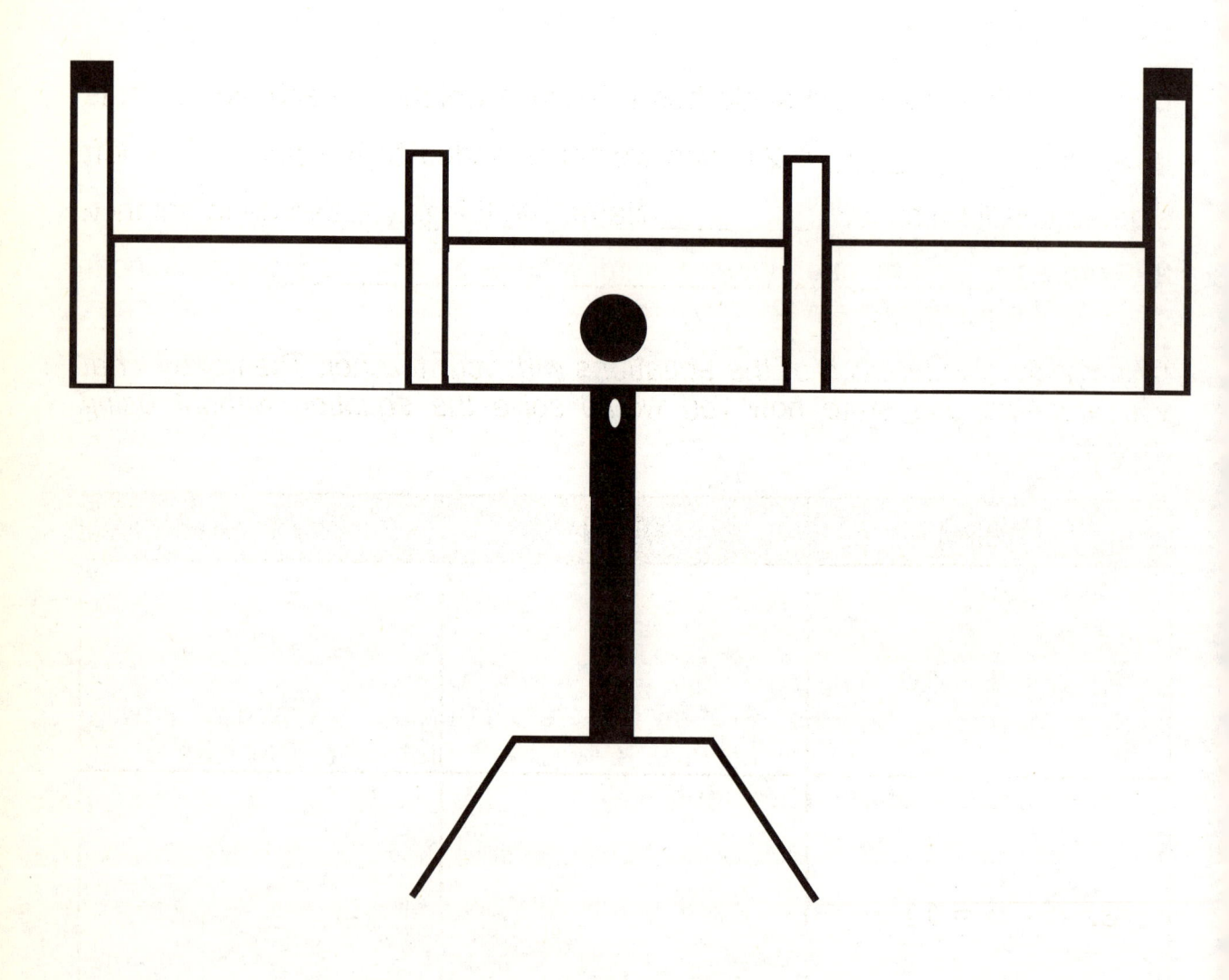

Algebraic Thinking • Foundations   Lesson 96

Keep it Balanced

A scale is balanced when it has equal weights on both sides. An equation is balanced if both sides of the equals sign have the same value.

Equation
An equation is a mathematical sentence containing an equals sign.

Consider this situation. A scale has a 5-ounce weight on each side of it. Is it balanced? _____ A 2-ounce weight is added to the pan on the left side. Is it still balanced? _____ Name two things you can do to balance the scale. _____

Directions: *Model each of the equations with your teacher. Then draw what you modeled and state how you would solve the equation without using models.*

Problem	Model	How to Solve
1. $n + 7 = 10$		
2. $c + 5 = 11$		
3. $t + 5 = 1$		

479

Lesson 96 **AlgebraicThinking** • Foundations

Problem	Model	How to Solve
4. $x + 4 = 3$		
5. $n + {}^-5 = 3$		
6. $q + {}^-2 = {}^-3$		
7. $c + 4 = 0$		
8. $x + {}^-3 = 6$		
9. $x + {}^-5 = {}^-10$		
10. $t + {}^-2 = 1$		

Algebraic Thinking • Foundations

Lesson 96

Directions: *Some students came up with the following solutions to these equations. Check their work by evaluating the equation with their solution. If the answer is wrong, find the correct solution.*

Equation	Solution	Check
11. $n + 4 = 12$	$n = 8$	
12. $x + {}^-3 = 4$	$x = 7$	
13. $y + 1 = {}^-4$	$y = 5$	
14. $b + 2 = {}^-2$	$b = {}^-4$	
15. $x + 4 = 2$	$x = 2$	

The method we have been using to solve these equations is called "isolate the variable." What does isolate mean? _____
_____

16. **Write a problem.** Write a problem that can be solved with $x + 3 = 15$.
_____
_____
_____
_____

481

Lesson 96

AlgebraicThinking • Foundations

Practice it!

Directions: Write the equation that matches the model and solve it.

1. [x] YY / YY = YYY / YYY	2. [x] YY = YYYY / YYYY
3. [x] YY / Y = RRRR / RRR	4. [x] RR / R = R

Directions: Draw a model for each equation. Then find the solution to the problem.

5. $x + 2 = 6$	6. $n + 3 = 2$
7. $y + {}^-2 = 9$	8. $x + {}^-4 = 7$
9. $x + {}^-5 = 1$	10. $c + {}^-3 = 4$

Algebraic Thinking • Foundations Lesson 96

Directions: *Solve each equation. Use any method.*

11. $7 + a = 5$ **12.** $f - 6 = 5$ **13.** $x + {^-2} = 4$

14. $y - 7 = 3$ **15.** $x - 20 = {^-12}$ **16.** $b + 10 = 18$

17. $x + 7 = 3$ **18.** $n + 6 = 1$ **19.** $x - 10 = {^-8}$

20. $p + 8 = 62$ **21.** $r - 3 = {^-7}$ **22.** $x + 12 = 4$

Directions: *Choose the equation that can be used to solve the word problem. Then answer the problem in a complete sentence.*

23. The Nelsons have 15 children in their family. Eight of the children are boys. How many are girls?

   a. $b + 15 = g$
   b. $8 + g = 15$
   c. $7 + g = 15$

24. Sally eats 15 pieces of fruit a week. This week she ate 2 bananas, 3 plums, and the rest apples. How many apples did she eat?

   a. $2 + 3 + a = 15$
   b. $2 + 3 + 15 = a$
   c. $10 + a = 15$

25. Write a problem: Write a problem that can be solved with $n + 5 = 25$.

_____
_____
_____
_____

483

Homework 96 — Algebraic Thinking • Foundations

Name _____

Directions: *In problems 1 – 4, put the decimals in order from least to greatest. In problems 5 – 10, put <, >, or = between the two decimals to make a true sentence.*

1. 6.45, 6.405, 6.41

2. 8.30, 8.29, 8.303

3. 0.55, 0.51, 0.551

4. 3.17, 3.13, 3.21

5. 0.5   ?   0.4

6. 4.9   ?   4.900

7. 0.37   ?   0.375

8. 10.05   ?   10.50

9. 5.15   ?   5.145

10. 0.051   ?   0.10

Algebraic Thinking • Foundations Warm Up 97

Warm Up 97: Choose a Trio

For each line below, use three of the four numbers from the box to complete a true sentence.

$$\boxed{5,\ 7,\ 8,\ 10}$$

_____ • _____ − _____ = 43

_____ + _____ ÷ _____ = 9

_____ + _____ • _____ = 47

_____ • _____ ÷ _____ = 4

_____ • _____ ÷ _____ = 3.5

Lesson 97 **AlgebraicThinking** • Foundations

Revenge of the Word Problems

These word problems are meant to challenge you. If you don't figure it out on the first or even the second and the third time you read it, don't give up! Organize the facts and you'll get it.

Directions: *S-O-L-V-E each word problem. Write an equation for each problem.*

1. The exploration team discovered an unexplored cave in the Ozark Mountains. They traveled down into the cave 432 feet before finding another tunnel. The radio could transmit to the surface through the rock structure for 650 feet. How much further could they travel before losing communication with the home-base research team?

S
O
L
V
E

2. On Friday evening the temperature was 82 degrees. A cold front was expected to enter the area before sundown on Saturday. The expected high for Saturday evening was to be 43 degrees. What was the temperature change?

S
O
L
V
E

Algebraic Thinking • Foundations

Lesson 97

3. The surface temperatures of the planets were measured and recorded. The range of temperatures was 682 degrees. What was the highest temperature recorded if the lowest temperature recorded was ⁻220 degrees? Explain your answer.

S
O
L
V
E

4. Mr. Sturdent worked as a stockbroker for a local finance company. On Tuesday the stock market recorded the stocks of Smith Agricultural Company at $45\frac{1}{2}$ per share. When the stocks had closed on Tuesday, the stocks had dropped $4\frac{3}{4}$ points per share. What were the stocks listed at on the opening of the day on Wednesday?

S
O
L
V
E

Lesson 97 AlgebraicThinking • Foundations

5. Jason wanted to purchase a coat from the catalog. The total cost of the coat including tax and shipping was $174. He cut lawns in the summer and had saved $97. How much will he need to earn before he can purchase the coat?

S
O
L
V
E

6. Teller Savings and Loan offers a free gift every time you deposit $220. Jill has an account and would like to receive the gift that the bank offers. She had earned $180 babysitting. How much more will she need in order to receive the free gift when she makes her deposit?

S
O
L
V
E

AlgebraicThinking • Foundations Lesson 97

Directions: *Solve the equations. Show your work.*

7. $n + 8 = 20$ 8. $x + {}^-11 = 15$ 9. $n + 1.6 = 3.4$

10. $x - \frac{3}{4} = \frac{1}{8}$ 11. $c - 3.7 = 8.1$ 12. $y - \frac{5}{6} = \frac{1}{4}$

13. $x - 9 = 16$ 14. $3 + q = 15$ 15. $x - \frac{11}{12} = \frac{5}{6}$

16. $d - \frac{1}{2} = \frac{9}{10}$ 17. $x - {}^-9 = 16$ 18. $t + 10 = 8$

19. $c - 9 = {}^-4$ 20. $12 = x + 5$ 21. $10 - 9 = n$

Homework 97 **AlgebraicThinking • Foundations**

Name _____

Directions: *Find each product or quotient.*

1. 0.4 • 7 =

2. 54 • 0.32 =

3. 9 • 0.8 =

4. 0.07 • 0.3 =

5. 16 ÷ 3.2 =

6. 34 ÷ 0.2 =

7. 0.68 ÷ 10 =

8. 0.68 • 10 =

9. 0.33 ÷ 6 =

10. 25.2 • 0.5 =

Algebraic Thinking • Foundations

Warm Up 98: Concentrate on Fractions

Cover up each fraction with counters or pieces of paper. Uncover them two at a time. When you uncover equivalent fractions, keep the counters. The person with the most counters wins.

(**HINT:** Matches will be on opposite sides of the center line.)

$\frac{70}{100}$	$\frac{6}{16}$	$\frac{9}{10}$	$\frac{7}{8}$
$\frac{2}{5}$	$\frac{1}{5}$	$\frac{5}{25}$	$\frac{8}{20}$
$\frac{1}{2}$	$\frac{27}{30}$	$\frac{2}{3}$	$\frac{4}{5}$
$\frac{12}{15}$	$\frac{4}{6}$	$\frac{7}{10}$	$\frac{4}{8}$
$\frac{21}{24}$	$\frac{5}{6}$	$\frac{9}{12}$	$\frac{3}{12}$
$\frac{3}{4}$	$\frac{1}{4}$	$\frac{3}{8}$	$\frac{10}{12}$

Lesson 98

AlgebraicThinking • Foundations

Solving Multiplication and Division Equations

Directions: *Model each equation with your teacher. Then draw what you modeled and state how you would solve the equation without using models.*

Problem	Model	How to Solve
1. $3n = 12$		
2. $2x = 10$		
3. $4d = 24$		
4. $2y = {}^-6$		
5. $3x = 15$		

Algebraic Thinking • Foundations Lesson 98

Directions: Some students came up with the following solutions to these equations. Check their work by evaluating the equation with their solutions.

Equation	Solution	Check
6. $4c = 32$	$c = 8$	
7. $^-3x = 27$	$x = {}^-9$	
8. $5x = 25$	$x = 5$	
9. $^-9n = 9$	$n = {}^-1$	
10. $12q = 24$	$q = 2$	

Practice it!

Directions: Write the equation represented by each model. Then solve the equation.

1.
$x \quad x = \begin{matrix} Y\;Y\;Y \\ Y\;Y\;Y \end{matrix}$

_____

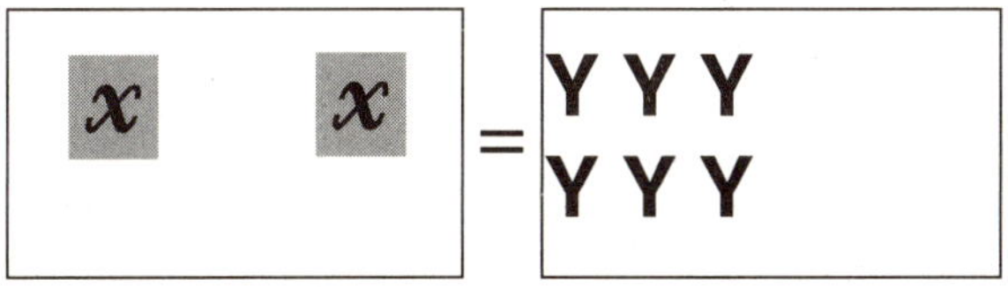

2.
$x \quad x \atop \quad x\quad\; = \begin{matrix} Y\;Y\;Y \\ Y\;Y\;Y \\ Y\;Y\;Y \end{matrix}$

_____

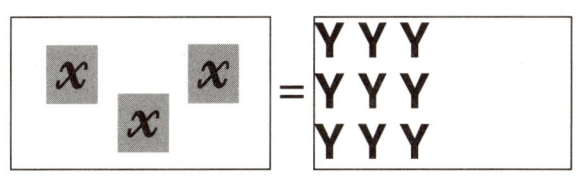

3.
$\begin{matrix} x & x \\ x & x \end{matrix} = \begin{matrix} YYYYYY \\ YYYYYY \end{matrix}$

_____

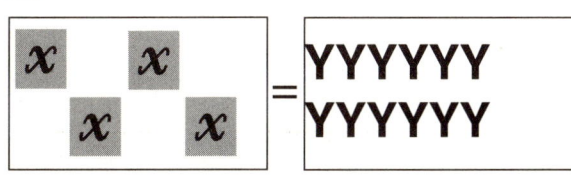

4.
$\begin{matrix} x & x & x \\ & x & x \end{matrix} = \begin{matrix} RRR \\ RR \end{matrix}$

_____

493

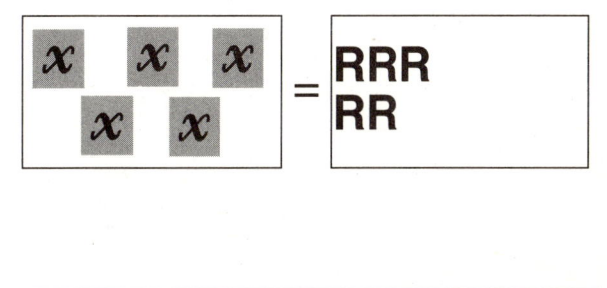

Lesson 98 Algebraic Thinking • Foundations

Directions: Draw a model for each equation. Then solve the equation.

5. $4n = 8$	**6.** $2x = 10$
7. $4x = {}^-12$	**8.** $3y = {}^-15$

Directions: Solve each equation. Use any method.

9. $2x = 22$ **10.** $6c = 18$ **11.** $3x = 15$

12. $4d = 16$ **13.** $2x = 8$ **14.** $3t = 9$

15. $5y = 45$ **16.** $4x = 28$ **17.** $9n = 72$

AlgebraicThinking • Foundations   Lesson 98

18. **S-O-L-V-E:** Rockford High School has twice as many students as Auburn High School. Rockford High School has 1,450 students. Write and solve an equation to show how many students go to Auburn High School.

S

O

L

V

E

19. **S-O-L-V-E:** Dr. Johnson gave six patients tetanus shots on Monday. His total revenue from the shots was $120. Write and solve an equation to show how much each patient was charged for the shot.

S

O

L

V

E

Lesson 98 **Algebraic Thinking • Foundations**

Directions: *Solve each equation. Check each answer.*

Solve	Check
20. $^-3x = 21$	
21. $5x = {}^-45$	
22. $\frac{3}{4}n = 16$	
23. $\frac{2}{5}n = 4$	
24. $\frac{f}{3} = 4$	
25. $12p = 4$	

AlgebraicThinking • Foundations

Homework 98

Name _____

Directions: *Complete each operation.*

1. ⁻28 ÷ 4 =

2. ⁻2 + ⁻8 =

3. 7 − ⁻8 =

4. ⁻7 • ⁻3 =

5. 5 + ⁻10 =

6. 9 − ⁻3 =

7. ⁻72 ÷ ⁻9 =

8. ⁻5 − ⁻5 =

9. ⁻7 • ⁻13 =

10. 4 • ⁻6 =

Warm Up 99: What Are the Questions?

Read the information below. Then write questions for the answers that are given below.

President William Henry Harrison's inaugural speech lasted for 2 hours in 1841. In contrast, George Washington's 2nd inaugural speech lasted 90 seconds in 1793.

1. One and a half minutes

2. 120 minutes

3. $118\frac{1}{2}$ minutes

4. 48 years

AlgebraicThinking • Foundations   Lesson 99

Return of the Word Problems

These word problems are meant to challenge you. If you don't figure it out on the first or even the second or third time you read it, don't give up! Organize the facts and you'll get it.

Directions: *S-O-L-V-E each word problem. Write an equation for each problem.*

1. Cheryl is making 6 batches of cupcakes. She has 3 pounds of icing to put on the cupcakes. How much icing will she use on each batch?

S

O

L

V

E

2. The custodian had to set up 320 seats for the assembly in the gym. How many chairs will he have to put into each row if he can only fit 20 rows in the gym?

S

O

L

V

E

Lesson 99　　　　　　　　　　　　**AlgebraicThinking** • Foundations

3. Jerry was traveling at a rate of 70 miles per hour to reach his new job. He left West Texas and drove 595 miles to a city in South Texas. How long did the trip take him? (distance = rate • time)

S

O

L

V

E

4. Beth works at the city clerk's office and presently makes $6.50 per hour. How many hours will she need to work each week to make $227.50?

S

O

L

V

E

AlgebraicThinking • Foundations   Lesson 99

5. The width of a piece of plywood is 4 feet. How long will the plywood have to be in order to have an area 32 ft²? (Area = length • width)

S

O

L

V

E

6. Using the information in problem #5, how many pieces of plywood would you need to cover an area of 345 ft²?

S

O

L

V

E

501

Lesson 99 — **AlgebraicThinking** • Foundations

7. Jillian has 6 boxes of materials to ship. She had to pay $4.36 per pound to have the packages shipped. How much did the packages weigh if the shipping cost was $73.60?

S

O

L

V

E

8. Using the information from problem #7, calculate the weight of each package if each package weighed the same amount.

S

O

L

V

E

Algebraic Thinking • Foundations

Lesson 99

Directions: *Solve each equation.*

9. $\frac{1}{4}x = 2$

10. $1.2x = 3.6$

11. $5y = 12$

12. $0.9x = 0.45$

13. $\frac{2}{3}n = 8$

14. $5x = 100$

15. $10c = 5$

16. $\frac{1}{3}x = 7$

17. $\frac{-1}{5}x = 6$

18. $\frac{3}{5}n = 6$

19. $25t = 150$

20. $12x = 6$

Homework 99 — **AlgebraicThinking • Foundations**

Name _____

Directions: *Find each product.*

1. $\frac{1}{2} \cdot \frac{1}{3} =$

2. $\frac{3}{8} \cdot \frac{1}{3} =$

3. $\frac{4}{5} \cdot \frac{1}{3} =$

4. $2 \cdot \frac{3}{4} =$

5. $\frac{1}{2} \cdot 7 =$

6. $1\frac{1}{2} \cdot 12 =$

AlgebraicThinking • Foundations　　　　　　　　　　Warm Up 100

Warm Up 100: Pyramids

Perform the operation from left to right. Put the answer for each pair of integers above and between.

Addition

```
                    _____
              _____      _____
         _____      _____      _____
   _____      _____      _____      _____
```

5　　　　　⁻8　　　　　3　　　　　8　　　　　⁻10

Multiplication

```
                    _____
              _____      _____
         _____      _____      _____
   _____      _____      _____      _____
```

⁻1　　　　　⁻2　　　　　3　　　　　1　　　　　⁻3

Subtraction

```
                    _____
              _____      _____
         _____      _____      _____
   _____      _____      _____      _____
```

3　　　　　⁻7　　　　　⁻5　　　　　2　　　　　4

505

Lesson 100 Algebraic Thinking • Foundations

Directions: Solve each problem below. Next, cut apart all of the 16 squares. Rearrange the squares so all solutions match up and form a new 4 x 4 square. Then, glue or tape the new 4 x 4 square pieces on a blank sheet of paper.

Mystery Squares

$\dfrac{x}{4} = {}^-4$ N $^-8$ 9 $y - 4 = 9$	5 L $g + 1 = 1$ $\dfrac{y}{^-2} = {}^-7$ 60	21 A $\dfrac{x}{^-1} = 5$ $\dfrac{s}{3} = 6$ $^-16$	$^-4$ B $y + 10 = {}^-8$ $a + 3 = 1$ $^-2$
8 O $q - {}^-1 = 4$ $\dfrac{m}{3} = 5$ $^-7$	$^-6$ W $6 + k = 10$ $\dfrac{b}{4} = 8$ $^-12$	$^-5$ A $c + {}^-8 = 12$ $5x = {}^-60$ 18	$^-9$ U $4x = 36$ $x + 2 = {}^-6$ 11
$n - 9 = 9$ O 15 22 $\dfrac{r}{3} = 7$	13 E $w + {}^-6 = 5$ $7 + y = 12$ $^-12$	$y - 3 = {}^-5$ K 14 0 $^-6p = 30$	$x + 5 = {}^-2$ C 14 $^-5$ $9y = {}^-81$
$5x = 55$ I 32 11 $9s = 36$	$y - 5 = 55$ Y $^-12$ 9 $^-2 + d = {}^-8$	$d \div 5 = {}^-20$ G $^-2$ 3 $4c = 20$	$\dfrac{f}{^-9} = {}^-2$ D 13 4 $^-8g = 56$

506

AlgebraicThinking • Foundations Warm Up 101

Warm Up 101: "Sum" Products

Find two integers that have the sum in the first column and the product in the second column.

Sum	Product	Integers
13	40	
7	⁻30	
⁻15	56	
⁻10	9	
⁻5	⁻24	

Warm Up 102: What's a Palindrome?

A palindrome is a number that is read the same backwards as forwards. For example: 252, 3,883, and 58,785 are palindromes.

1. How many 2-digit palindromes are there?

2. How many 3-digit palindromes are there?

Algebraic Thinking • Foundations   Lesson 102

Solving Proportions

A **proportion** is a statement that two ratios are equal. Consider the following proportion.

$\dfrac{2}{3} = \dfrac{4}{6}$ This proportion can be rewritten 2:3 as 4:6. It is read "2 is to 3 as 4 is to 6."

In the ratio, 2:3 as 4:6, which two numbers are in the middle? _____ They are called the **means**.

Which two numbers are on the outside? _____ They are called the **extremes**.

Directions: Fill in the chart with your teacher.

Proportion	Means	Extremes	Product of the Means	Product of the Extremes
1. $\dfrac{1}{4} = \dfrac{2}{8}$				
2. $\dfrac{3}{5} = \dfrac{12}{20}$				
3. $\dfrac{6}{8} = \dfrac{12}{16}$				
4. $\dfrac{7}{10} = \dfrac{70}{100}$				
5. $\dfrac{15}{20} = \dfrac{3}{4}$				

6. What do you notice about the product of the means and the product of the extremes? (Write your answer in a complete sentence.)

Lesson 102　　　　　　　　　　　　　　　**AlgebraicThinking • Foundations**

Sometimes the product of the means and the product of the extremes are called the **cross products** of the proportion. Since the cross products are always equal in the proportion, it becomes easy to rename fractions, to write equal ratios, and to find unit rates. All of those things can be accomplished by solving a proportion.

Directions: *Solve the following proportions with your teacher.*

1. $\frac{4}{5} = \frac{12}{n}$	2. $\frac{3}{5} = \frac{x}{12}$
3. Find the unit rate for typing 75 words in 5 minutes.	4. Use a proportion to show how to rewrite $\frac{2}{3}$ as a fraction with a denominator of 15.
5. $\frac{3}{10} = \frac{x}{25}$	6. $\frac{1.4}{2.8} = \frac{x}{2}$

7. **S-O-L-V-E:** Daniel drove 250 miles in 4 hours on the highway. At this rate how far can he drive in 10 hours?

S
O
L
V
E

Algebraic Thinking • Foundations

Lesson 102

Practice it!

Directions: State whether or not the following ratios form a proportion. Find the cross products to answer.

1. $\dfrac{10}{5} = \dfrac{12}{6}$

2. $\dfrac{4}{8} = \dfrac{7}{16}$

3. $\dfrac{3}{5} = \dfrac{4}{9}$

4. $\dfrac{4}{8} = \dfrac{5}{10}$

5. $\dfrac{6}{2} = \dfrac{21}{7}$

6. $\dfrac{8}{3} = \dfrac{12}{4}$

Directions: Solve each proportion.

7. $\dfrac{x}{4} = \dfrac{5}{10}$	8. $\dfrac{3}{8} = \dfrac{d}{10}$	9. $\dfrac{c}{6} = \dfrac{12}{8}$
10. $\dfrac{4}{8} = \dfrac{5}{k}$	11. $\dfrac{5}{12} = \dfrac{e}{15}$	12. $\dfrac{x}{7} = \dfrac{5}{3}$

511

Lesson 102 **AlgebraicThinking • Foundations**

13. $\frac{12}{6} = \frac{8}{t}$	14. $\frac{h}{6} = \frac{5}{10}$	15. $\frac{7}{6} = \frac{g}{12}$
16. $\frac{6}{9} = \frac{4}{y}$	17. $\frac{r}{3} = \frac{12}{4}$	18. $\frac{s}{8} = \frac{5}{10}$
19. $\frac{6}{4} = \frac{r}{6}$	20. $\frac{h}{3} = \frac{6}{2}$	21. $\frac{4}{6} = \frac{i}{12}$

S-O-L-V-E each word problem.

22. A bicycle travels 29 meters for every 14 turns of the wheel. If a wheel has turned 42 times, how far has the bicycle traveled?

S

O

L

V

E

Algebraic Thinking • Foundations Lesson 102

23. At our middle school, 2 out of every 5 students walk to school. If there are 900 students enrolled at our school, how many students walk to school?

S
O
L
V
E

24. Yum Yum Bakery uses 8 apples for every 3 apple turnovers it bakes. If 36 turnovers were baked, how many apples were used?

S
O
L
V
E

Lesson 102

AlgebraicThinking • Foundations

25. Tina can type 45 words per minute. How many words can she type in an hour?

S

O

L

V

E

AlgebraicThinking • Foundations Homework 102

Name _____

Directions: *Write each fraction as a decimal and a percent.*

1. $\dfrac{1}{2}$

2. $\dfrac{3}{4}$

3. $\dfrac{4}{5}$

4. $\dfrac{13}{20}$

5. $\dfrac{1}{20}$

6. $\dfrac{1}{25}$

7. $\dfrac{9}{25}$

8. $\dfrac{3}{8}$

9. $2\dfrac{7}{10}$

10. $5\dfrac{17}{20}$

Warm Up 103: Coded Message

What person has won the most Oscars?

A $\frac{1}{2}n = 10$

D $8n = 56$

N $^-4n = 96$

T $\frac{n}{9} = 4$

Y $7n = 7$

W $6n = 78$

S $n - 13 = {}^-1$

E $n - 9 = 2$

L $n + 7 = 3$

I $n + 4 = {}^-12$

__	__	__	__
13	20	$^-4$	36

__	__	__	__	__	__
7	$^-16$	12	$^-24$	11	1

AlgebraicThinking • Foundations   Lesson 103

The Word Problems Return

Directions: *S-O-L-V-E each problem. Try to use a proportion.*

1. A canary's heart beats 130 times in 12 seconds. At this rate, how many times will it beat in 1 minute?

S

O

L

V

E

2. An average adult's heart beats 8 times every 6 seconds. At this rate, how many times does it beat in 2 minutes?

S

O

L

V

E

Lesson 103   Algebraic Thinking • Foundations

3. Mr. Johnson likes his tea strong. He uses 5 tea bags for a gallon of tea. At this rate, how many bags would he use on 4 gallons of tea?

S

O

L

V

E

4. Kristin walks on a 4-mile trail in Big Bend National Park. She walks the first 1.5 miles in 25 minutes. At this rate, how long will it take her to walk the 4 miles?

S

O

L

V

E

AlgebraicThinking • **Foundations** Lesson 103

5. A 453-gram box of cereal suggests a serving size of $\frac{3}{4}$ cup (30 grams). It states that there are 1.5 grams of fat per serving. How many grams of fat would you eat if you ate the whole box while watching cartoons on Saturday morning?

S

O

L

V

E

6. Elizabeth drove her car about 350 miles on 14 gallons of gas. Find the unit rate of miles per gallon for her car.

S

O

L

V

E

519

Lesson 103 **AlgebraicThinking • Foundations**

7. The drama club bought carnations for a fundraiser. They bought the flowers for $9.50 for a bundle of 25. How much did they pay for the 1,500 carnations that they bought?

S

O

L

V

E

8. At a carnival, you can buy 5 tickets for $1.50. You can buy 25 tickets for $6.00. Find the unit rate per ticket to determine which is the better buy.

S

O

L

V

E

520

Algebraic Thinking • Foundations

Lesson 103

9. During the summer Brandon paints houses. He needs to paint 5,000 square feet on a building. When he goes to buy paint, he finds that he can buy a 5-gallon bulk can of Painter's Primer that covers a total of 1,000 square feet for $59.95. He can buy a 1-gallon can of Painter's Choice that covers 300 square feet for $18.95. Find the unit price for each brand. Which is the better buy?

S

O

L

V

E

10. Use the information from #9 to determine what he would spend on paint to complete the job. Show the price for both brands of paint.

S

O

L

V

E

Lesson 103 — Algebraic Thinking • Foundations

Directions: *Solve each proportion.*

11. $\dfrac{x}{10} = \dfrac{12}{25}$

12. $\dfrac{12}{5} = \dfrac{5}{t}$

13. $\dfrac{15}{20} = \dfrac{a}{100}$

14. $\dfrac{8}{b} = \dfrac{20}{25}$

15. $\dfrac{1}{y} = \dfrac{3.8}{27}$

16. $\dfrac{10}{x} = \dfrac{12}{1.50}$

17. $\dfrac{20}{28} = \dfrac{k}{8}$

18. $\dfrac{x}{12} = \dfrac{\frac{3}{4}}{25}$

19. $\dfrac{h}{5} = \dfrac{12}{9}$

Algebraic Thinking • Foundations Homework 103

Name _____

Directions: *Solve each equation.*

1. $x + 5 = 12$

2. $x - 8 = 3$

3. $3n = 21$

4. $x - 12 = {}^-10$

5. $\dfrac{y}{3} = 9$

6. $x + {}^-7 = 3$

7. Borrow a dollar from your parents. Measure the length and width of the dollar in inches. Find the area of the dollar bill. Smile at your parents and ask if you can keep the dollar bill. ☺ (Try for a twenty!)

Directions: *S-O-L-V-E the following problem.*

8. A rectangular rose garden has a base of 5 meters and a height of 6 meters. If each rose bush needs at least 0.5 m² of space, how many rose bushes can be planted in this garden?

523

Warm Up 104 — Algebraic Thinking • Foundations

Warm Up 104: Empty Squares

Fill in the empty squares with numbers so that each row, column, and diagonal will have the same sum.

135	37	
65		121
79		

AlgebraicThinking • Foundations   Lesson 104

Finding a Percent of a Number

Recall that percent means "per 100" or "out of 100." So write each of these percents as a fraction.

a. 47%   **b.** 83%   **c.** 49%

Since a percent is a fraction with a denominator of 100, proportions can be used to convert a fraction to a percent. Convert the fractions to a percent using a proportion.

d. $\frac{3}{5}$ **e.** $\frac{7}{8}$ **f.** $\frac{11}{25}$

S-O-L-V-E: The 300 sixth graders at school were asked, "If money were no object, where would you like to go on a field trip?" Fifty percent of the students chose a theme park. How many chose a theme park?

The problem involves finding 50% of 300. Twenty-five percent of the students chose going to the Super Bowl. How many students chose the Super Bowl?

It is fairly easy to find 50% or 25% of a number. Try these percentages. Fifteen percent of the students chose the NBA All-Star Game. How many students chose the NBA?

Ten percent of the students chose the Mall of America in Minnesota. How many students chose the Mall?

525

Lesson 104 AlgebraicThinking • Foundations

Directions: *Complete the chart.*

10% of 300 is	60% of 300 is
20% of 300 is	70% of 300 is
30% of 300 is	80% of 300 is
40% of 300 is	90% of 300 is
50% of 300 is	100% of 300 is

The percentages above can be represented with models. Let's do the problem, 40% of 300. First start out with a fraction bar. Divide the bar into 10 sections. The whole bar will represent 100% or 300 students from the survey. Each section will represent 10%. How many students does each section represent?

0%   100%

0   300

Shade 4 sections to represent 40%. Since each section represents 30 people, 40% of 300 people is 120 people.

Algebraic Thinking • Foundations

Lesson 104

Directions: *Use the models to find the percent of a number. Remember that each section represents 10%.*

a. 60% of 200

0%   100%

0   200

b. 70% of 50

0%   100%

0   50

c. 30% of 20

0%   100%

0   20

d. 80% of 40

0%   100%

0   40

e. 75% of 20

0%   100%

0   20

f. 65% of 1,000

0%   100%

0   1,000

527

Lesson 104   Algebraic Thinking • Foundations

g. 15% of 10

0%   100%

0   10

Practice it!

Directions: Write a percent sentence that is represented by each model. Number 1 has been done for you.

1. 40% of 50 is 20

0%   100%

0   50

2.

0%   100%

0   500

3.

0%   100%

0   20

4.

0%   100%

0   200

5.

0%   100%

0   30

6.

0%   100%

0   90

7.

0%   100%

0   5

8.

0%   100%

0   12

9.

0%   100%

0   20

10.

0%   100%

0   120

528

Algebraic Thinking • Foundations

Lesson 104

Directions: *Draw a model to help you find each amount.*

11. 90% of 40

0%

12. 40% of 90

0%

13. 75% of 200

0%

14. 30% of 150

0%

15. 5% of 10

0%

16. 50% of 10

0%

17. 35% of 20

0%

18. 75% of 60

0%

19. 80% of 600

0%

20. 60% of 60

0%

529

Lesson 104

AlgebraicThinking • Foundations

Directions: *Find the amount. You may construct a model if you need it.*

21. 20% of 200   **22.** 20% of 300   **23.** 20% of 400

24. 60% of 90   **25.** 80% of 300   **26.** 40% of 400

27. 30% of 50   **28.** 35% of 1,000   **29.** 95% of 20

30. 1% of 200   **31.** 65% of 500   **32.** 20% of 1

33. S-O-L-V-E: On a 20-problem multiple-choice test a student answered 15% of the problems incorrectly. How many problems did he answer correctly?

S

O

L

V

E

Algebraic Thinking • Foundations   Homework 104

Name _____

Directions: *Solve each equation. Check your answers.*

1. $9 + x = {}^-7$

2. $a + {}^-8 = {}^-3$

3. $f + {}^-5 = 12$

4. $n + 16 = {}^-42$

5. $c + 12 = 20$

6. $p + 2 = {}^-20$

7. $b + {}^-8 = 5$

8. $4 + n = 1$

9. $y + {}^-13 = 0$

10. $n + 30 = {}^-6$

Warm Up 105: Coded Message

What is the largest carnivore? (A carnivore is a meat-eating animal.)

R $\frac{3}{8} + \frac{1}{3} =$

P $\frac{2}{3} + \frac{1}{4} =$

A $\frac{1}{6} + \frac{5}{8} =$

L $\frac{2}{5} + \frac{1}{3} =$

E $\frac{1}{2} + \frac{2}{5} =$

B $2\frac{1}{3} + 4\frac{3}{4} =$

O $3\frac{2}{5} + 3\frac{7}{10} =$

___   ___   ___   ___   ___
$\frac{11}{12}$ $7\frac{1}{10}$ $\frac{11}{15}$ $\frac{19}{24}$ $\frac{17}{24}$

___   ___   ___   ___
$7\frac{1}{12}$ $\frac{9}{10}$ $\frac{19}{24}$ $\frac{17}{24}$

Algebraic Thinking • Foundations   Lesson 105

Using Proportions to Find the Percent of a Number

Many times the percent that you are trying to find is a multiple of 10 or even 5. When it is, the models we used yesterday are a good tool to use. But what about when you have a percent that is not a multiple of 10 or 5? For example, what if you need to find 33% of 24.99 or 44% of 39.95? You can still estimate with the models, or you can find an accurate answer by using a proportion.

> **S-O-L-V-E:** Janna wants to buy a stereo. She gets $300 from her savings account and then goes to an electronics store. The stereo she wants to buy has a price tag of $285 plus tax. If the tax rate is 8%, will she have enough money to buy the stereo?
>
> **S**
>
> **O**
>
> **L**
>
> **V**
>
> **E**

Consider this problem. What is 8% of 285? This is a question you must answer to solve the problem above. In the last lesson we drew a model like the one below to solve it.

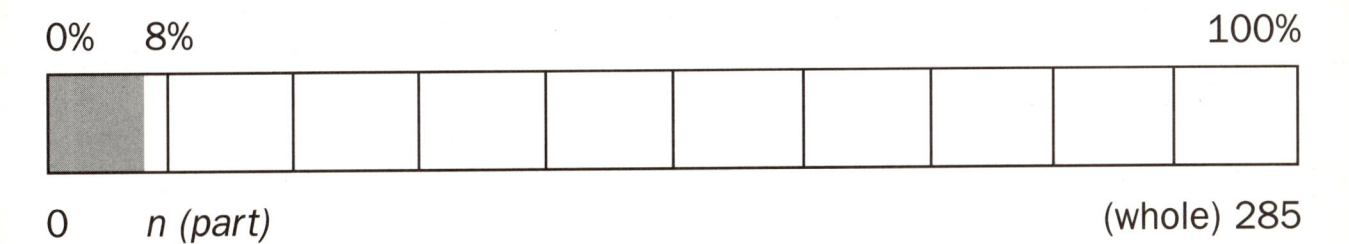

0%   8%   100%

0   n (part)   (whole) 285

The model may not be the best way to solve this problem. However, it will help to estimate and to set up a proportion. The percents will be one of the ratios and the other numbers will be the other ratio.

533

Lesson 105 AlgebraicThinking • Foundations

a. What is the ratio that represents 8%? (It doesn't have to be put in simplest form.)

b. What is the ratio? (**HINT:** It is part of a whole.)

c. Those ratios are equal. Write a proportion and solve it.

Algebraic Thinking • Foundations

Lesson 105

✎ When solving a percent problem will the percent always be "over 100"?
✎ Will the other ratio always be part over the whole?

Directions: *Solve these percent problems with your teacher. You will use a proportion.*

a. What is 44% of 150?	b. Find 58% of 80.
c. What is 88% of 200?	d. 24 is 25% of what number?
e. 18 is 30% of what number?	f. 12 is 24% of what number?
g. 25 is what percent of 100?	h. What percent of 40 is 12?
i. 45 is what percent of 200?	j. 45 is what percent of 50?

Lesson 105 — **AlgebraicThinking • Foundations**

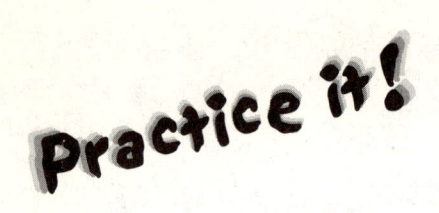

Practice it!

Directions: *Solve these percent problems using a proportion.*

1. What is 10% of 90?
2. What is 20% of 30?
3. What is 25% of 72?

4. 38 is what percent of 200?
5. What percent of 60 is 12?
6. What is 44% of 25?

7. What is 38% of 50?
8. 19 is what percent of 50?
9. 5 is what percent of 15?

10. Find 20% of 40.
11. What is 28% of 200?
12. What is 13% of 150?

13. What is 10% of 75?
14. What is 95% of 20?
15. What is 92% of 25?

AlgebraicThinking • Foundations　　　　　　　　　　　　　　　Lesson 105

Directions: *Use S-O-L-V-E to solve each word problem.*

16. In a recent survey about toothbrushes, 23% of those surveyed prefer blue toothbrushes. There are about 50 million people ages 5 to 17 in our country. Estimate how many of them prefer blue toothbrushes.

S

O

L

V

E

17. David bought a CD player that had a retail price of $80. He had to pay sales tax of 8%. How much tax did he pay? What was the total cost of the CD player?

S

O

L

V

E

Homework 105

AlgebraicThinking • Foundations

Name _____

Directions: *Solve each proportion.*

1. $\dfrac{6}{4} = \dfrac{x}{2}$

2. $\dfrac{x}{12} = \dfrac{3}{9}$

3. $\dfrac{5}{6} = \dfrac{10}{x}$

4. $\dfrac{4}{x} = \dfrac{8}{10}$

5. $\dfrac{2}{3} = \dfrac{x}{9}$

6. $\dfrac{3}{x} = \dfrac{10}{20}$

7. $\dfrac{4}{12} = \dfrac{2}{x}$

8. $\dfrac{x}{15} = \dfrac{1}{3}$

9. $\dfrac{2}{x} = \dfrac{7}{21}$

10. $\dfrac{3}{6} = \dfrac{x}{10}$

AlgebraicThinking • Foundations

Warm Up 106: S-O-L-V-E the Problem

Use the S-O-L-V-E method to solve this problem.

Old McDonald had a farm. On that farm he grew potatoes that he would use for french fries in a fast food restaurant he was thinking of starting. But, it seems that Old McDonald had a problem – the rabbits were eating his potatoes. So, he has decided to enclose his field with a fence. The field is 400 feet wide and 600 feet long. The fencing material will cost $3.98 per foot. How much will he pay for the fencing he is going to buy?

S

O

L

V

E

Lesson 106　　　　　　　　　　AlgebraicThinking • Foundations

Finding Percents Using Equations

S-O-L-V-E: Thirty-one percent of the seventh graders in a survey said that they prefer to bring a sack lunch to school rather than eat school food. How many of the 286 7th graders might you expect to bring their lunch to school?

Key Words for Translating Sentences to Equations	
Word	Mathematical Meaning
Is	= (equals)
Of	• (multiply)
Percent	per 100
What	n (any variable)

S

O

L

V

E

Directions: *Do these problems with your teacher. Translate each sentence to an equation and then solve it.*

a. What is 38% of 200?	**b.** What is 54% of 250?
c. 39 is 75% of what number?	**d.** 45 is 45% of what number?
e. 8.5 is what percent of 10?	**f.** What percent of 3 is 5?

540

Algebraic Thinking • Foundations — Lesson 106

Practice it!

Directions: *Solve each percent problem below with an equation. Show your work.*

1. What is 55% of 400?	**2.** 15 is what percent of 75?
3. 33 is what percent of 300?	**4.** What is 24% of 150?
5. 6 is 37.5% of what number?	**6.** What is 12% of 50?
7. 31.5 is what percent of 450?	**8.** 30 is 25% of what number?
9. What is 70% of 60?	**10.** 153 is 85% of what number?
11. What is 66% of 400?	**12.** What percent of 310 is 124?
13. 140 is what percent of 400?	**14.** 144 is 24% of what number?
15. 54 is what percent of 300?	**16.** What is 35% of 270?

Lesson 106 AlgebraicThinking • Foundations

Directions: *Use S-O-L-V-E to solve each word problem.*

17. In a recent survey, 876 people, 73%, said that popcorn was their favorite snack at the movies. How many people were surveyed?

S
O
L
V
E

18. Shannon sold a house for $125,000. What percent commission did she receive if she got $8,750?

S
O
L
V
E

19. Kathy earns a 3% royalty on sales of a book that she wrote. How much money did her book earn if she got $39,000?

S
O
L
V
E

20. Daniel earns $200 a week in base salary plus 6% commission on all sales. What were his sales last week if he earned $317?

S
O
L
V
E

Algebraic Thinking • Foundations   Homework 106

Name _____

Directions: *Solve each proportion.*

1. $\dfrac{7}{x} = \dfrac{5}{8}$

2. $\dfrac{5}{9} = \dfrac{x}{4}$

3. $\dfrac{x}{2} = \dfrac{3}{7}$

4. $\dfrac{10}{11} = \dfrac{5}{x}$

5. $\dfrac{2}{x} = \dfrac{7}{9}$

6. $\dfrac{x}{3} = \dfrac{5}{6}$

7. $\dfrac{8}{9} = \dfrac{3}{x}$

8. $\dfrac{5}{x} = \dfrac{4}{7}$

9. $\dfrac{1}{2} = \dfrac{x}{6}$

10. $\dfrac{x}{4} = \dfrac{1}{6}$

Warm Up 107   Algebraic Thinking • Foundations

Warm Up 107: Galois

What is a Galois? Actually, the question is, *who* is Galois. He was a French mathematician. As a young boy he read every book on mathematics he could get his hands on. He did poorly in school because he could not focus on the lessons since he was daydreaming about mathematical theories!

He got a good teacher and by 18 he was making exciting changes in the theory of equations. However, he become interested in politics and other things and didn't spend time writing down his ideas on math. While in politics he got many political enemies. One of them challenged him to a duel over a sweetheart.

The night before the duel, he began writing down the ideas he had thought about while participating in his various activities. He had a lot of thoughts, but had never had the motivation to write them down. He stayed up all night writing and was killed in the duel because he was so tired. He was only 20 years old.

Legend has it that there was a bloody will in his pocket when he died. It read something like this. *"I leave all my money to my mother, my sister, my sweetheart, and my old teacher. The money is to be divided in the following way: My sister and my sweetheart are to get half the money, but they must share the amount in the ratio of 4:3 (4 parts for my sister and 3 parts for my love). My mother is to get twice as much as my sweetheart and my teacher is to get 500 francs.)*
(**HINT:** The total inheritance is 7,000 francs.)

How much money is each of his heirs to get?

AlgebraicThinking • Foundations

Warm Up 108: Same Answer

Draw a line from one column to the other to match problems with the same answer.

1. 3 • 0.25

2. 120 ÷ 10

3. 3 – 12

4. 8 – ⁻7

5. 25 • 0.01

6. ⁻10 – 17

7. 10 ÷ 2

A. 8 + 7

B. 25 ÷ 100

C. 3 ÷ 4

D. 120 • 0.1

E. ⁻10 + ⁻17

F. 10 • 0.5

G. 3 + ⁻12

Congruent and Similar Figures

The two polygons below are exactly the same. All of the sides are equal. All of the angles are equal. If you don't believe me, measure them. If two polygons are equal, they are said to be congruent.

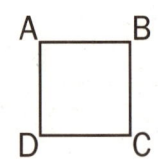

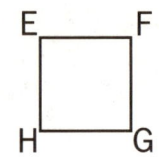

If you turn one of the polygons, the sides are still equal and the angles are still equal. The two polygons will still be _____.

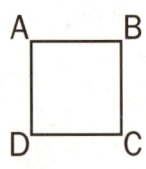

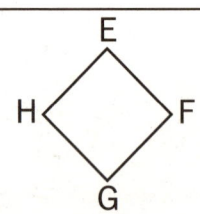

We could write that the polygons are congruent like this. ▱ ABCD ≅ ▱ EFGH.

The ≅ symbol means congruent.

The first two polygons had all four sides equal and all four angles equal. Do you know the name for a four-sided polygon with equal sides and equal angles?
_____

Now let's look at two more polygons. They are congruent also. If you know they are congruent, answer the questions below about them.

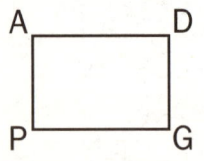

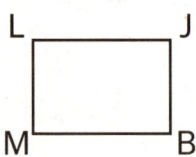

1. ▱ ADGP ≅ ▱ _____

2. ∠A ≅ _____

3. ∠G ≅ _____

4. $\overline{LM}$ ≅ _____

5. $\overline{PG}$ ≅ _____

6. ∠B ≅ _____

Algebraic Thinking • Foundations — Lesson 108

Look at the following polygons with your partner and answer the following questions.

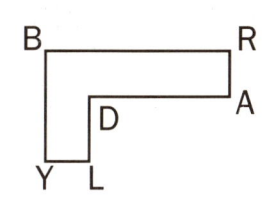

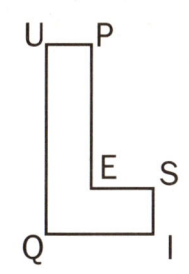

◻ BRADLY ≅ ◻ QUPESI

1. ◻ DARBYL ≅ ◻ _____
2. ◻ SIQUPE ≅ ◻ _____
3. ∠E ≅ ∠ _____
4. ∠B ≅ ∠ _____
5. ∠Y ≅ ∠ _____
6. ∠P ≅ ∠ _____
7. $\overline{BR}$ ≅ _____
8. $\overline{UP}$ ≅ _____
9. $\overline{LY}$ ≅ _____
10. $\overline{EP}$ ≅ _____

Parts in polygons that are the same are called **corresponding parts.**

All of the angles and line segments that are congruent above are corresponding parts.

Go back to the figures on the first page and name their corresponding parts.

Here are a few more examples. Find the corresponding parts for the given angles and line segments.

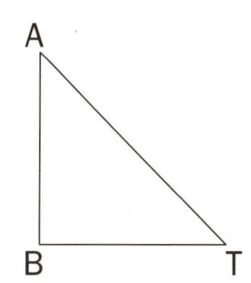

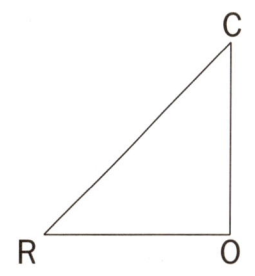

△ABT ≅ △COR

11. ∠A ≅ ∠ _____
12. ∠O ≅ ∠ _____
13. $\overline{BT}$ ≅ _____
14. $\overline{AT}$ ≅ _____

Are there any other corresponding angles or line segments? _____

547

Lesson 108   **Algebraic Thinking** • Foundations

The two polygons below are the same shape and have equal angles; however, one of the polygons is larger than the other. If two polygons are the same shape, but one is larger than the other, they are **similar polygons.** We use the symbol ~ to say that two polygons are similar.

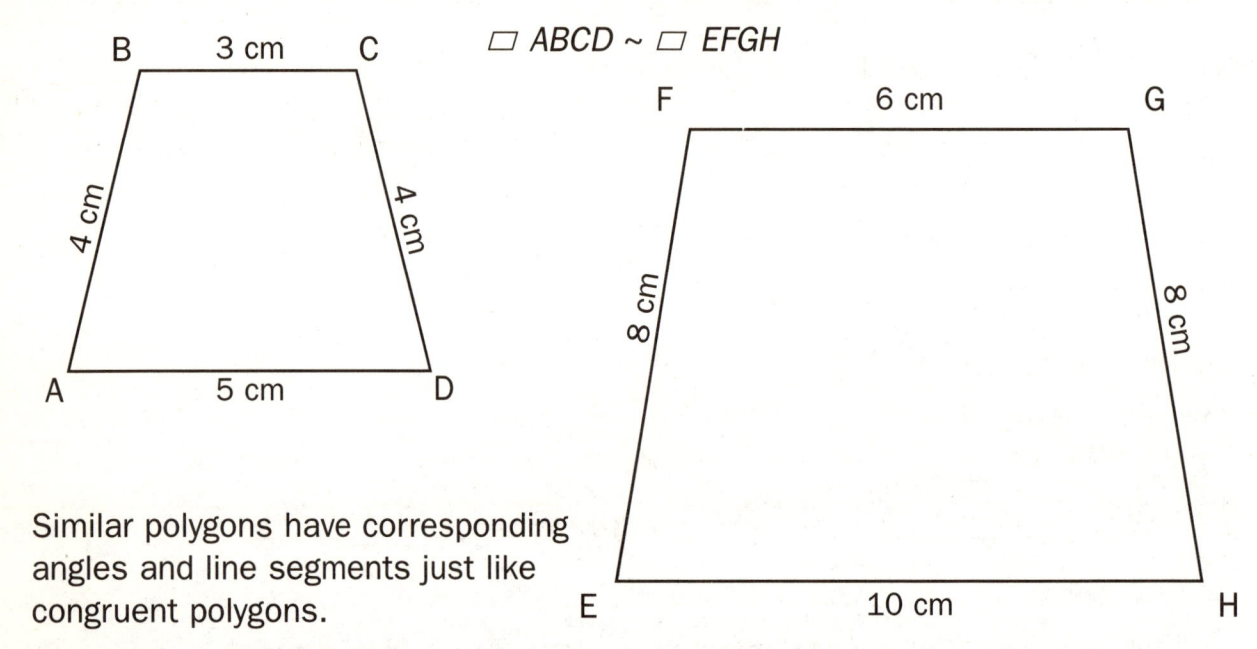

▱ ABCD ~ ▱ EFGH

Similar polygons have corresponding angles and line segments just like congruent polygons.

The angles are congruent, so we can still use the same symbol, ≅.

∠A ≅ ∠E   ∠B ≅ ∠F   ∠C ≅ ∠G   ∠D ≅ ∠H

We cannot use the same symbol to discuss the corresponding sides because they are not equal. We are going to write them this way.

$\overline{AB}$ ~ $\overline{EF}$ $\overline{BC}$ ~ $\overline{FG}$ $\overline{CD}$ ~ $\overline{GH}$ $\overline{DA}$ ~ $\overline{HE}$

Even though the sides are not equal, they do have something in common. If you compare the lengths of corresponding sides of similar polygons they have the same ratio. What does that mean? Look at the ratios below.

$\frac{AB}{EF} = \frac{4 \text{ cm}}{8 \text{ cm}} = \frac{1}{2}$ $\frac{BC}{FG} = \frac{3 \text{ cm}}{6 \text{ cm}} = \frac{1}{2}$ $\frac{CD}{GH} = \frac{4 \text{ cm}}{8 \text{ cm}} = \frac{1}{2}$ $\frac{DA}{HE} = \frac{5 \text{ cm}}{10 \text{ cm}} = \frac{1}{2}$

If you notice, they all have the same ratio, or if you divide the length of a side from the smaller polygon by the length of its corresponding side, you will always get the same ratio.

You also can divide the sides of the larger polygon by the corresponding sides of the smaller polygon. If you did this for the first example, what would be the ratio?

Algebraic Thinking • Foundations   Lesson 108

Use the following similar figures to find the corresponding angles and sides.

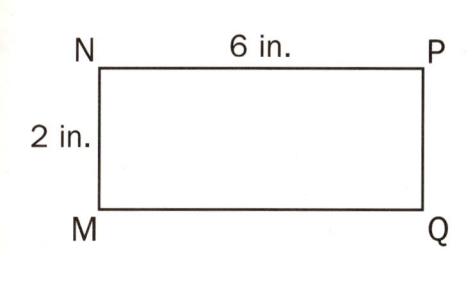

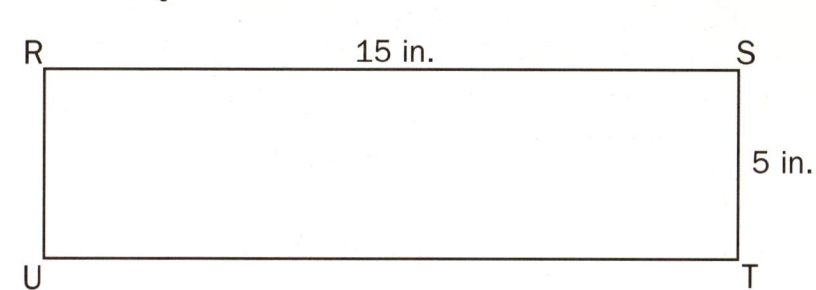

▱MNPQ ~ ▱URST

1. ∠N ≅ ∠_____
2. ∠P ≅ ∠_____
3. ∠Q ≅ ∠_____
4. ∠M ≅ ∠_____

5. $\overline{MN}$ ~ _____
6. $\overline{NP}$ ~ _____
7. $\overline{PQ}$ ~ _____
8. $\overline{QM}$ ~ _____

Now find the ratio created by the corresponding sides. I will get you started.

$\dfrac{MN}{\_\_\_} = \dfrac{2 \text{ in.}}{\_\_\_} =$

Here are two more similar figures. List the corresponding sides and corresponding angles. Then find the ratio created by the corresponding sides.

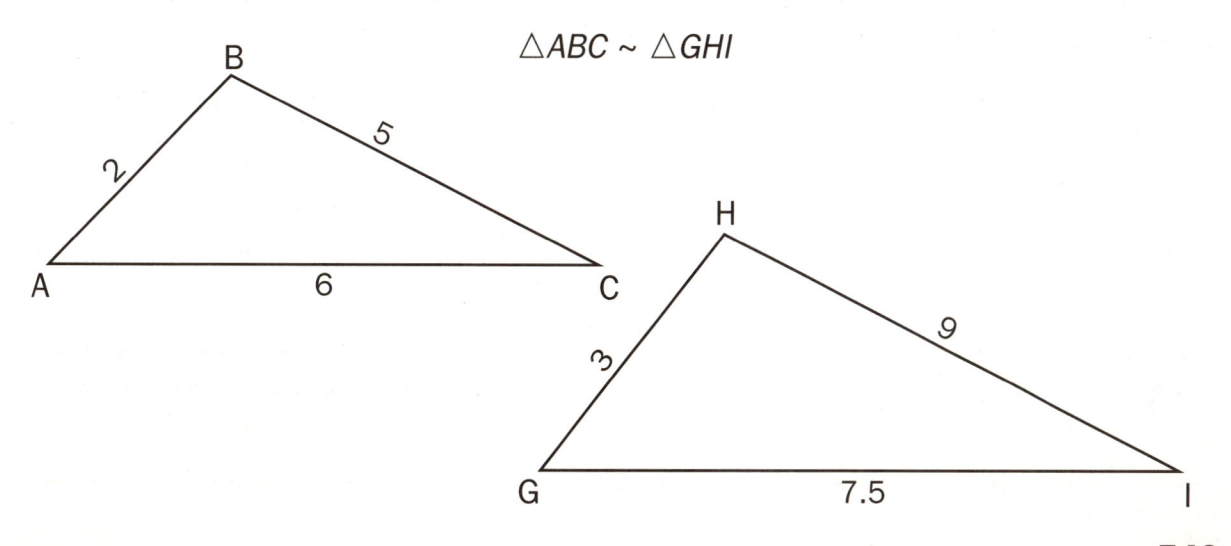

△ABC ~ △GHI

549

Lesson 108 **AlgebraicThinking • Foundations**

When we know we have similar triangles, we are able to figure out unknown side measurements by using the ratio of the sides. We create a proportion.

Look at the following similar triangles.

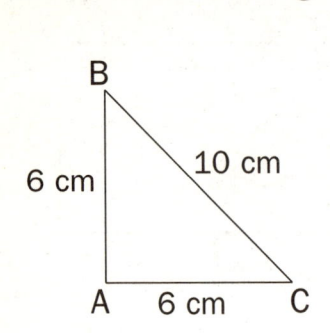

△ABC ~ △DEF

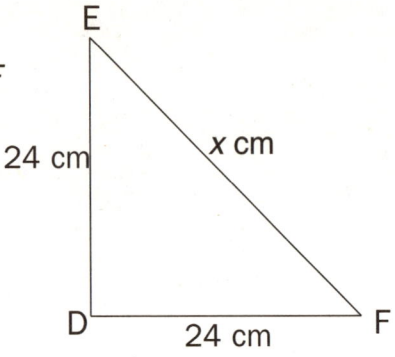

We know that $\overline{AB}$ ~ $\overline{DE}$ and $\overline{BC}$ ~ $\overline{EF}$. We know all of the measurements except that of the line segment EF.

We can set up a proportion which allows us to find the measurement of $\overline{EF}$.

$$\frac{\overline{AB}}{\overline{DE}} = \frac{\overline{BC}}{\overline{EF}} \qquad \frac{6}{24} = \frac{10}{x}$$

$$\frac{6x}{6} = \frac{240}{6} \qquad \text{When you cross multiply,}$$
$$x = 40 \qquad \text{divide both sides by 6.}$$

$\overline{EF}$ = 40 cm

Use a proportion to find the measure of the missing side.

1. ▱ABCD ~ ▱EFGH

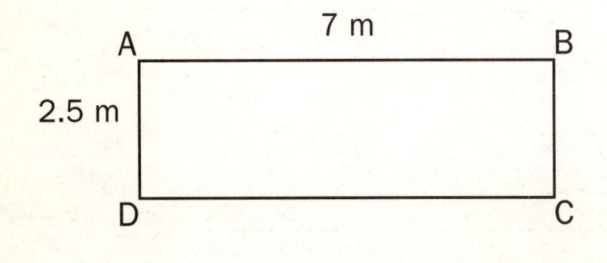

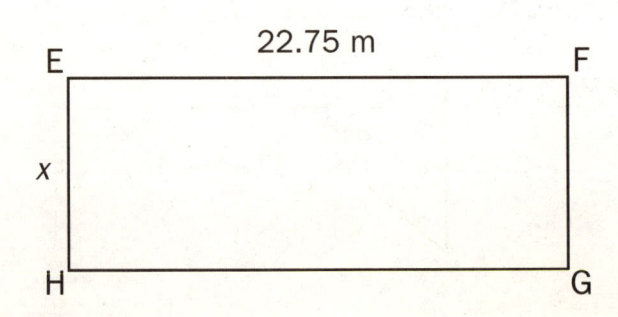

550

AlgebraicThinking • Foundations

Lesson 108

Use a proportion to find the measure of the missing side.

2. The polygons given are similar.

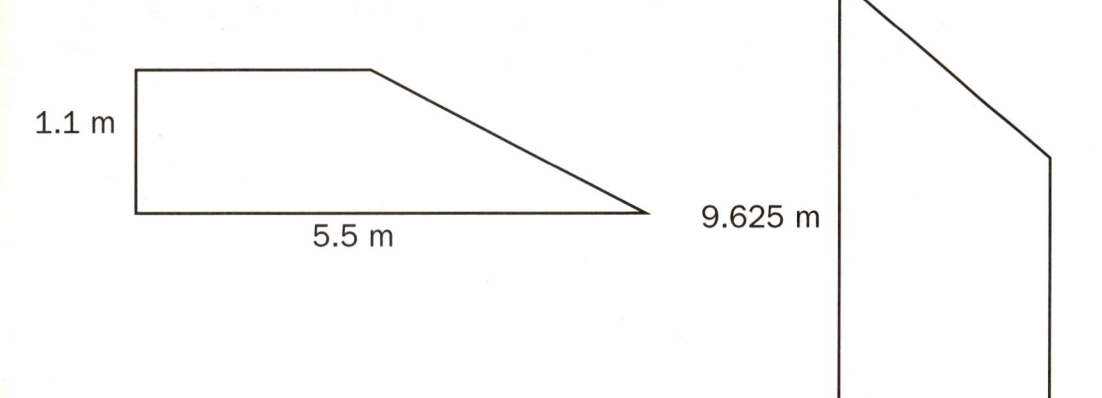

1.1 m

5.5 m

9.625 m

n

3. The polygons given are similar.

80 m

20 m

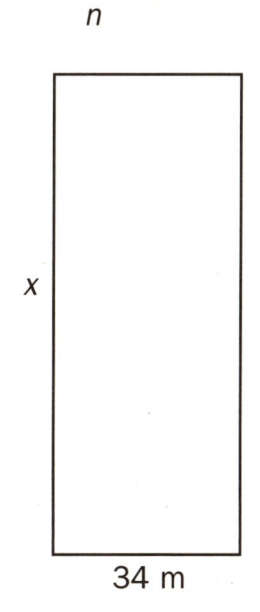

x

34 m

4. The polygons given are similar.

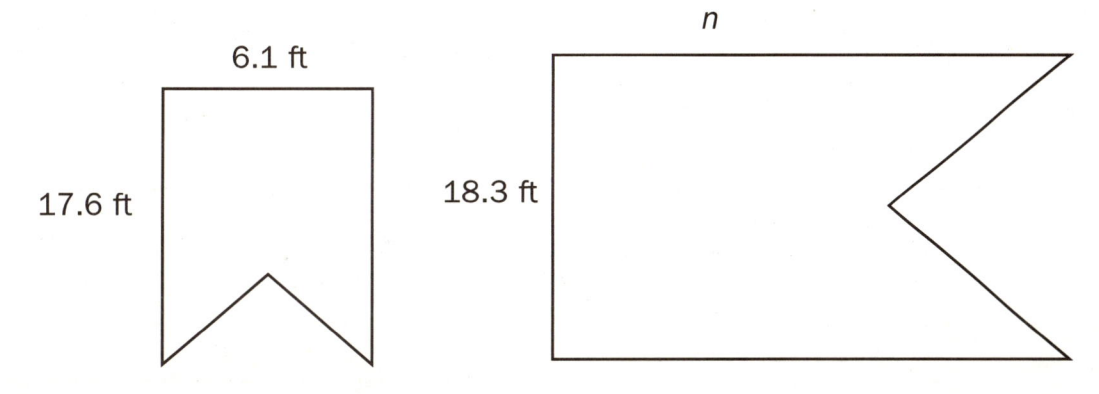

6.1 ft

17.6 ft

n

18.3 ft

551

Lesson 108

AlgebraicThinking • Foundations

SOLVE

5. Brett bought a model car which was 12 inches long and 5 inches high. The model car was built exactly to the same scale as the real car. If the real car is 5 feet high, how long is it?

S

O

L

V

E

Algebraic Thinking • Foundations   Homework 108

Name _____

Directions: *Solve each equation.*

1. $x - \frac{2}{3} = \frac{1}{4}$

2. $8 + x = {}^-4$

3. $x - 4.3 = 9.8$

4. $x + {}^-7 = 3$

5. $8 - 10 = x$

6. $5x = 60$

7. $x + 2 = {}^-11$

8. $3x = {}^-21$

9. $5x = {}^-20$

10. $x - \frac{1}{6} = \frac{2}{9}$

Warm Up 109: Did You Know?

Uniquely You

1. Who is your favorite cartoon character? Why do you like him/her the best?

2. Do you collect anything? If so, what?

3. What is your best friend's name? Why do you like them?

Crazy Questions

4. Which number is funnier, 4 or 5? (Be creative.)

5. Which number is better, one or one million? Why?

AlgebraicThinking • Foundations Lesson 109

Metric Units of Length

Two units of measure for length are the _____ and the _____ . The **centimeter** is longer than the **millimeter.** In fact, it is 10 times longer than the millimeter. The thickness of a penny is about one millimeter. Can you think of something that has the length of one centimeter?

_____

In the picture above, the pencil is ____ cm long or _____ mm long.

EXPLORE! Measurement

Your teacher will assign you several objects to measure. You will then use a ruler, meter stick, or tape measure to measure the length, height, or width of the object. Record all information in the chart below. Be sure to include a diagram (picture) of the object on a separate sheet of paper. The last object your teacher selects will be a rectangle. Measure all four sides of it.

Object	Measurement(s)

Lesson 109 **Algebraic Thinking • Foundations**

Ask your teacher for a dictionary to define the following units of measure.
- cubit
- fathom
- chain
- furlong
- micrometer
- nanometer

You probably used centimeters to measure most of the objects. List a few objects that you would use millimeters to measure.

I would use millimeters to measure the following items:

1. _____   2. _____

3. _____   4. _____

5. _____

On your Own!

Directions: *Use a ruler to measure each of the following objects in cm.*

1. Nail **2.** Paintbrush  **3.** Pencil

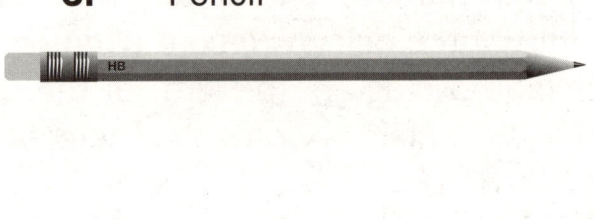

4. Ball point pen  **5.** Hardware

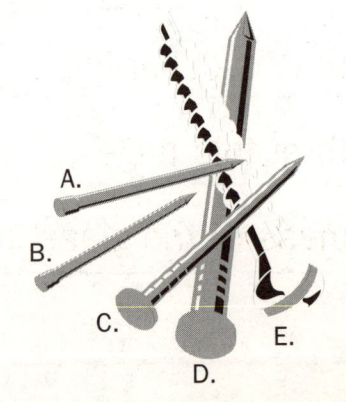

556

Algebraic Thinking • Foundations   Lesson 109

At the beginning of this lesson, you measured all four sides of a rectangle. If you add all four measures of the rectangle together, it is called the **perimeter.** Can you find the perimeter of the following door?

Rectangles aren't the only shapes with a perimeter. In fact, **polygons,** or *all closed shapes in one plane with straight edges,* have a perimeter. Draw five shapes and measure the perimeter of each. (Be creative. Try shapes other than rectangles.)

Directions: *Circle the more reasonable unit of measure for each item.*

1. thickness of your fingernail   cm *or* mm

2. length of a pencil   cm *or* mm

3. length of a dollar bill   cm *or* mm

4. length of this page   cm *or* mm

5. thickness of the glass in a window   cm *or* mm

Lesson 109 **AlgebraicThinking** • Foundations

Directions: *Estimate the length of each segment in centimeters. Then measure each segment with a ruler.*

6. _____   Estimate: _____

   Actual: _____

7.   ____   Estimate: _____

   Actual: _____

8.   _____   Estimate: _____

   Actual: _____

9.   _____   Estimate: _____

   Actual: _____

10. Estimate the perimeter of this **pentagon.** Then measure it. (Use centimeters.)

   Estimate: _____
   Actual: _____

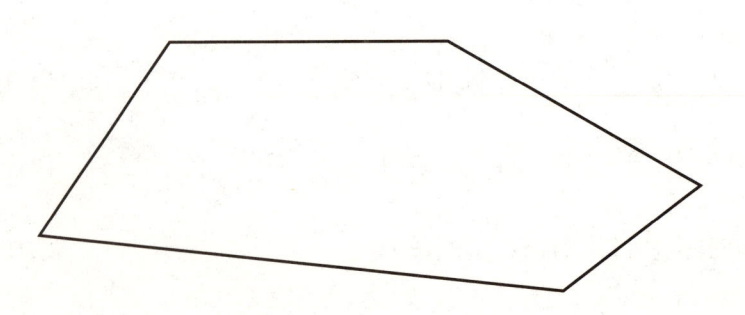

558

AlgebraicThinking • Foundations Lesson 109

Today we have talked about two units which are used to measure lines or parts of lines. These kind of units are used for **linear measurement.** Now we are going to talk about two more linear measurement units. There are many more metric units, but we will focus on two of the more common ones. These are used to measure longer distances. For instance, the distances of races in track meets are measured in _____. In countries that use the metric system, distances between cities are measured in _____.

PSSSSST! There are 100 cm in a meter and 1,000 meters in a kilometer

Complete the following charts.

Meters	Centimeters
1	100
	200
	300
4	
5	
	1,000
15	

Kilometers	Meters
1	1,000
2	
3	
	4,000
	5,000
45	
	100,000

Directions: *Choose the more reasonable estimate.*

11. the height of your desk   1 cm   or   1 m   or   1 km

12. the length of 6 city blocks   1 cm   or   1 m   or   1 km

13. the height of a flagpole   9 cm   or   9 m   or   9 km

14. the length of a sheet of paper   26 cm   or   26 m   or   26 km

15. the length of a mountain trail   6 cm   or   6 m   or   6 km

559

Homework 109 — Algebraic Thinking • Foundations

Name _____

Directions: *Solve.*

1. What percent of 75 is 15?

2. 6 is what percent of 50?

3. What is 42% of 50?

4. What percent of 20 is 5?

5. What is 65% of 140?

6. What is 80% of 60?

7. 72 is what percent of 120?

8. What percent of 60 is 12?

9. 4 is what percent of 50?

10. What is 35% of 80?

AlgebraicThinking • Foundations

Warm Up 110: Triangle Times

If you added five more rows to the bottom of this figure, how many "small" triangles would you have in all?

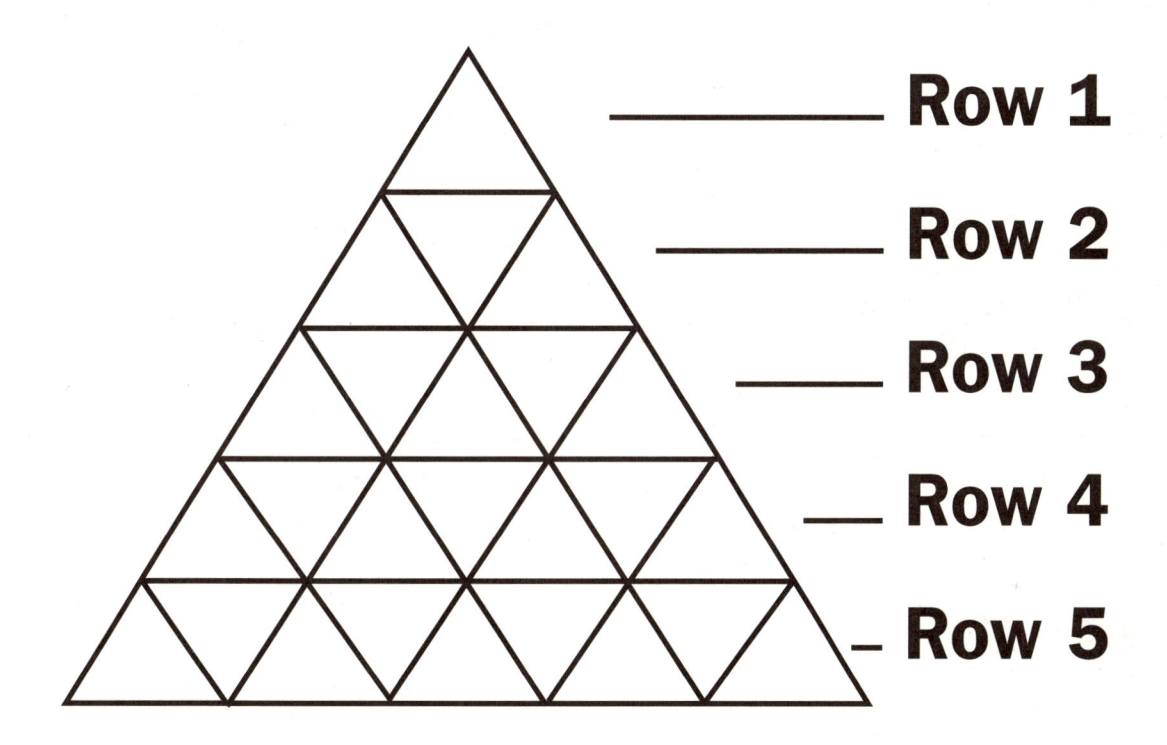

———— Row 1

———— Row 2

———— Row 3

———— Row 4

– Row 5

Lesson 110 Algebraic Thinking • Foundations

Metric Units of Capacity and Weight

The _____ is the metric unit used to measure the weight of lighter objects. A paper clip weighs about one gram and a nickel weighs about 5 grams. *Take a minute to list several things that you think weigh less than 10 grams.*

The _____ is the metric unit used to measure the weight of heavier objects. A school textbook weighs about 1 kilogram. *Take a minute to list several objects which you would use kilograms to measure.*

What are we gonna measure now?

1 kilogram = 1,000 grams
1 kilometer = 1,000 meters

Your teacher will give you several objects. Record the weight of each object in the chart below. Be sure to include the unit you used!

Name of Object	Weight

Directions: *Choose the more reasonable unit for measuring the weight of each object.*

1. your pencil
   g   kg

2. a person
   g   kg

3. this paper
   g   kg

4. an aspirin
   g   kg

5. a car
   g   kg

6. an elephant
   g   kg

562

Algebraic Thinking • Foundations Lesson 110

The _____ is the metric unit used to measure the capacity of smaller objects. A drop of water from an eye dropper is about one milliliter. *Take a minute to list several objects whose capacity you would measure in milliliters.*

The _____ is the metric unit used to measure the capacity of larger objects. *A quart milk container is about 1 liter. Take a minute to list several objects whose capacity you would measure in liters.*

Hey, man, like, what's the capacity?

Your teacher will give you several objects. Record the capacity of each object in the chart below. Be sure to include the unit you used!

Name of Object	Capacity

1 liter = 1,000 milliliters
1 meter = 1,000 millimeters

Directions: *Choose the most reasonable unit for measuring.*

7. a soda bottle
   L   mL

8. a raindrop
   L   mL

9. water in a fish tank
   L   mL

563

Directions: *Complete the following conversions.*

10. 4 kg = ____ g

11. 6.4 kg = ____ g

12. 3,000 mL = ____ L

13. 250 g = ____ kg

14. 5.8 L = ____ mL

15. 8,250 g = ____ kg

16. 10.75 kg = ____ g

17. 500 mL = ____ L

18. 3 L = ____ mL

Directions: *Choose the best answer.*

19. How much soda pop is in a large plastic bottle?
a. 3 mL
b. 3 L
c. 30 mL
d. 30 L

20. What is the weight of a person?
a. 8 g
b. 8 kg
c. 80 g
d. 80 kg

21. How much water is in a raindrop?
a. 10 L
b. 10 mL
c. 2 L
d. 2 mL

22. What is the weight of an apple?
a. 50 g
b. 50 kg
c. 25 kg
d. 25 g

23. What is the weight of a quarter?
a. 5 g
b. 5 kg
c. 50 g
d. 50 kg

24. What is the capacity of a jug of milk?
a. 3.78 mL
b. 3.78 L
c. 25 mL
d. 25 L

AlgebraicThinking • Foundations

Homework 110

Name _____

Directions: *Find each product.*

1. 6 • ⁻3 =

2. ⁻8 • 7 =

3. $\frac{2}{3}$ • ⁻9 =

4. ⁻5 • ⁻9 =

5. ⁻2$\frac{1}{2}$ • 4 =

6. ⁻8 • $\frac{3}{4}$ =

Directions: *Find at least four objects at home. Read the label and record the weight or capacity in metric units.*

Item	Weight/Capacity
7.	
8.	
9.	
10.	

565

Warm Up 111

Warm Up 111: Pyramids

Perform the operations from left to right. Put the answer for each pair of integers above and between them.

Addition

```
              _____
           _____   _____
        _____   _____   _____
     _____   _____   _____   _____
   3       ⁻8       ⁻6        0       ⁻2
```

Multiplication

```
              _____
           _____   _____
        _____   _____   _____
     _____   _____   _____   _____
  ⁻3       12       ⁻1       ⁻2        5
```

Subtraction

```
              _____
           _____   _____
        _____   _____   _____
     _____   _____   _____   _____
  ⁻7       ⁻7       10        3        2
```

Algebraic Thinking • Foundations Lesson 111

Customary Units of Length

Throughout U.S. history, the Customary System which is inherited from, but now different from, the British Imperial System, has been customarily used as the primary system of measurement. The inch (in.), foot (ft), yard (yd), and mile (mi) are used to measure length in the customary system.

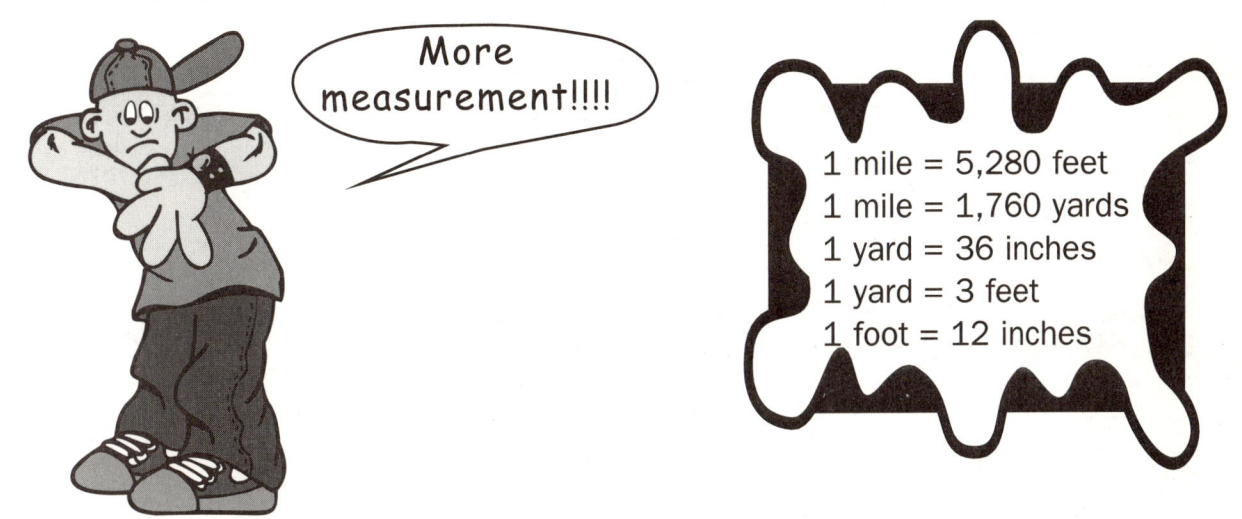

More measurement!!!!

1 mile = 5,280 feet
1 mile = 1,760 yards
1 yard = 36 inches
1 yard = 3 feet
1 foot = 12 inches

EXPLORE! Measurement

Your teacher will assign you several objects to measure. You will then use a ruler, yard stick, or tape measure to measure the length, height, or width of the object. Record all information in the chart below. Be sure to include a diagram (picture) of the object on a separate sheet of paper. The last object your teacher selects will be a rectangle. Measure all four sides of it.

Object	Measurement(s)

567

Lesson 111 Algebraic Thinking • Foundations

Directions: *Choose the more reasonable unit for measuring.*

1. the length of a football field
   mi   yd   ft   in.

2. the height of an adult
   mi   yd   ft   in.

3. the distance to England
   mi   yd   ft   in.

4. the thickness of a text book
   mi   yd   ft   in.

5. the length of a cricket
   mi   yd   ft   in.

6. the distance to the moon
   mi   yd   ft   in.

Directions: *Complete the following conversions.*

7. 4 yd = ____ ft

8. 4 yd = ____ in.

9. 2.5 mi = ____ ft

10. 36 in. = ____ ft

11. 18 in. = ____ ft

12. 10 ft = ____ in.

13. 10.5 ft = ____ in.

14. 40 in. = ____ ft

15. 3 in. = ____ ft

At the beginning of this lesson and in a previous lesson, you measured all four sides of a rectangle. Do you remember what the sum of the measures of all four sides of a rectangle is called?

What is the perimeter of the rectangle that you measured?

Algebraic Thinking • Foundations   Lesson 111

Directions: *Estimate the length of each segment in inches. Then measure each segment with a ruler.*

16. _____   Estimate: _____

    Actual: _____

17.   _____   Estimate: _____

    Actual: _____

18.   _____   Estimate: _____

    Actual: _____

19.   _____   Estimate: _____

    Actual: _____

20. Estimate the perimeter of this **pentagon.** Then measure it. (Use inches.)

    Estimate: _____
    Actual: _____

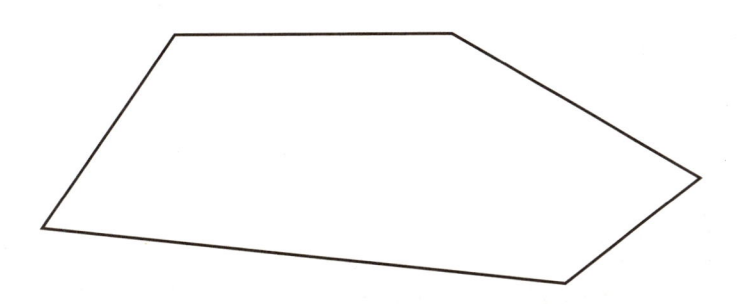

569

Homework 111 **AlgebraicThinking** • Foundations

Name _____

Directions: *Find each sum or difference.*

1. $\dfrac{1}{2}$
   $+\dfrac{2}{3}$

2. $\dfrac{3}{4}$
   $+\dfrac{2}{5}$

3. $\dfrac{7}{8}$
   $-\dfrac{3}{4}$

4. $2\dfrac{1}{3}$
   $+3\dfrac{3}{4}$

5. $4\dfrac{1}{5}$
   $-3\dfrac{7}{10}$

6. 1
   $-\dfrac{2}{3}$

Directions: *Use a ruler to measure the length or width of any four items in your house. Use feet or inches.*

Item	Measure
7.	
8.	
9.	
10.	

AlgebraicThinking • Foundations   Warm Up 112

Warm Up 112: Triangles, Triangles, Triangles

How many triangles can you find in the figure below?

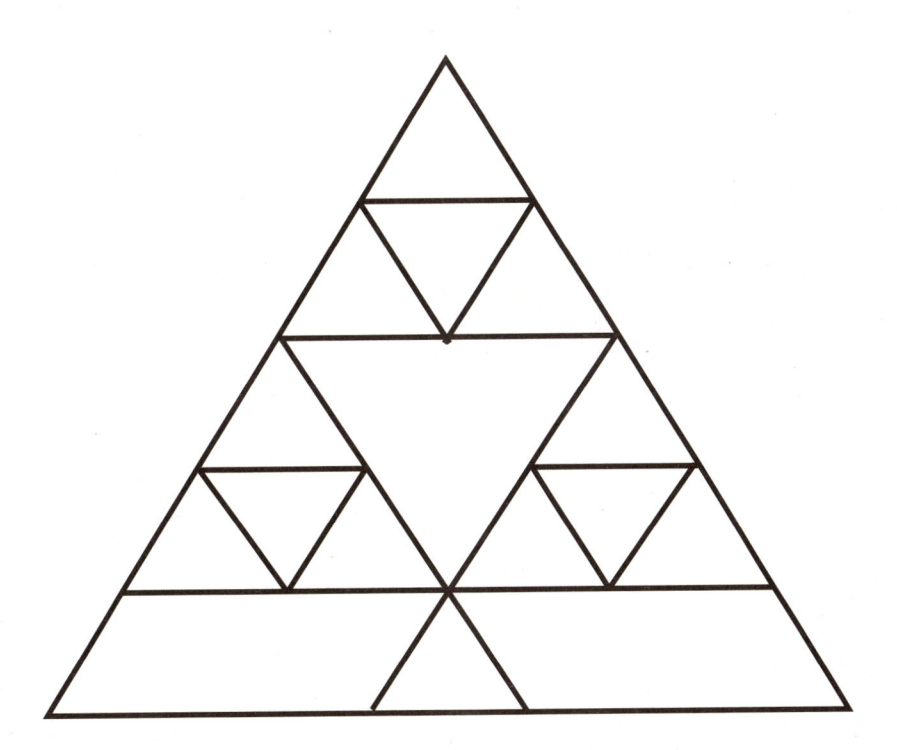

Lesson 112   Algebraic Thinking • Foundations

Customary Units of Capacity and Weight

In the Customary System, the _____ , _____ , _____ ,

_____ , and _____ are used to measure capacity.

Directions: Your teacher will give you several objects. Record the capacity of each object in the chart below. Be sure to include the unit you used!

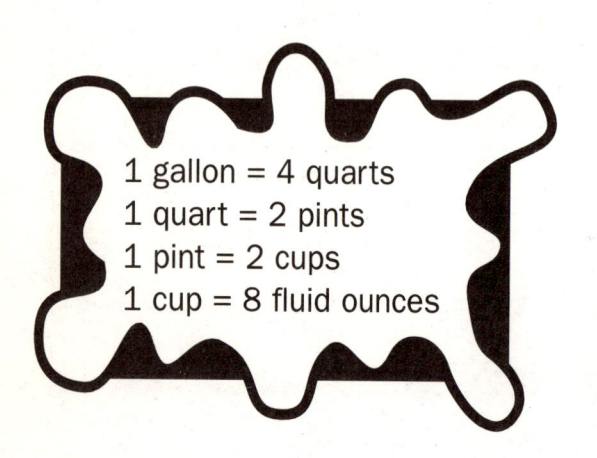

1 gallon = 4 quarts
1 quart = 2 pints
1 pint = 2 cups
1 cup = 8 fluid ounces

Name of Object	Capacity

Directions: Choose the most reasonable unit for measuring.

1. capacity of a car's gas tank
fl oz   c   pt   qt   gal

2. water in a water tower
fl oz   c   pt   qt   gal

3. capacity of a fountain drink
fl oz   c   pt   qt   gal

4. sugar in a recipe
fl oz   c   pt   qt   gal

Directions: Complete the following conversions.

5. 128 fl oz = ____ c

6. 16 c = ____ pt

7. 8 pt = ____ qt

8. 4 qt = ____ gal

9. 1 gal = ____ fl oz

10. 1 gal = ____ c

11. 1 gal = ____ pt

12. 30 c = ____ pt

13. 3 qt = ____ gal

AlgebraicThinking • Foundations

Lesson 112

In the Customary System, the _____ , _____ , and _____ are used to measure weight.

Directions: This time, record the weight of the objects in the chart below. Don't forget the units!

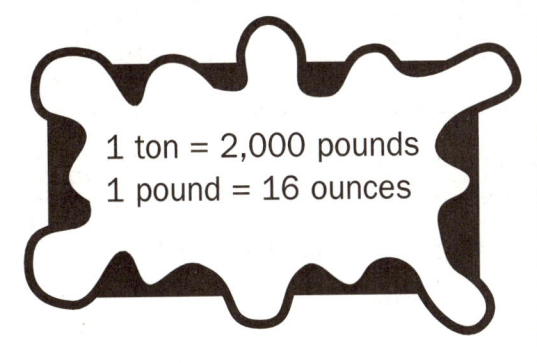

1 ton = 2,000 pounds
1 pound = 16 ounces

Name of Object	Weight

Directions: Choose the most reasonable unit for measuring.

14. weight of your teacher (be nice)
    oz   lb   t

15. weight of an elephant
    oz   lb   t

16. weight of a can of vegetables
    oz   lb   t

17. weight of a dog
    oz   lb   t

Directions: Complete the following conversions.

18. 20,000 lb = _____ t

19. 43 oz = _____ lb _____ oz

20. 4 t = _____ lb

21. 1,000 lb = _____ t

22. 1,500 lb = _____ t

23. 8 oz = _____ lb

573

Warm Up 113: Did You Know?

1. The Pilgrims sailed from Plymouth, England, on the *Mayflower* on September 6, 1620 (some sources say September 13). The ship weighed 180 tons. How many pounds did the *Mayflower* weigh?

2. That's nothing! On April 14, 1912, the ocean liner, *Titanic*, ran into an iceberg. Less than three hours later it sank. The *Titanic* weighed 46,328 tons. How many pounds did the *Titanic* weigh?

3. On September 14, 1959, the Soviet Space Probe Luna II became the first man-made object to reach the moon. On average, the moon is 384,400 kilometers away from the earth. How many meters is this?

4. How many people do you think it would take to reach the moon if they stood on each other's shoulders?

Algebraic Thinking • Foundations   Lesson 113

Geometric Solids

Today we will learn about solid figures with only flat surfaces and later we will learn about solids with some flat and some curved surfaces. Solids that have flat surfaces only are called polyhedrons. A **polyhedron** *is a solid formed by polygons that enclose a part of space.* Look at the pictures below.

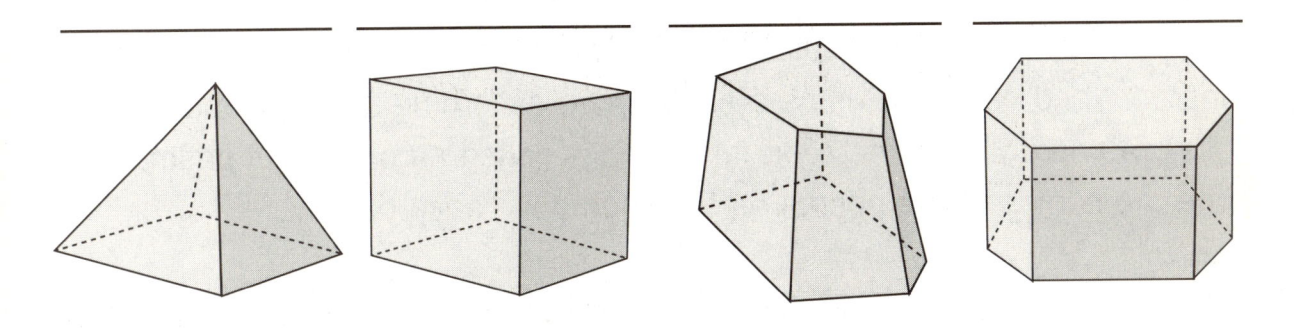

Each figure is a polyhedron. The flat surfaces are called **faces.** Notice that there are no curved surfaces. All faces in polyhedrons are made of *polygons*. Take a minute to list all the polygons you see in the polyhedrons.

A segment where two faces intersect is called an **edge.** A point where three or more edges intersect is called a **vertex** of the polyhedron. Polygons are named by the number of sides they have. Polyhedrons are named by the number of faces they have. The same prefixes used for polygons are used for polyhedrons, except for quadrilaterals. A polyhedron with four faces is called a **tetrahedron.** The prefix *hexa* means six, so a polyhedron with six faces is called a hexahedron. What do you call a polyhedron with 8 faces?

List the names for the polyhedrons pictured above on the line above the polyhedron.

Lesson 113   **Algebraic Thinking** • **Foundations**

The first type of polyhedron that we will talk about is called a **prism.** The polyhedrons below are examples of prisms.

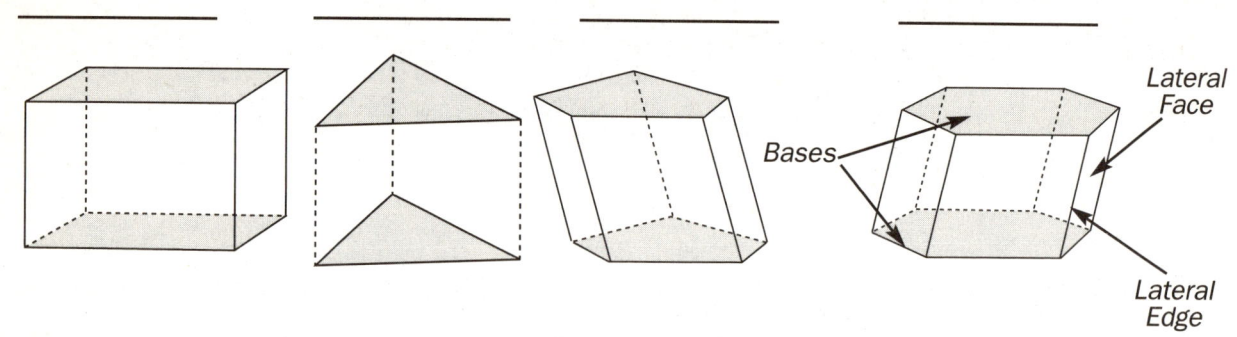

The two shaded faces are called **bases.** The bases of a prism are congruent and parallel. Prisms are classified according to the shape of the bases. A prism with an octagon for bases is called an octagonal prism. Write the names of the prisms on the line above each drawing.

The faces that are not bases are called **lateral faces.** The intersection of lateral faces form **lateral edges.** When the lateral edges are perpendicular to the base, the prism is a **right prism.** When the lateral edges are not perpendicular to the bases, it is called an **oblique prism.** (This is not true for pyramids.)

Now, we will talk about **pyramids.** The following polyhedrons are pyramids.

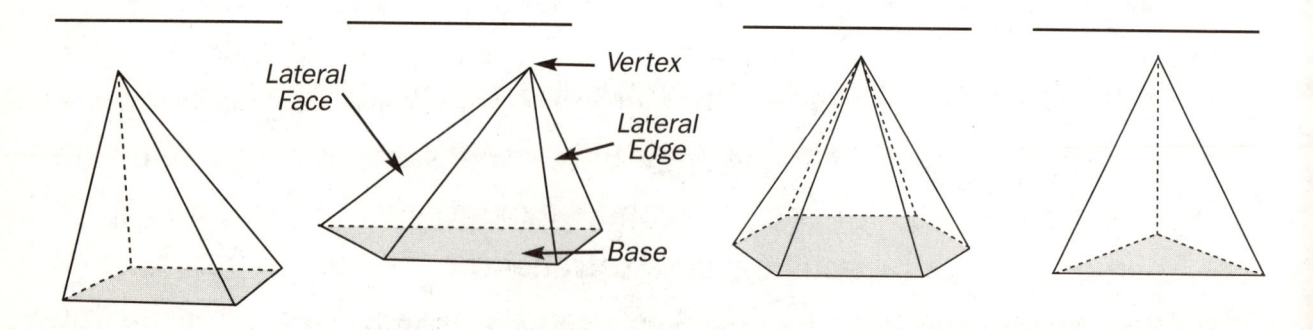

The shaded face is called a **base.** The faces that are not bases are called **lateral faces.** The intersection of lateral faces form **lateral edges.** Pyramids are also classified according to the shape of the base. What are the names of the pyramids above?

Algebraic Thinking • Foundations Lesson 113

Let's Build Some Polyhedrons!

We will build polyhedrons with toothpicks or spaghetti. We will connect them with clay, gumdrops, or marshmallows. You may have to cut or break some of the sticks. Save all the polyhedrons you make.

1. Build a square pyramid.

2. Build a hexagonal pyramid.

3. Build a cube (a cube is a square prism).

4. Build a hexagonal prism.

5. Build an oblique prism.

6. Build a tetrahedron.

7. How are prisms and pyramids alike? *List at least 2 ways.*

8. How are prisms and pyramids different? *List at least 2 ways.*

9. The lateral faces of pyramids are always what shape?

10. The lateral faces of prisms are always what shape?

Lesson 113   Algebraic Thinking • Foundations

Cylinders and **cones** are two examples of solids that have curved surfaces. Since they have surfaces that are not formed by polygons, they are not polyhedrons. Below are pictures of them. Can you think of items that are cylinders or cones?

Out of the two solids at the right, which is more like a prism? Why?

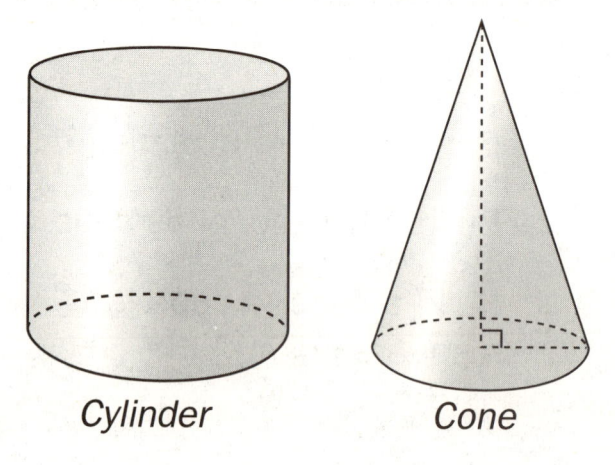

Cylinder   *Cone*

Which is more like a pyramid? Why?

Algebraic Thinking • Foundations

Homework 113

Name _____

Directions: *Use a straightedge to draw each of the following.*

1. a 35° angle

2. an obtuse triangle

3. a parallelogram with no right angles

4. a concave hexagon

5. an isosceles triangle

6. a trapezoid with only one right angle

7. What is the area of a trapezoid with bases of 10 inches and 7 inches and a height of 8 inches?

8. What is the area of a triangle with a base 12 inches and a height of 4 inches?

Warm Up 114

Warm Up 114: Division Tower

Follow the division problems from top to bottom. Use the answer for each problem as the dividend in the next problem.

20,160 ÷ 10 = ____

____ ÷ 9 = ____

____ ÷ 4 = ____

____ ÷ 8 = ____

____ ÷ 7 = ____

Algebraic Thinking • Foundations   Lesson 114

Volume of Prisms

Volume is the amount of space that a figure takes up. It is measured in cubic units. Complete the following activity to learn more about volume.

You will need some small cubes and scratch paper to complete this activity.

1. Make a single layer rectangular prism that is 5 cubes long and 4 cubes wide. The prism's dimensions are 5 units by 4 units by 1 unit. What is the area of the prism's base? _____ How many cubes are in the prism? _____

2. Add another layer to the prism to make the dimensions 5 units by 4 units by 2 units. What is the area of the prism's base? _____ How many cubes are in the prism? _____

3. Add another layer to the prism to make the dimensions 5 units by 4 units by 3 units. What is the area of the prism's base? _____ How many cubes are in the prism? _____

4. Add another layer to the prism to make the dimensions 5 units by 4 units by 4 units. What is the area of the prism's base? _____ How many cubes are in the prism? _____

Lesson 114 AlgebraicThinking • Foundations

5. If you added one more layer to your prism, how many cubes would there be? _____

6. How many cubes would be in the prism if it had 10 layers?

7. What would be the volume of a prism that had 30 cubes in its base and 5 layers of cubes?

8. To find the volume of a prism, multiply the area of the _____ times the _____.

AlgebraicThinking • Foundations

Lesson 114

Directions: *Find the volume for each prism.*

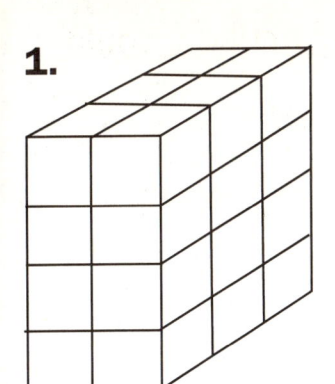

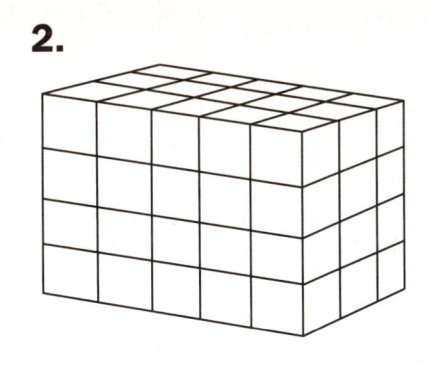

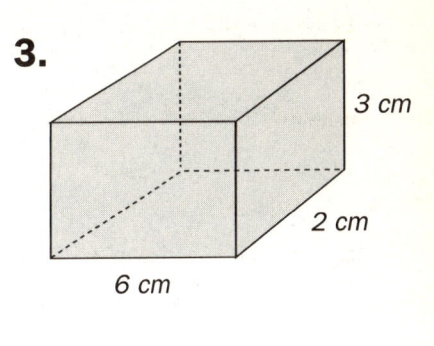

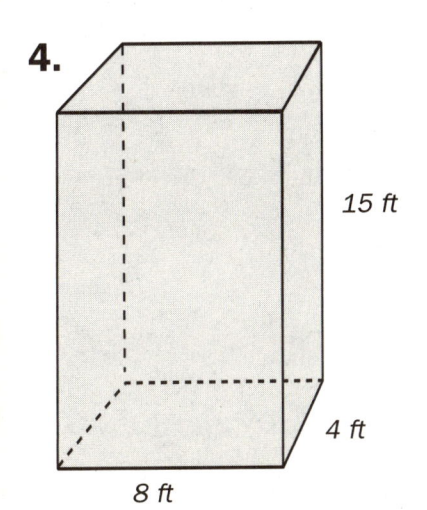

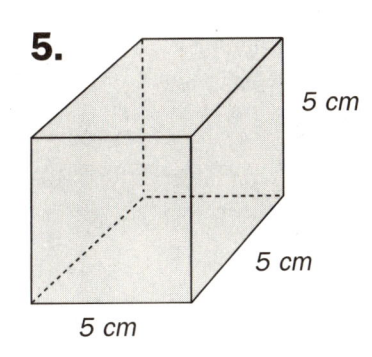

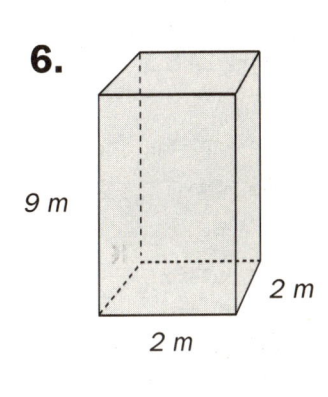

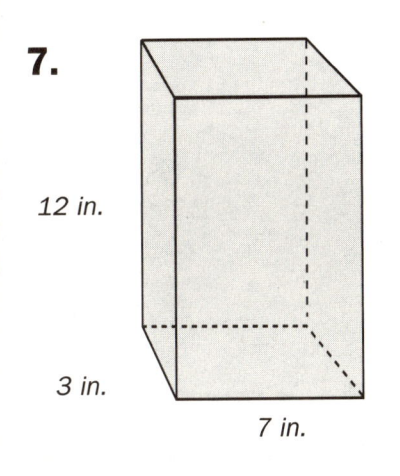

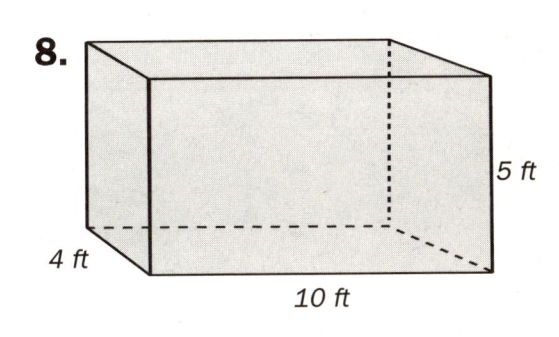

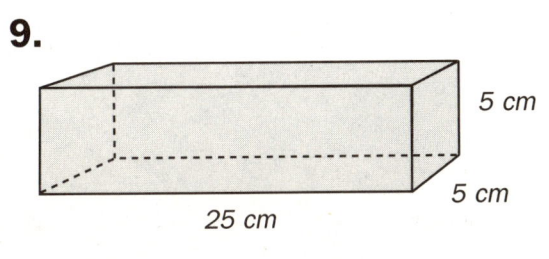

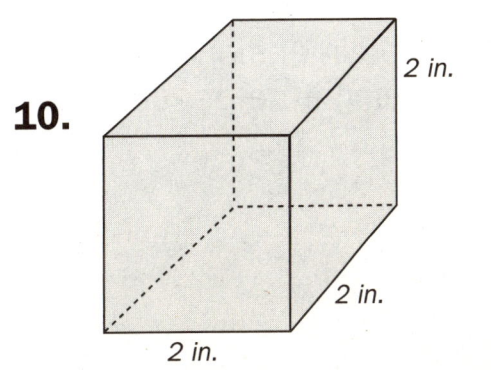

1.

2.

3.
3 cm
2 cm
6 cm

4.
15 ft
4 ft
8 ft

5.
5 cm
5 cm
5 cm

6.
9 m
2 m
2 m

7.
12 in.
3 in.
7 in.

8.
5 ft
4 ft
10 ft

9.
5 cm
5 cm
25 cm

10.
2 in.
2 in.
2 in.

583

Homework 114 **AlgebraicThinking** • Foundations

Name _____

Directions: *S-O-L-V-E the following problems.*

1. Sally Baker the cake maker is baking me a cake. It will be a huge rectangular cake with icing on the top only. The top of the cake measures 3 feet by 5 feet. It is 6 inches tall. In square inches, what is the area to be covered by icing?

2. What is the volume of a rectangular prism 5 meters by 4 meters by 3 meters high?

3. Hector's mother is forcing him to build a pen for his pet ferret. What are the dimensions of the largest pen Hector can make with 30 feet of fencing if he uses an existing wall as part of the pen?

Algebraic Thinking • Foundations

Warm Up 115: Tic-Tac-Toe

Simon and Omar played a game of tic–tac-toe. Find out who won the game by solving each equation. Put the appropriate letter on the board.

<u>Simon played the X</u>
$n + 6 = 15$
$n + 3 = {}^-12$
$n - 8 = {}^-7$
$n - {}^-2 = 0$

<u>Omar played the O</u>
$n + {}^-6 = 4$
$n - 8 = {}^-12$
$n - 14 = 8$
$n + 12 = 0$

9	2	⁻2
22	⁻15	⁻12
1	⁻4	10

Who won the game? _____

585

Warm Up 116: Pyramids

Perform the operations from left to right. Put the answer for each pair of integers above and between them.

Addition

7   ⁻18   ⁻6   11   ⁻8

Multiplication

⁻2   4   1   ⁻3   7

Subtraction

8   ⁻9   8   5   7

586

AlgebraicThinking • Foundations　　　　　　　　Lesson 116

Solving Two-Step Equations

Directions: *Model these equations with your teacher. Then draw what you modeled and state how you would solve the equation without using models.*

Problem	Model	How to Solve
1. $2c + 4 = 6$		
2. $3c + {}^-5 = 10$		
3. $4c + 4 = 16$		
4. $5c + 3 = 13$		
5. $2c + {}^-8 = 0$		

Lesson 116 — **AlgebraicThinking** • Foundations

Directions: *Solve each equation with your partner. Make sure you show all of your work and check the problem.*

1. $3n + 2 = 14$ Check

2. $2d + {}^-7 = 9$ Check

3. $5y + 3 = 63$ Check

4. ${}^-4x + 3 = 27$ Check

5. ${}^-2t + 5 = 15$ Check

6. $7x - 6 = 50$ Check

Algebraic Thinking • Foundations Lesson 116

Directions: *Solve the equations and then answer each question with your partner.*

$$2x + 5 = 7 \qquad 3x + 4 = {}^-11$$

1. How many steps are there to solve each equation?

2. What operations did you do first each time?

3. What operation did you do second each time?

4. What is your goal each time?

5. What is the opposite of each operation?

   Addition _____

   Subtraction _____

   Multiplication _____

   Division _____

6. Explain why you must do the same operations to both sides of an equation when solving it.

   _____

   _____

589

Homework 116

AlgebraicThinking • Foundations

Name _____

Directions: *Find the area of each shape. Write the formula to show your work.*

1.

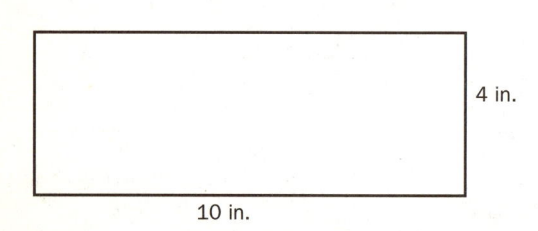

4 in.
10 in.

2.

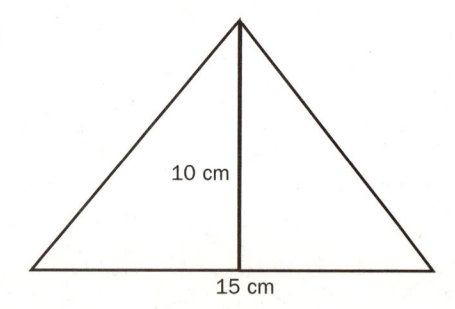

10 cm
15 cm

3.

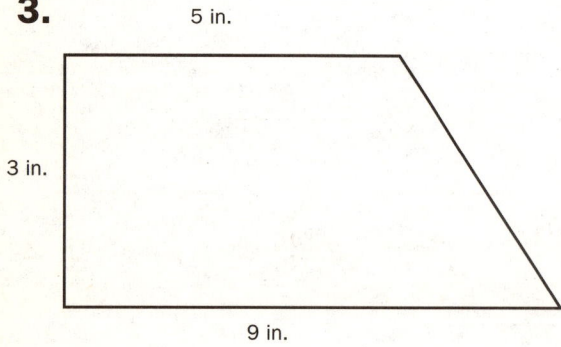

5 in.
3 in.
9 in.

4.

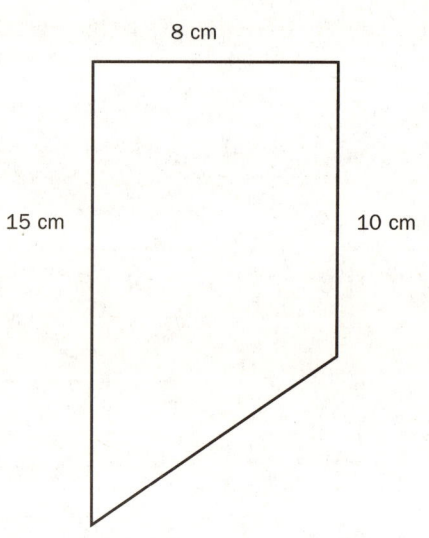

8 cm
15 cm
10 cm

5.

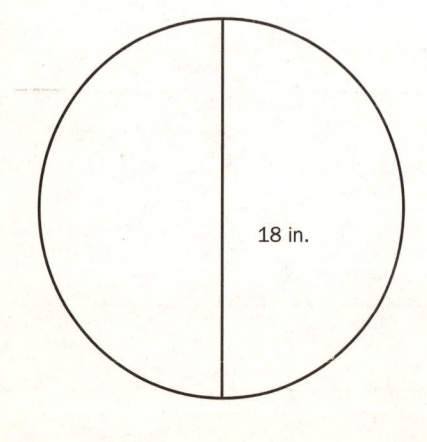

18 in.

6.

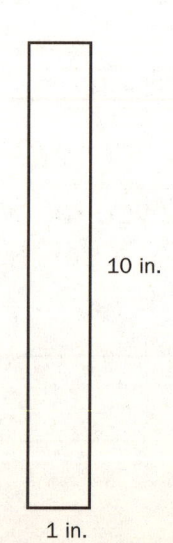

10 in.
1 in.

590

AlgebraicThinking • Foundations　　　　　　　　　　　　　　Warm Up 117

Warm Up 117: Pyramids

Perform the operations from left to right. Put the answer for each pair of integers above and between them.

Addition

```
                    _____
                _____    _____
            _____    _____    _____
        _____    _____    _____    _____
   ⁻8        ⁻7         8         3        ⁻2
```

Multiplication

```
                    _____
                _____    _____
            _____    _____    _____
        _____    _____    _____    _____
   ⁻2         1         3        ⁻2         2
```

Subtraction

```
                    _____
                _____    _____
            _____    _____    _____
        _____    _____    _____    _____
    8        10        ⁻4        ⁻3         6
```

591

Lesson 117 Algebraic Thinking • Foundations

Two-Step Equations

Directions: *Follow along with your teacher to solve each equation.*

1. $3x - 7 = 8$　　　　　　　　　　　　　　　Check

2. $\frac{x}{2} + 3 = 4$　　　　　　　　　　　　　Check

3. $^-4m + 3 = {^-9}$　　　　　　　　　　　　Check

4. $\frac{n}{5} - 12 = {^-8}$　　　　　　　　　　　Check

5. $\frac{f}{^-3} + 1 = 7$　　　　　　　　　　　　Check

6. $7d - 6 = 8$　　　　　　　　　　　　　　Check

AlgebraicThinking • Foundations   Lesson 117

Directions: Solve each equation with your partner. Make sure you show all of your work and check.

1. $\frac{x}{5} + 28 = 18$ Check

2. $3x - 12 = {}^-21$ Check

3. $\frac{c}{2} - 6 = 8$ Check

4. $2y + 5 = 23$ Check

5. $\frac{y}{3} - 2 = {}^-2$ Check

6. **S-O-L-V-E:** Last night at El Parrel, Gina bought 6 dinner specials for each person in her family. She left a $12 tip for the waiter. If she spent a total of $54, how much did each dinner cost?

S

O

L

V

E

Homework 117   **AlgebraicThinking • Foundations**

Name _____

Directions: *Find each quotient.*

1. $\frac{2}{3} \div \frac{1}{3} =$

2. $3 \div \frac{1}{4} =$

3. $\frac{3}{4} \div \frac{1}{8} =$

4. $\frac{1}{2} \div \frac{3}{4} =$

5. $2\frac{3}{5} \div \frac{1}{10} =$

6. $\frac{5}{8} \div \frac{5}{8} =$

Directions: *Find at least four objects at home. Read the label and record the weight or capacity in standard units.*

Item	Weight/Capacity
7.	
8.	
9.	
10.	

AlgebraicThinking • Foundations

Warm Up 118: Did You Know?

1. On October 11, 1984, Kathleen Sullivan became the first American woman to walk in space. If she weighed 115 pounds 6 ounces, her space suit weighed 25 pounds 8 ounces, and her oxygen tanks weighed 40 pounds 9 ounces, what was her total weight with all her gear?

2. The Statue of Liberty was unveiled on October 28, 1886. From pedestal to torch it is over 300 feet tall. The statue is over 151 feet tall. The right arm is 42 feet long and the index finger is 8 feet long. Use a ruler to measure your index finger. How many times longer is Lady Liberty's finger than yours?

Lesson 118   Algebraic Thinking • Foundations

Scavenger Hunt

Directions:
1. Begin at the poster that the teacher instructs.
2. Solve the equation on the poster.
3. Find another poster that has the solution to the equation at the bottom of the poster.
4. Keep going through each of the posters, always moving to the poster with the solution of the equation you just solved.
5. Be sure to show all work and record the order in which you traveled from one poster to the next.

1. Poster _____   2. Poster _____

3. Poster _____   4. Poster _____

5. Poster _____   6. Poster _____

7. Poster _____   8. Poster _____

AlgebraicThinking • Foundations — Lesson 118

9. Poster _____

10. Poster _____

11. Poster _____

12. Poster _____

13. Poster _____

14. Poster _____

15. Poster _____

597

Warm Up 119　　　　　　　AlgebraicThinking • Foundations

Warm Up 119: Think Maximum

In this game of "Think Maximum" you will subtract each number that you pick. The highest score still wins!

8	⁻10	⁻4	5	⁻2	8
2	⁻4	8	2	15	⁻3
0	5	**M**	0	⁻3	⁻10
6	12	2	⁻5	⁻4	3
⁻7	3	⁻3	10	0	7
⁻5	⁻1	5	⁻7	⁻5	2

598

Algebraic Thinking • Foundations

Warm Up 120: Order Up

Directions: *Solve each equation. Put the letters with the equations in the blanks at the bottom of the page in order from the one with the smallest answer to the one with the largest answer.*

E $\dfrac{x}{-3} = 2$

O $-8p - 4 = 4$

A $x + 5 = -13$

S $-8x = 32$

E $-x - 5 = -18$

W $2y + 4 = -14$

M $\dfrac{x}{-3} + 6 = 3$

____ ____ ____ ____ ____ ____ ____

Lesson 120　　　　　**AlgebraicThinking** • Foundations

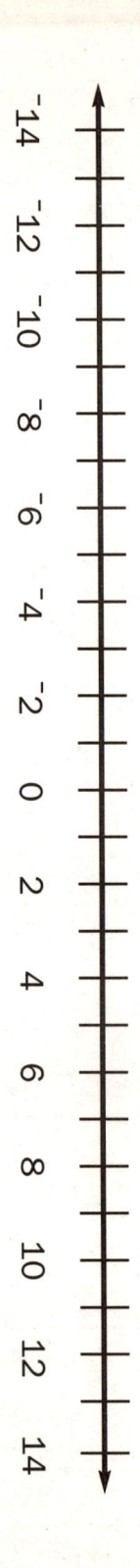

Algebraic Thinking • Foundations　　　　　　　　　　Lesson 120

Directions: *Graph each phrase on a number line.*

1. all integers less than 5

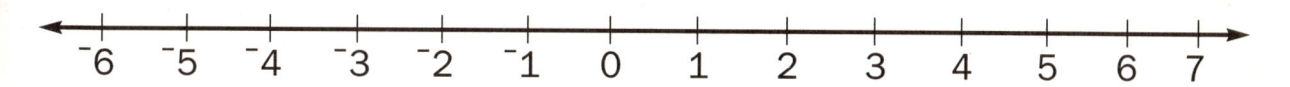

⟵―+―+―+―+―+―+―+―+―+―+―+―+―+―⟶
⁻6 ⁻5 ⁻4 ⁻3 ⁻2 ⁻1　0　1　2　3　4　5　6　7

2. all positive real numbers

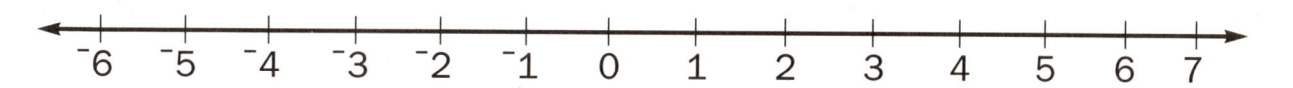

⟵―+―+―+―+―+―+―+―+―+―+―+―+―+―⟶
⁻6 ⁻5 ⁻4 ⁻3 ⁻2 ⁻1　0　1　2　3　4　5　6　7

3. all real numbers greater than or equal to ⁻4

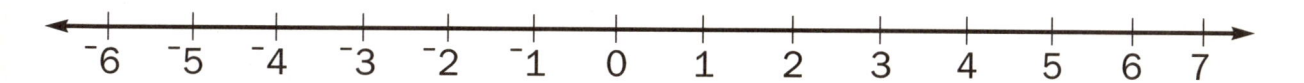

⟵―+―+―+―+―+―+―+―+―+―+―+―+―+―⟶
⁻6 ⁻5 ⁻4 ⁻3 ⁻2 ⁻1　0　1　2　3　4　5　6　7

4. all integers less than or equal to 2

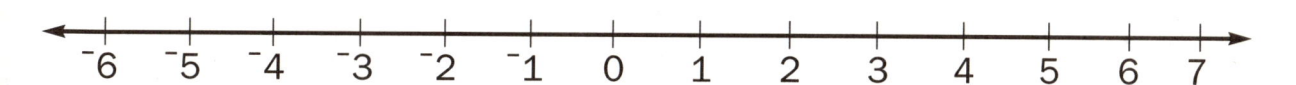

⟵―+―+―+―+―+―+―+―+―+―+―+―+―+―⟶
⁻6 ⁻5 ⁻4 ⁻3 ⁻2 ⁻1　0　1　2　3　4　5　6　7

5. all real numbers greater than 4

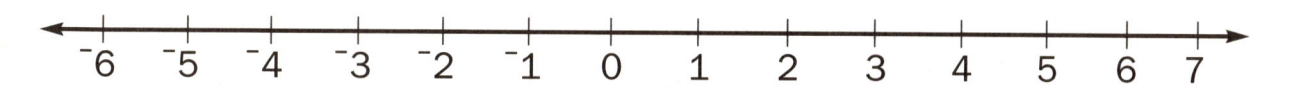

⟵―+―+―+―+―+―+―+―+―+―+―+―+―+―⟶
⁻6 ⁻5 ⁻4 ⁻3 ⁻2 ⁻1　0　1　2　3　4　5　6　7

6. all integers less than ⁻2

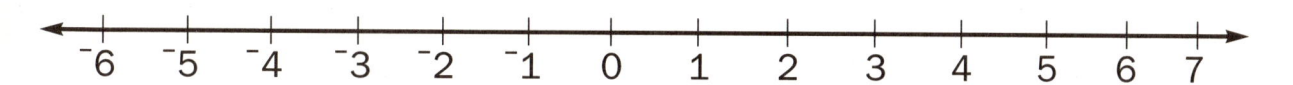

⟵―+―+―+―+―+―+―+―+―+―+―+―+―+―⟶
⁻6 ⁻5 ⁻4 ⁻3 ⁻2 ⁻1　0　1　2　3　4　5　6　7

7. all real numbers greater than or equal to 0

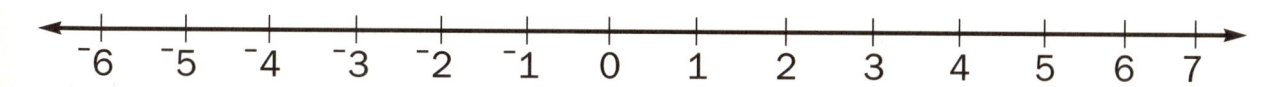

⟵―+―+―+―+―+―+―+―+―+―+―+―+―+―⟶
⁻6 ⁻5 ⁻4 ⁻3 ⁻2 ⁻1　0　1　2　3　4　5　6　7

Lesson 120 **AlgebraicThinking** • Foundations

Directions: *Match each phrase to the correct graph.*

1. all integers less than 3

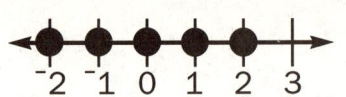

2. all real numbers greater than or equal to 2

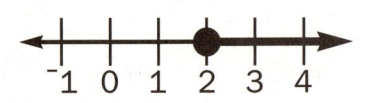

3. all real numbers less than 4

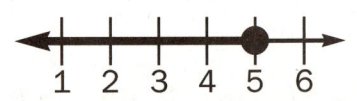

4. all integers less than or equal to 2

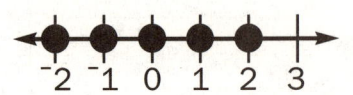

5. all real numbers greater than 3

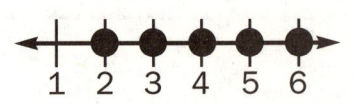

6. all real numbers less than or equal to 5

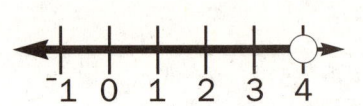

7. all integers greater than 1

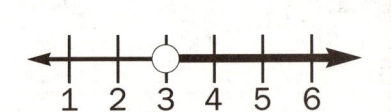

8. all integers greater than or equal to 4

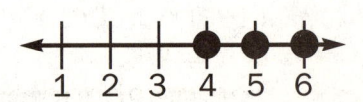

602

AlgebraicThinking • Foundations Homework 120

Name _____

Directions: *Find the volume for each prism.*

1. 9 cm, 4 cm, 7 cm _____

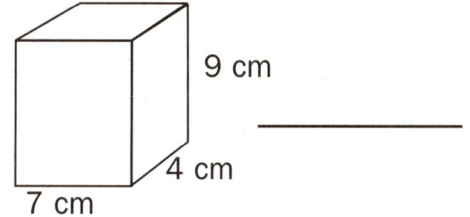

2. 5 in., 5 in., 5 in. _____

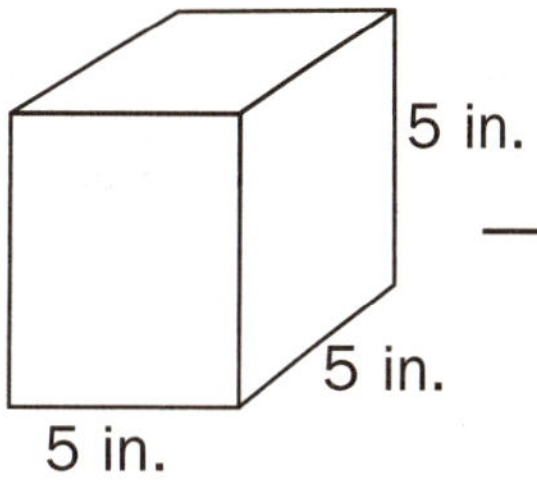

3. 6 m, 6 m, 12 m _____

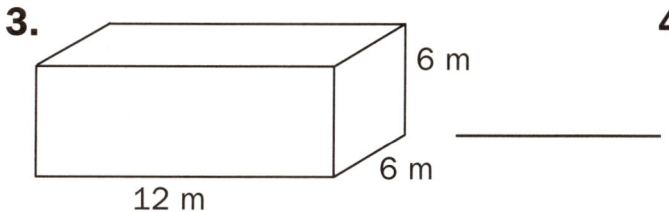

4. 13 ft, 9 ft, 8 ft _____

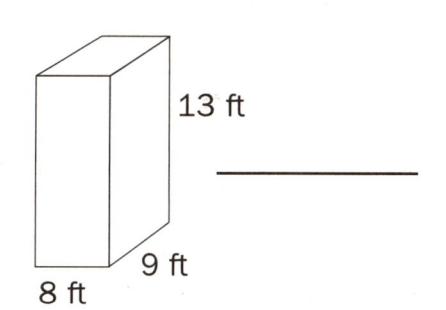

5. 2 m, 14 m, 3 m _____

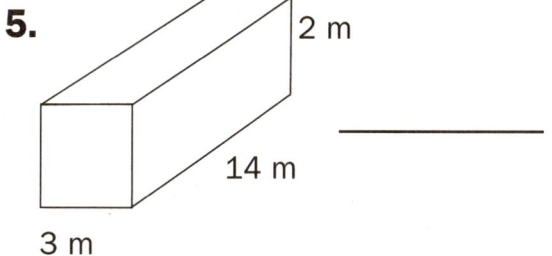

6. 7 in., 3 in., 7 in. _____

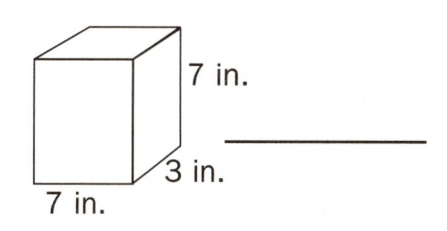

7. S-O-L-V-E
   The neighborhood swimming pool is 25 yards long, 14 yards wide, and 6 feet deep. How much water will the pool hold? (**Hint:** Careful with the dimensions.)

Warm Up 121: Perplexing Parentheses

Directions: *If the problems are correct, leave the letter with the expression. If they are not, mark out the letter with the expression. Those letters that are left should spell a message.*

I $6 + (10 - 7) \div 3 = 7$

S $(4 + 10) \cdot {}^-3 + 7 = 56$

N ${}^-8 + (7 - 5) = {}^-10$

D $\dfrac{{}^-9 - (5 - 2)}{{}^-4} = 3$

A $4 \cdot {}^-5 + (2 - 6) = {}^-24$

O $6 + {}^-7(4 - 6) = 20$

T $9 \div (3 - 6) = 3$

R $6^2 + 3 \cdot ({}^-6 + {}^-2) = {}^-12$

E $4^2 + (9 + {}^-2) + 8 = 23$

N $12 \cdot (0 + 7) - 8 = 76$

M $\dfrac{2 - 3^2}{(4 + 3) \cdot {}^-1} = 1$

E $(6 - 11) \cdot {}^-7 - 4 + 2 = 33$

Algebraic Thinking • Foundations   Lesson 121

Directions: *Follow along with your teacher to solve the problems below.*

Example 1:

Mark has $30 to spend. He will either go to the movies or buy a new DVD. It will cost less to buy a ticket to the movies and have a $6 popcorn and soda than it would for him to buy the $19 DVD. How much is a movie ticket?

Example 2:

Robert has to pay Jewels America $3,000 for the ring he has just purchased. His bank requires that he maintain a balance of at least $1,000 in order to receive free checking. How much should Robert have in his account to be sure that he will continue to have free checking after buying the gift for his girlfriend?

Lesson 121 **AlgebraicThinking • Foundations**

Directions: *Follow along with your teacher to solve the problems below.*

Example 1:

Meg is going with her two children to the circus. The cost of the tickets for everyone is more than $18. What is the least that a circus ticket may cost? You need to assume all ticket prices are the same.

Example 2:

A box of cookies was split evenly among four children. What is the minimum number of cookies in the box, if each child received at least 4 cookies?

AlgebraicThinking • Foundations

Lesson 121

Directions: *Work with your partner to solve each inequality.*

1. Six cartons weigh less than 48 pounds. If all of the cartons weigh the same amount, what is the most that a carton can weigh?

⟵─────────────────────────────⟶

2. $x + 15 < 22$

⟵─────────⟶

3. $7x \geq 21$

⟵─────────⟶

4. $\frac{x}{3} > 6$

⟵─────────⟶

5. $x - 14 \leq 5$

⟵─────────⟶

607

Homework 121   Algebraic Thinking • Foundations

Name _____

Directions: *Solve each equation. Make sure you show all your work and check your answers.*

1. 2x + 4 = 12

2. 3d − 5 = 10

3. $\frac{x}{3}$ − ⁻7 = 2

4. $\frac{n}{⁻4}$ + 6 = 3

5. ⁻8a + 4 = 20

6. ⁻9y + ⁻3 = 6

7. S-O-L-V-E
   Michael took 3 friends to the movies for his birthday. He paid for the tickets and refreshments that cost $15. Michael's total bill was $47. What was the price of each ticket?

AlgebraicThinking • **Foundations**　　　　　　　　　　　　　　　Warm Up 122

Warm Up 122: Cross It

Directions: *Using the numbers from 1 – 12 only once, fill in the rest of the boxes in the double cross below, so that the numbers in each row and each column of four blocks add up to 26.*

		8		
	11		1	
6		9		
		5		

609

Lesson 122   **AlgebraicThinking** • Foundations

I. When solving inequalities, you must _____ the inequality symbol when you _____ or _____ by a _____ integer.

II. Solve each inequality below. Check each one by plugging in a value from your answer for the variable to make sure it works.

1. $^-7d < 63$ **2.** $5y \leq 25$

3. $\dfrac{c}{^-4} \geq ^-8$ **4.** $^-6n \leq ^-54$

5. $\dfrac{m}{8} < 6$ **6.** $\dfrac{v}{^-1} \geq ^-12$

AlgebraicThinking • Foundations — Lesson 122

Directions: Choose the correct answer for each inequality.

1. $^-4x > 12$
   a) $x > {}^-3$ b) $x > 3$
   c) $x < 3$ d) $x < {}^-3$

2. $b + 7 \leq 11$
   a) $b \leq 4$ b) $b \leq {}^-4$
   c) $b \geq {}^-4$ d) $b \geq 4$

3. $\dfrac{5k \geq 9}{{}^-5}$
   a) $k \geq {}^-45$ b) $k \geq 45$
   c) $k \leq 45$ d) $k \leq {}^-45$

4. $m - 9 \leq {}^-6$
   a) $m \leq {}^-3$ b) $m \geq 3$
   c) $m \geq {}^-3$ d) $m \leq 3$

5. $^-10g < {}^-50$
   a) $g < 5$ b) $g < {}^-5$
   c) $g > 5$ d) $g > {}^-5$

6. $\dfrac{r}{3} > {}^-6$
   a) $r > 18$ b) $r > {}^-18$
   c) $r < 18$ d) $r < {}^-18$

Homework 122   **AlgebraicThinking • Foundations**

Name _____

Directions: *Solve each equation. Show all your work and check your answers.*

1. $5x - 7 = 28$

2. $\dfrac{m}{^-2} - 7 = 11$

3. $6n + 12 = {^-18}$

4. $\dfrac{a}{4} + 9 = 5$

Directions: *Graph each inequality.*

5. $n > 3$

6. $x \leq {^-2}$

7. $y < 4$

8. $b \geq {^-4}$

AlgebraicThinking • Foundations Warm Up 123

Warm Up 123: S - O - L - V - E

Manuel went to the mall. He bought four t-shirts and had lunch for $5. Manuel spent less than $57. What is the most that each of the equally priced t-shirts could cost?

S

O

L

V

E

Lesson 123 Algebraic Thinking • Foundations

Directions: *Cut apart the inequalities below. Then, solve and graph each of them. Finally, put them in trios (groups of threes) that have the same answers.*

A. ⁻4x < ⁻16	B. 7 + x > 4	C. ⁻9x > ⁻27
D. $\frac{x}{^-3} < 1$	E. x − 8 < ⁻12	F. ⁻5x < 15
G. x − 5 > ⁻1	H. $\frac{x}{^-3} > {^-1}$	I. x − 13 < ⁻10
J. $\frac{x}{4} < {^-1}$	K. 6 + x > 10	L. ⁻8x > 32

Algebraic Thinking • Foundations

Lesson 123

Directions: *Solve and graph each inequality.*

1. $x - {}^-5 \leq {}^-6$

2. ${}^-9n > {}^-54$

⟵——————⟶   ⟵——————⟶

3. $\dfrac{v}{5} \geq {}^-8$

4. ${}^-11 + f < 6$

⟵——————⟶   ⟵——————⟶

5. $7b > 49$

6. $\dfrac{c}{{}^-3} \leq {}^-5$

⟵——————⟶   ⟵——————⟶

615

Lesson 123

AlgebraicThinking • Foundations

STUDENT QUIZ

Name: _____

#1–6: Solve and graph each inequality. Show all work for full credit.

1. $8x < {}^-40$

2. $x + {}^-7 \geq 1$

⟵―――――――――⟶   ⟵―――――――――⟶

3. $\dfrac{x}{{}^-6} \leq 2$

4. $x - 8 < {}^-3$

⟵―――――――――⟶   ⟵―――――――――⟶

5. $x - {}^-8 > {}^-2$

6. ${}^-9x \geq 54$

⟵―――――――――⟶   ⟵―――――――――⟶

AlgebraicThinking • Foundations   Lesson 123

STUDENT QUIZ

Name: _____

For #7 – 9, use the SOLVE method to answer each problem.

7. Jenny spent less than $65 for gifts for her brothers and sisters. What is the most that she could have spent equally on each of her 5 siblings?

   S

   O

   L

   V

   E

8. Sally divided her weekly allowance into equal amounts to spend daily at the food cafe. What is the least Sally's allowance can be if her usual lunch costs $5?

   S

   O

   L

   V

   E

9. Jon spent less than $15 on a movie ticket and a box of popcorn. The popcorn costs $3 and candy cost $2. What was the most he spent on his ticket?

   S

   O

   L

   V

   E

617

Appendix A   **Algebraic**Thinking • Foundations

Prime and Composite Numbers

Complete the following table using the graph paper on the following page.

Create rectangles given that number of squares. The table shows different rectangles that can be made using 3 or 4 squares. A 1 x 3 rectangle is the same as a 3 x 1 rectangle.

Number of Squares	Sketch of Rectangle Formed	Dimension of Each Rectangle
2		1 x 2
3		1 x 3
4		1 x 4, 2 x 2
5		
6		
7		
8		
9		
10		
11		
12		
13		
14		
15		
16		
17		
18		
19		
20		

AlgebraicThinking • Foundations

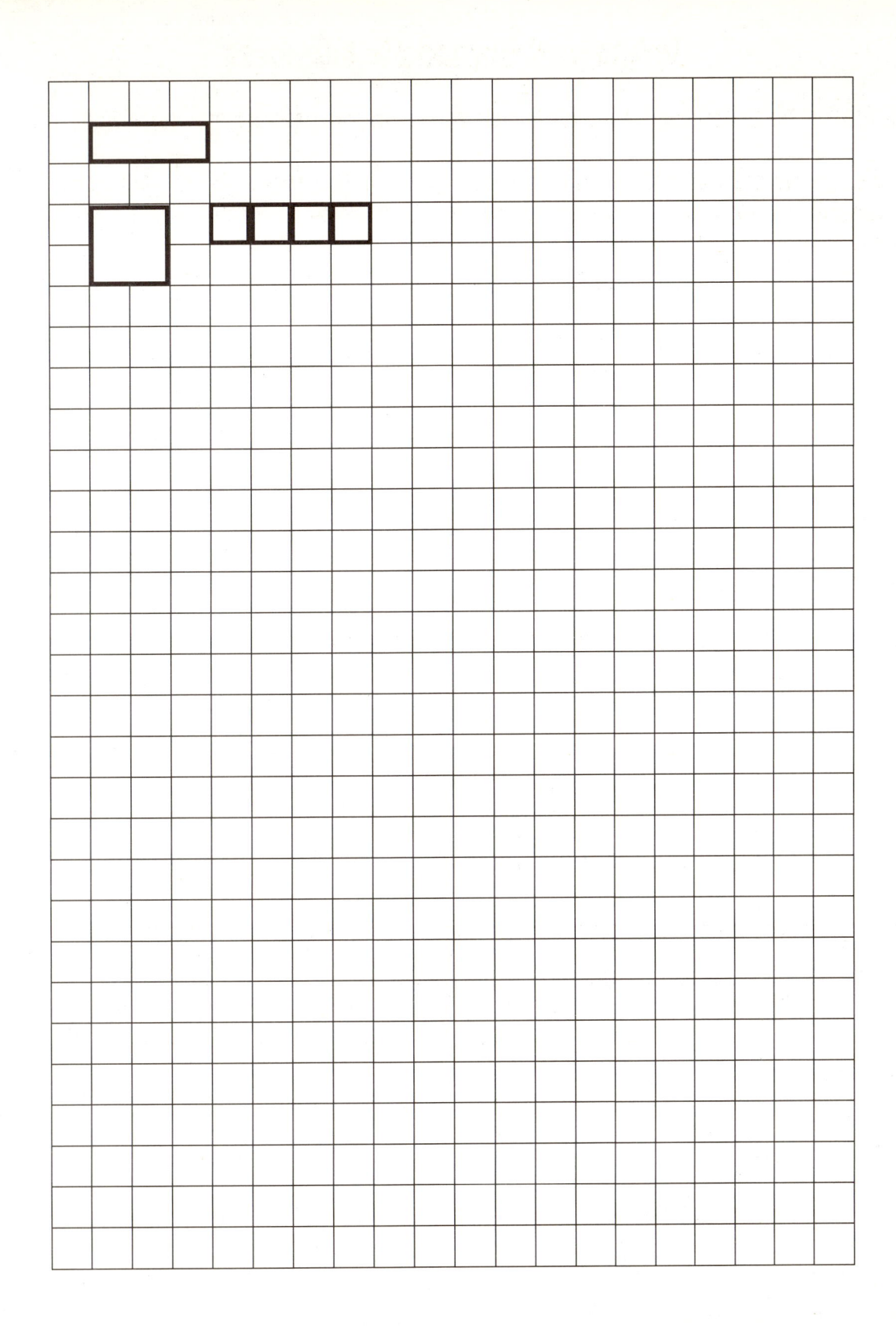

Appendix A

619

Appendix A   **AlgebraicThinking** • Foundations

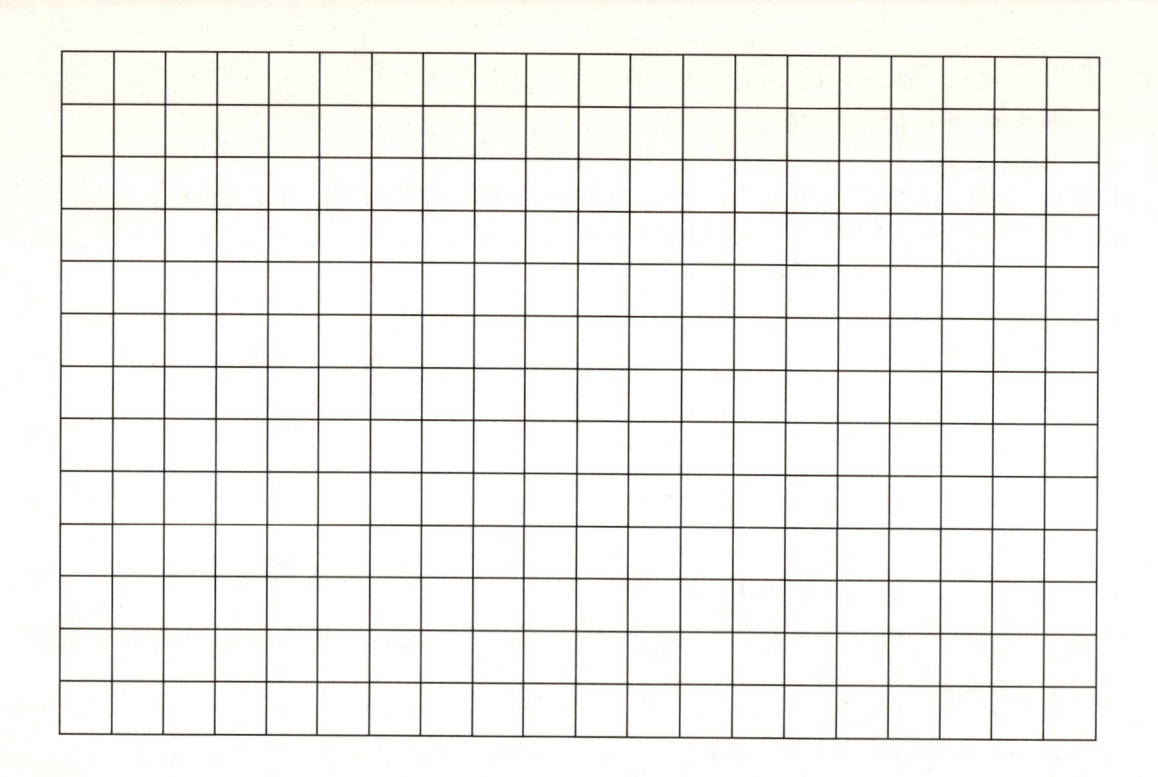

1. For what numbers can more than one rectangle be formed?

2. For what numbers can only one rectangle be formed?

3. For the numbers in which only one rectangle is formed, what do you notice about the dimensions of the rectangle?

If a number has only two different factors, one and itself, it is a _____ number.

If a number has more than two different factors, it is a _____ number.

AlgebraicThinking • Foundations

Appendix A

Erathosthenes (276–195 B.C.) developed a method of finding prime numbers by sifting out the primes.

Follow the instructions below to find all the prime numbers between 1 and 100 by using the method developed by Erathosthenes.

1	2	3	4	5	6	7	8	9	10
11	12	13	14	15	16	17	18	19	20
21	22	23	24	25	26	27	28	29	30
31	32	33	34	35	36	37	38	39	40
41	42	43	44	45	46	47	48	49	50
51	52	53	54	55	56	57	58	59	60
61	62	63	64	65	66	67	68	69	70
71	72	73	74	75	76	77	78	79	80
81	82	83	84	85	86	87	88	89	90
91	92	93	94	95	96	97	98	99	100

1. Cross out 1, since it is not classified as a prime number.
2. Draw a circle around 2, the smallest prime number. Then cross out every second number after 2.
3. Draw a circle around 3, the next prime number. Then cross out every third number after. Some numbers will be crossed out more than once.
4. Circle the next open number, 5. Then cross out every fifth number after 5.
5. The next open number is 7. Circle 7 and then cross out every seventh number after 7.
6. Go through the grid and draw a circle around every number that has not yet been crossed out. The circled numbers are all the prime numbers between 1 and 100.
7. You should have found a total of 25 primes between 1 and 100.

Prime numbers up to 100 are:

Appendix A

Algebraic Thinking • Foundations

Prime Triangles

To express a number using prime factorization, divide the number by the smallest prime factor and repeat until all factors listed are prime.

For example: 81 = 3 • 27
             = 3 • 3 • 9
             = 3 • 3 • 3 • 3
             = 3^4

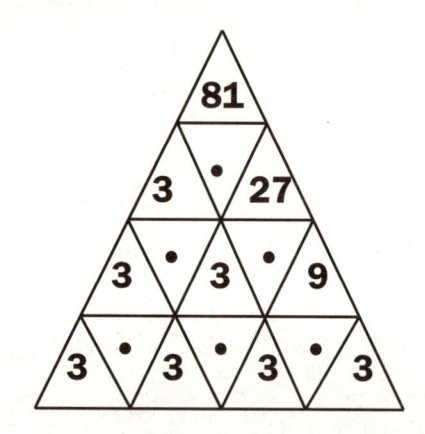

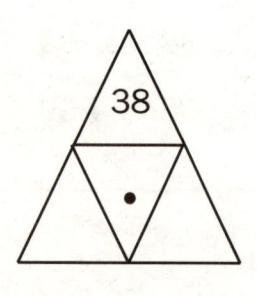

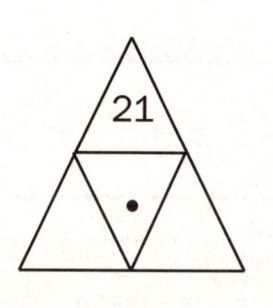

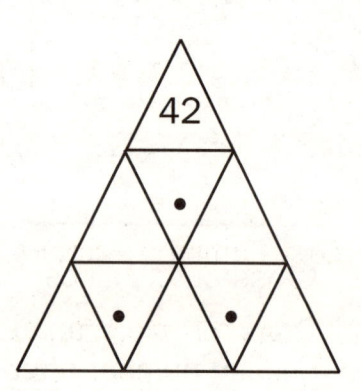

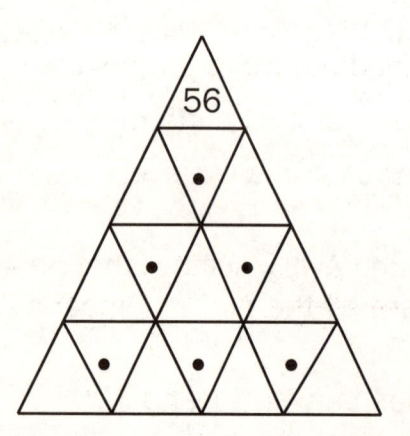

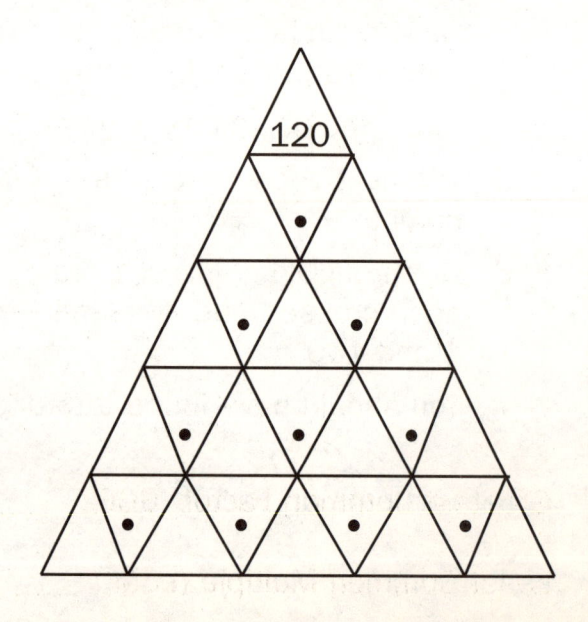

AlgebraicThinking • Foundations Appendix B

Finding the Greatest Common Factor and the Least Common Multiple

1. | 56   72

Greatest Common Factor (GCF): _____

Least Common Multiple (LCM): _____

2. | 15   30

Greatest Common Factor (GCF): _____

Least Common Multiple (LCM): _____

3. | 24   36

Greatest Common Factor (GCF): _____

Least Common Multiple (LCM): _____

Appendix B

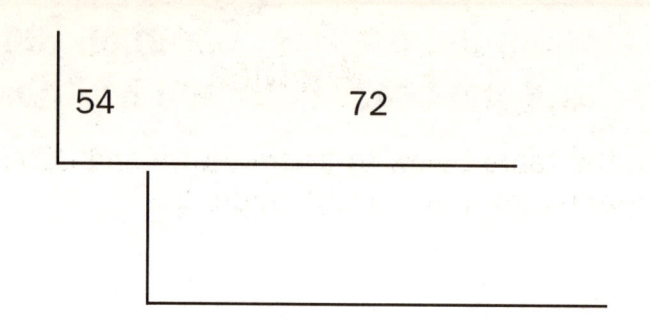

4. | 54   72

Greatest Common Factor (GCF): _____

Least Common Multiple (LCM): _____

5. | 24   56

Greatest Common Factor (GCF): _____

Least Common Multiple (LCM): _____

6. | 20   36

Greatest Common Factor (GCF): _____

Least Common Multiple (LCM): _____

Algebraic Thinking • Foundations

Appendix B

Practice

Directions: Fill in the table below to find the GCF and LCM. Use the slide method you just learned to find the GCF and LCM.

		GCF	LCM
1	12, 15		
2	20, 36		
3	15, 25		
4	20, 32		
5	30, 80		
6	33, 44		
7	12, 20		
8	18, 27		
9	64, 120		

Algebraic Thinking • Foundations

Appendix 1: Stem and Leaf Plots

Warm Up – Mean, Median, Mode

1. Calculate the mean, median and mode for the following set of data.

4, 5, 10, 4, 2, 4, 3, 7, 8, 5

Stem and Leaf Plots

Take turns with your partner rolling two number cubes. Record the sum of each roll in the table below. Once you and your partner have finished all ten of your turns, find the total and record.

Name	Roll 1	Roll 2	Roll 3	Roll 4	Roll 5	Roll 6	Roll 7	Roll 8	Roll 9	Roll 10	Total

Follow along with your teacher and record the data of your fellow classmates' totals below.

_____

Rewrite the data set in order from least to greatest.

_____

- Underline the digit in the ones place of each piece of data.
- Circle all numbers that are not underlined in each piece of data.
- The circled value on the lowest number tells you the value of your first stem.
- List all circled digits from the first stem to the value of the greatest stem.
- List the digits in the ones place for the leaves next to the appropriate stem. (There may be stems with no leaves. They still need to be shown.)
- Add a key and a title.

Algebraic Thinking • Foundations

Stem	Leaves

Key:

Example 1:

Ms. Young recorded the scores for the last math test. She thinks that a stem and leaf plot would be the best way to present the data to the class. Make a stem and leaf plot using the test scores from Ms Young's class.

82, 74, 78, 88, 92, 82, 85, 94, 58, 86, 75, 91, 55, 87

Ms Young's Class Test Scores

Stem	Leaves

Key: |

By looking at the stem and leaf plot, most of the scores are in what stem? _____

Why is there an empty space on the stem and leaf plot? _____

AlgebraicThinking • Foundations

Example 2:
The students at Alexander Mills Middle School are selling candy bars for a school fundraiser. The top 13 students' sales are represented.

Number of Candy Bars Sold at Alexander Mills

Stem	Leaves
9	4
10	
11	2 9
12	4 6 7
13	8
14	0 5
15	0 3 3
16	1

Key: 14 | 5 = 145

List the values from the stem and leaf plot in order from least to greatest.
_____

What is the range of the candy bar sales? _____

What is the median number of the data set? _____

What is the mode of the number of candy bars sold? _____

Find the mean of the top candy bar sales. _____

Example 3:
The stem and leaf plot shows the number of songs that are played on 15 radio channels in the Baltimore area in two hours.

Songs Played in Two Hours on Radio Channels in Baltimore

Stem	Leaves
1	8
2	0 2 5 6 6
3	1 3 4 6 7 9 9
4	0 2

Key: 3 | 4 = 34

You can also find measures of central tendency by taking the data directly from the stem and leaf plot. Use the directions to answer the questions.

What is the range of the number of songs played? _____

628

Algebraic Thinking • Foundations

Cross out the leaf for the least value and the leaf for the greatest value. Cross out the leaf for the next smallest and next greatest values. Continue to do this until you find the median. What is the median number of songs played in two hours? _____

Look for more than one of the same digit in the same stem. What is the mode number of songs played? _____

Find the mean number of songs played. _____

Directions: Work with your partner to answer the following questions.

Pizzas Ordered at Pizza Palace Each Day for Two Weeks

Stem	Leaves
2	6 7 9
3	1 3 6
4	0 2 2 3 4 7
5	2 4

Key: 3 | 1 = 31

How many days were there less than 40 pizzas ordered? _____

What is the range number of pizzas ordered in two weeks? _____

What is the mode number of pizzas ordered? _____

What is the median number of pizzas ordered? _____

What was the mean number of pizzas sold during the two weeks at Pizza Palace? _____

Algebraic Thinking • Foundations

Homework

Directions: Use the steps of S-O-L-V-E to find the answer to the following word problem.

Jabari has been saving money from his weekly paychecks to buy a new video game system and three new games. He needs to save at least $750 (including tax) to make his purchase. So far, he has saved the following amounts over the last five weeks: $125, $101, $98, $247, $178. Has Jabari saved enough money to make his purchase?

S- Highlight the question.

O- Identify the facts.
Eliminate the unnecessary facts.
List the necessary facts.

L- Choose an operation.
Write in words what your plan of action will be.

V- Estimate your answer.
Carry out your plan.

E- Did you answer what you were asked to find?
Is your answer reasonable?
Is your answer accurate?
Write answer as a complete thought.

AlgebraicThinking • Foundations

Appendix 2: Divisibility

Warm Up: SOLVE the Problem

Use the **S-O-L-V-E** method to answer the following word problem.

Janay is working on her science project. She needs to purchase materials to complete the project. Janay goes to the store and buys paint for $3.49, plastic cups for $1.89, and a piece of wood for $4.59. She is going to enter her science project in the school science fair. If her mother gave her $10.00, does she have enough money to purchase all her supplies?

S- Highlight the question.

O- Identify the facts.
Eliminate the unnecessary facts.
List the necessary facts.

L- Choose an operation.
Write in words what your plan of action will be.

V- Estimate your answer.
Carry out your plan.

E- Did you answer what you were asked to find?
Is your answer reasonable?
Is your answer accurate?
Write answer as a complete thought.

AlgebraicThinking • Foundations

Divisibility

Today we are going to talk about divisibility of numbers. What do the following numbers have in common?

    124   58   60   2,134

They all end in an even number which means they can be divided evenly by 2. In other words, they are divisible by 2. If a number is not divisible by 2 then it is an odd number. To determine whether a number is even or odd, you look at the digit in the one's place. If the digit is even, (0, 2, 4, 6, 8) then the number is even. If the digit in the one's place is odd (1, 3, 5, 7, 9) then the number is odd.

Look at the following numbers and determine whether they are odd or even.

  25   374   101   87   1,567   624

What is Divisibility?

A whole number is **divisible** by another whole number if, after dividing, the quotient is a whole number with no remainder.

    $24 \div 2 = 12$ 24 is **divisible** by 2 because when you divide 24 by 2 there is no remainder.

    $19 \div 2 = 9\ r.\ 1$ 19 is **not divisible** by 2 because when you divide 19 by 2 there is a remainder.

What do you think? Look at the following numbers with your partner and decide whether they are divisible by two. Show your division work and be prepared to explain your answer.

  16   28   112

Another way that you can determine the divisibility of a number is to use a **divisibility test**. A **divisibility test** is a way of deciding whether one whole number is divisible by another.

The **divisibility** test for 2 is this: If the last digit of a number is an even number (0,2,4,6,8) then the number is **divisible** by 2.

Use the **divisibility test** for 2 to determine if these numbers are **divisible** by 2.

  2,682   3,458   243   57

Algebraic Thinking • Foundations

Divisibility

A divisibility test is a way to determine whether a whole number is divisible by another whole number. It can help you find the factors of large numbers.

Look at the chart below. It shows the **divisibility tests** for the numbers 2, 3, 5, 6, 9, 10. The multiples of a number can help you find patterns for **divisibility**.

	Multiples	Observation	A number is divisible by …	Example:
2	2, 4, 6, 8, 10, 12, 14…	Last digit is even, even numbers, divide evenly by 2	2 – If the last digit is even (0, 2, 4, 6, 8)	78 ends in 8 (even number),
3	3, 6, 9, 12, 15, ___, ___…	Divide evenly by 3, counting by 3's	3 – If the sum of the digits is divisible by 3	54 5+ 4 = 9 9 is divisible by 3
4	4, 8, ___, ___, ___…		4 – If the last two digits form a number divisible by 4.	216 16 is divisible by 4
5	5, ___, ___, ___, ___, ___, ___…			
6	6, ___, ___, ___…			
9	9, ___, ___, ___, ___, ___…			
10	10, ___, ___, ___, ___, ___…			

633

Algebraic Thinking • Foundations

Directions: Use the divisibility tests to determine whether each of the numbers is divisible by 2, 3, 4, 5, 6, 9, and 10. Write *yes* if the number is divisible. Write *no* if it is not. Explain your answer.

Number	2	3	4	5	6	9	10
345	no	yes	no	yes	no	no	no
Why or why not?	345 does not end in an even number	3+4+5=12 Twelve is divisible by 3	45 is not divisible by 4	345 ends in a 5	345 is not divisible by both 2 and 3	3+4+5=12 Twelve is not divisible by 9	345 does not end in a 0

Number	2	3	4	5	6	9	10
2,740	yes	no					
Why or why not?	2,740 ends in an even number (0)	2+7+4=13 Thirteen is not divisible by 3					

Number	2	3	4	5	6	9	10
852							
Why or why not?							

If a number is divisible by both 4 and 2, does that mean it is divisible by 8?

Explain your answer.

Something to think about....

Algebraic Thinking • Foundations

Homework

Directions: Use the order of operations to evaluate each expression.

1. $16 + 8 \cdot 2 - 7 =$

2. $(5 \cdot 4) + 2^3 \div 4 =$

3. $(3 \cdot 3)^2 + 6 \cdot 5 =$

4. $24 \div 3 - (19 - 16) =$

5. $7^2 + (2 + 3)^3 - 50 =$

6. $84 \div 12(13 - 6) - 1 =$

Algebraic Thinking • Foundations

Appendix 3: Sample Space

Warm Up: You're the Teacher – Order of Operations

Directions: You are the teacher. Check each of the following problems. If the answer is correct, mark it correct. If the answer is incorrect, find the mistake and correct it.

$60 \div (8 + 2) \cdot 4^2 - 23$
$60 \div 10 \cdot 4^2 - 23$
$60 \div 10 \cdot 8 - 23$
$6 \cdot 8 - 23$
$48 - 23$
25

$(52 + 8 \div 2) \cdot (40 \div 5 - 2)$
$(60 \div 2) \cdot (8 - 2)$
$30 \cdot 6$
180

$28 \div (7 + 7) \cdot 8 - 2^3$
$28 \div 14 \cdot 8 - 2^3$
$28 \div 14 \cdot 8 - 8$
$2 \cdot 8 - 8$
$16 - 8$
8

$(12 - 4)^2 - 24 \div 3$
$8^2 - 24 \div 3$
$64 - 24 \div 3$
$64 - 8$
56

AlgebraicThinking • Foundations

Directions: Construct a tree diagram to display the sample space of the problem below. After completing the tree diagram, answer the probability questions about the sundaes. Write each probability as a fraction, decimal and percent.

At the end of the school year, the sixth graders had an ice cream sundae party. The ice cream flavor choices were chocolate, vanilla, and strawberry. Topping choices were hot fudge, strawberry, and pineapple. Students could choose to complete their sundae with or without chopped peanuts.

What is the total number of possible sundae choices?

What is the probability of choosing a sundae with strawberry topping?

What is the probability of choosing a sundae made with chocolate ice cream?

What is the probability of choosing a sundae without chopped peanuts?

What is the probability of choosing a sundae made with vanilla ice cream?

637

Algebraic Thinking • Foundations

Highland Middle School is choosing new school uniforms. The girls can wear navy pants, navy shorts or a navy skirt. Their shirts must be red, white, yellow or navy.

Directions: Make a list of all the possible outcomes for the school uniforms. Answer the probability questions about the uniforms. Write each probability as a fraction, decimal and percent.

How many different outfits will make up the sample space?

What is the probability of choosing an outfit with a navy skirt?

What is the probability of choosing an outfit with a red shirt?

What is the probability of choosing an outfit with navy shorts?

Algebraic Thinking • Foundations

Directions: Use the frequency table below to determine the experimental probability of the following questions. Write each probability as a fraction, decimal and percent.

Dana tossed a fair number cube 25 times and recorded her results in the frequency table.

Number	1	2	3	4	5	6
Frequency	3	4	6	3	7	2

What is the probability that Dana rolled a 3?

What is the probability that Dana rolled an even number?

What is the probability that Dana rolled a prime number?

What is the probability that Dana rolled a number less than 4?

Algebraic Thinking • Foundations

Homework

Directions: Order the fractions from least to greatest.

1. $\frac{7}{8}, \frac{2}{3}, \frac{5}{6}$

2. $\frac{5}{4}, \frac{9}{11}, \frac{5}{7}$

3. $\frac{3}{4}, \frac{3}{8}, \frac{7}{16}$

4. $\frac{1}{3}, \frac{4}{9}, \frac{2}{11}$

Algebraic Thinking • Foundations

Appendix 4: Probability - Results as Decimals, Percents, and Ratios

Warm Up

Directions: Use the SOLVE method for the following word problem.

Gina went out to breakfast with her family. She had a choice of eggs, cereal or pancakes. With her breakfast she could choose a side item of toast, bacon, muffin or ham. Gina could select either juice or hot chocolate as her drink. How many different breakfast combinations did she have to choose from?

S- Highlight the question.

O- Identify the facts.
Eliminate the unnecessary facts.
List the necessary facts.

L- Choose an operation.
Write in words what your plan of action will be.

V- Estimate your answer.
Carry out your plan.

E- Did you answer what you were asked to find?
Is your answer reasonable?
Is your answer accurate?
Write answer as a complete thought.

Algebraic Thinking • Foundations

Activity: Probability with Color Tiles

Part 1:
Directions: You and your partner will receive a lunch bag with 3 red tiles, 2 yellow tiles, 4 green tiles and 1 blue tile. Answer the following questions and make some predictions about your results.

Questions:

1. Which color tile do you expect to draw the least number of times? Why?

2. Which color tile do you expect to draw the most number of times? Why?

Predictions:

Find the theoretical probability of the following events. Assume that you choose 1 tile randomly out of the bag.

$P(red) =$ _____ $P(green) =$ _____

$P(blue) =$ _____ $P(yellow) =$ _____

Part 2:
Directions: One partner will draw 20 tiles, one at a time, returning the tile to the bag after each draw. The other partner will record the results in this chart.

Red	Yellow	Blue	Green

Algebraic Thinking • Foundations

Record the results of your experiment in the following chart. Please write the experimental probability as a fraction, decimal and percent.

	Fraction	Decimal	Percent
Red			
Yellow			
Green			
Blue			

Questions:

1. Compare the theoretical probability of choosing a red tile with your experimental probability of choosing a red tile. Are they the same? How could you explain the difference between the two probabilities?

2. What changes could be made to the experiment that may alter the experimental probability?

Algebraic Thinking • Foundations

Homework

Directions: Evaluate each expression.

1. 3 • 4 − 5

2. 7 + 2 • 9

3. 24 − 4 ÷ 2

4. 10 ÷ 5 • 2

5. 18 − 4 • 2

6. 15 + 9 ÷ 3

7. 6 • 7 − 2 • 3

8. 77 ÷ 7 − 6 ÷ 2

9. 13 − 3 + 1

AlgebraicThinking • Foundations

Appendix 5: More Probability

Warm Up:

Directions: Find the quotient or product of the following problems.

1. $\dfrac{3}{4} \div \dfrac{1}{2} =$

2. $\dfrac{1}{7} \cdot \dfrac{3}{5} =$

3. $\dfrac{4}{5} \cdot \dfrac{2}{3} =$

4. $\dfrac{6}{7} \div \dfrac{1}{3} =$

5. $\dfrac{2}{5} \div \dfrac{1}{8} =$

6. $\dfrac{3}{7} \cdot \dfrac{5}{12} =$

7. $\dfrac{4}{9} \cdot \dfrac{5}{6} =$

8. $\dfrac{4}{11} \div \dfrac{8}{22} =$

Algebraic Thinking • Foundations

Today you will be working with your partner to conduct experiments with candy. The results of your experiments will be graphed and written as fractions, decimals and percents.

Part 1: Graphing (With your partner)

1. Open your candy and put it into the plastic bag. Make sure you seal the bag.
2. Count the number of candies in the bag. _____
3. List the colors of your candies in the chart below. Chart the fraction, decimal, and percent of each color.

Color	Fraction	Decimal	Percent

4. Create a bar graph based on the colors of your candy. Remember to include all the parts of the graph.

Colors

AlgebraicThinking • Foundations

Part 2: Probability

1. Divide your candies with your partner.

2. Chart the color and numbers that you have.

Colors	Number	Theoretical Probability	Experimental Probability

3. If you were to put all your candies in a paper bag and pull out one candy, what color would you be most likely to pull out? _____

4. What color would you be least likely to pull out? _____

5. In the chart above, record the theoretical probability of selecting each color. (Remember theoretical probability is a fraction with the numerator being the number of a certain color and the denominator being the total number of candies.) Don't forget to simplify the fraction.

6. Now put all your candies into a paper bag and pull one piece of candy out. Keep a tally of each color that is pulled. Put the candy back in the bag and repeat this 30 times.

Colors	Tally

AlgebraicThinking • Foundations

7. Use your tally marks to record the experimental probability in the chart at the top of the previous page. (Remember experimental probability is a fraction with the numerator as the tallies of each color and the denominator being the total number of candies.)

8. How do the theoretical numbers compare to the experimental numbers?

9. Pull one candy from the bag and, without replacing it, select another candy. Determine the compound probability of choosing those two candies.

    Would this be an example of dependent or independent events? Explain your answer.

10. Pull one candy from the bag, replace it and then select another candy. Determine the compound probability of choosing those two candies.

    Would this be an example of independent or dependent events? Explain your answer.

11. Make up two probability questions about your candies and have your partner answer the questions.

AlgebraicThinking • Foundations

Homework:

Directions: Answer the following probability questions.

1. At the local restaurant, there are 3 dessert choices: apple pie, cherry pie or blueberry pie. Customers can choose to have their pie with ice cream, whipped cream or plain. Use a tree diagram to show all the possible combinations of pies and toppings.

2. How many possible outcomes are there?

3. What is the probability of selecting a dessert with ice cream?

4. What is the probability of selecting a dessert with apple pie?

649

Algebraic Thinking • Foundations

Appendix 6: Identify and Compare the Relationship Between Parts of a Circle

Warm Up – Perimeter of a rectangle:

Find the width of the following rectangles.

1. Perimeter = 40 cm

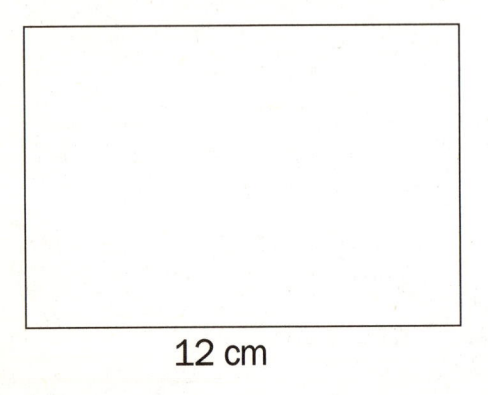

12 cm

2. Perimeter = 24 ft

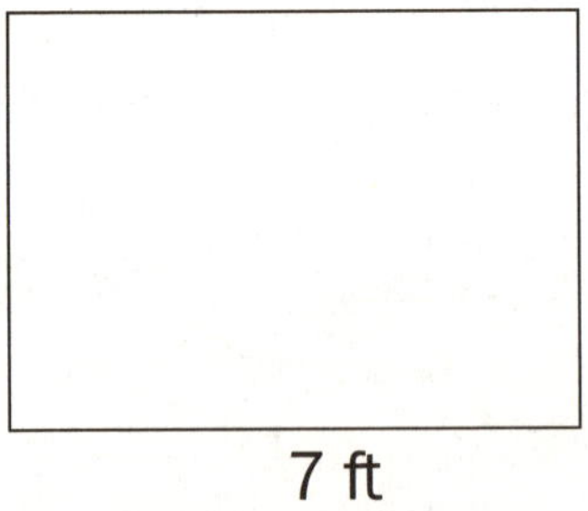

7 ft

Calculate the perimeter of the following rectangles.

3.

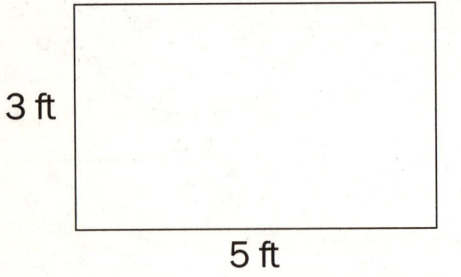

3 ft

5 ft

4.

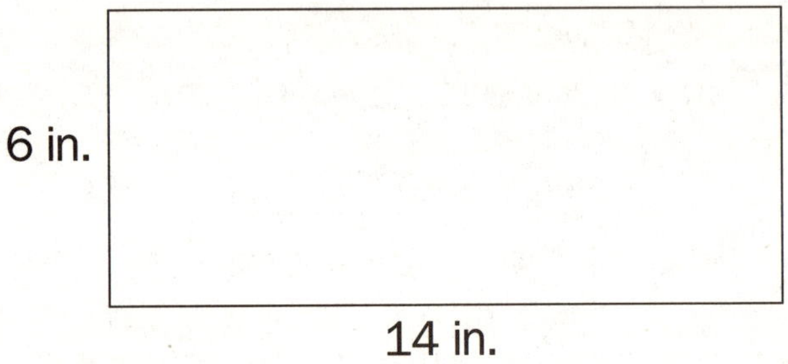

6 in.

14 in.

Algebraic Thinking • Foundations

Label the parts of the circle: center, radius, diameter, and a chord.

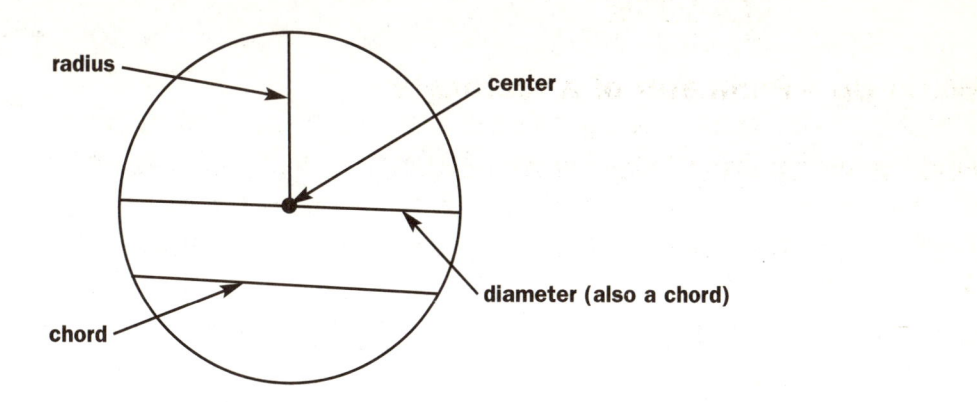

Explain the relationship between the radius and the diameter of a circle.

The radius is _____

The diameter is _____

What is the longest chord of any circle called? _____

What is the radius of the following circles?

8 cm   12 yd   15 ft

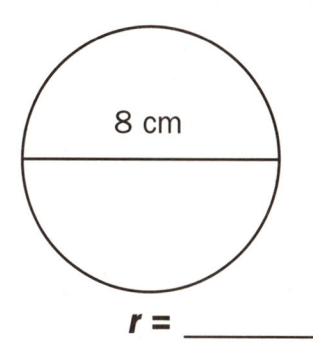

r 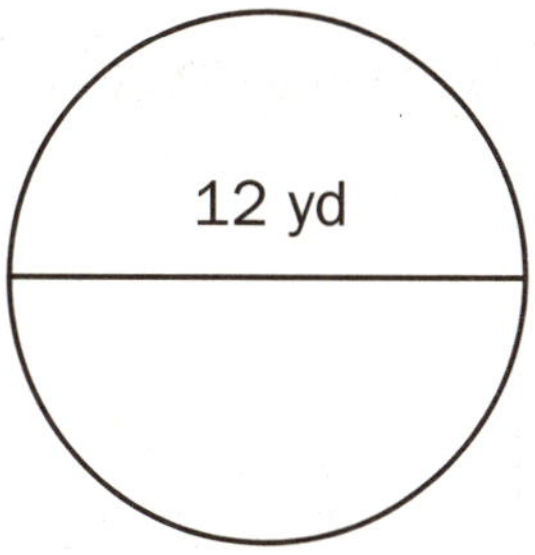 = _____   r 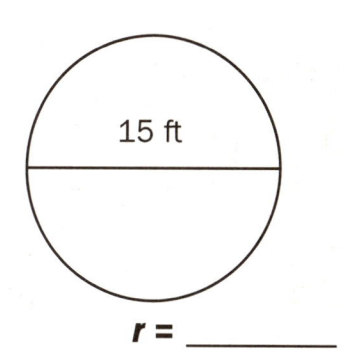 = _____   r = _____

What is the diameter of the following circles?

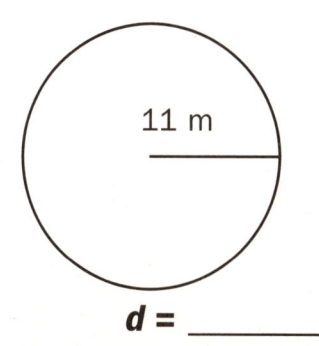

11 m   16 yd   4 cm

d 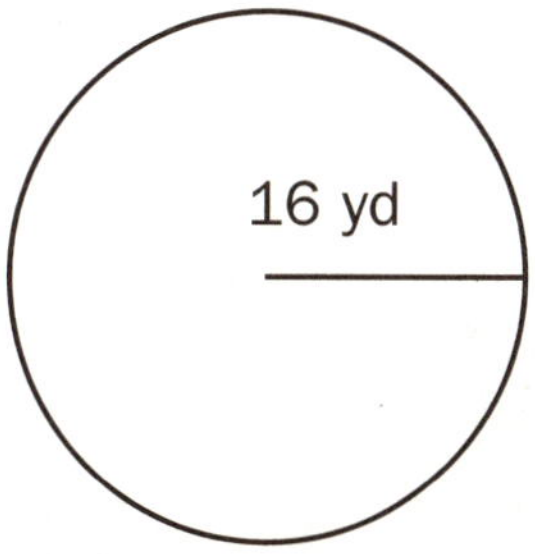 = _____   d 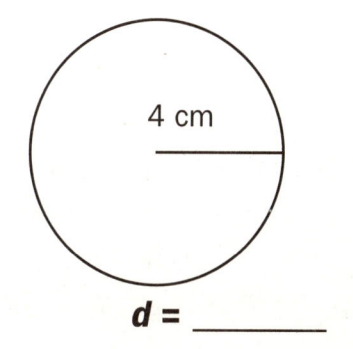 = _____   d = _____

651

Algebraic Thinking • Foundations

Homework:

Directions: Use the Order of Operations to SOLVE the following problem.

Nancy, an accountant, charges a flat fee of $50 plus $75 per hour for every hour worked up to ten hours. After the first ten hours, her rate jumps to $100 per hour. She worked fifteen hours for one of her clients, Experts, Inc. How much did she make altogether?

S- Highlight the question.

O- Identify the facts.
Eliminate the unnecessary facts.
List the necessary facts.

L- Choose an operation.
Write in words what your plan of action will be.

V- Estimate your answer.
Carry out your plan.

E- Did you answer what you were asked to find?
Is your answer reasonable?
Is your answer accurate?
Write answer as a complete thought.

AlgebraicThinking • Foundations

Appendix 7: Determine the Area and Perimeter of Composite Figures

Warm Up: The Marble Game

Laverne has a bag of marbles. The bag contains the following: 4 blue, 3 red, 5 purple, 3 yellow, and 10 green marbles. Find the probability of the following outcomes and write each as a fraction, decimal and percent.

1. P(purple)

2. P(green)

3. P(green or blue)

4. P(not green)

Any figure (or shape) that can be divided into more than one basic figure is said to be a _____.

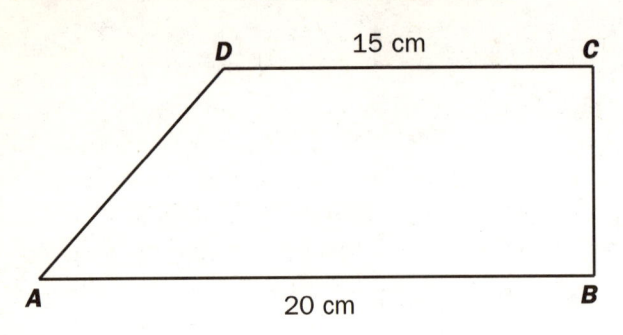

Trapezoid *ABCD* is a composite figure because it consists of two basic figures.

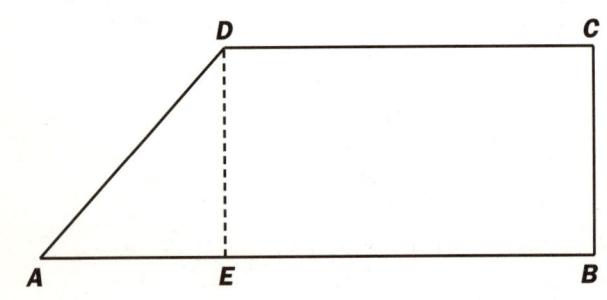

trapezoid *ABCD* = triangle *ADE* and rectangle *CBDE*

The area of a composite figure is found by adding together the areas of the individual figures.

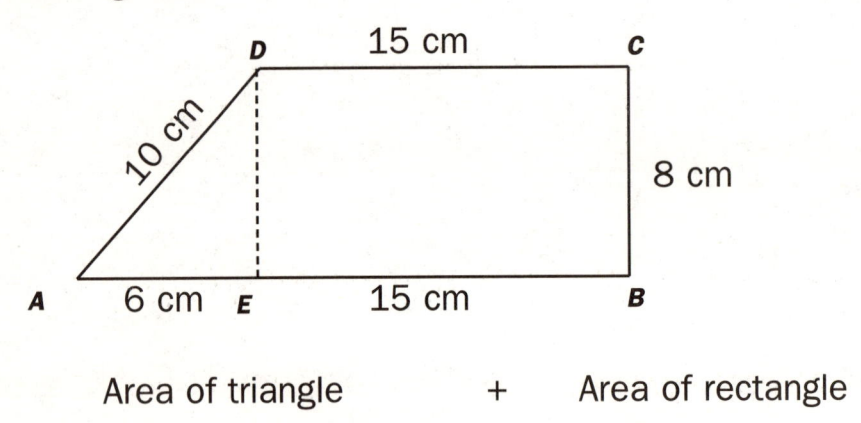

Area of triangle   +   Area of rectangle

The perimeter is found by adding the measures of each side. What is the perimeter of the composite figure?

AlgebraicThinking • Foundations

Directions: Find the area of each composite figure.
Examples:

1.

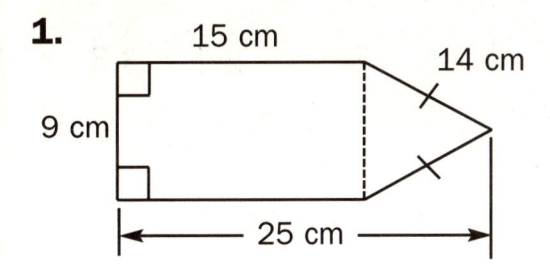

15 cm
14 cm
9 cm
25 cm

2.

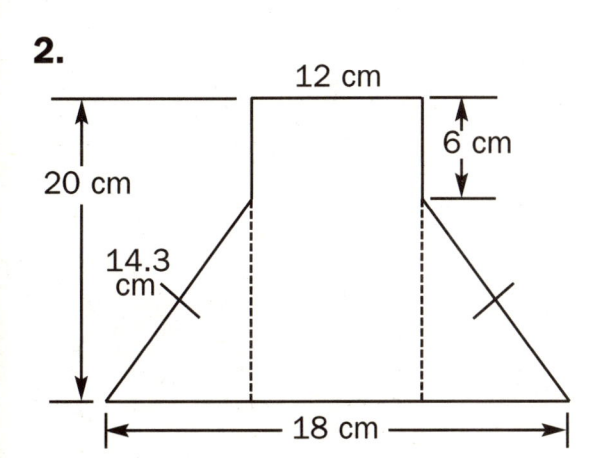

12 cm
6 cm
20 cm
14.3 cm
18 cm

655

3.

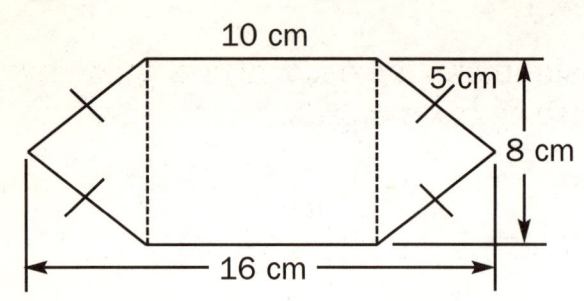

```
   10 cm
   ┌─────┐ 5 cm
  ╱│     │╲ ↑
 ╱ │     │ ╲ 8 cm
 ╲ │     │ ╱ ↓
  ╲│     │╱
   └─────┘
   ← 16 cm →
```

Find the perimeter of each of the composite figures below.

1.

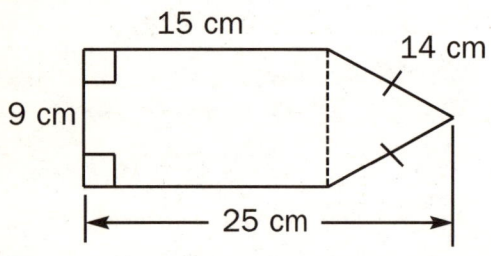

```
      15 cm
  ┌─────────┐ 14 cm
9 cm         ╲
  │          ╱
  └─────────╱
   ← 25 cm →
```

2.

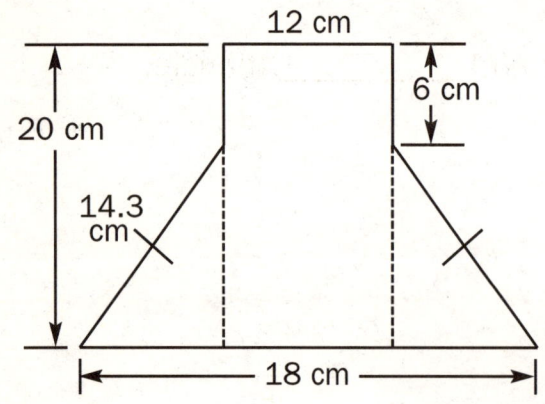

```
        12 cm
   ┌────┬────┐
   │    │    │ 6 cm
20 cm   │    
   │ 14.3 cm
   │  ╲      ╲
   └───┴──────┘
      ← 18 cm →
```

3.

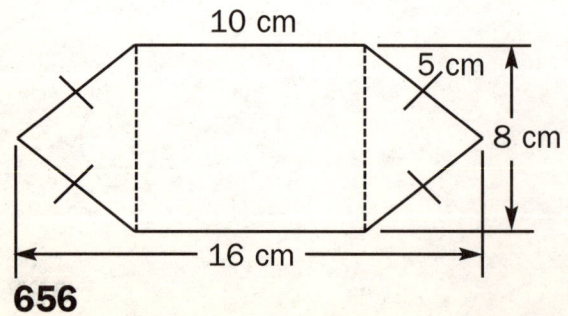

```
   10 cm
   ┌─────┐ 5 cm
  ╱│     │╲ ↑
 ╱ │     │ ╲ 8 cm
 ╲ │     │ ╱ ↓
  ╲│     │╱
   └─────┘
   ← 16 cm →
```

656

AlgebraicThinking • Foundations

Homework

Directions: Find the missing angle measurement for each of the following triangles, and then name the triangle according to its angles.

1. 90°, 60°, _____°   This is a(n) _____ triangle.

2. 110°, 35°, _____°   This is a(n) _____ triangle.

3. 73°, 58°, _____°   This is a(n) _____ triangle.

4. 60°, 60°, _____°   This is a(n) _____ triangle.

5. 45°, 45°, _____°   This is a(n) _____ triangle.

6. 38°, 47°, _____°   This is a(n) _____ triangle.

Appendix 8: Comparing and Ordering Rational Numbers on a Number Line

Warm Up: Scientific Notation

Directions: Convert each problem to scientific notation or standard form.

1. $3.4 \cdot 10^{3}$

2. $6.05 \cdot 10^{-2}$

3. $1.234 \cdot 10^{7}$

4. 0.0000437

5. 12,345,678

6. 0.00000000065

Algebraic Thinking • Foundations

Comparing and Ordering Rational Numbers

Did you know that fractions, decimals and percents can be negative numbers? Just as you can jump one and a half feet high (1½ feet), you can also dive one and half feet below the surface of the water (⁻1½ feet).

Fractions, decimal fractions, percent fractions and their opposites are all examples of rational numbers. _____ are numbers that can be written as a fraction of two integers.

Here are some examples of rational numbers:

$\frac{1}{3}$ Both 1 and 3 are integers.

⁻4.5   ⁻4.5 can be written as a fraction of $\frac{-450}{100}$. Both ⁻450 and 100 are integers.

0.24   0.24 can be written as a fraction of $\frac{24}{100}$ which simplifies to $\frac{6}{25}$.
Both 6 and 25 are integers.

$\frac{-2}{5}$ Both the numerator and the denominator are integers.
Both 3 and 4 are integers.

0.75   0.75 can be written as a fraction of $\frac{75}{100}$ which simplifies to $\frac{3}{4}$.
Both 3 and 4 are integers.

All rational numbers can be graphed on a number line. Let's look at the following two examples:

Graph the fractions $2\frac{1}{2}$ and $\frac{-4}{5}$.

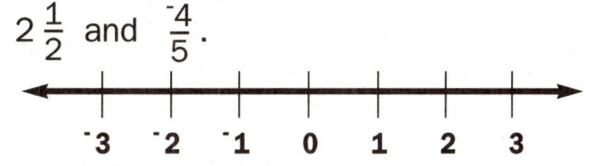

⬅———|———|———|———|———|———|———➡
   ⁻3 ⁻2 ⁻1   0   1   2   3

When you graph fractions, decide between which two integers you will find the fraction. $2\frac{1}{2}$ will be between ____ and ____ on the number line. Because $2\frac{1}{2}$ is exactly halfway between the two numbers, it is located halfway between ____ and ____.

$\frac{-4}{5}$ will be placed to the _____ of zero on the number line because it is a negative number. $\frac{-4}{5}$ will be placed on the number line between ___ and ___. Because $\frac{-4}{5}$ is closer to ___ than ___, it will be placed closer to ___.

Now try this: Graph the following fractions on the number line.
$1\frac{1}{3}$, ⁻$2\frac{1}{2}$, $\frac{5}{8}$, ⁻1

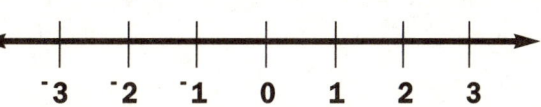

⬅———|———|———|———|———|———|———➡
   ⁻3 ⁻2 ⁻1   0   1   2   3

659

Algebraic Thinking • Foundations

When you graph decimals, you will follow the same steps as graphing fractions. Decide between which two integers you will find the decimal and then place the decimal on the number line. Remember to consider which integer it is closest to when you place it on the number line.

Directions: Graph the following decimals on the number line.

⁻3.2, 0.6, 2.4, ⁻1.75

If you are going to graph a percent, change to the decimal equivalent and then graph.

Comparing rational numbers

Directions: Make each number sentence true by using one of the following math verbs <, >, =. (You may want to draw a number line.) If you use a number line, remember that on a number line, the numbers to the left of the number line are smaller than those to the right.

1. $\frac{-11}{2}$ ◯ $-2\frac{1}{3}$ 2. 2.67 ◯ $2\frac{9}{10}$ 3. $-2\frac{5}{8}$ ◯ ⁻3.4

4. 42% ◯ 0.9   5. ⁻0.67 ◯ ⁻0.24   6. $1\frac{1}{8}$ ◯ 0.95

Ordering rational numbers

When ordering rational numbers it is helpful to put all the numbers in the same form. Many times it is easiest to change them all to decimals. Because some of the numbers you are ordering will be negative it is also helpful to place the numbers on a number line.

Example: Order the following rational numbers from least to greatest:
1.62, $\frac{3}{5}$, ⁻$1\frac{1}{2}$, ⁻200%

1. Change all numbers to the same form. In this case it would easiest to change to decimals. 1.62 = ___, $\frac{3}{5}$ = ___, ⁻$1\frac{1}{2}$ = ___, ⁻200% = ___

2. Draw a number line and place your decimals on the number line.

3. List the numbers in order from least to greatest in their original form.
   _____

Algebraic Thinking • Foundations

Directions: Order the following rational numbers from least to greatest.

1. 0.5, ⁻0.63, 20%, ⁻0.1

2. ⁻35%, ⁻1.34, ⁻2, $\frac{^-12}{10}$

3. $^-1\frac{1}{3}$, $^-2\frac{3}{4}$, 100%, 1.7

4. 0.07, $^-1\frac{5}{7}$, 0.7, ⁻23%

5. ⁻2.83, ⁻250%, $^-1\frac{9}{10}$, ⁻2

661

Algebraic Thinking • Foundations

Homework

The custodian at Maryland Middle School must refinish the schools basketball court. In order to determine how much sealer and stain to buy, he needs to know the area of the court. If the floor is 75 feet long and 40 feet wide, what is the area of the basketball court?

S- Highlight the question.

O- Identify the facts.
Eliminate the unnecessary facts.
List the necessary facts.

L- Choose an operation.
Write in words what your plan of action will be.

V- Estimate your answer.
Carry out your plan.

E- Did you answer what you were asked to find?
Is your answer reasonable?
Is your answer accurate?
Write answer as a complete thought.

AlgebraicThinking • Foundations

Appendix 9: Functions Without Integers

Warm Up: Patterns

Directions: Find the missing value in each problem below.

1. 1, 4, 9, 16, ___, 36;

2. 1, 8, 27, ___, 125;

3. 1, 4, 13, 40, 121, ___;

4. 1, 2, 1, 2, 3, 1, 2, 3, ___;

5. red, yellow, blue, yellow, red, _____;

6. w, s, a, f, w, ___, a;

AlgebraicThinking • Foundations

IN

?

OUT

AlgebraicThinking • Foundations

Directions: Use this page to make up four functions, and inputs and outputs for each function. Do not show your partner.

Input	Output	Rule Options

Function: _____

Input	Output	Rule Options

Function: _____

Input	Output	Rule Options

Function: _____

Input	Output	Rule Options

Function: _____

Algebraic Thinking • Foundations

Directions: Work with your teacher to complete this page.

Operation: $x - 3$

Input (x)	Output (y)
12	9
10	7
8	
7	
6	
5	
4	
3	

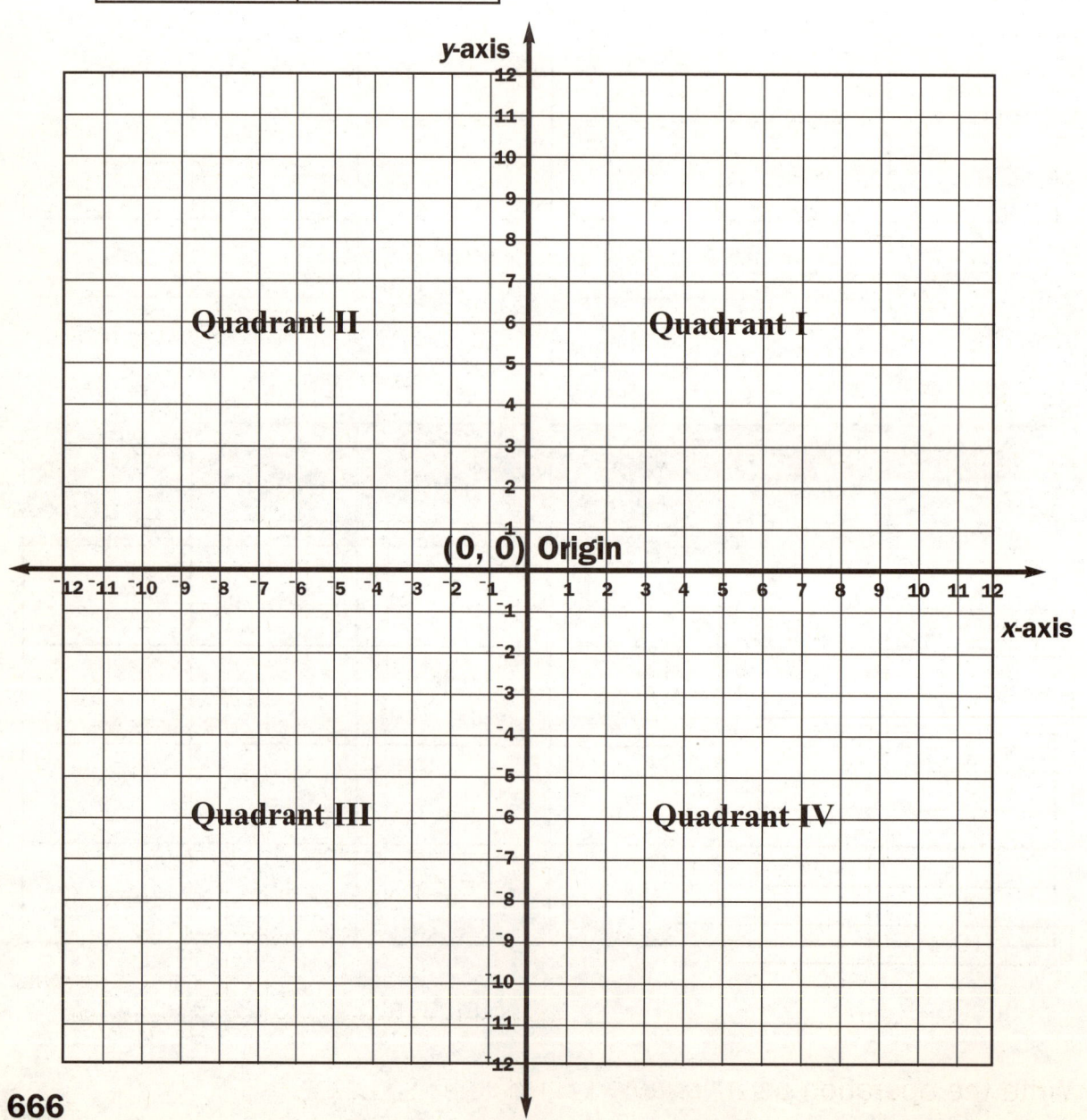

AlgebraicThinking • Foundations

Directions: Complete the next four function tables with your partner, including the graph. Also answer any questions relating to the tables and graphs.

1. Operation: $3x$

Input (x)	Output (y)
0	
1	
2	
3	
4	

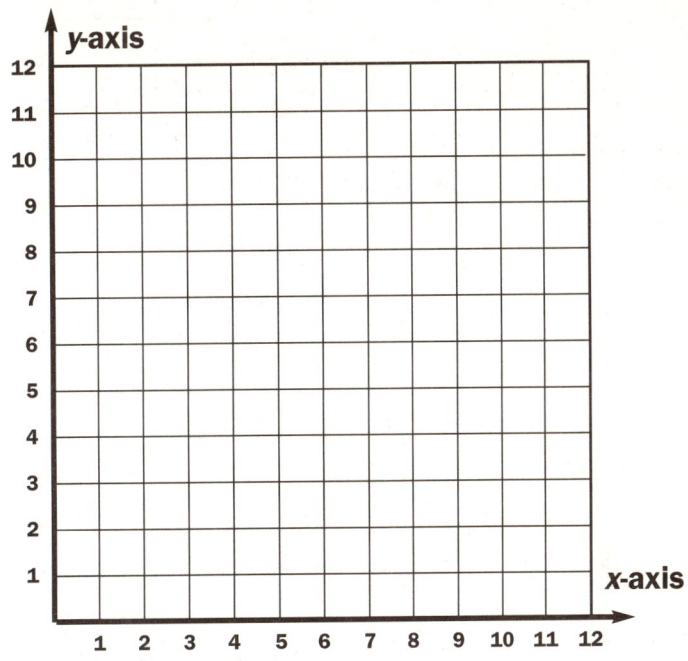

If the input (x) were 6 what would the output (y) be? _____
What would the ordered pair be for an input of 6? _____
Would this ordered pair be on the line of the graph you made for the table? _____

2. Operation: Input times itself

Input (x)	Output (y)
1	
2	
3	
4	
5	
7	
8	
10	

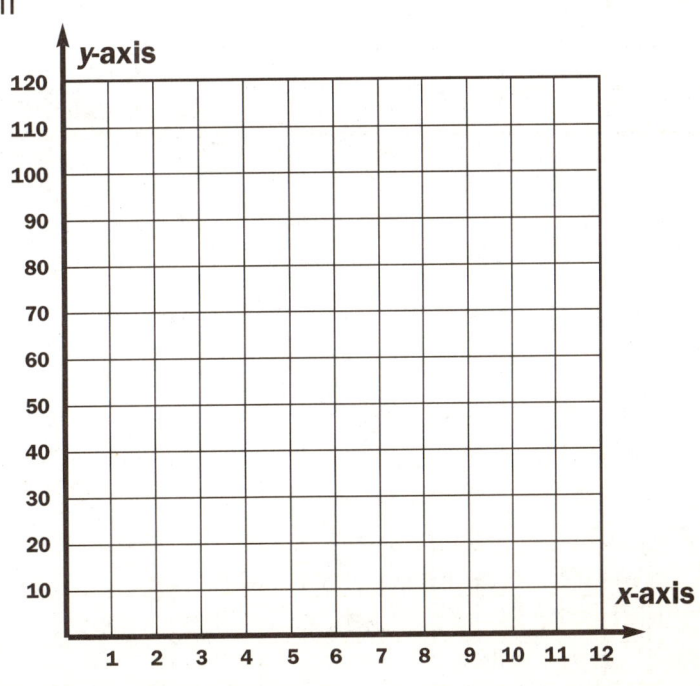

Write the operation as a variable expression: _____

667

Algebraic Thinking • Foundations

3. Operation: _____
   (Fill in the operation based on the x and y values in the table.)

Input (x)	Output (y)
0	0
2	1
4	2
6	3
8	4
10	5
12	6

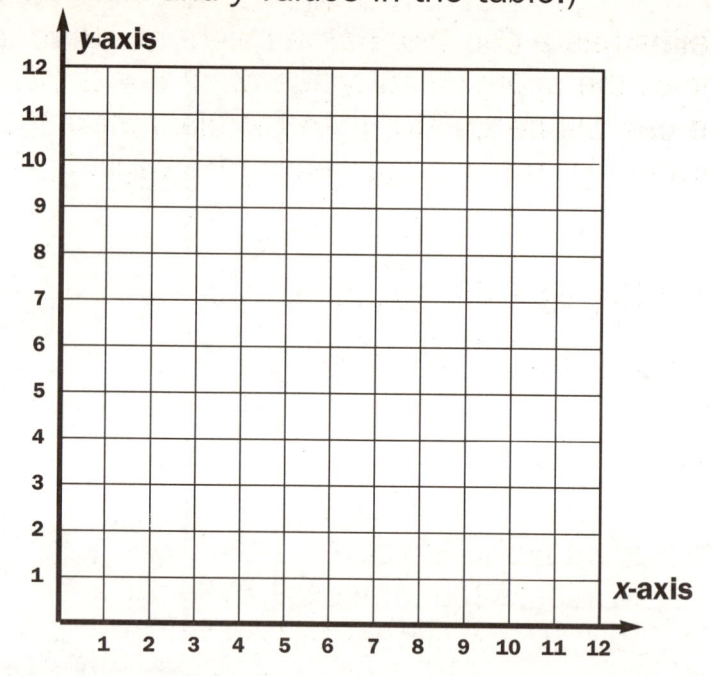

What rule could the function table have been if you just looked at the first input/output? _____

4. Operation: 2x + 2

Input (x)	Output (y)
0	2
1	4
3	8
4	10
6	14
7	16
9	20
11	24

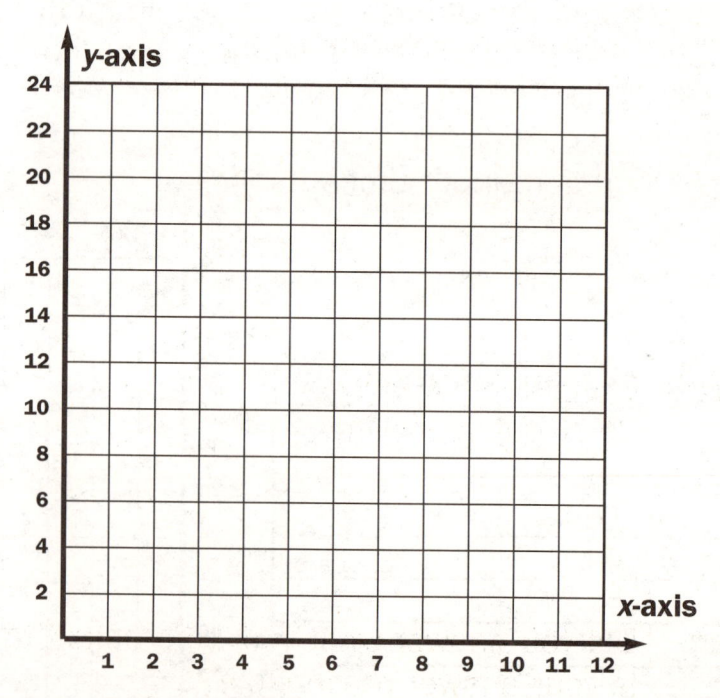

If the input (x) were 8, what would the output (y) be? _____
What would the ordered pair be for an input of 8? _____
Would this ordered pair be on the line of the graph you made for the table? _____
Why do you think so? _____

668

Algebraic Thinking • Foundations

Homework: Circumference of a Circle

Melina has a can that has a height of 20 cm and a radius of 4 cm. She knows the approximate value of pi: $\pi = 3.14$. She believes the height of the can will be greater than the circumference. Is she correct? Hint: Formula for the circumference of a circle is $C = 2\pi r$.

S- Highlight the question.

O- Identify the facts.
Eliminate the unnecessary facts.
List the necessary facts.

L- Choose an operation.
Write in words what your plan of action will be.

V- Estimate your answer.
Carry out your plan.

E- Did you answer what you were asked to find?
Is your answer reasonable?
Is your answer accurate?
Write answer as a complete thought.

AlgebraicThinking • Foundations

Appendix 10: Plotting Points in the Coordinate Plane

Warm Up: Tic – Tac – Toe - Decimal Operations

Directions: Solve each decimal problem and place the correct letter in the tic-tac-toe box to find the winner.

Kelly Played the X

1. 1.73 + 12. 1 =
2. 2.5 • 4.8 =
3. 10.06 – 8.57 =
4. 1.3 • 5.9 =

Jamilah played the O

1. 26.083 + 11.96 =
2. 35.4 – 16.85 =
3. 4.3 + 5.7 =

38.043	13.83	9.5
3.15	10	12
7.67	1.49	18.55

AlgebraicThinking • Foundations

Directions: Follow along with your teacher to label your coordinate plane.

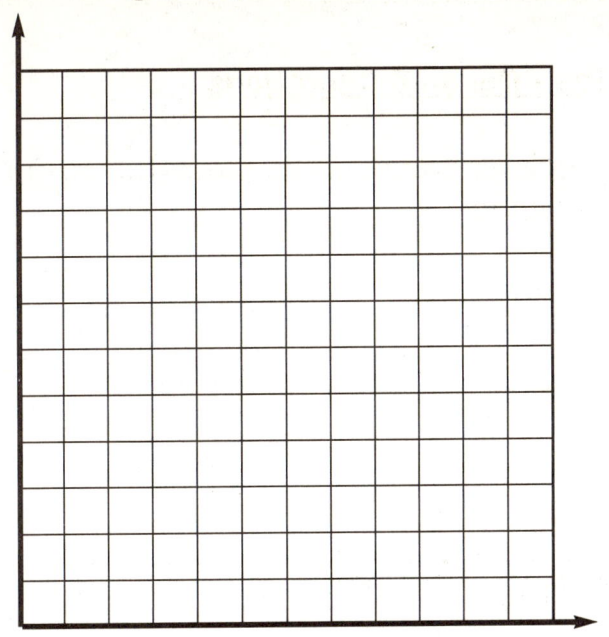

1. Label the horizontal line going across as the _____

2. Label the vertical line going up and down as the _____

3. Label the point that the two lines meet as the _____

4. Number the *x*-axis and *y*-axis.

   An **ordered pair** is a set of two numbers that describes how to graph a point. The first number in an ordered pair is known as the <u>x-coordinate</u> and the second number in an ordered pair is known as the <u>y-coordinate</u>. The origin is always (0, 0).

The *x*-coordinate tells you where to go on the *x*-axis.

The *y*-coordinate tells you where to go on the *y*-axis.

5. In the ordered pair (6, 3), what number is the *x*-coordinate? _____
   What number is the *y*-coordinate? _____

6. Graph the ordered pair (6, 3).

671

Algebraic Thinking • Foundations

Label the graph below as you did with your teacher on the last page. Make sure that you do the following things:

- Label the *x*-axis
- Label the *y*-axis
- Label the origin
- Number both the *x*-axis and the *y*-axis

Follow along with your classmates as each cooperative pair plots their point on the coordinate grid your teacher has displayed in the room. Each time a new point is given, write it down and connect it to the last point drawn with a line.

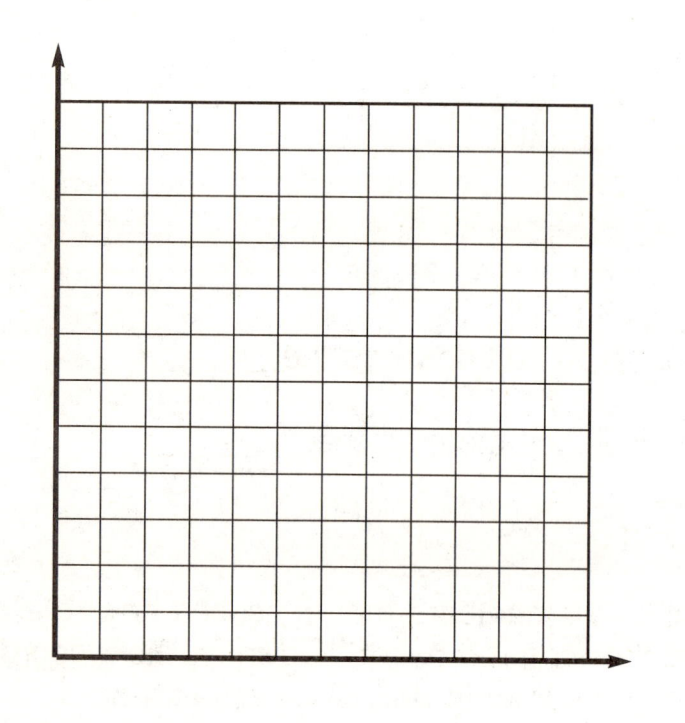

1. (9,4)
2. (8,5)
3. (6,6)
4. (3,6)
5. (1,4)
6. (3,3)
7. (1,2)
8. (3,1)
9. (6,1)
10. (9,2)
11. (12,1)
12. (11,3)
13. (12,5)
14. (9,4)

What does the set of ordered pairs make a picture of? _____

Describe what you would need to do to plot the point (8,2).

_____

_____

_____

AlgebraicThinking • Foundations

In the activity that you just completed, you were able to see that you can use ordered pairs on a coordinate grid to create a picture. It is also possible to make geometric figures. "Figure it out" by answering the following questions with your partner.

1. Use the graph to the right to plot the points (4, 8), (9, 8), (8, 10) and (5, 10). Connect the points with lines. What shape do the points connect to form?

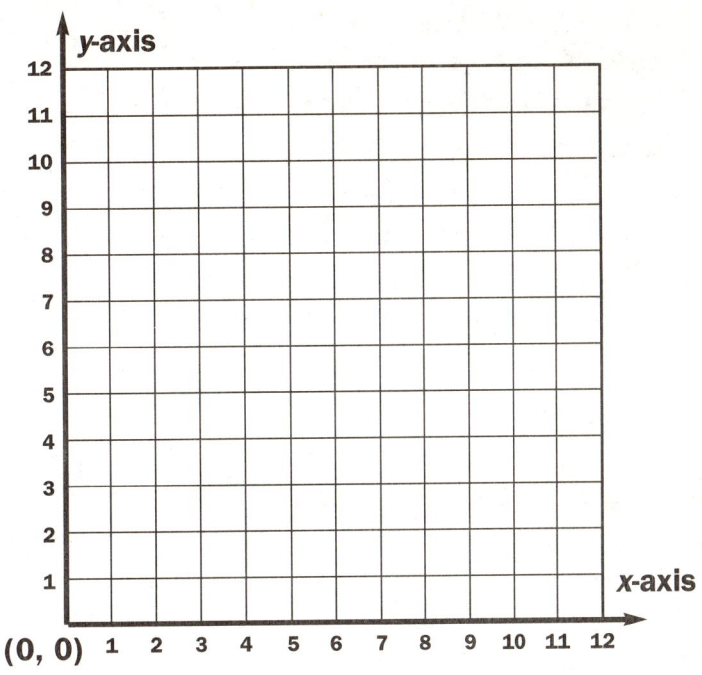

   _____

2. Use the graph to the right to plot the points (2, 2), (4, 2), (4, 6) and (2, 6). Connect the points with lines. What shape do the points connect to form?

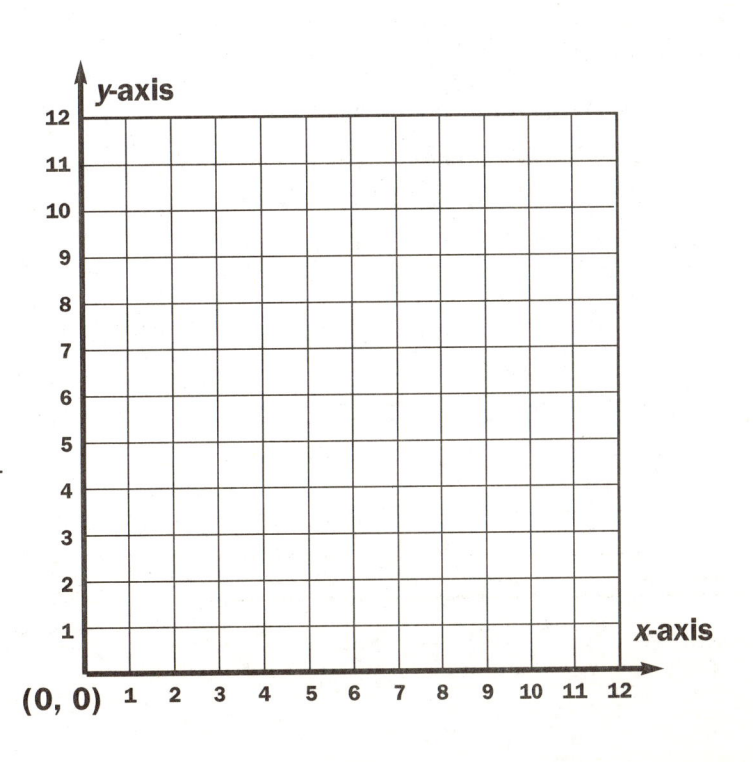

   _____

AlgebraicThinking • Foundations

Follow along with your teacher to complete the next two graphs.

3. Graph the ordered pairs (5,3), (8,3), and (8,6). These points are three of the four vertices of a square. Plot the fourth point to make a square.

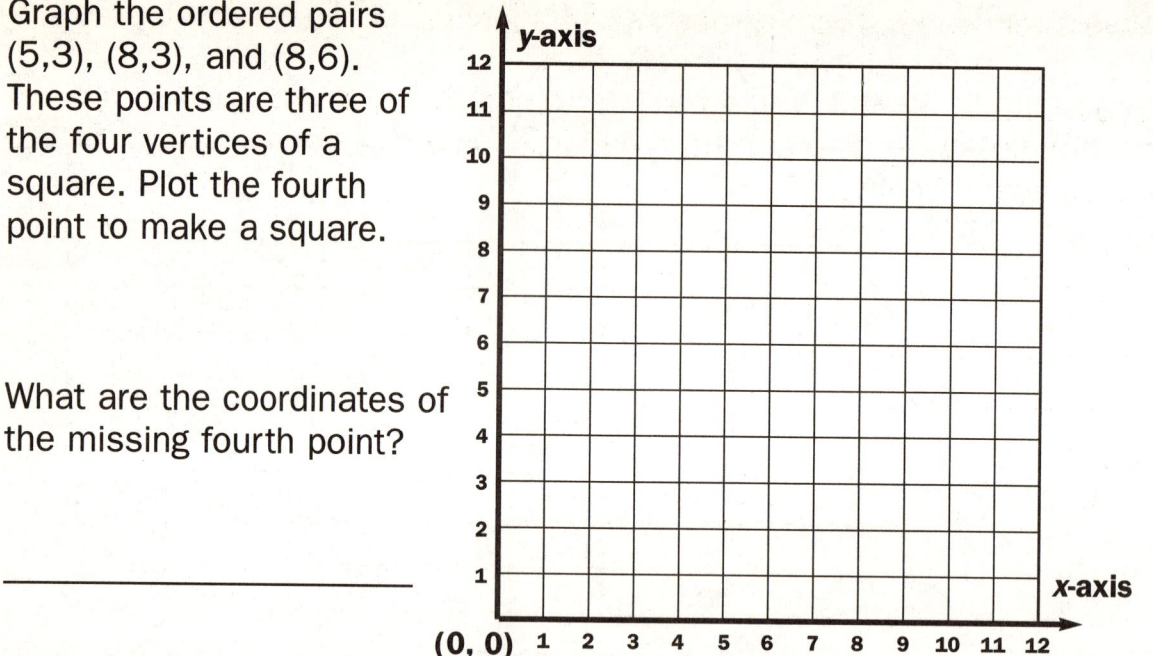

   What are the coordinates of the missing fourth point?

   _____

4. Graph the ordered pairs (10,3), (10,7), and (4,7). These points are three of the four vertices of a rectangle. Plot the fourth point to complete the shape.

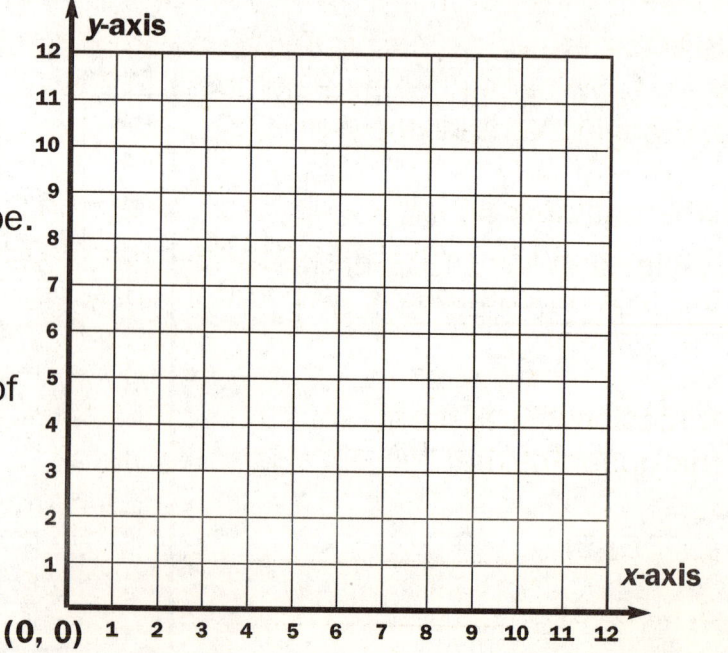

   What are the coordinates of the missing fourth point?

   _____

674

Algebraic Thinking • Foundations

Below is an example of a four quadrant graph. Quadrant I is located in the upper right section of the grid. This is the same part of the graph that you have been working with throughout this lesson.

Quadrants II, III, and IV can be determined by going around the graph in a counterclockwise direction from quadrant 1. Label the remaining quadrants on the graph below.

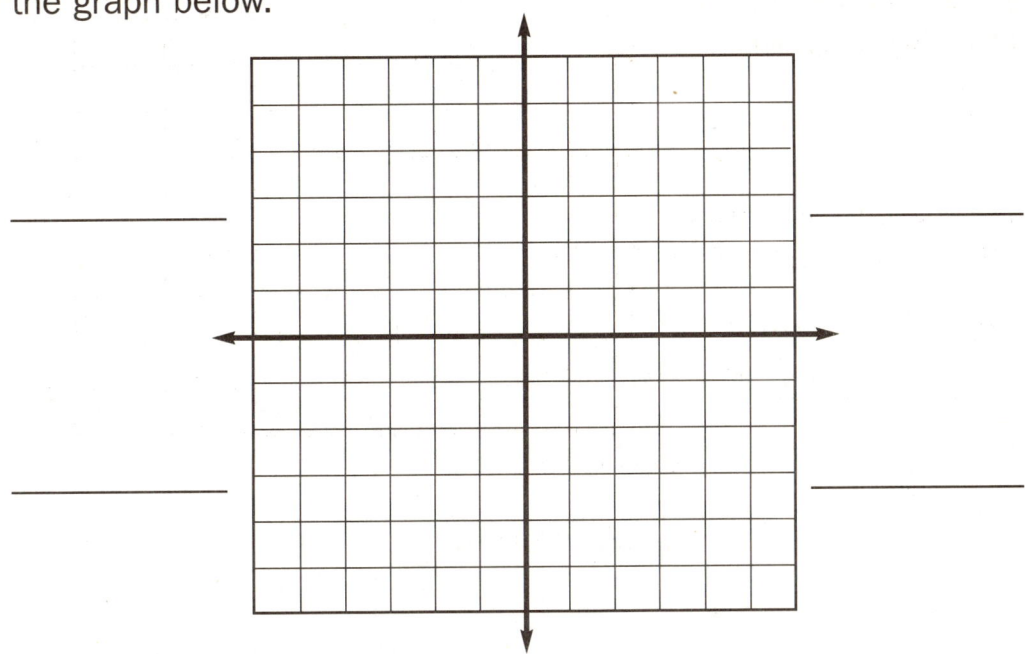

Label the *x*-axis, *y*-axis, and origin on the coordinate grid above.

When numbering the *x*-axis, it is the same as numbering a number line. Start at the origin and write the positive numbers to the _____, beginning with 1. Write the negative numbers to the _____, beginning with ⁻1 next to the origin. Number the *x*-axis.

When numbering the *y*-axis, start at the origin. The values going up are positive and the values going down are negative. Beginning at the origin, the first number above is 1 and the first number going down is ⁻1. Number the *y*-axis.

Directions: Graph each of the ordered pairs. Next to the ordered pair, write the quadrant that the point is in.

1. (5, 3) _____
2. (⁻5, ⁻3) _____
3. (⁻5, 3) _____
4. (5, ⁻3) _____
5. (2, 6) _____
6. (1, ⁻4) _____
7. (⁻1, ⁻2) _____
8. (⁻4, 4) _____

Algebraic Thinking • Foundations

Homework: Fraction Addition

Victoria wants to bake her mother a cake for her birthday. The recipe requires $3\frac{1}{4}$ cups of flour and $2\frac{2}{3}$ cups of sugar. How many cups of flour and sugar does she need altogether?

S- Highlight the question.

O- Identify the facts.
Eliminate the unnecessary facts.
List the necessary facts.

L- Choose an operation.
Write in words what your plan of action.

V- Estimate your answer.
Carry out your plan.

E- Did you answer what you were asked to find?
Is your answer reasonable?
Is your answer accurate?
Write answer as a complete thought.

AlgebraicThinking • Foundations

Appendix 11: Polygons in the Coordinate Plane

Warm Up: Plotting Points in the first quadrant

1. Plot the following points on the graph below; then connect the dots to form a picture.

   (2, 6), (5, 5), (5, 7), (6, 2), (6, 10), (7, 5), (7, 7), (10, 6)

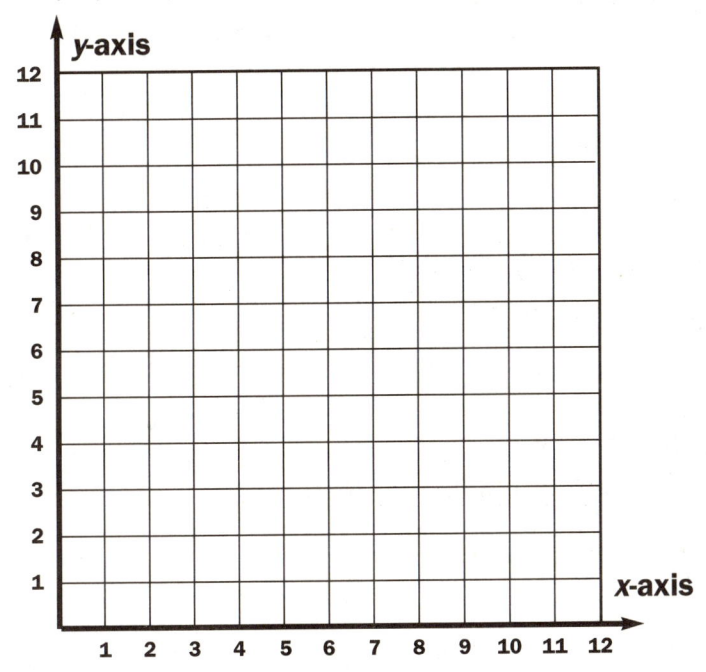

Connect the points in the following order; (2, 6), (5, 7), (6, 10), (7, 7), (10, 6), (7, 5), (6, 2), (5, 5) and back to (2, 6).

Algebraic Thinking • Foundations

In the last lesson, we reviewed how to plot points in the coordinate plane. The x-coordinate is the first number in the ordered pair (x, y) and tells how to move horizontally. The y-coordinate is the second number in the ordered pair (x, y) and tells how to move vertically.

Determining the distance between two ordered pairs.

During today's lesson we are going to find the distance between two points both on the x and y axis, as well as the points on a polygon created on the coordinate grid.

Let's start with finding the distance between two ordered pairs that lie on the same axis. When ordered pairs are plotted directly on either the x-axis or y-axis, you can determine the distance by subtracting the values in the two ordered pairs, or by simply counting the number of spaces between the two points.

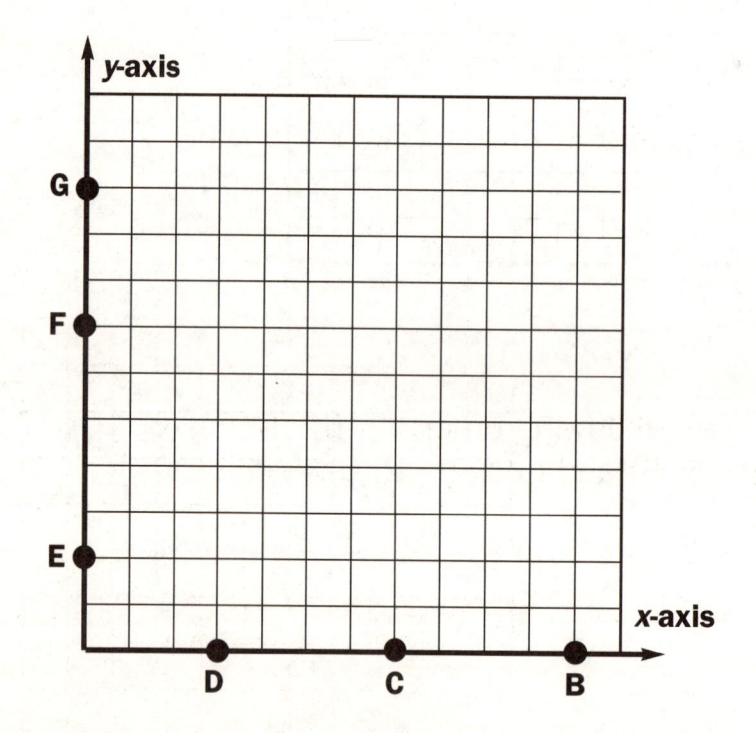

How would we find the distance between points E and G?

We will first determine the distance by subtracting the values of the two ordered pairs. What is the ordered pair for G? _____

What is the ordered pair for E? _____

Algebraic Thinking • Foundations

Since the points lie on the *y*-axis, you will only need to subtract the *y*-values: _____

Now try the counting method. Place your finger on point *E*. Count how many units it takes to reach point *G*. _____

Determine which axis the points lie on. Calculate the distance between the two given points.

    B and *C* _____   *B* and *D* _____

    E and *F* _____   *G* and *F* _____

You can also draw polygons in the coordinate plane by connecting ordered pairs with straight lines. Look at the examples below with your teacher.

Example 1:

Write the ordered pair for each vertex of the rectangle.

A _____

B _____

C _____

D _____

What do you notice about the numbers in the ordered pairs of the rectangle?
_____
_____

679

Algebraic Thinking • Foundations

What is the distance between Point *A* and *D* of the rectangle? _____

How do you know? _____

This is also called the _____ of the rectangle.

What is the distance between Point *A* and *B* of the rectangle? _____

How do you know? _____

This is also called the _____ of the rectangle.

What is the perimeter of the rectangle? _____

What is the area of the rectangle? _____ How do you know?
_____

Example 2:

Plot and connect the following points in order and identify the polygon.

    F (5, 0) *G* (9, 0) *H* (9, 5) *J* (7, 8) *K* (5, 5)

The polygon you have just drawn has ____ sides and is a _____.

What is the distance between Point *G* and Point *H*? _____

What is the distance between Point *F* and Point *G*? _____

What is the area of this figure? (Hint: Think of this as two separate figures and add the areas together.) _____

680

AlgebraicThinking • Foundations

Example 3:
Here are three vertices of rectangle *LMNP*. What ordered pair would name vertex *P*?

   L (0, 4)   *M* (0, 7)   *N* (10, 7)

To answer this question, you can use two methods.

Method 1: Plot the three points on a coordinate plane. Connect the points you have. Decide where the fourth point should be in order to make a rectangle. Remember that a rectangle has four 90° angles, and two pair of congruent sides.

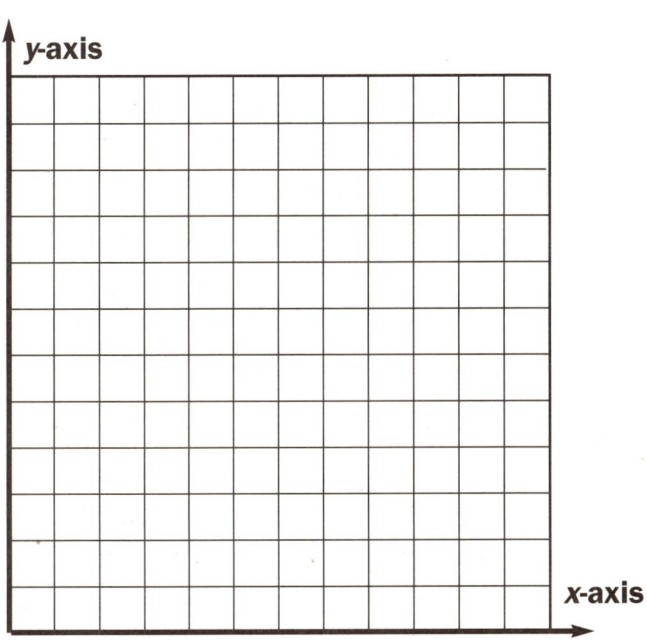

Point *P* must be directly across from point ____, and directly below point ____. The ordered pair for P is _____.

What is the area of the rectangle formed? _____

Method 2:
Look back at example 1 (pg 2). Ordered pairs of rectangles have two pair of points with the same *x*-coordinate, and two pair of points with the same *y*-coordinate.

Points *L* and *M* both have an *x*-coordinate of _____. Point *N* has an *x*-coordinate of _____, so *P* must have an *x*-coordinate of _____.
Points *M* and *N* both have a *y*-coordinate of _____. Point *L* has a *y*-coordinate of _____, so *P* must have a *y*-coordinate of _____.
Point *P* is _____

681

AlgebraicThinking • Foundations

Directions: With your partner, try the problems below.

1. What are the ordered pairs for the vertices of parallelogram *ABCD*?

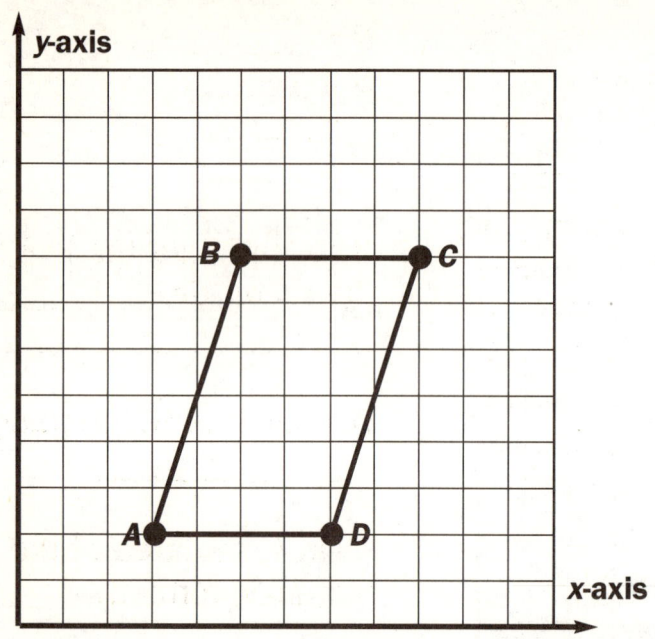

   A _____
   B _____
   C _____
   D _____

   Now give the measure of the height: 8 – 2 = 6 units
   and the base: _____

   What is the area of the parallelogram? _____

2. The following points are part of square *MNPQ*. What are the coordinates of point *M*? Plot the coordinates on the graph below.

   N (1, 10)   *P* (6, 10)   *Q* (6, 5)   *M* _____

   How did you know the location of point *M*?

   _____
   _____

   What is the area?
   _____

682

Algebraic Thinking • Foundations

3. What are the ordered pairs for rectangle *RSTV*? Find the ordered pair for *V*.

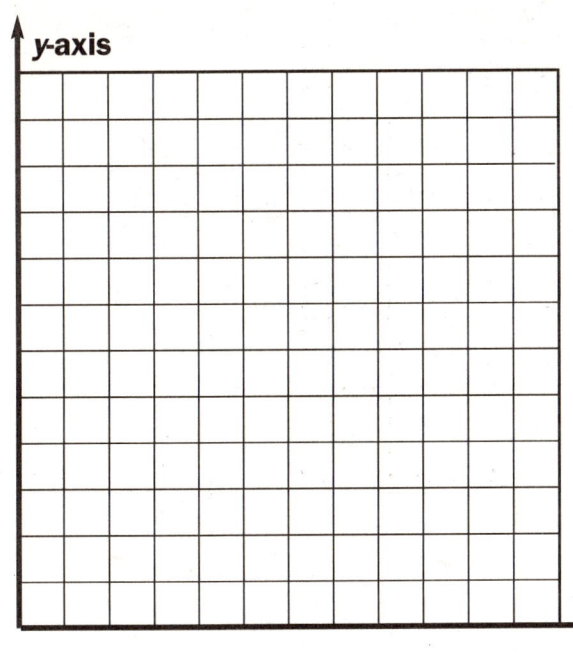

R = _____
S = _____
T = _____
V = _____

Now, calculate the length of the rectangle. _____
_____

The width of the rectangle:
_____

What is the area of the rectangle formed? _____
_____

4. Plot and connect the points given below in order. What type of polygon have you drawn? _____

W (1, 7)   X (2, 10)   Y (8, 10)   Z (7, 7)

Calculate the length of the base of the parallelogram:
_____

Calculate the height of the parallelogram: _____

The area of the parallelogram is
_____

683

Algebraic Thinking • Foundations

Homework – Bar Graph

The Miller Middle School basketball coach was analyzing data from other basketball teams. He charted the average free throw statistics for five other schools. What is the range of points scored by free throws from the five schools?

Free Throw Points

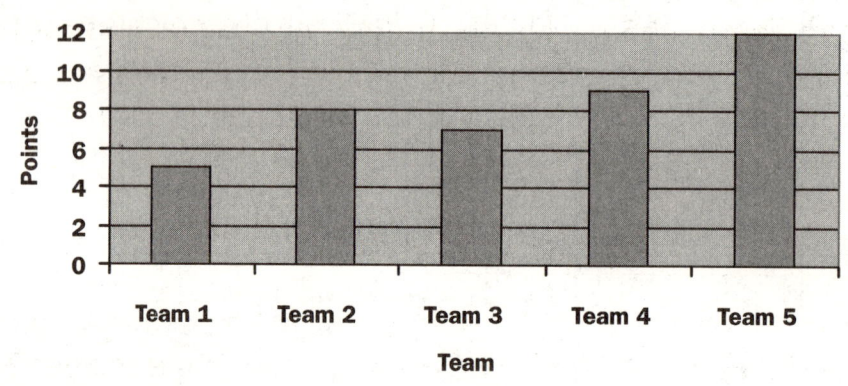

Team	Points
Team 1	5
Team 2	8
Team 3	7
Team 4	9
Team 5	12

S- Highlight the question.

O- Identify the facts.
List the necessary facts.

L- Choose an operation.
Eliminate the unnecessary facts.
Write in words what your plan of action will be.

V- Estimate your answer.
Carry out your plan.

E- Did you answer what you were asked to find?
Is your answer reasonable?
Is your answer accurate?
Write answer as a complete thought.

Algebraic Thinking • Foundations

Appendix 12: Rotations

Warm Up:

Directions: The answers to the following word problem have been given. Give a question for each answer.

The Georgetown Bulls football team made it to the state championship game this year. The prices for tickets to the game were $6 for students and $9 for adults. There were 850 adults and 1,000 students who attended the game. All proceeds from the game went to buy the team new uniforms for next season.

Answers:	Sample Questions
1. $7,650	
2. 1,850	
3. $6,000	
4. $13,650	

Algebraic Thinking • Foundations

Directions: Follow along with your teacher to complete this page.

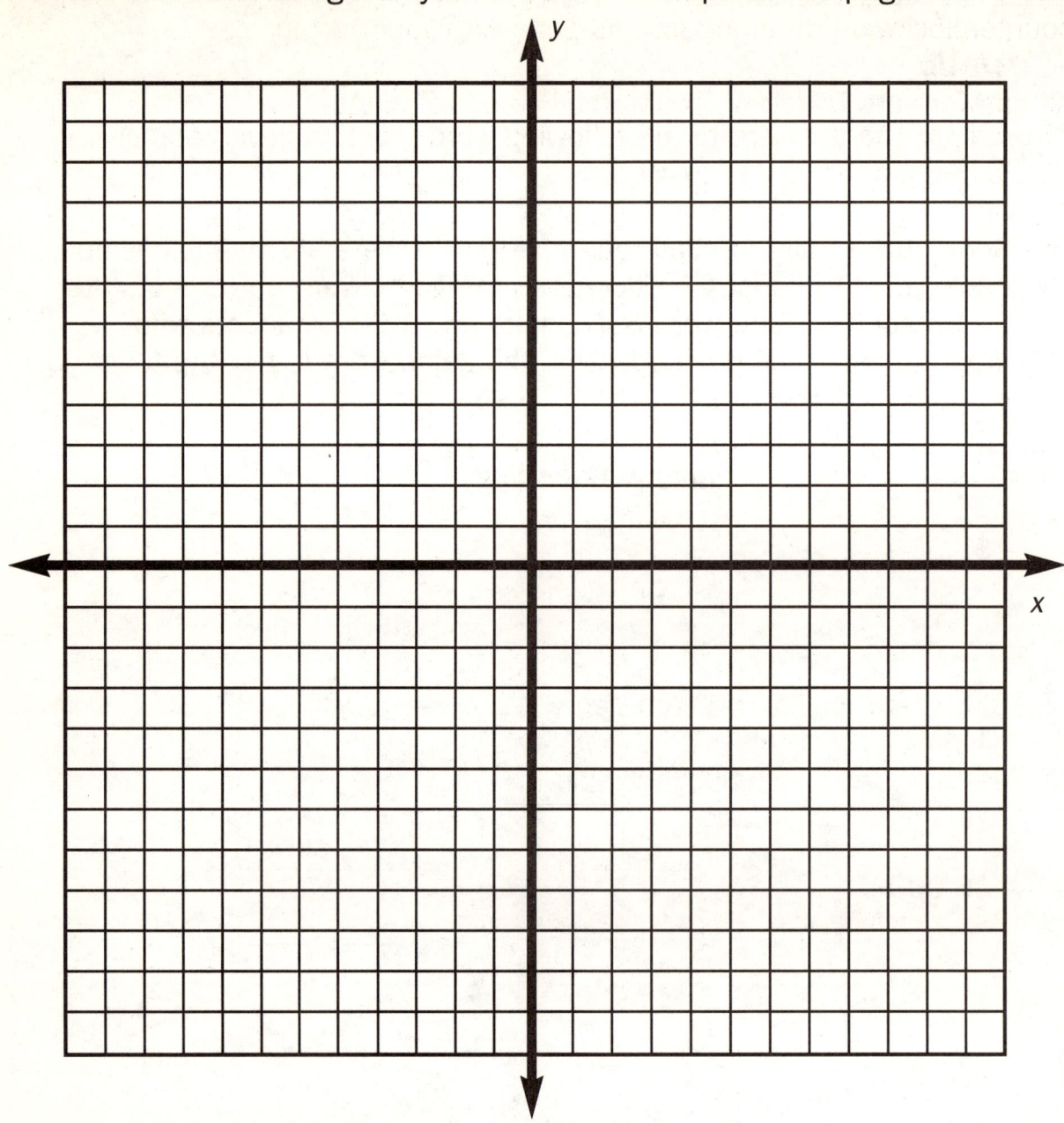

All answers are based on counterclockwise rotations.

(1, 3)   —   90° rotation   —   (____, ____)

(1, 3)   —   180° rotation   —   (____, ____)

(1, 3)   —   270° rotation   —   (____, ____)

(1, 3)   —   360° rotation   —   (____, ____)

AlgebraicThinking • Foundations

Use the coordinate plane on the previous page to complete the counterclockwise rotations on this page with your partner.

All answers are based on counterclockwise rotations.

(⁻1, ⁻6) – 90° rotation – (____, ____)

(⁻1, ⁻6) – 180° rotation – (____, ____)

(⁻1, ⁻6) – 270° rotation – (____, ____)

(⁻1, ⁻6) – 360° rotation – (____, ____)

(2, ⁻3) – 90° rotation – (____, ____)

(2, ⁻3) – 180° rotation – (____, ____)

(2, ⁻3) – 270° rotation – (____, ____)

(2, ⁻3) – 360° rotation – (____, ____)

(x, y) – 90° rotation – (____, ____)

(x, y) – 180° rotation – (____, ____)

(x, y) – 270° rotation – (____, ____)

(x, y) – 360° rotation – (____, ____)

Algebraic Thinking • Foundations

Directions: Describe the rotation from Column A to Column B as a 90°, 180°, 270°, or 360° rotation.

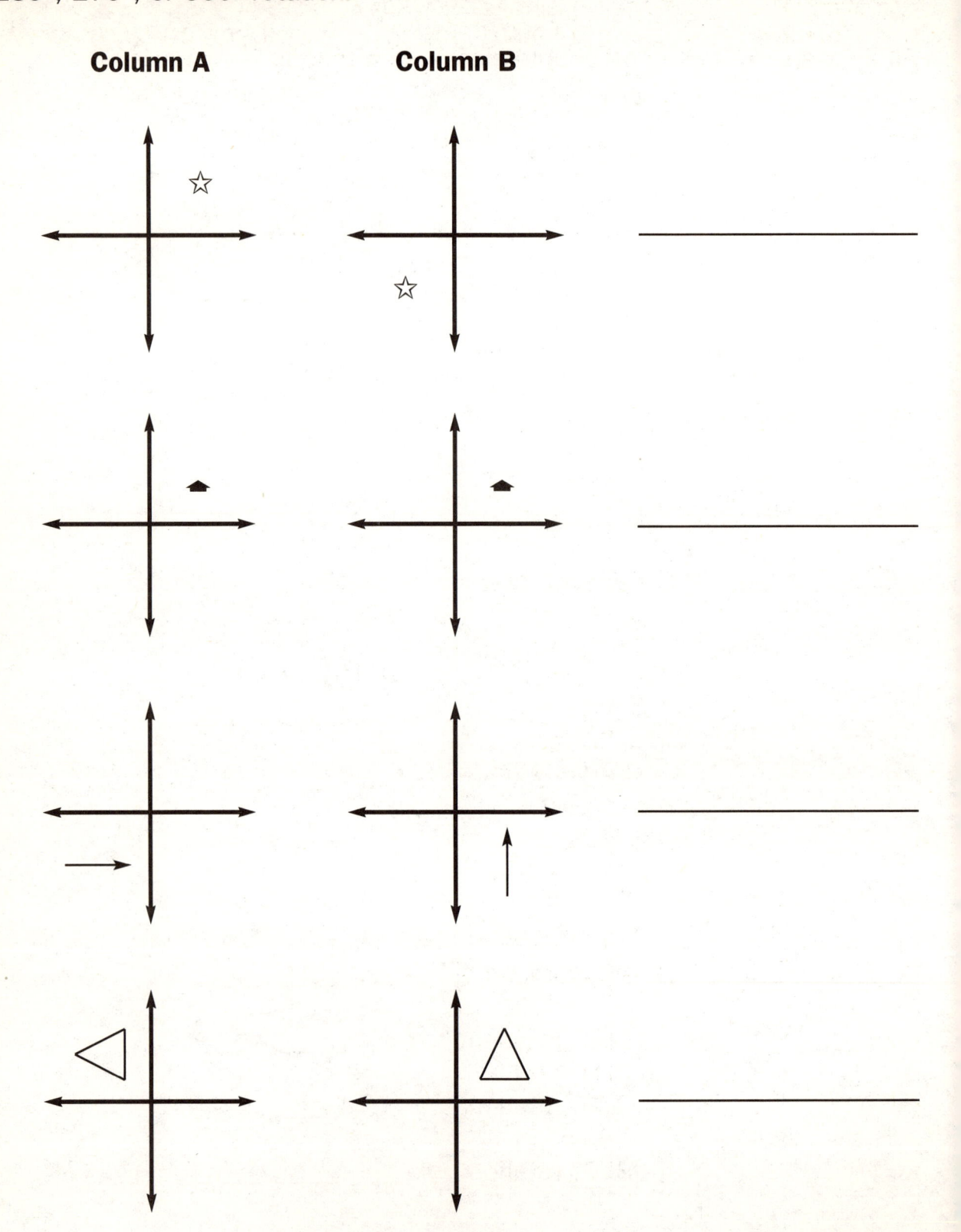

Column A   **Column B**

Algebraic Thinking • Foundations

Homework

1. $4 + 5 \cdot 2 =$

2. $14 - 40 \div 5 =$

3. $1 + 6 \cdot 2 - 8 =$

4. $7^2 - 8 \div 4 =$

5. $16 + (14 - 2) \div 3 =$

6. $9 \div (7 - 4) + 3 =$

7. $(32 - 11) \div 7 =$

8. $\dfrac{16}{12 + 4} =$

9. $56 \div 2^2 =$

Algebraic Thinking • Foundations

Appendix 13: One-Step Equations – No Integers

Warm Up: What Am I?

1. I am a four-digit number. All of my digits are different and less than 7. My first and third digits are odd. My second and fourth digits are even. The sum of my digits is 18. What number am I?

2. I am a three-digit number. My last digit is twice my first digit. My middle digit is half my first digit. What number am I?

3. I am a two-digit number. The sum of my digits and the product of my digits are the same. My first digit and my second digit are both even. What number am I?

AlgebraicThinking • Foundations

Algebraic Thinking • Foundations

Keep it Balanced

A scale is balanced when it has equal weights on both sides. An equation is balanced if both sides of the equal sign have the same value.

Equation
An equation is a mathematical sentence containing an equal sign.

Consider this situation. A scale has a 5 ounce weight on each side of it. Is it balanced? _____ A 2 ounce weight is added to the pan on the left side. Is it still balanced? _____ Name two things you can do to balance the scale. _____

Directions: *Model each of the equations with your teacher. Then draw what you modeled and state how you would solve the equation without using models.*

Problem	Model	How to Solve
1. $n + 7 = 10$		
2. $c + 5 = 11$		
3. $t + 5 = 14$		

AlgebraicThinking • Foundations

Problem	Model	How to Solve
4. $x + 4 = 8$		
5. $n + 2 = 3$		
6. $q + 7 = 10$		
7. $c + 4 = 10$		
8. $x + 3 = 6$		
9. $x + 5 = 10$		
10. $t + 2 = 6$		

AlgebraicThinking • Foundations

Directions: Some students came up with the following solutions to these equations. Check their work by evaluating the equation with their solution. If the answer is wrong, find the correct solution.

Equation	Solution	Check
11. $n + 4 = 12$	$n = 8$	
12. $x + 3 = 8$	$x = 5$	
13. $y + 1 = 4$	$y = 5$	
14. $b + 2 = 2$	$b = 4$	
15. $x + 4 = 12$	$x = 8$	

The method we have been using to solve these equations is called "isolate the variable." What does isolate mean? _____

_____

16. Write a problem. Write a problem that can be solved with $x + 3 = 9$

_____

_____

_____

_____

AlgebraicThinking • Foundations

Practice it!

Directions: Write the equation that matches the model and solve it.

1. $x + 4y = 6y$

2. $x + 2y = 8y$

3. $x + 3y = 6y$

4. $x + 3y = 4y$

Directions: Draw a model for each equation. Then find the solution to the problem.

5. $x + 2 = 6$	6. $n + 3 = 5$
7. $y + 2 = 9$	8. $x + 4 = 7$
9. $x + 5 = 11$	10. $c + 3 = 4$

695

AlgebraicThinking • Foundations

Directions: *Solve each equation. Use any method.*

11. $7 + a = 10$

12. $f + 6 = 15$

13. $x + 2 = 4$

14. $y + 7 = 11$

15. $x + 20 = 21$

16. $b + 10 = 18$

17. $x - 4 = 2$

18. $n - 6 = 6$

19. $x - 10 = 1$

20. $p - 14 = 21$

21. $r - 7 = 10$

22. $x - 5 = 12$

Directions: *Choose the equation that can be used to solve the word problem. Then answer the problem in a complete sentence.*

23. The Nelsons have 10 children in their family. Eight of the children are boys. How many are girls?
    a. $b + 10 = g$
    b. $8 + g = 10$
    c. $7 + g = 10$

24. Sally eats 10 pieces of fruit a week. This week she ate 2 bananas, 3 plums, and the rest apples. How many apples did she eat?
    a. $2 + 3 + a = 10$
    b. $2 + 3 + 10 = a$
    c. $10 + a = 10$

25. **Write a problem:** Write a problem that can be solved with $n + 5 = 15$.

Algebraic Thinking • Foundations

Homework:

Directions: *In problems 1 – 4, put the decimals in order from least to greatest. In problems 5 – 10, put <, >, or = between the two decimals to make a true sentence.*

1. 7.103, 7.13, 7.3

2. 9.02, 9.2, 9.002

3. 0.554, 1.5, 0.6

4. 4.12, 4.21, 4.093

5. 0.7 ◯ 0.8

6. 3.1 ◯ 3.100

7. 0.07 ◯ 0.037

8. 9.02 ◯ 9.20

9. 1.0 ◯ 0.983

10. 0.062 ◯ 0.10

Algebraic Thinking • Foundations

Appendix 14: One-Step Equations – Revenge of the Word Problems – No Integers

Warm Up: Choose a Trio

For each line below, use three of the four numbers from the box to complete a true sentence.

$$\boxed{4,\ 5,\ 9,\ 10}$$

_____ • _____ – _____   31

_____ + _____ ÷ _____   11

_____ + _____ • _____   41

_____ • _____ ÷ _____   8

_____ • _____ ÷ _____   4.5

Algebraic Thinking • Foundations

Revenge of the Word Problems

These word problems are meant to challenge you. If you don't figure it out on the first or even the second and the third time you read it, don't give up! Organize the facts and you'll get it.

Directions: S-O-L-V-E each word problem. Write an equation for each problem.

1. The exploration team discovered an unexplored cave in the Ozark Mountains. They traveled into the cave 432 feet before finding another tunnel. The GPS (Global Positioning System) could transmit to the surface through the rock structure for 150 feet. How many feet has the exploration team been traveling without the GPS communication?

S

O

L

V

E

2. On Friday evening the temperature was 64 degrees. A warm front was expected to enter the area on Saturday. The expected high for Saturday evening was to be 89 degrees. What was the temperature change?

S

O

L

V

E

AlgebraicThinking • Foundations

3. The surface temperatures of the planet Mercury were measured and recorded. The range of temperatures was 740 degrees between the sunlit side and the dark side of the planet. What was the temperature of the sunlit side if the dark side was 210°F? Explain your answer.

S

O

L

V

E

4. Mr. Moneymaker worked as a stockbroker for a local finance company. On Tuesday the stock market recorded the stocks of DJ Mix Recording Company at $58\frac{5}{8}$ per share. When the stocks had closed on Tuesday, the stocks went up $4\frac{3}{8}$ points per share. What were the stocks listed at on the opening of the day on Wednesday?

S

O

L

V

E

Algebraic Thinking • Foundations

5. Andrew wanted to purchase athletic shoes from the Internet. The total cost of the shoes including tax and shipping was $96.56. He washed cars in the summer and had saved $78. How much will he need to earn before he can purchase the shoes?

S

O

L

V

E

6. Jackson Savings and Loan offers a free $20 check card every time you deposit $500. Jack has an account and would like to receive the gift that the bank offers. He has earned $325 delivering newspapers. How much more will he need in order to receive the free gift when he makes his deposit?

S

O

L

V

E

Algebraic Thinking • Foundations

Directions: *Solve the equations. Show your work.*

7. $n + 2 = 24$

8. $x + 11 = 15$

9. $n + 2.1 = 3.3$

10. $x - \frac{2}{3} = \frac{1}{9}$

11. $c - 4.3 = 6.4$

12. $y - \frac{3}{4} = \frac{1}{4}$

13. $x - 26 = 15$

14. $3 + q = 14$

15. $x - \frac{7}{8} = \frac{1}{16}$

16. $d - \frac{1}{2} = \frac{5}{6}$

17. $x - 12 = 16$

18. $t + 1 = 1$

19. $c - 7 = 7$

20. $23 = x + 5$

21. $29 - 9 = n$

AlgebraicThinking • Foundations

Homework:

Directions: *Find each product or quotient.*

1. 0.8 • 0.7 =

2. 28 • 0.51 =

3. 12 • 0.22 =

4. 0.02 • 0.1 =

5. 15 ÷ 3.75 =

6. 38 ÷ 0.4 =

7. 0.02 ÷ 10 =

8. 0.642 • 1,000 =

9. 1.001 ÷ 5 =

10. 251 • 0.35 =

Algebraic Thinking • Foundations

Appendix 15: Solving Multiplication and Division Equations – No Integers

Warm Up: Concentrate on Fractions

Cover up each fraction with counters or pieces of paper. Uncover them two at a time. When you uncover equivalent fractions, keep the counters. The person with the most counters wins. (**HINT:** Matches will be on opposite sides of the center line.)

$\frac{7}{10}$	$\frac{12}{32}$	$\frac{9}{10}$	$\frac{7}{8}$
$\frac{2}{5}$	$\frac{1}{5}$	$\frac{7}{35}$	$\frac{6}{15}$
$\frac{1}{2}$	$\frac{45}{50}$	$\frac{2}{3}$	$\frac{4}{5}$
$\frac{28}{35}$	$\frac{6}{9}$	$\frac{14}{20}$	$\frac{26}{52}$
$\frac{14}{16}$	$\frac{5}{6}$	$\frac{21}{28}$	$\frac{9}{36}$
$\frac{3}{4}$	$\frac{1}{4}$	$\frac{3}{8}$	$\frac{15}{18}$

AlgebraicThinking • Foundations

Solving Multiplication and Division Equations

Directions: *Model each equation with your teacher. Then draw what you modeled and state how you would solve the equation without using models.*

Problem	Model	How to Solve
1. $3n = 15$		
2. $2x = 8$		
3. $4d = 12$		
4. $2y = 6$		
5. $3x = 18$		

705

AlgebraicThinking • Foundations

Directions: *Some students came up with the following solutions to these equations. Check their work by evaluating the equation with their solutions.*

Equation	Solution	Check
6. $4c = 36$	$c = 9$	
7. $3x = 27$	$x = 9$	
8. $5x = 30$	$x = 6$	
9. $9n = 9$	$n = 1$	
10. $12q = 36$	$q = 3$	

Practice it!

Directions: *Write the equation represented by each model. Then solve the equation.*

1. [box with x, x, x] = [box with 6 y's]

2. [box with x, x, x] = [box with 12 y's]

3. [box with 6 x's] = [box with 10 y's]

4. [box with 5 x's] = [box with 5 y's]

706

AlgebraicThinking • Foundations

Directions: *Draw a model for each equation. Then solve the equation.*

5. $4n = 12$	**6.** $2x = 2$
7. $4x = 16$	**8.** $3y = 6$

Directions: *Solve each equation. Use any method.*

9. $2x = 20$ **10.** $6c = 30$ **11.** $3x = 30$

12. $4d = 44$ **13.** $2x = 44$ **14.** $3t = 39$

15. $5y = 100$ **16.** $4x = 76$ **17.** $9n = 18$

AlgebraicThinking • Foundations

18. **S-O-L-V-E:** Central High School has three times as many students as South High School. Central High School has 2,616 students. Write and solve an equation to show how many students go to South High School.

    S-

    O-

    L-

    V-

    E-

19. **S-O-L-V-E:** Maxine gave six customers hair cuts on Monday. Her total revenue from the hair cuts was $192. Write and solve an equation to show how much each customer was charged for their hair cut.

    S-

    O-

    L-

    V-

    E-

AlgebraicThinking • Foundations

Directions: *Solve each equation. Check each answer.*

Solve	Check
20. $3x = 21$	
21. $5x = 45$	
22. $\frac{1}{2}n = 15$	
23. $\frac{3}{5}n = 9$	
24. $\frac{f}{4} = 3$	
25. $\frac{p}{4} = 12$	

Algebraic Thinking • Foundations

Homework:

Directions: *Complete each operation. Simplify.*

1. $\frac{3}{4} \div \frac{1}{4} =$

2. $\frac{7}{8} + \frac{3}{16} =$

3. $2 \cdot \frac{1}{3} =$

4. $1\frac{1}{5} - \frac{4}{5} =$

5. $\frac{2}{3} \div \frac{2}{9} =$

6. $\frac{9}{10} + 4\frac{5}{6} =$

7. $\frac{1}{4} \cdot \frac{8}{9} =$

8. $2\frac{7}{15} - 1\frac{4}{5} =$

9. $\frac{11}{12} \div 22 =$

10. $\frac{3}{5} \cdot \frac{2}{3} =$

AlgebraicThinking • Foundations

Appendix 16: One-Step Equations - Return of the Word Problems – No Integers

Warm Up: What Are the Questions?

Read the information below. Then write questions for the answers that are given below.

A marathon is a 26.4-mile race. In 1984, Carlos Lopes of Portugal won the Olympic gold medal for running the marathon in 2 hours 9 minutes and 21 seconds.

1. about 13 miles per hour

2. about 129 minutes

3. 7,761 seconds

AlgebraicThinking • Foundations

Return of the Word Problems

These word problems are meant to challenge you. If you don't figure it out on the first or even the second or third time you read it, don't give up! Organize the facts and you'll get it.

Directions: *S-O-L-V-E each word problem. Write an equation for each problem.*

1. Latrenda is making 8 dozen baked potatoes for a pot luck dinner fundraiser. She has 2 cups of butter to put on the baked potatoes. How much butter will she use on each dozen?

S

O

L

V

E

2. The drama club had to set up 575 seats for the assembly in the gym. How many chairs will they have to put into each row if they can only fit 25 rows in the gym?

S

O

L

V

E

Algebraic Thinking • Foundations

3. The Travlynn family took a summer cross-country vacation. They drove from New York City, NY, to San Francisco, CA, 2,925 miles away. The rate at which they traveled was 65 miles per hour on their trip. How long did the trip take them? (distance = rate • time)

S

O

L

V

E

4. Beth works at the Coffee Talk Cafe and presently makes $6.25 per hour. How many hours will she need to work to make $218.75 per week?

S

O

L

V

E

Algebraic Thinking • Foundations

5. The width of a piece of wallpaper is 3 feet. How long will the wallpaper have to be in order to have an area of 27 ft²? (Area = length • width)

S

O

L

V

E

6. If each piece of wallpaper is 27 ft², how many pieces of wallpaper would you need to cover an area of 405 ft²?

S

O

L

V

E

Algebraic Thinking • Foundations

7. Hank has 9 boxes of materials to ship. He had to pay $12.60 per pound to have the packages shipped overnight delivery. How much did the packages weigh if the shipping cost was $214.20?

S
O
L
V
E

8. Using the information from Problem 7, calculate the weight of each package if each package weighed the same amount.

S
O
L
V
E

Algebraic Thinking • Foundations

Directions: *Solve each equation.*

9. $\frac{1}{4}x = 3$ 10. $1.2x = 4.8$ 11. $5y = 25$

12. $0.9x = 0.63$ 13. $\frac{2}{3}n = 10$ 14. $5x = 75$

15. $10c = 2$ 16. $\frac{1}{3}x = 3$ 17. $\frac{1}{5}x = 1$

18. $\frac{3}{5}n = 9$ 19. $25t = 250$ 20. $12x = 12$

AlgebraicThinking • Foundations

Homework:

Directions: *Find each quotient.*

1. $\frac{1}{2} \div \frac{1}{3} =$

2. $\frac{3}{8} \div \frac{1}{3} =$

3. $\frac{4}{5} \div \frac{1}{3} =$

4. $2 \div \frac{3}{4} =$

5. $\frac{1}{2} \div 7 =$

6. $1\frac{1}{2} \div 12 =$

AlgebraicThinking • Foundations

Appendix 17: Review of One-Step Equations

Warm Up: Pyramids

Perform the operation from left to right. Put the answer for each pair of integers above and between.

Addition

5   8   3   8   10

Multiplication

1   2   4   1   0

Subtraction

100   20   5   1   0

Algebraic Thinking • Foundations

Directions: Solve each problem below. Next, cut apart all of the 16 squares. Rearrange the squares so all solutions match up from a new 4 × 4 square. Then, glue or tape the new 4 × 4 square pieces on a blank sheet of paper.

Mystery Squares

$x = 3$ **P** $x = \frac{1}{2}$ ... $x = 121$ $\frac{x}{4} = 8$	$x = 94$ **W** $x = 12$ ... $x + 2 = 4$ $3x = 9$	$x - 4 = 6$ **O** $\frac{x}{11} = 11$ ... $6x = 36$ $x + 20 = 35$	$x = 32$ **M** $x = 17$ ... $x - 20 = 63$ $x - 15 = 32$
$\frac{x}{14} = 28$ **H** $x = 1$ ... $x = 20$ $x = 5$	$14 + x = 90$ **Q** $x = 12$ ... $x - 1 = 0$ $3x = 12$	$x = 4$ **A** $x = 6$ ... $2x = 18$ $\frac{x}{10} = 7$	$x = 15$ **R** $x = 83$ ... $\frac{x}{20} = 5$ $x = 29$
$x = 42$ **Z** $x = 2$ ... $\frac{1}{2}x = 6$ $x = 10$	$5x = 25$ **H** $x = 9$ ... $x = 71$ $x = 8$	$x = 70$ **R** $x = 100$ ... $x = 24$ $x = 14 + 75$	$\frac{x}{2} = 4$ **W** $\frac{x}{3} = 8$ ... $x = 0$ $x = 114$
$x = 89$ **T** $x = 84$ ... $5x = 0$ $\frac{x}{5} = 35$	$x = 47$ **D** $\frac{x}{10} = 8$ ... $x + 3 = 10$ $3x = 99$	$x = 128 - 14$ **K** $x = 0$ ... $x = \frac{1}{3}$ $x + 1 = 64$	$x - 15 = 14$ **S** $x = 7$ ... $\frac{x}{12} = 7$ $14x = 28$

AlgebraicThinking • Foundations

Cards for "Chain Reaction"

Rules:
1. Get the answer to the equation on one of the cards.
2. Find the answer at the top of one of the other cards.
3. Lay that card below the first one, and find the answer to the equation on it.
4. Find the answer at the top of another card. Lay it below the second card. Keep going until you have a vertical "chain."

19

$x + 7 = 16$

9

$7y = 84$

12

$a - 17 = 27$

44

$\dfrac{x}{4} = 10$

40

$d - 2 = 8$

Algebraic Thinking • Foundations

Cards for "Chain Reaction"

10 $8f = 56$	7 $3x = 24$
8 $14 + z = 28$	14 $15 + g = 17$
2 $\frac{q}{8} = 9$	72 $1k = 19$

Algebraic Thinking • Foundations

Appendix 18: Interpreting Circle Graphs

Warm – Up: Multiplication

Complete the following multiplication problems. Fill in the letter that matches the answer in the puzzle below.

R 8 • 6 =   O 9 • 9 =

D 8 • 7 =   L 7 • 6 =

E 6 • 5 =   T 4 • 7 =

A 3 • 9 =   P 2 • 8 =

K 6 • 9 =   U 10 • 7 =

C 5 • 4 =   J 2 • 5 =

What is the answer to a multiplication problem called?

_____
16   48   81   56   70   20   28

722

Algebraic Thinking • Foundations

Use the following circle graph. Answer the questions based on the data given.

100 people were surveyed about their favorite soft drink. The results are on the following circle graph.

Favorite Soft Drinks

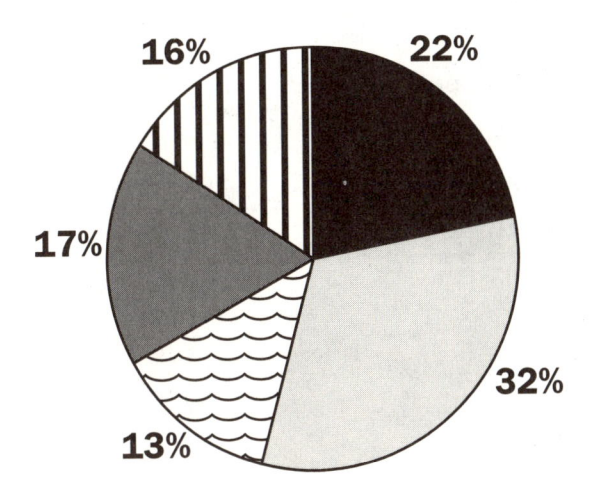

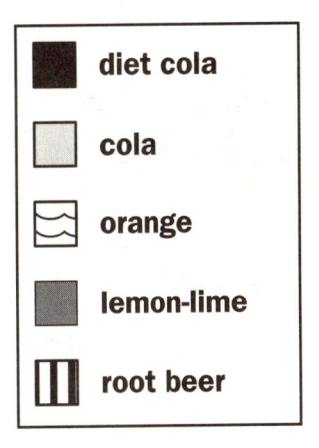

- diet cola: 22%
- cola: 32%
- orange: 13%
- lemon-lime: 17%
- root beer: 16%

1. What is the most popular soft drink?

2. What percent of people did not choose cola or diet cola?

3. What is the difference of the percent of people who chose lemon-lime over orange?

4. What percent of the people chose root beer or orange?

AlgebraicThinking • Foundations

Using the following circle graph, answer the questions based on the data given.

A group of drivers were polled about the vehicles that they drive. Answer the questions about these statistics using the graph below.

Types of Vehicles

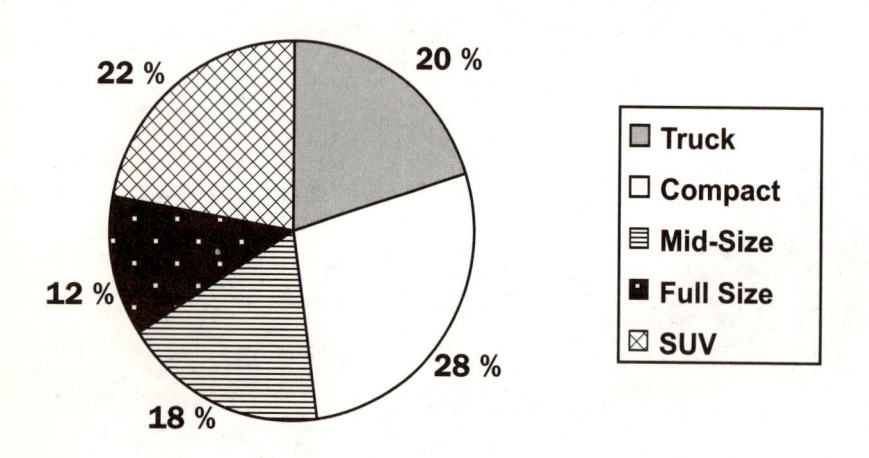

Pie chart values: Truck 20%, Compact 28%, Mid-Size 18%, Full Size 12%, SUV 22%

Legend:
- Truck
- Compact
- Mid-Size
- Full Size
- SUV

1. What percent of people own a truck or SUV ?

2. Which type of vehicle is owned by the least amount of people?

3. What percent of people do not own trucks?

4. What percent of people do not own mid-size or full size cars?

AlgebraicThinking • Foundations

Mr. Caskey collected data from his students about their favorite color. He created a circle graph to display the data. Work with your partner to write three questions that can be answered using the data on the graph.

Favorite Colors

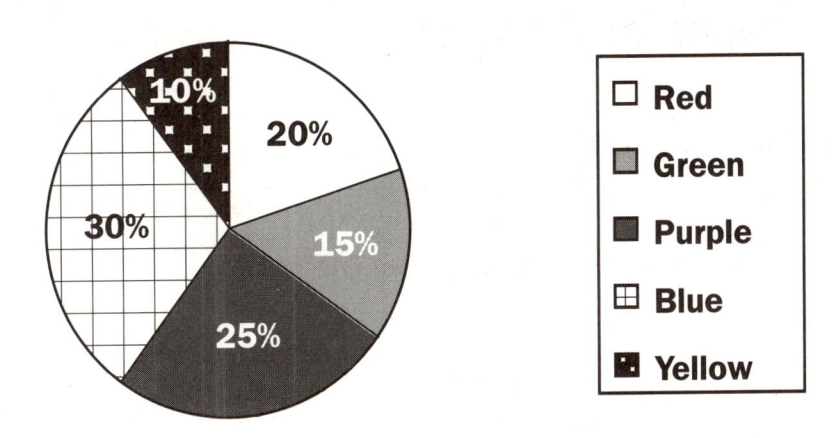

☐ Red
■ Green
■ Purple
⊞ Blue
▩ Yellow

Questions:

1.

2.

3.

Algebraic Thinking • Foundations

Homework:

1. 54 + 36 = _____

2. 100 − 78 = _____

3. 32 • 5 = _____

4. 25 ÷ 5 = _____

5. 29 + 13 = _____

6. 36 − 18 = _____

7. 14 • 3 = _____

8. 42 ÷ 6 = _____

Algebraic Thinking • Foundations

Appendix 19: Percent of Discount, Sales Tax

Warm Up

Directions: Match the fraction in the left hand column to its decimal equivalent in the right hand column.

$\frac{1}{4}$	0.4
$\frac{3}{8}$	0.5
$\frac{2}{5}$	0.9
$\frac{1}{2}$	0.375
$\frac{4}{5}$	0.04
$\frac{7}{20}$	0.8
$\frac{9}{10}$	0.25
$\frac{1}{25}$	0.35

Algebraic Thinking • Foundations

Understanding how to find the percent of a number is very important when you are making purchases if you want to get the best deal for your money. Complete the SOLVE problem below with your teacher to find the best deal.

SOLVE

Juanita wants to buy a leather jacket, and has found that the same exact jacket is on sale at two different stores. The jacket has a regular price of $150 at Store A, and $160 at Store B. Store A has a 20% sale on all jackets, and Store B's jackets are 25% off. Juanita lives on the border of two states, so the sales tax for each store is different. Store A's sales tax is 7%, and store B's sales tax is 6%. Which store will give Juanita the best price?

S- Highlight the question.

O- Identify the facts.
Eliminate the unnecessary facts.
List the necessary facts.

L- Choose an operation.
Write in words what your plan of action will be.

V- Estimate your answer.
Carry out your plan.

E- Did you answer what you were asked to find?
Is your answer reasonable?
Is your answer accurate?
Write answer as a complete thought.

Algebraic Thinking • Foundations

Below you will see sales ads for two different sports stores. Work with your partner to pick three items that you would like to purchase, and figure out which store you should go to if you want to spend the least amount of money. You must buy all three items at the same store. Use the worksheet after the ads to help you organize your information.

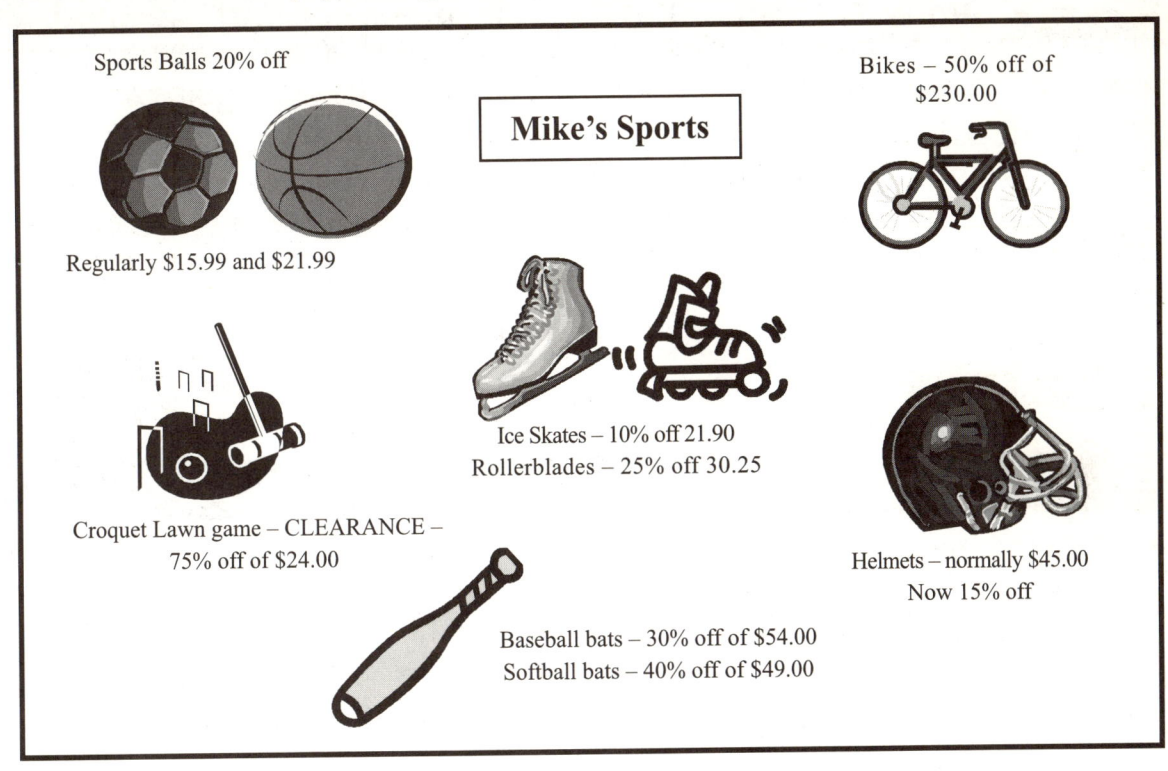

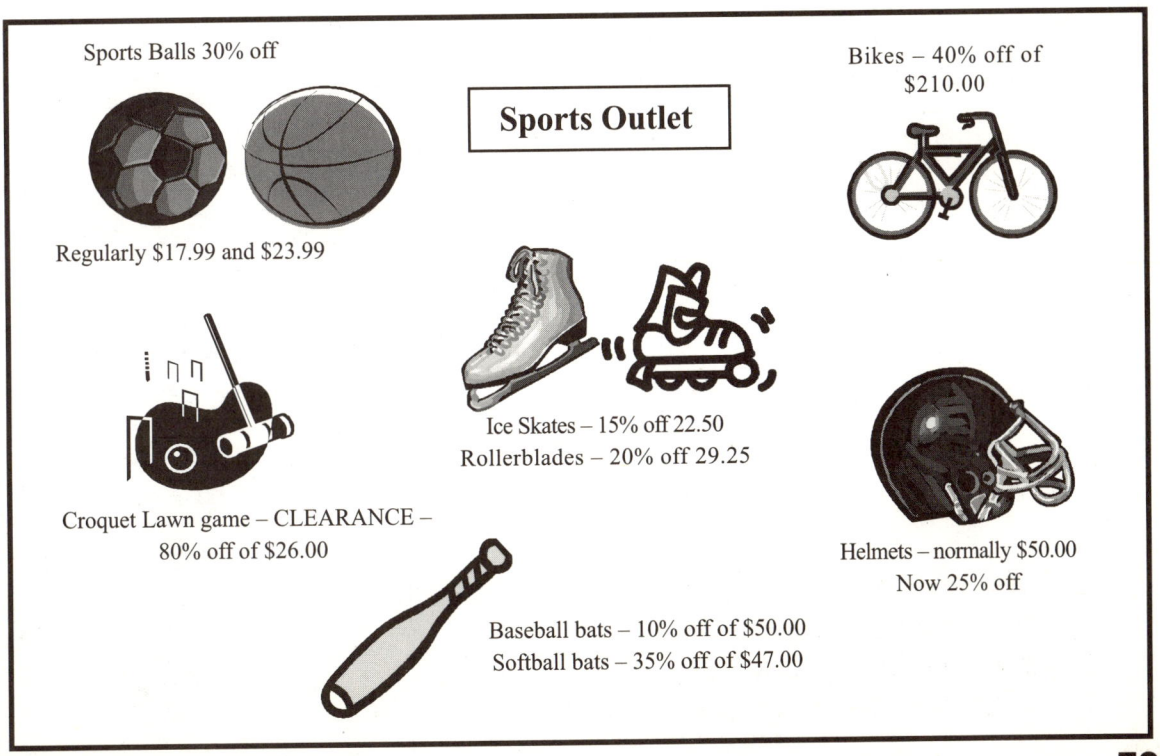

Mike's Sports

Sports Balls 20% off
Regularly $15.99 and $21.99

Bikes – 50% off of $230.00

Ice Skates – 10% off 21.90
Rollerblades – 25% off 30.25

Croquet Lawn game – CLEARANCE – 75% off of $24.00

Helmets – normally $45.00 Now 15% off

Baseball bats – 30% off of $54.00
Softball bats – 40% off of $49.00

Sports Outlet

Sports Balls 30% off
Regularly $17.99 and $23.99

Bikes – 40% off of $210.00

Ice Skates – 15% off 22.50
Rollerblades – 20% off 29.25

Croquet Lawn game – CLEARANCE – 80% off of $26.00

Helmets – normally $50.00 Now 25% off

Baseball bats – 10% off of $50.00
Softball bats – 35% off of $47.00

729

Algebraic Thinking • Foundations

Worksheet for Sports Items

	Mike's Sports			Sports Outlet		
	Regular Price	Percent Off	Discounted Price	Regular Price	Percent Off	Discounted Price
Item 1						
Item 2						
Item 3						
Subtotal						
Tax		8%			7%	
Total						

Which store is the better bargain for your three items?
_____

What is the difference in the total price for the two stores?
_____

730

Algebraic Thinking • Foundations

Homework: SOLVE Problem

Denise is picking out her new school supplies. She can choose from 3 backpacks, 4 different notebooks and 3 different boxes of crayons. How many different combinations of school supplies are possible?

S- Highlight the question.

O- Identify the facts.
Eliminate the unnecessary facts.
List the necessary facts.

L- Write in words what your plan of action will be.

V- Estimate your answer.
Carry out your plan.

E- Did you answer what you were asked to find?
Is your answer reasonable?
Is your answer accurate?
Write your answer as a complete thought.

AlgebraicThinking • Foundations

Appendix 20: Distance Between Two Points Using a Drawing and a Scale

Warm Up – Proportions – "You're the Teacher"

Justin's Quiz	What's his mistake?	Correct Solution

1. 20 is 25% of what number?

$\frac{25}{100} = \frac{20}{x}$;

$x = 800$

2. What is 35% of 50?

$\frac{35}{100} = \frac{x}{50}$;

$x = 1.75$

3. 8 is what percent of 40?

$\frac{8}{x} = \frac{100}{40}$;

$x = 3.2$

4. What is 42% of 75?

$\frac{42}{75} = \frac{x}{100}$;

$x = 56$

AlgebraicThinking • Foundations

You have probably all seen a map with a scale while reading in your Social Studies text. But, what exactly is a scale? See if you can use the example below to write your own definition of a scale.

Example 1: Becky lives on the same street as her school, and a store. From Becky's house to the store is 3 cm on the diagram below (check it with your ruler). The actual distance is 600 feet. The diagram is drawn with a scale of
3 cm : 600 ft, or 1 cm : 200 ft.

Store   Becky's   School

Scale: 1 cm = 200 ft

Scale: _____

Based on your definition above, can you find the actual distance from Becky's house to the school? _____

How do you know? _____
_____

A scale drawing or a map is a proportional drawing of an object. You can also use a proportion to solve for the actual measurement. To find the distance from Becky's house to the school, you would set up a proportion where one ratio is the scale factor, and the other is the distance you measured on the drawing over the unknown actual distance.

Scale Factor → $\dfrac{1 \text{ cm}}{200 \text{ ft}} = \dfrac{2 \text{ cm}}{x \text{ ft}}$

Using cross products, we see that $1x$ is equal to 400, so the actual distance is 400 feet.

We can also use a scale to make something larger than it is in real life.

Example 2: In science class you might be asked to make a drawing of a worm's digestive system. The actual distance of your worm's digestive system is 2 cm, but in order to draw and label it, you may want to use the following scale: 3 in. = 1 cm. With your teacher, use a proportion to find how long the digestive system would be on your drawing.

$\dfrac{drawing}{actual} = \dfrac{3 \text{ in.}}{1 \text{ cm}} = \dfrac{x}{2 \text{ cm}}$

Algebraic Thinking • Foundations

Directions: Try the following with your teacher.

1. Ming is riding his bike to get some exercise. He rode to his friend Ben's house, and then rode back to his house. The map below shows his route. How far did he ride? (Round to nearest foot.)

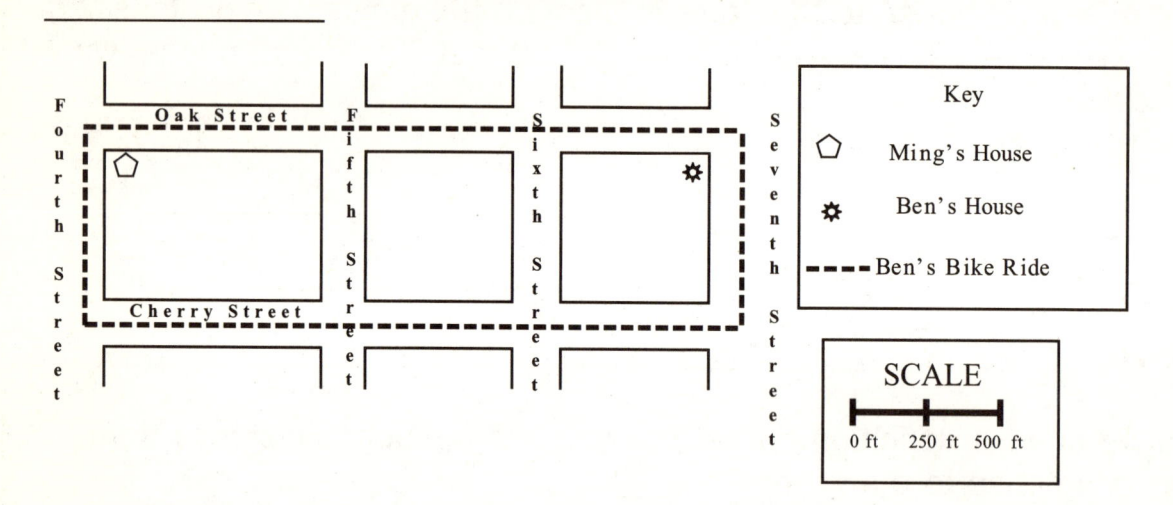

   _____

   Key
   - ⬠ Ming's House
   - ✺ Ben's House
   - ---- Ben's Bike Ride

   SCALE
   0 ft   250 ft   500 ft

2. The two cities below are 225 miles apart. What number is missing from the scale? _____

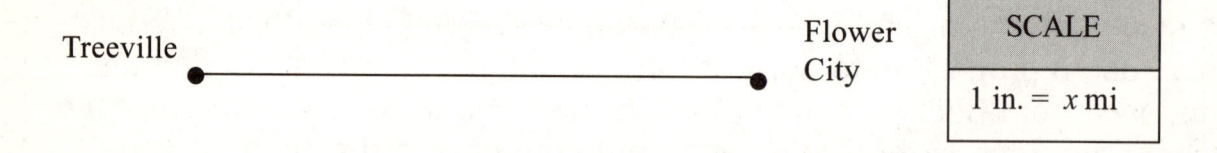

   Treeville • ————————————— • Flower City

   SCALE
   1 in. = x mi

3. Using the diagram below, whose house is 385 feet from Marisol's?

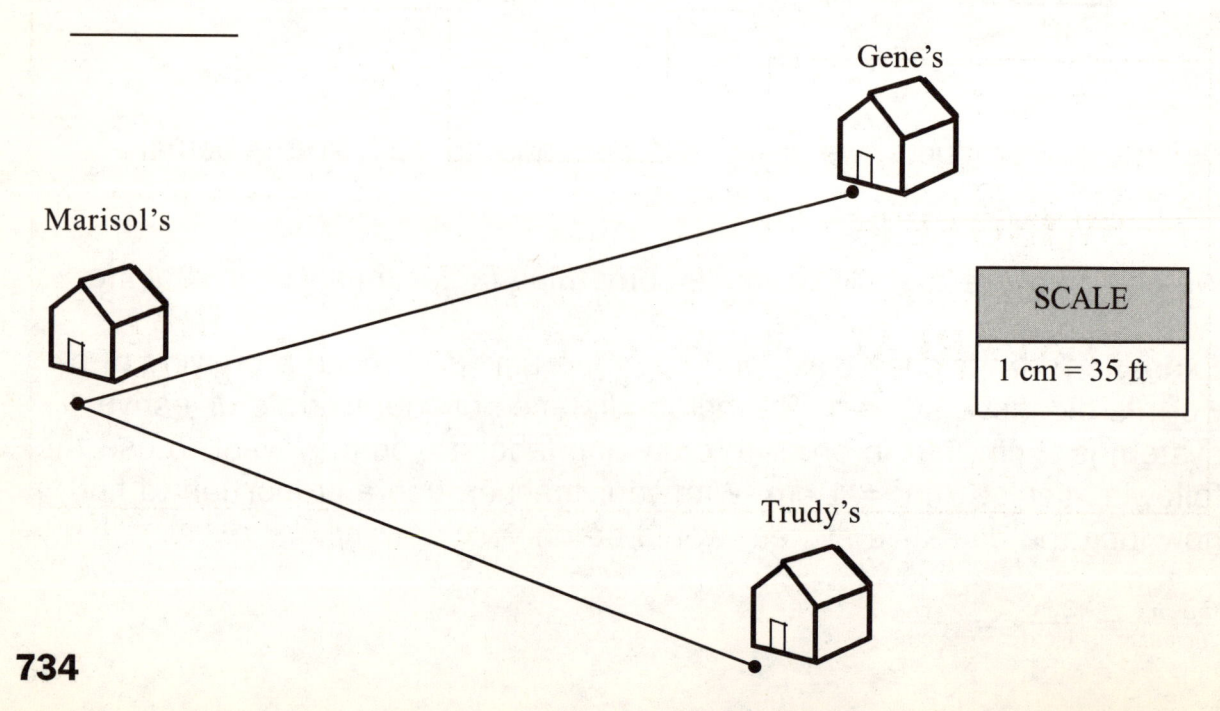

   _____

   SCALE
   1 cm = 35 ft

734

Algebraic Thinking • Foundations

Directions: Use the scale drawing below to answer the questions on the next page.

Jerome's Backyard

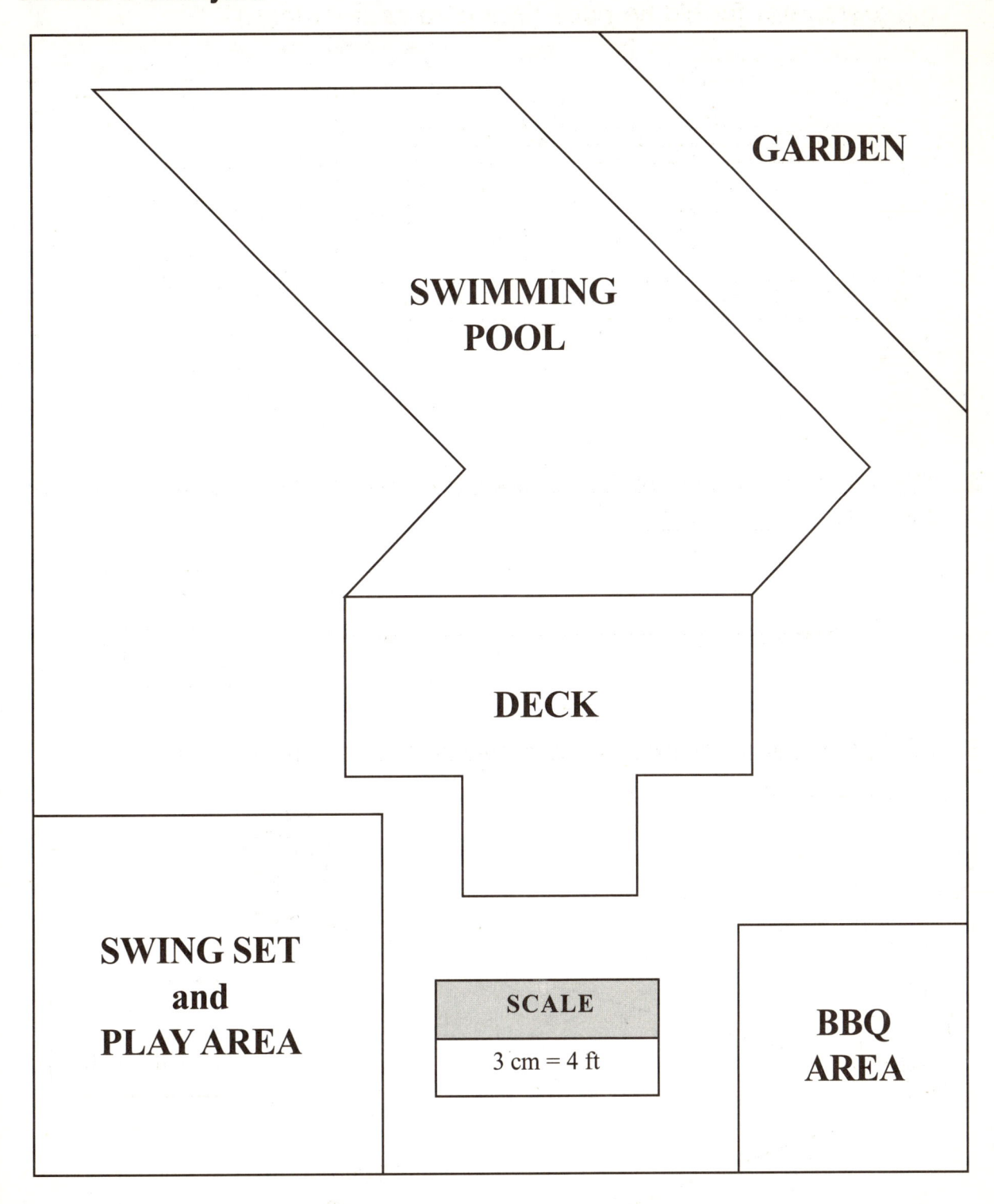

GARDEN

SWIMMING POOL

DECK

SWING SET and PLAY AREA

SCALE
3 cm = 4 ft

BBQ AREA

Algebraic Thinking • Foundations

Jerome's backyard is completely enclosed by a fence. The outer rectangle on the diagram represents the fence.

1. Jerome's mom needs to put up a small fence for the side of the garden closest to the swimming pool.

   What would the length of the small fence be in cm? _____

   What would the actual length of the small fence be? _____

2. What is the actual area of the swing set and play area? _____

3. What is the actual perimeter of the swimming pool? _____

4. Gerome's dad wants to add a rectangular awning (like a tent) to the left of the pool. If the awning is 16 feet by 12 feet, what would its measurements be on the drawing?

Algebraic Thinking • Foundations

Homework:

Four friends had $15.23, $7.98, $101.67, and $0.84 between them. They wanted to combine their money to buy a house-warming gift for a mutual friend. How much money do they have to spend on the gift?

S- Highlight the question.

O- Identify the facts.
Eliminate the unnecessary facts.
List the necessary facts.

L- Choose an operation.
Write in words what your plan of action will be.

V- Estimate your answer.
Carry out your plan.

E- Did you answer what you were asked to find?
Is your answer reasonable?
Is your answer accurate?
Write your answer as a complete thought.

Algebraic Thinking • Foundations

Appendix 21: Finding the surface area of cubes and rectangular prisms

Warm Up: Pick Two

Directions: Evaluate the following expressions if: $a = \frac{3}{8}$, $b = 6.75$, $c = 12$, $d = 112$

1. $d - 29 =$

2. $a + 2\frac{1}{2} =$

3. $12.6 + b =$

4. $c - 2.9 =$

5. $6\frac{1}{8} + a =$

6. $5.8 + c =$

7. $13.25 - b =$

8. $d - 44\frac{1}{2} =$

Which two problems have equivalent answers? _____

AlgebraicThinking • Foundations

Geometric solids are formed by polygons which enclose the space forming the solid. The **surface area** of any three-dimensional object or geometric solid can be found by finding the total area of the polygons used to construct the solid

Discovery Activity: Constructing a cube.

In the discovery activity you learned that a cube is made up of six congruent squares. By finding the area of one square and multiplying it by six you found the total surface area of the cube. The pattern that you started with is called the **net**. A **net** is a two-dimensional pattern of the solid and shows all the faces that make up the surface area.

Try These:
Directions: Find the surface area of each of the following cubes.

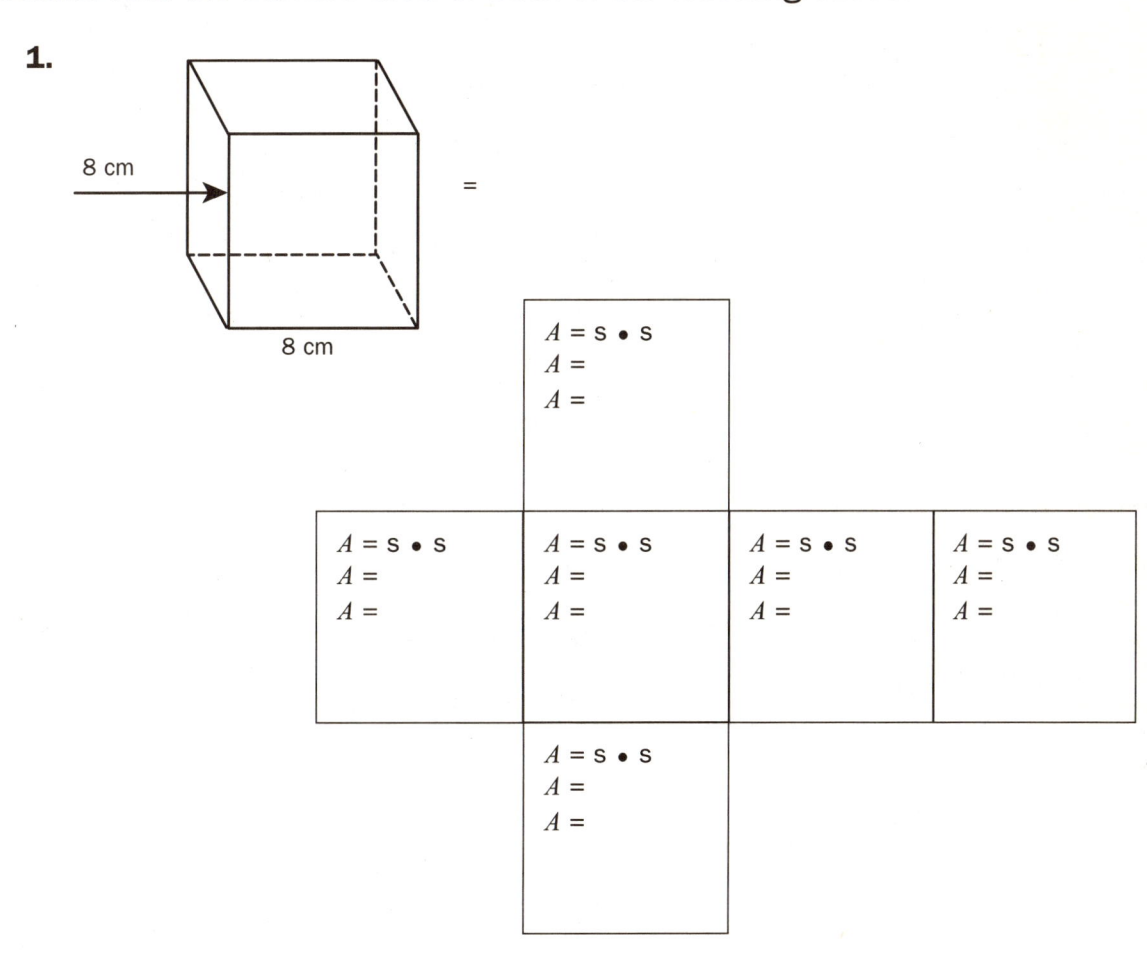

1.

8 cm
8 cm

=

$A = s \cdot s$
$A =$
$A =$

$A = s \cdot s$ $A = s \cdot s$ $A = s \cdot s$ $A = s \cdot s$
$A =$ $A =$ $A =$ $A =$
$A =$ $A =$ $A =$ $A =$

$A = s \cdot s$
$A =$
$A =$

AlgebraicThinking • Foundations

2. Find the surface area of a cube that has an edge that measures 5 inches. Draw the net of the cube. (See problem one.)

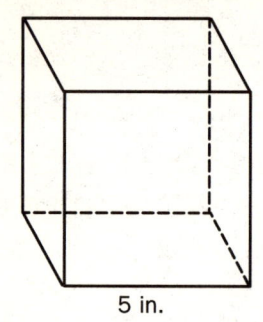

5 in.

AlgebraicThinking • Foundations

Rectangular Prisms

You can also find the surface area of other geometric solids such as a rectangular prism. In a rectangular prism, opposite sides are congruent. Look at the net of the box shown below. The dimensions of the box are: length – 6 cm, width – 5 cm, and height – 4 cm.

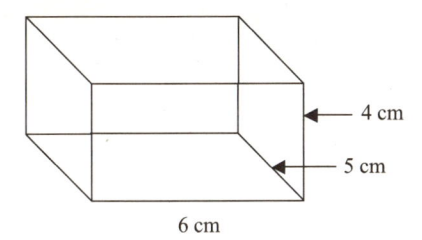

If you unfolded the box, the net of the box looks like this:

You can find the surface area of the box by finding the area of each of the sides. Because the opposite sides are congruent, the top and bottom will have the same area, the front and back will have the same area and the right and left sides will have the same area.

The bottom side has dimensions of 6 cm and 5 cm, so the area will be:

$A = lw$
$A = 6$ cm • 5 cm $= 30$ cm^2

The left side has dimensions of 5 cm and 4 cm so the area will be:

$A = lw$
$A = 5$ cm • 4 cm $= 20$ cm^2

The front side has dimensions of 6 cm and 4 cm so the area will be:

$A = lw$
$A = 6$ cm • 4 cm $= 24$ cm^2

We then add the areas of the sides to find the surface area of the box. (Remember that the opposite sides are congruent, so we multiply each area we found by 2 before adding for the total surface area.)

$SA = 2(30$ cm$^2) + 2(20$ cm$^2) + 2(24$ cm$^2) = 148$ cm^2

Algebraic Thinking • Foundations

Example:

1. Find the surface area of a rectangular box that is formed by the pattern below.

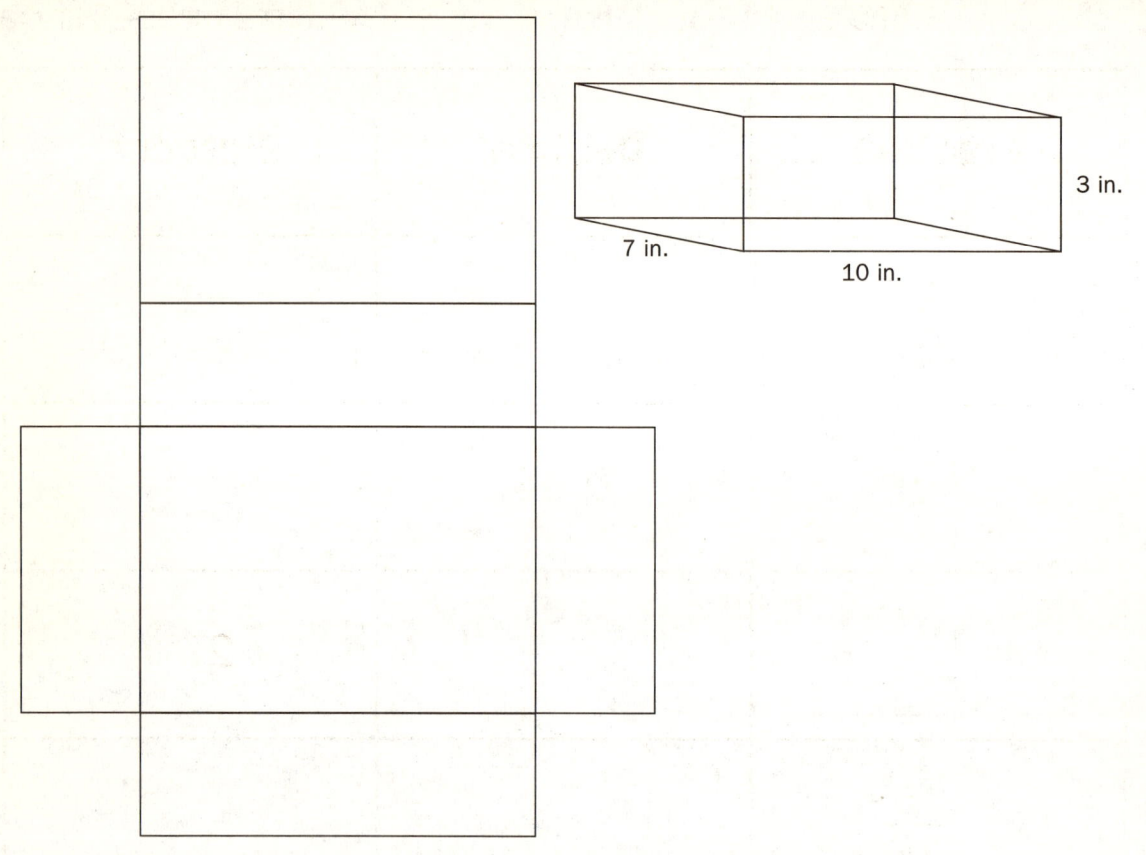

7 in. 10 in. 3 in.

Identify the three different rectangles that make up the box

What is the surface area?

2. Find the surface area of the following rectangular prism.

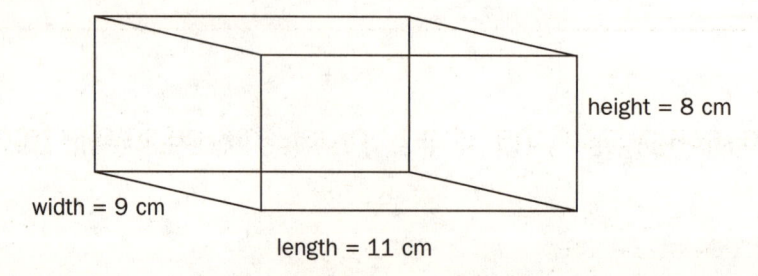

width = 9 cm
length = 11 cm
height = 8 cm

AlgebraicThinking • Foundations

Homework:

Directions: Convert the following fractions, decimals and percents.

Fraction	Decimal	Percent
$\frac{3}{6}$		
	0.34	
		27%
$\frac{7}{10}$		
	0.15	
		45%

Now that you have completed the chart, order the decimals from least to greatest.

Algebraic Thinking • Foundations

Appendix 22: Histograms

Warm Up

Put a third number in each box to get the sum of 87 in each one.

```
┌─────────────────┐
│ 36              │
│                 │
│          21     │
│                 │
│ ___             │
└─────────────────┘
```

```
┌─────────────────┐
│                 │
│ 32       ___    │
│                 │
│          23     │
└─────────────────┘
```

```
┌─────────────────┐
│ 36              │
│                 │
│          14     │
│                 │
│ ___             │
└─────────────────┘
```

AlgebraicThinking • Foundations

Statistics have become an important part of everyday life. We see them in newspapers and magazines, on television and in general conversations. We use them when we discuss the cost of living, unemployment, medical breakthroughs, weather predictions, sports, politics and the state lottery.

Although we are not always aware of it, each of us is an informal statistician. We are constantly **gathering, organizing and analyzing** information and using this data to make judgments and decisions that will affect our actions.

Groups of data have little value until they have been placed in some kind of order. Usually measurements are arranged in ascending or descending order.

One way to organize your data is to place your data into a category or group. This can be displayed in a **Frequency Table**. To create a Frequency Table, you must select an appropriate interval. The intervals used must be equal or consistent.

Children	Children in Family Tally	Frequency
1–2	llll	4
3–4	llll l	6
5–6	lll	3

Using this data, we can also create a **histogram** to pictorially show the frequency. A **histogram** is a method of displaying data that uses intervals. A **histogram** must have a **title** and **labels** on the x-axis and y-axis. A histogram uses intervals. You can use the same intervals you determined to use in the frequency table.

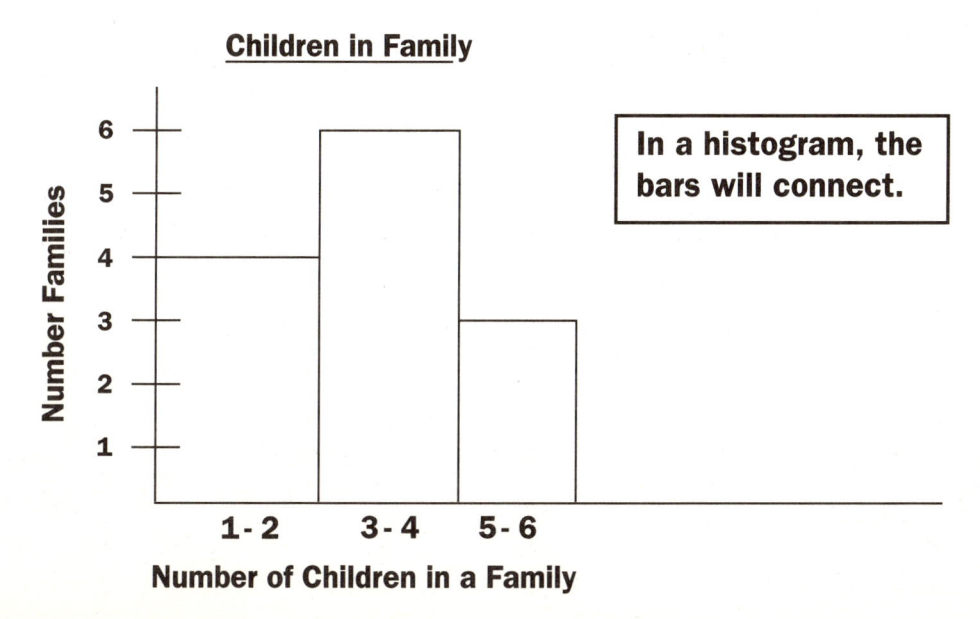

Children in Family

In a histogram, the bars will connect.

745

AlgebraicThinking • Foundations

Use the Frequency Table to Create a Histogram

HOW MANY HOURS DO YOU SLEEP EACH NIGHT?

Number of Hours	5 – 6	7 – 8	9 – 10	11 – 12
Frequency	4	12	9	1

How many students sleep more than 8 hours? ____

How many students were surveyed? ____

How many students get 6 hours or less? ____

What interval is being used? ____

Cell Phone Usage in Minutes

Interval	Frequency
0 – 19	3
20 – 39	7
40 – 59	9
60 – 79	5

How many phone calls lasted 60 minutes or more? ____

How many phone calls lasted less than 40 minutes? ____

How many phone calls lasted at least 40 minutes? ____

How many phone calls were made in all? ____

AlgebraicThinking • Foundations

Directions: Use the data below to create a histogram.

Number of hours spent studying

Interval	Frequency
0 – 1	5
2 – 3	8
4 – 5	4
6 – 7	10
8 – 9	4

How many students studied more than 5 hours? ____

How many students were surveyed? ____

Which interval contains the most students? _____

Conduct a survey of how hours students spend on homework in a week. Select an appropriate scale and interval that best fits your data. Organize your data in both a frequency table and histogram.

Algebraic Thinking • Foundations

Homework

Write each algebraic expression.

1. Three more than twice a number.

2. A number doubled decreased by 4.

3. The quotient of a number and 4 increased by 2.

4. 6 less than three times a number.

NOTES

NOTES